Zapolska's Women: Three Plays
Malka Szwarcenkopf, The Man and Miss Maliczewska

Dedication

For Irena, Jola and Mała Murjas

Zapolska's Women: Three Plays
Malka Szwarcenkopf, The Man and Miss Maliczewska

Teresa Murjas

intellect Bristol, UK / Chicago, USA

First published in the UK in 2009 by
Intellect Books, The Mill, Parnall Road, Fishponds, Bristol, BS16 3JG, UK

First published in the USA in 2009 by
Intellect Books, The University of Chicago Press, 1427 E. 60th Street, Chicago,
IL 60637, USA

Anyone wishing to perform the translated version of the plays in this
publication should contact Teresa Murjas for permission at the following address:

Teresa Murjas
Department of Film, Theatre & Television
The University of Reading
Bulmershe Court, Woodlands Avenue
Reading, RG6 1HY, UK

A catalogue record for this book is available from the British Library.

Series editor: Roberta Mock
Cover designer: Holly Rose
Copy-editor: Rebecca Vaughan-Williams
Typesetting: Mac Style, Beverley, E. Yorkshire

ISBN 978-1-84150-236-6

Printed and bound by Gutenberg Press, Malta.

Contents

... Zapolska was endlessly talking herself into lots of things – feminism and patriotism, socialism and modernism, naturalism and mysticism. That is the shallowest aspect of her work. Her strength will forever reside in contempt, in loathing, will reside in a profound disgust for life, a spasmodic cry of pain, in mocking and bitter laughter...

Stanisław Brzozowski, 1906 (trans. T.M.)

... When the houselights had already gone down and they were about to raise the curtain for the third act... a teacher... in the stalls... got up... let's call him Kowalski... and in a voice quivering with emotion shouted: As someone responsible for educating today's youth I protest against the staging of this cynical play! Then someone from the gallery shouted: Sit down, Kowalski. The speaker, who had wanted to say something else, became confused, and sat down like an obedient pupil. The curtain rose, amidst general mirth, which rather surprised the actors...

Jan Parandowski, a Lvovian student, 1910 (trans. T.M.)
recalling the first production of Miss Maliczewska in his home town

17th December
... Julian tells me often, that I am "stupid". That's strange! At school and at home I passed as someone very intelligent...

Gabriela Zapolska, 1899 (trans. T. M.) from her short story
'Memoirs of a newly married Young Woman'

... We are most accustomed to thinking of translation as an empirical linguistic maneuver, but excavating burial sites or ruins in order to reconstruct traces of the physical and textual past in a new context is also a mode of translation, just as resurrecting a memory or interpreting a dream are acts of translation. In the process of being transferred from one realm or condition to another, the source event or idea is necessarily reconfigured; the result of translation is that the original, also inaccessible, is no longer an original per se; it is a pretext whose identity has been redefined...

Bella Brodzki, 2007 (p. 4)

ACKNOWLEDGEMENTS

With special thanks to Mike Stevenson, Melanie Harrison, Doug Pye, Lisa Clark, Pamela Wiggin, Ashley Thorpe, Lib Taylor, Matt Ager, Elwira Grossman, the actors who took part in the Reading/London production of *The Man* and the Woman's Hour interview with Jenny Murray; Victoria Brown, Francesca Clarke, Sophie Green and Sam Milsom, the actors who took part in the Reading/London production of *The Mistress*; Andrew Baker, Michael Day, Peter Dodds, Phoebe Garrett, Daniel Harding, Ben Mitchell, Lauren McKinstry, Michael Muncer, Matthew van Niftrik, Saskia Solomons, Karina Thresh, Samantha Tye, all technicians and designers involved in realizing the two productions in Reading and London, and all staff at POSK, especially technician Marek Titov.

Figure 1: Zapolska in 1884, costumed as the sprite Chochlik in Juliusz Słowacki's poetic drama, *Balladyna*. By kind permission of Warsaw Theatre Museum.

INTRODUCTION

Translating Zapolska

This book is the outcome of a five-year translation project relating to Zapolska's work. It follows my 2007 book, also published by Intellect, which includes a translation of and introduction to this prolific playwright's best-known dramatic text, *Moralność Pani Dulskiej* (*The Morality of Mrs Dulska*) (1906). The reader wishing to obtain more specific information about the playwright's biography and the various relevant critical and historical contexts for her literary and theatrical activities should also refer to my extensive introduction to *Dulska*.[1]

The three plays included in this volume have been grouped together both because of their thematic contiguities – for example, a preoccupation with the economic influences determining the lives and loves of women – and because they represent different stages in Zapolska's career. What is revealed via this collection is how her use of form and particularly her approach to dialogue, subtext and characterization developed over time.

The translation of the first play, *Małka Szwarcenkopf* (1897)[2] came about thanks to a period of AHRC funded research leave at the University of Reading, where I have worked as a Lecturer in Theatre since 2002. Translations of the remaining plays, *Mężczyzna* (*The Man*) (1901) and *Panna Maliczewska* (*Miss Maliczewska*) (1910), have in their current form arisen as the result of two research productions which originated in my department and which I directed. Of these three plays, the latter has been most frequently revived in Zapolska's native Poland.

My research into Polish theatre of the late nineteenth/early twentieth century has drawn together six symbiotic methodological strands, aspects of which have informed both the selection of material for inclusion in this book and also its structure.

The first involves identification of a requisite historiographical and critical context for the purpose of facilitating readings of late nineteenth/early twentieth century, predominantly naturalist,

Figure 2: Two sisters torment their 'dissolute' brother. Research performance of Zapolska's *The Morality of Mrs. Dulska*. University of Reading and POSK Theatre, London, 2003/4. Rose Walton as Mela, Laura Farrell as Hesia, John Lynch as Zbyszko. Photo by Lib Taylor.

theatre practice in partitioned Poland. Naturalism was the form most consistently employed by Zapolska, who produced nearly 40 play texts, a core body of which are frequently revived in Polish.

The second strand involves archival research, which is a somewhat complex endeavour, since there is no single archive holding the playwright's work. The investigation focuses on the performance history of Zapolska's plays up to the present day, specifically consideration of their likely practical realization, their reception and critical responses to their staging. An awareness of these issues facilitates the visualization of previous staging solutions, speculation about contexts and theatrical conventions and informs the decisions I subsequently make as a translator and director of these works.

The third strand comprises their initial, pre-rehearsal, first-draft translation into English. So far seven translations exist, four of which are published by Intellect.

The fourth strand involves staging translated works as research productions, translation in its broader sense ultimately constituting, as a result, both a research method (that in these instances is fundamentally collective) and an outcome. Research productions at the University of Reading represent examples of what is referred to in the field of UK Theatre Studies as 'practice as research' or 'research through practice'. This involves the structured critical exploration of particular research or theoretical questions or problems through workshops and/or the staging of a production/performance, which may have evolved from a written play text or a process of devising. Accordingly, a formalized, annual nine-week slot is available each autumn term for extra curricular, staff-led research projects of a practical nature. This opportunity provides an arguably indispensable experimental forum for the theatre translator. With my cast I work on staging productions of my new translations. Rehearsals become a way of developing the translated text, which changes week by week in response to this collaborative process. A developmental, rehearsal-based working method of this kind is not dissimilar from that employed by the playwright herself.

The fifth strand involves sometimes extensive re-fashioning of the text following the witnessing of public performances of its first 'incarnation', with particular focus on rhythm, tone, visual and verbal humour (absolutely crucial to and very complex in Zapolska's work) and specificity of 'voice' in the definition of character. I usually engage in this re-fashioning following a few months' break, returning to the Polish original, the contextual research I have amassed and, importantly, memories of actors' movements, gestures, voices and audience response. The performances, or sometimes readings or workshops, which take place in national and international contexts, are inscribed to a large degree in the final published text, which is itself by no means, of course, 'fixed' or 'stable'.

Characterizing the sixth strand of my research is interrogation of how interactions between so-called source and target cultures and languages problematically manifest themselves as theatre, since my research productions are staged in contrasting environments – in spaces occupied by the academic community and in spaces occupied by what might be classed as

Figure 3: A friend of the family arrives, aggravating marital problems. Research performance of Zapolska's *Four of Them*. University of Reading, POSK Theatre London and Łódź Theatre Festival, 2006/7. Kelly Wines as the Seamstress. Photo by Lib Taylor.

the 'Polish community', both in the United Kingdom and abroad. In addition, as the daughter of Poles deported from their country at the start of World War II, the translation and direction of dramatic literature written in Polish involves extensive consideration of my own work within narratives of emigration, deportation and exile from Poland and post-WWII processes of Polish/ British identity formation.

I am, in 2009, extending my research activities to the translation and direction of work by other Polish modernist playwrights – specifically those late nineteenth/early twentieth-century writers working within the theatrical form of naturalism, many of whose plays do not exist in English translation. A related book, *Invisible Country* (Intellect Press), will appear in 2010.

Maria Gabriela Stefania Korwin-Piotrowska, who later took the stage name Gabriela Zapolska and occasionally wrote under the pseudonym Józef Maskoff, was born in 1857 and died in 1921, in Polish Galicia. She grew up in Podhajce, near Łuck, in the area called Wołyń, once part of Eastern Poland, which is now Volhynia, part of Ukraine. She was a commercially successful playwright, an actor, a journalist, a prolific prose writer and a glamorous social

Figure 4: The daughter of the house tries to make friends with the servant. Research performance of Zapolska's *The Morality of Mrs. Dulska*. University of Reading and POSK Theatre, London, 2003/4. Zoe Gamon as Hanka, Rose Walton as Mela. Photo by Lib Taylor.

outcast. Her divorce from a military man and an attempt to sue a national newspaper provoked scandals, as did her willingness to discuss identity politics and economics from a fundamentally left-wing perspective. Dubbed by her many and varied critics as an immoral actress, she and her work became a site for emotive debates about the role of woman in Polish society.

During the playwright's lifetime Poland was subject to its third partition, brought about by Russia, Austria (later Austro-Hungary) and Prussia. It did not exist on the map until after World War I. This socio-geographic fragmentation had profound consequences in all private and public spheres, though events in one partition did impact on the functioning of the other two. The nature of government and law enforcement within each partition varied immensely, particularly given the repeated insurrections that characterized the Russian partition specifically throughout the nineteenth century.

Any attempt to recount and encompass the events of 123 years of cartographic invisibility presents a considerable challenge. Polish historiography has its nationalist, Romantic and Marxist variants. Post-colonial theorists and revisionists may continue to provide important strategies for re-generating and re-defining the historiography of this period, particularly taking account of Poland's cultural diversity. The key for the translator must be to interrogate

Figure 5: A married journalist and a working girl consider the options. Research performance of Zapolska's *The Man*. University of Reading and POSK Theatre, London, 2004/5. Sam Milsom as Karol and Sophie Green as Elka. Photo by Lib Taylor.

her ideological position in relation to events during those 123 years. To what extent should an outline of previous geographical boundaries be permitted to hover in the consciousness over maps drawn up between 1795 and 1918 from which it was eradicated, given that many of the same families, including those who identified themselves as Polish, continued to occupy what might be referred to as a sort of shape-shifting – or even occasionally 'virtual' – country.

Indeed, one might say that the concept of liminality – a state of ambiguity or in-between space – is of direct consequence in relation to several aspects of my research into Zapolska's work and its various contexts. Geographically speaking, boundaries had, during the period in question, shifted. This engendered complex debates about the terms in which definitions of national identity ought to be formulated. The theatre, specifically in the Russian partition, was, following the January Insurrection of 1863, the only public forum where Polish language use was permitted, though theatrical institutions of varying kinds were subjected to increasingly strict state censorship. Consequently, theatre itself – as a series of concepts, practices, institutions – arguably became a contested space; both a site of resistance *and* constraint, of potentially subversive or revolutionary public interaction *and* the enactment of varying levels of imperialist control over cultural discourse. Zapolska's plays reflect these conditions and focus on the representation of characters contemporary to her, existing in so-called 'liminal states' – in and

Figure 6: Two sisters overcome their oppressor. Research performance of Zapolska's *Miss Maliczewska*. University of Reading, POSK Theatre, London, 2007/8. Dan Harding as Daum, Phoebe Garrett as Stefka, Sam Tye as Michasiowa. Photo by Lib Taylor.

between – and often torn between – political systems, languages, social roles and conventions, modes of cultural discourse and religious practice, and linguistic and conceptual frameworks for self-definition and self-realization.

Polish scholars, predominantly discussing the work of male writers, have frequently identified the unifying characteristic of native Polish literature written during the period following the brutally suppressed January Insurrection of 1863 as tension between neo-Romantic nationalism and compromise. It has been noted that they were forced to communicate via metaphor, allusion and subtext. This is seen as a culturally specific problem posing an insurmountable challenge to the historiographer and scholar of dramatic literature written in Polish. This challenge is regarded as particularly acute for theatre translators and directors of Polish texts outside Eastern Europe, including those written after World War II. Norman Davies, the British historian, is in agreement, and maintains that Polish politics (of the nineteenth century) was

> driven from the public arena by an army of police and censors. It developed its own vivid literary code, a corpus of symbols and conventions which assumed a life of their own. For this reason, nineteenth-century Polish Literature ... comparable to all the great literatures of Europe, has proved markedly unsuitable for export and largely untranslatable.[3]

Though to some degree I appreciate this assessment of the situation, and can acknowledge also the inevitable losses incurred by the censor's activities, at the same time I remain unconvinced that the politics of translation and publication of Polish (or any) literature is thus easily reducible, most particularly in relation to drama and live performance. The material and ideological systems within which translators have had to function have inevitably affected the dissemination and reception of this work. In this context, it is interesting to bear in mind that in Britain only 3% of all published texts are translations. Contrast this with 'other European countries, which are happy to publish roughly 25% of their books in translation'.[4] Zapolska's work complicates Davies' position and may provide access to a rather different reading of the period. This may apply equally to the work of other fundamentally naturalist playwrights who were her contemporaries, such as Jan August Kisielewski, whose plays are rarely the subject of critical investigation within Poland itself, let alone abroad.

Zapolska's formal and stylistic preoccupations as a playwright stem directly and vividly from the political and social circumstances in which she functioned. What is additionally intriguing is the popularity of her work in live performance and her ability to unite in appreciation or condemnation readers and audiences whose objections to her work appear to emerge from apparently politically or ideologically incompatible perspectives. She has been referred to as both the 'Polish Zola' and the 'Polish Moliere' given the formal tensions between satire and realism in her work. Her plays may be grouped into four main categories. There are, of course, other possibilities, but the following categories, not reliant on chronology, may be the most useful starting point for an Anglophone reader.

Firstly, the short one-act plays, demonstrating a tension between naturalism and symbolism, such as Car Jedzie (Here Comes the Tzar) (1901). Secondly, those plays written predominantly before 1900, requiring casts of roughly 50 actors or substantially more and dealing with issues relating to the exploitation of the so-called lower classes or minority communities, such as Małaszka (1886). These texts encapsulate a tension between the forms of melodrama and naturalism, with visual spectacle residing not in dramatic shifts in location or complex theatrical devices, but in crowd scenes and the representation of large-scale social events, such as weddings, to create, via a kind of attempt at 'ethnographic accuracy' (as it was often referred to by contemporary critics) both a strong sense of realism and visually striking spatial and proxemic arrangements. An example is Małka Szwarcenkopf (1897), written predominantly in

Polish and set in Russian Warsaw, in the north-west part of the city, an area largely inhabited by Jews speaking a variety of languages; Yiddish, Polish, Russian, German and Hebrew. The play also contains very small sections written in Yiddish, which Zapolska could not speak (see my introduction to this particular translation for further information), specifically a betrothal ceremony during which the petrified groom tries to flee the building. The play is about arranged marriage and divorce and explores the pressures Małka, the protagonist, and her future husband, Jojne are exposed to. It ends with her suicide. These themes are arguably explored in a dialectical, non-didactic fashion. Issues relating to the Jewish enlightenment, or Haskalah, are raised, including questions around assimilation, acculturation, self-identification, ethnic origin, nationality, orthodoxy, secularism, patriarchal imperatives and their impact on gender roles. For readers keen to research the socio-cultural contexts for the play I would very strongly recommend a fascinating body of research into Jewish life in Poland in the nineteenth century, by writers Ewa Hoffman and Antoni Polonsky.[5] These sources include close examination of the development of the Yiddish language and of Yiddish literature and theatre in Poland during this period.

The third group of plays centres on the representation of more public settings, including those associated with the military and overtly politically active characters. These plays, such as

Figure 7: A failed attempt at persuasion. Research performance of Zapolska's *The Morality of Mrs. Dulska*. University of Reading and POSK Theatre, London, 2003/4. Cassie Earl as Juliasiewiczowa and Emma Ankin as Dulska. Photo by Lib Taylor.

Sybir (*Siberia*) (1899) are also naturalistic in form and tackle contemporary subject matter, for example, Polish–Russian relations. However, in addition, they draw strongly on the historical epic, thus attaining greater breadth of narrative scope and a more explicit politicization of the domestic sphere. *Tamten* (*The Other*) (1898), for example, which is written in Polish with some Russian, was completed in 1898, a year after *Małka Szwarcenkopf*, and is worth dwelling on in relation to the latter play, which is included in this collection.

The play was commissioned by the Kraków director Tadeusz Pawlikowski and reflected contemporary circumstances in the Russian partition. Fearing that she would not be able to return to the Russian partition as a result of the play's potentially politically inflammatory references (the characters were rather overtly modelled on senior Imperial military officers of her acquaintance) Zapolska took the pseudonym Józef Maskoff in order to protect herself. However, hearing of a rapidly spreading rumour that the play had been written by a young Russian playwright, she retracted with considerable rapidity. In 1907, the possibility arose of the play being staged in Warsaw but because of difficulties at the censor's office, this did not occur for many years.

In *The Other*[6] Zapolska tackles the topic of conspiratorial activity for the cause of Polish independence and the counter-active machinations of the Russian military secret police. The text contains a memorable scene in which policemen enter a room where several women

Figure 8: A mother resorts to force. Research performance of Zapolska's *The Morality of Mrs. Dulska*. University of Reading and POSK Theatre, London, 2003/4. Emma Ankin as Dulska, John Lynch as Zbyszko. Photo by Lib Taylor.

are seated, some of whom are highly politicized, pretending they are engaged in domestic, feminine activities. One of them has hidden an incriminating note in her hair, which is pinned up. The women are instructed to let their hair down and the letter is discovered.

The Russian employed by Zapolska in the play might be described as 'polonized' – the Cyrillic alphabet has been transliterated and what might be described as a 'jostling between' two languages is at times achieved. One of the central characters, Kornilov, a military policeman whose job it is to root out anti-imperial conspirators, is bi-lingual and bi-cultural. The fact that his mother might be identified as 'ethnically Polish' problematizes his professional activities, rendering him both particularly dangerous and particularly vulnerable. His ability to move between two linguistic forms and registers and to 'own' them in a very particular way is used by Zapolska to anchor her exploration of themes of internal and political conflict, otherness, duplicity and performativity within power relations in both private and public environments. The politicized practice of translation in contexts where many characters understand both languages to varying degrees (partially accounted for by considerable phonetic correspondences within the context of so-called Russification) is a central feature and problem of the play.

In *Siberia*, written shortly afterwards, the playwright created a 'fusion' of the Polish and Russian languages – a 'theatrical language' of sorts – in order to parody, for a Galician audience, the nature and extent of linguistic and political 'complication' experienced by Poles in the Russian partition, as a result of oppressive policies of Russification. Rurawski describes this language as Zapolska's 'volapuk' – a sort of 'esperanto' (with considerable ideological differences, of course) referencing the constructed language of nineteenth-century priest Johann Schleyer.[7] Interestingly, the work 'volapuk' is now used to describe the transliteration of the Cyrillic alphabet using the roman.

The challenges of translating such plays are considerable. They were written directly about political circumstances relating to the Russian partition for the Polish reader, *Siberia* most specifically for a Galician audience, because this would have been the only partition where live performance, and publication, was likely to have been, and was, sanctioned. Significant semantic and therefore political and ethical issues are raised, in terms of achieving relational equivalence between languages.

Bringing certain stages of the translation process into the rehearsal room allows me to engage dynamically, spatially and physically with theoretical questions about ideology and the ethics of theatrical representation. The relationship between actor and character that is implied within these naturalist play texts renders such a process particularly important. Such a working method also facilitates the identification of potential strategies for animating these plays in a new context in such a way that the full import and context for the relationships in question is at once expressed with immediacy *and* historicized. The main question being – where and when, conceptually, spatially, physically, linguistically, within the here and now, can one 'situate' these plays, particularly given the fact that many are being translated into English for the first time and finding reference points and relevant paradigms that might 'chime' with the Anglophone reader and audience member is difficult.

Figure 9: One sister helps another. Research performance of Zapolska's *The Man*. University of Reading and POSK Theatre, London, 2004/5. Sophie Green as Elka, Francesca Clarke as Julka. Photo by Lib Taylor.

In the fourth remaining category of plays Zapolska focused intently on a critique of capitalism, the bourgeoisie and the urbanized domestic sphere. Once again, the reader may be interested in referring to my translation *The Morality of Mrs. Dulska* as an example. *Żabusia* (*Little Frog*) (1896) (discussed briefly in the introduction to *Małka*), *Ich Czworo* (*Four of Them*) (1907), *The Man* and *Miss Maliczewska* can all be located within this category. I have now translated all these texts and realized them theatrically. This is partly because their small cast sizes make it possible and convenient for me to work on them within my own professional environment. It is also partly a consequence of their specific focus on the representation of gender and domestic spaces, which interests me greatly in relation to other European dramatic texts of the period, particularly those written by Githa Sowerby, Ibsen, Strindberg, Chekhov, Shaw and Granville-Barker.

The former three plays focus on family relationships and involve an exploration, in a register that frequently shifts towards bedroom farce, of the impact adult relationships, secrecy and infidelity have on children. *The Man* and *Miss Maliczewska*, though they share many thematic similarities, are different in tone, the latter including one of the playwright's few explicit

Figure 10: A mother lavishes her son with affection. Research performance of Zapolska's *The Morality of Mrs. Dulska*. University of Reading and POSK Theatre, London, 2003/4. Emma Ankin as Dulska, John Lynch as Zbyszko. Photo by Lib Taylor.

dramatic representations of physical violence perpetrated against a woman, at the end of Act 1. Importantly both plays of this category which are included in this collection focus on the lives of single women and the economic, professional and social pressures and opportunities with which they are faced. As such they hark back to *Małka Szwarcenkopf*. There are ten years between these two texts and in comparison a distinct shift in Zapolska's approach to crafting dialogue is evident. This predominantly relates to her greater confidence in allowing visual imagery and subtext to play as significant a role as language and the more dynamic, more precisely wrought verbal interactions. Both texts rely significantly on lapses in time between acts as a strategy for exploring complexity within relationships. This is evident in *The Man*, in which Elka's changing body arguably acts as a 'locus' around which a complex relational dynamic between four characters evolves – namely, Elka herself, her sister Julka, her lover Karol and his wife, Nina. Elka's body, its transforming shape, as expressed through her pregnancy, for example, and the way she clothes it, is at once a fixed *and* unstable sign, read as a 'vessel' that absorbs and a 'surface' that reflects the desires of others. Temporal lapses in the dramatic structure allow the reader or audience to visualize or observe contrasts in her appearance as it alters and 'mutates' in juxtaposition with the apparently greater visual 'stability' of her sister's body and physical appearance and the highly 'costumed', constructed and performed femininity of Karol's wife.

In *Miss Maliczewska* spatial changes reflect the shifts in Stefka's status as she moves from impoverished chorus member to the mistress of one lawyer, then another. The most disturbing and intriguing shift occurs between the first and second acts. At the end of Act 1, Daum attempts to force himself on Stefka, but she narrowly manages to escape, cutting her hand on a broken window pane. As he is leaving, he drops a banknote which Stefka picks up. She announces, as she exits the basement laundry where she lodges with Edek and her sister before the act closes, that she will use it to pay off her debts. In the second act, we are introduced immediately to a different space in which she is 'installed' as Daum's mistress. No discussion of what transpired in the interim subsequently occurs. However, any production of the play must in many ways hinge on decision-making relating to this 'absent' information.

Figure 11: Gabriela Zapolska in 1909. By kind permission of Warsaw Theatre Museum.

Zapolska died in 1921, in Lwów. It has been documented[8] that she was at the time planning to write a three-act play – never completed – that was to share many of the themes she tackled in the works included in this book. Entitled *Likwidacja* (*Liquidation*), it was to be a three-hander, in which an upper-class woman demands that her lover, a fifth-year medical student, should break off ties with her lower-class rival before she agrees to marry him. The protagonist was to be based on a doctor, Eugeniusz Kapitain, who was then treating the playwright. The play would perhaps have reflected and extended many of the ideas she had explored throughout her distinguished and difficult career as a playwright; class distinction, romantic and sexual rivalry; the impossibilities and difficulties of nurturing and sustaining love in a cold economic climate; the possibility of loving more than one person at the same time and the tensions and stresses that arise when one tries to juggle a fulfilling professional life with a fulfilling private one.

Shortly after Zapolska's death, suspicions were raised that this was not due to natural causes. It was insinuated that the will she had written during her last days, in which she left everything to Eugeniusz Kapitain, had been composed and signed by a woman not in possession of her full faculties and under duress. Following a court-case, the will was declared null and void, though Kapitain was not sentenced or punished. Zapolska's brother and sister, with whom she had had difficult relationships since her divorce and so-called illegitimate pregnancy in her late teens/ early twenties, took over her personal effects and subsequently auctioned everything off. A plan to collect and archive for the city of Lwów all that had belonged to her was never realized.[9]

Notes

1. Murjas, T. (trans.), *The Morality of Mrs. Dulska* by Gabriela Zapolska, Bristol/Chicago: Intellect, 2007.
2. This is the name of the central character and consequently I have not translated the title.
3. Davies, N., *The Heart of Europe*, Oxford: OUP, 1986, p. 177.
4. Crace, J., 'Move over, Ian Rankin', g2 (*The Guardian*), 23.01.09, p.14.
5. Hoffman, E., *Shtetl*, London: Vintage, 1999. Polonsky, A., *The Jewish Community in Warsaw*, Oxford: Blackwell, 1988.
6. This title might also be translated as *That One* but I have opted for *The Other* given that the play is about cultural difference and national allegiances – indeed, about 'otherness'.
7. Rurawski, *Gabriela Zapolska*, Warszawa: Wiedza Powszechna, 1981, p. 215.
8. See Czachowska, *Gabriela Zapolska*, Kraków: Wydawnictwo Literackie, 1966, p. 495.
9. See Kallas, A., *Zapolska*, Warszawa: Renaissance, 1931; Czachowska, J., *Gabriela Zapolska*, Kraków: Wydawnictwo Literackie, 1966; Rurawski, J., *Gabriela Zapolska*, Warszawa: Wiedza Powszechna, 1981.

'To You, it is Light – To Me, Darkness'

Małka Szwarcenkopf (1897)

In the late 1890s Zapolska returned to Poland from Paris where she had been attending actor training classes, including at the Comédie Française, and had performed, in spite of the limitations imposed by a strong Polish accent, in both André Antoine's Théâtre Libre and Lugné Poe's Théâtre de l'Oeuvre, on one occasion playing a foreign aristocrat. She had also successfully made contact with Polish émigré circles, emigration by Polish artists and intellectuals to Paris being a frequent occurrence during the nineteenth century, due to the repeated failure of insurrections and the quashing of freedoms of expression. She had, in addition, sent journalistic articles back to Poland, which had been published in the Galician press, portraying scenes of Paris life.

In 1897, the year *Małka Szwarcenkopf*, the play that secured Zapolska's gradual rise to national fame, was written, the playwright, now aged forty was living in Warsaw, then in the Russian partition. It turned out to be a period of prolific literary and theatrical activity. At the beginning of the year she was invited to participate in a series of guest performances with provincial touring companies. In January she performed to critical acclaim in Lublin as a member of Felicjan Feliński's company. In February she took part in a charity concert organized in Warsaw, reciting extracts from a poem by the Polish writer Kazimierz Tetmajer. In the second half of March she was associated, for a series of appearances in Płock and Włocławek, with Lucjan Dobrzański's company. It is clear, from the engagements she received and available reviews of her work, that at this point she was increasingly respected as a significant literary and theatrical figure. Indeed, her stay in Paris had to some degree served to bolster her reputation. She frequently received standing ovations and it was commented, in relation to her work with Antoine, that she had become the prime exponent of a new, more naturalistic and unaffected performance style in Poland. This innovation, however, associated primarily with somewhat controversial naturalistic play texts, was not to every critic's taste – particularly those associated with the conservative press. Zapolska's reputation as a vindictive prima donna was still in formation – this aspect of her public persona was to develop to its fullest over time, based chiefly on an anecdote that she had struck a female co-star with the wrong (solid) part of a stage prop (an axe) deliberately during a performance.

At the beginning of April she travelled, with Członkowski's company, to St Petersburg, in order to perform at the Kononov theatre. In April and May she starred in, among other plays, Meilhac & Halévy's Frou Frou (1869), Jan Słowacki's Mazepa (1840) and her own hugely popular Żabusia (Little Frog) (1896).[1] This play is set in Warsaw and tells the story of a clandestine extra-marital 'affair', conducted mainly in the Botanical Gardens, by an infantilized, seductive bourgeois mother of one, full of affectations, whose husband is, by her own estimation, a somewhat unsophisticated, overly direct man with rural roots. Little Frog – as she is playfully nicknamed by her doting, comical and aged parents – is drawn into conflict with her sister-in-law, Maria, who constitutes the austere polar opposite to her highly contrived, exaggerated femininity. Maria happens to be the fiancée of slippery Little Frog's lover. She falls desperately ill when she learns of the 'affair' and her hair is shaved off during a period of high fever. When she recovers she effectively kidnaps her niece for complex reasons, including revenge. The play includes some brilliant comic scenes involving the lover's visits to the house in the absence of Little Frog's husband, Little Frog's thoroughly wicked, apparently sexually sophisticated neighbour and several frantic entrances and exits through – and concealments on – a balcony.

Zapolska's touring performances were highly successful and on this basis she made plans, reported in the Polish press, to remain in St Petersburg and sign a contract with the state Imperial theatres, via which she would have reaped considerable financial rewards and achieved a greater stability of sorts, though invariably far less creative autonomy. However, these plans never came to fruition and she herself broke the connection.

As a consequence, upon returning to Warsaw, she had effectively eliminated the possibility of performing in the state theatres of any city in the Russian Empire. What followed was a period of intensive focus on playwriting. It was in June that she wrote Małka Szwarcenkopf, in Polish, with some Yiddish, for the Eldorado Theatre, which was a 'garden theatre' (see p. 62, f. 94). Kazimierz Braun points out that 'the history of productions in the Yiddish language within the Jewish communities in Poland goes back to 1876 when Abraham Goldfaden (1840-1908), actor and playwright, created the first professional theatre company'. He adds that during the period in question (specifically 1885-1905) the Russian authorities imposed a ban on plays written in Yiddish in Russia itself and the Russian partition and that this 'hampered, but did not stop Goldfaden's work'.[2] It is clearly important to take this information into account in relation to the play's performance histories. The Eldorado was the nineteenth-century equivalent of a 'fringe venue', situated on the borders of the Jewish district. Interestingly, it is referred to as a location, reflexively, within the fictional play world, as the place where Małka's father, Old Szwarcenkopf, sells his matches and cigarettes. The phenomenal success of the play – which fuses melodramatic and naturalistic conventions – led to Zapolska's completion, the following year, of a sequel, *Jojne Firułkes*, in which Małka – who commits suicide in the closing act of the first play – appears as a ghost and her former husband, the pitiful, broken Jojne, as the protagonist. The sequel was, in relative terms, a flop. During this period Zapolska also completed another play, a melodrama entitled *Antek Nędza*, hoping that a state theatre might stage it. However, this plan did not come to fruition.

During the summer season of 1897, working as a freelance actress, Zapolska performed several times in the Warsaw garden theatres; at the Bagatela, or Bagatelle, also managed by Dobrzański, in the play *Karpaccy Górale* (*Carpathian Mountaineers*) (1843) by Korzeniowski (the father of Joseph Conrad); at the Eldorado in her own play *Małka Szwarcenkopf* (she also contributed towards the direction of the premiere); and at the Wodewil, or Vaudeville, managed by Michał Wołowski, in E. Grange and L. Thiboust's *The Thief* (c.1857).

Małka Szwarcenkopf premiered in Warsaw on 10 July 1897 with an all-Polish cast and was first published in 1903. Different versions of the play's genesis exist. Dobrzański, manager of the Eldorado, claimed that Zapolska approached him with the idea shortly after the opening of the season (1 June). Aleksander Rajchman, on the other hand, claimed in a review that Dobrzański first approached Zapolska, requesting that she should write a play representing the life of Warsaw Jews in order to address a lack of relevant available performance texts, thinking particularly of the theatre's location, its politics and the community it was intended to serve. As Rurawski[3] comments, by choosing this subject matter, the playwright keyed in to debates very much 'of the moment' in intellectual and political circles, and framed by an increasingly oppressive programme of late nineteenth-century Tsarist 'Russification', regarding Polish-Jewish assimilation and what form(s) this might take. This perhaps seems the most likely version though, as Aniela Kallas, who knew the playwright, suggests, Zapolska had an idea for a similar play much earlier on, between 1883 and 1885, in Lwów, where she lived in the Jewish district and reportedly met a woman called Jenta (who appears as a character in the play) who recounted the story of 'some Małka's marriage to a stupid Jojne'. Zapolska had also known a tradeswoman called Pake Rozenthal in 1884/85, whom she had owed a considerable sum of money.[4] Characters based on these figures first appeared in Zapolska's earlier short stories – Jenta in *We Krwi* (*In the Blood*) (1891) and Pake in *Wodzirej* (1895). Zapolska's interest in the life of Polish Jews is also expressed in her 1887 novella, *Peri i Raj* (*Peri and Paradise*), in which she traces the life of a Małka Feigenzwejg, whose fate bears strong similarities to Małka Szwarcenkopf's.

The scenes in *Małka Szwarcenkopf* containing the betrothal ceremony arose, according to Zapolska, as follows

the betrothal scene, Jojne's arrival, the arrival of the girls, the handling of the kerchiefs, the singing, the character of Mowsze [the elder], and finally of the Marszelik himself, have been written by me, and only the words of the Marszelik, written by me in Polish, have been translated by Mr Modzelewski into Yiddish, which in my own copy has not been crossed out, but has been added (I mean in Yiddish). I left this [decisions about Yiddish usage] to the director [Dobrzański] and the actor playing the part of the

Marszelik [Modzelewski]. The wedding couplets and the tuchim [this is a mistake and should read tenaim] were written by an authentic Marszelik, Mr Jukiel (I will not mention his surname). I on the other hand wrote my betrothal scene on the basis of information from two street dealers in second hand goods, to which I have witnesses.[5]

The hand-written copy of the play appears to confirm this version of events – next to the playwright's Polish text is written, in a different hand and in pencil, a Yiddish translation. Zapolska felt compelled to defend her intellectual property when Modzelewski sued her (and lost) suggesting that he had written aspects of the scene. In her defence, Zapolska claimed that prior to his involvement with the production, and even at her first acquaintance with him, she had presented the completed play in its entirety to the Russian censor.

This argument is significant. We know that Zapolska could not speak fluent Yiddish but that she was attempting to write for a mixed, often bi-lingual, audience of Yiddish and Polish speakers – this, indeed, was part of the political remit of the Eldorado, at a time when the public performance of plays written entirely in Yiddish was banned. We know from other sources (for example reviews) that as part of live performances of this play, Yiddish usage is likely to have been considerably greater than the traces we have in both hand-written and published versions. Zapolska wrote extremely quickly and often for an upcoming performance and so this type of scenario was arguably inevitable and it is now difficult to retrieve completely reliable information about the exact nature of the live performances in question, each one of which would, in any case, have differed, irrespective of the level of improvisation allowed or encouraged. This series of events might also account for some irregularities in terms of both Yiddish and French language usage in the published versions.

The popular success of the play at the garden theatres can be expressed in material terms. There were 88 performances altogether, most of them at the Eldorado, but also including twenty at the Bagatela and twelve at the Wodewil. The number of tickets sold for the premiere exceeded 1,600 (the previous day the theatre had sold 347 tickets for another performance, which was more usual). On the 12 July the performance was sold out. Sales remained extremely high throughout the run, always exceeding 1,000 tickets. Zapolska had been paid an advance of 300 roubles, whereas the production grossed 22,000 in one season. This was, in relative terms, a theatrical phenomenon, and the play soon attracted the attention of directors of permanent theatres and touring provincial companies across the former Polish territories. Zapolska asserted her intellectual property rights in a statement in the *Daily Courier* on the 30 July. By the end of August, the main theatres in Lwów, Kraków, Łódź and Lublin had acquired performance rights. The play was also performed in several more theatres in these cities, as well as in Poznań, Wilno, Łuck, Bydgoszcz, Toruń, Kiev and New York (in Polish and Yiddish). It was translated into Czech and performed in 1907 in Prague, into German around 1899 and performed in Vienna, into Russian in 1901 and performed in Moscow and Odessa and into Yiddish and performed in Warsaw in 1917.

Jadwiga Czachowska[6] understands the success of the performance chiefly within the context of a particular version of Polish theatre history, rather than Yiddish theatre history (probably due to the lack of information available to her about the latter in the 1950s, when she completed her bio-bibliography). A more unified approach might on the whole be infinitely more desirable given that both strands can be seen as developing in the same city. She quotes from the *Warsaw Courier* and the *Izraelite* newspapers, where agreement was expressed that the playwright had, in *Małka*, achieved an effective juxtaposition of contrasting perspectives via strong characterization and had captured some of the complexity of questions of identity being debated in the potentially inflammatory political climate. Both publications identified the playwright's apparent attempt at impartiality as a positive strategy. In addition, she was commended by several reviewers for representing 'new subject matter' in a theatrical context. Others suggested that the play balanced precariously between gritty realism and melodramatic pathos and that the protagonists as a consequence did not arouse sympathy. Yet others, however, most harbouring a strongly right-wing, Polish nationalistic tone, expressed objections to the use of Yiddish in the theatre, it being regarded as 'inferior' and the 'language of the gutter', not suitable for a Polish stage. In addition, the fact that actors appeared to be adding more Yiddish than may have been suggested by the manuscript itself, in an improvisatory fashion, was regarded with suspicion.

Michael C. Steinlauf, in a fascinating book that brings together a series of articles about the representation of Jews in Eastern Europe, locates the play and its initial performances more firmly in a different set of highly significant and under-explored contexts crucial for gaining an understanding of its history. He cites Eliza Orzeszkowa's *Meir Ezofowicz* (1878)[7] and Karl Gutzkow's *Uriel Acosta* (1846) as 'influential predecessors' of *Małka* in Polish literature and theatre and writes that

> in focusing on the custom of arranged marriages as the instrument of Małka's destruction, Zapolska chose a theme hardly foreign to Jewish audiences but placed it in a modern context. Arranged marriages (as well as hadorim [traditional elementary schools], the object of her concern in *Jojne Firułkes*...) had been regularly attacked by Polish and Jewish reformers since the beginning of the nineteenth century and were constantly parodied in Yiddish literature and theatre.

Also important in this context is the consideration that Małka's motivation might have been drawn by Zapolska as more nuanced than Steinlauf implies, though this may be something that emerges to a greater degree in performance. She is portrayed as a highly complex figure – arguably irrationally stubborn – someone who is, up to a point, aware of her limitations of understanding in relation to her own background. Indeed, negative attitudes towards arranged marriage are arguably also critiqued throughout the play. Steinlauf suggests that there is 'nothing particularly Jewish' about the protagonist (it might also be interesting to ask whether there is anything particularly Polish about her), though what precisely these categories might mean or might have meant is somewhat difficult to quantify. In addition this may arguably have been Zapolska's intention. In what sense, we are prompted to ask, is Małka Jewish, or not, since Zapolska perhaps uses the character, given her own cultural and political position, as a way of mediating between different sets of social and cultural conventions theatrically and problematizing notions of fixed categories and boundaries in relation to questions if identity.

The result is, as Steinlauf expresses it, the character's 'universality' – a difficult concept that one might wish to interrogate further. He continues; 'for many turn-of-the-century Warsaw Jews, whose lives had begun to be rent by profound intergenerational and domestic conflicts' (those Zapolska indeed seeks to explore) 'Małka's simple declaration that "every human being has the right to live and be happy" probably struck a chord'. He argues that in this play: 'Warsaw Jews gained something even Goldfaden had not been able to give them: the first, however flawed, theatrical reflection – several years before the production of comparable Yiddish plays – of themselves.' Steinlauf explores extensively what may have 'appealed so mightily to Jewish as well as Polish audiences'.[8] Framing his argument with the suggestion that Polish perceptions of Jews remained consistently rooted in ideas around 'exoticism', he puts forward the idea that Polish critics of the play assumed that what rendered it additionally popular with its various audience members was Zapolska's so-called 'ethnographic approach'. It may be argued, for example, that they read it in terms of concepts of realism and authenticity – as a kind of 'historical' or 'social document' – rather than, perhaps, in terms of theatricality and representation, which is arguably what Jewish critics also did, from a different perspective. Note also Steinlauf's phrase *flawed theatrical reflection*. Steinlauf asserts, however, that Zapolska's 'ethnography was problematic' and suggests that the betrothal ceremony written by Zapolska 'bears little resemblance to any known Jewish ceremony', that it is 'filled with errors of ritual … and language … and is written in stylized Polish-Yiddish jargon, with which, indeed, the whole play is filled'.[9] One might in addition assert that, given the play's form, which expresses a tension between naturalism and melodrama, issues of stylization, authenticity, representation and who should engage in it, both textually speaking and in live performance, are brought into sharper focus. For example, questions concerning whether the actors involved in any production were, should and could have been Jewish (particularly the actor playing Małka) would have been of central importance during the staging of the play. These questions would have affected the ways in which the performance was read, as well as practitioners' perceptions about possible target audiences. Inflecting and fuelling these questions was the broader political context, with its fermenting debates concerning nationhood, as well as the daily re-enactment of social inequality and discrimination, which the play's naturalism purported to express and explore. Arguments concerning identity formation and its destabilization, tradition and progressivity, authenticity and dissimulation would have been key concerns, particularly given the perceived national and political identity of the playwright and her gender.

Stylization in terms of patterning, emphasis, rhythm and expression is common in varying degrees to all Zapolska's plays, whether they include Yiddish, or Russian, for example, or are written exclusively in Polish, as are characters that might be described as verging on – or engaging with the conventions of – 'stock' or 'type'. My issue with Steinlauf's argument is that he moves almost immediately to the following assertion:

> Jewish audiences may have sensed Zapolska's good intentions, but their laughter, well noted by Polish critics, was doubtless not that of delight. Ironic and indicative of the cultural abyss that continued to separate Poles and Jews is the Polish interpretation of this Jewish mirth, as well as the writing of a 'Jewish play' which, with the best of intentions, could only parody actual Jewish customs.

Without asserting that Zapolska, or the many directors of Małka, achieved ethnographic accuracy (it is impossible, I think, to assert the 'authenticity' of the latter given the ephemeral nature of performances that occurred so long ago, and my own position of limited knowledge of the history of Jewish custom in practice prevents me from asserting the former) I would suggest that the following two issues might be considered, which are key to developing readings of the play and its performance histories. Firstly, why might a non-Jewish playwright be perceived as incapable of representing Polish-Jewish customs, in any language, and is it only possible to represent these in one particular way – or are they utterly inflexible, never having been subject, in reality, to any culturally and historically specific intervention of any kind? In what sense is the fact that Steinlauf knows of no Jewish betrothal ceremony in which a group of girls actually danced around the bride and presented her with flowers problematic? Does the inclusion of these actions theatrically signify a particular kind of failure, betrayal and transgression? It is also worth pointing here towards a suggestion that a source for the betrothal ceremony, a rabbi, was said to have avoided giving specific details for fear of giving rise to the blasphemous theatrical treatment of religious material.[10] It also seems unlikely, given the Eldorado's remit, that the directors would not respond to perceived production problems as any given run progressed at the risk of alienating potential audiences. Secondly, I believe it is impossible to determine why the many thousands of Jewish audience members of several productions may have been laughing (it is very difficult to quantify the nature or volume of this laughter and how exactly it differed from 'Polish laughter' from the theatre reviews). However, I would like to add another suggestion as to why a diverse Polish audience might additionally have laughed at the acts in question, and that is, that the betrothal is represented as failing, that there is an extremely potentially comic role reversal involved – that it is, in short, a potentially very entertaining and highly theatrical series of scenes which are, in their perhaps, as Steinlauf argues, limited context, already intended by the playwright to contain strong elements of parody. Małka remains silent almost continuously throughout, with arguably rather stereotypically masculine self-restraint and Jojne is forced into the space, like a stereotypically shy young bride, weeping and protesting. Without disputing Steinlauf's reservations, I would suggest that some further qualification might be required and accept that it is difficult to make this given the limited information about live performance now available. In addition, tracing responses to the performance of Zapolska's sequel to the play, *Jojne Firułkes*, discussed later, Steinlauf records the fact that the play closed after only nineteen performances; that, in spite of efforts to attract a Jewish audience, they came reluctantly; and that Zapolska herself recorded the fact that Jewish audience members appeared extremely offended by the play, Orthodox Jews walked out of the Kraków theatre and at the second performance there was even hissing. If audience members were indeed at liberty to make decisions such as these in relation to theatrical performances, albeit in a different partition, then the popularity of *Małka* with a range of audiences appears to imply that the opposite of offence was true in the case of this particular play. It is likely that it would quite simply have closed.[11]

The Galician premiere of *Małka* in fact took place in Lwów on 6 October 1897 and until 1900, 35 performances took place. Critical opinion was divided and the production did not 'take off' in the same way as it had in Warsaw, perhaps because its comparatively urbanized setting was not so immediate and recognizable to the inhabitants of this city and thus did not key into debates about identity politics. Some critics claimed that it was one of the best contemporary plays to have been written, on account of its strong visual effects and characterization. Others asserted that its only significance lay in the fact that Zapolska had introduced 'new subject matter' – the representation of Jewish characters in a naturalistic fashion – to the stage. Yet other critics claimed that only Acts 3 and 4, with their 'ethnographic originality' were worthy of praise, contending that, in other places, the play was badly (even 'naively' and 'stupidly') written. Catholic and overtly nationalistic publications expressed contempt with regard to 'the staging of a play about Jews', claiming that Zapolska was adding fuel to the 'philo-semitic' movement. The use of Yiddish in a public forum was again severely criticized. In association with the staging of *Małka Szwarcenkopf* by the Lwów Theatre, at the beginning of November, Zapolska herself visited the city and was present at the fourteenth performance. During her stay she talked with the director Ludwik Heller about the possibility of staging her new play *Antek Nędza* and the forthcoming *Jojne Firułkes*. The outcome of the discussions appears to have been positive, since soon after Zapolska began her research for *Jojne*.

In addition, towards the end of August the playwright had signed a contract with the reputable Kraków director Tadeusz Pawlikowski. They planned to stage a cycle of plays from Antoine's repertoire, drawing on her Paris experiences. Her first appearance in Kraków was in the role of Laura in Hervieu's play *The Law of Man* (1897) and took place on 9 October. It received positive reviews. In total, Zapolska took on a further six leading roles during the remainder of 1897. Three of the plays in question she had translated herself and as such is credited for introducing them to the Polish stage, namely G. Courteline's *Boubouroche* (1893), A. Belot's dramatization of A. Daudet's novel *Sappho* (1884) and a play by T. Gautier & A. Silvestre. Interestingly, only the first of these had featured as part of Antoine's repertoire at the Théâtre Libre.

Whilst in Galicia, Zapolska also intensified her literary efforts. She became part of a circle of both prominent and emerging writers and artists who together published the weekly *Życie* (*Life*), which had announced her arrival in Kraków. It is important not to underestimate the significance of this publication, which has achieved iconic status in terms of its impact on cultural life of the city as well as the modernist movement as a whole. Extracts from Zapolska's plays, short stories and her reviews were printed in the weekly. In addition, she belonged to the editorial team, working with chief editor and publisher Ludwik Szczepański (with whom she had a close personal relationship) and alongside Artur Górski, Władysław Orkan, Adolf Nowaczyński, Ludwik Solski (who later played Jojne Firułkes in the play of that name) and the artists Włodzimierz Tetmajer and Jan Stanisławski. The hugely influential playwright and artist Stanisław Wyspiański was also on good terms with her and painted a decorative curtain for her theatre dressing room. Other close acquaintances linked with this group were the poet Maciej Szukiewicz and the painter Stanisław Janowski, whom she later married.

Zapolska's strong association with an essentially left-wing publication facilitated the public expression of persistent conflicts she encountered concerning her literary and theatrical treatment of Jewish themes, specifically in relation to the Kraków production of *Małka Szwarcenkopf*. The premiere took place on 16 October 1897 and over the next two years the text was staged 23 times. The right-wing, anti-Semitic daily, *Głos Narodu* (*Voice of the Nation*), which was edited by Kazimierz Ehrenberg, had expressed offence at the prospect of a forthcoming production, following its unrivalled success in Warsaw, and subsequently began a vicious, though in actual fact rather isolated, campaign against the management of the Kraków theatre and the playwright, publishing defamatory comments and criticizing Zapolska's performances in the most personal terms. The affair did indeed have a personal dimension, since the theatre critic of the *Voice* was actually related to Zapolska – Józef Łoziński – and wrote under the pseudonym 'Minos'. It was claimed that Zapolska 'unashamedly showed Jews in a positive light' and that the 'patience of a Christian audience would be taxed'.[12] Most other Polish publications, however, responded positively. As in the Warsaw press, Zapolska's 'objectivity', the new subject matter and strong characterization was commended by critics. To celebrate the success of the play on 18 October the Jewish-owned Hotel Metropol held a function, at which Jewish food was served and the menu was printed in Yiddish and Polish. Nevertheless, *Life* retaliated against *Voice of the Nation*, most specifically Szczepański, who defended Zapolska's work. The playwright produced a rather more visceral response. She laid a dog's muzzle on each theatre seat reserved for a reviewer from *Life*. In addition, she formulated her answer in her short story 'Antysemitnik' ('The Anti-Semite'), also published in *Life*.

'The Anti-Semite' is arguably a strongly polemical short story set during the late autumn in Kraków, with the late nineteenth-century Dreyfus case and anti-Semitic demonstrations in Algiers acting as a broader context for the narrative. Zapolska traces the rising career of a somewhat unfocused, neurasthenic, rootless, politically vague, ambitious and, most crucially, very poor twenty-year-old journalist, Zygmunt Szatkiewicz, who has just arrived at the *National Courier*, a right-wing newspaper, to work as a theatre critic. She based the character of Szatkiewicz on her relative, Łoziński. Szatkiewicz, the root of whose surname is the verb 'szatkować' – to chop something finely or grate it – is introduced to the reader drinking at a late-night restaurant with his choleric friend, almost to the point of oblivion, transfixed by the shape of a mirror hanging on the wall rather than his own reflection in it and worrying about his debts whilst letting money idly slip through his fingers. Zapolska represents Kraków as a downtrodden, oppressive place, full of grimy shadows, half-light and poverty-stricken characters that emerge from the alleyways like spectres, as in this description of the exterior of one of the theatres:

> …The young people stand, indecisive and laughing, without quite knowing why. He alone purses his lips and tightens his fists in the pockets of his autumn coat, feeling a kind of boundless sorrow trickling into his soul.

> Yet there, before him, the autumn night impinged upon the yellowish blackness of the square. In the centre, like the body of a gigantic beast with tautened haunches, the theatre – a single lantern blinking, attached to its side, like a dying star. The melancholy air of vast lunatic asylums and their sleeping inmates lingers about this beast. Behind the walls tragic moans and despairing howls still echo. Night falls suddenly, like a dark opiate and dulls momentarily the despair, the sobbing, the violent longing…

We watch Szatkiewicz moving through a series of indoor and outdoor locations – restaurants, hotels, theatres, domestic interiors, press offices and the medieval market square – almost as if in a dream, clutching at straws in order to render his life meaningful amidst the destitute people scrabbling about in order to make a living. He makes a little money as a journalist but appears unable to accumulate any savings, spending almost impulsively on decadent luxuries as rewards to himself for half-achieved 'goals' at work. The publication for which he works is clearly based on the *Voice of the Nation*, whose journalists caused Zapolska so much aggravation in relation to the production of *Małka Szwarcenkopf* – she reworks the name in this case to the *National Courier* and gives the editor Binder certain characteristics of Kazimierz Ehrenberg. The two main tenets of this apparently fictional publication are stirring up anti-Semitic and anti-socialist sentiment, both in the sphere of culture, where plays or performances remotely connected with Jews or Jewish subject matter are criticized irrespective of their perceived quality, and in the sphere of direct political activism, where racial hatred is fuelled and attacks on Jews provoked, resulting in the loss of life and a threat to already limited civil liberties. Many of the situations described in the story have their root in real events, most particularly the vicious, career-wrecking critiques of Jewish actresses who had, for example, played roles of Christian religious figures or had, as part of their performances, been required to make the sign of the cross on stage, which was seen as a profanity. Zapolska makes it clear that the professional environment Szatkiewicz works in, and his consciousness, is framed by a society in which, in order to advance, it is essential to act out anti-Semitism, no matter how shallow a root this 'tendency' might have in terms of personal conviction, and likewise to conceal one's Jewish identity in order to remain safe and beyond reproach. Szatkiewicz does the former – since he is not as far as we know a Jew – and builds his career on it, irrespective of the fact that his unarticulated political tendencies (except to the reader) are clearly somewhat in opposition (insofar as they are formed) to those he at first passively, then increasingly actively, condones and perpetuates at work. In other words, as far as Szatkiewicz is concerned (if Zapolska ever gave him the voice to articulate it consciously) there is no acceptable 'space' for him to act out his left-wing tendencies, since this would equal absolute poverty and vulnerability.

Consequently he puts himself at the mercy of his superiors, who instruct him in what he should write about and how he should write it. Szatkiewicz is, for them, a 'blank canvas', someone who is clearly dispossessed but determined not to see himself in this way. He turns the hatred evident in his environment on himself – if he does not churn out anti-Semitic, anti-socialist invective it is made clear that he will lose his job – and as such he writes with vitriol almost in his sleep; at one point the sentences appear on the page almost without any sense of his agency. He scorns Hauptmann's *Die Weber* (*The Weavers*)[13] in a review without ever having seen it performed (he gets his ideas from German reviews), he dreams of 'bringing down' Ibsen and at the same time fantasizes about writing a play about 'the masses' or 'the proletariat', in which dispossessed characters he encounters in his daily life on the streets of Kraków might appear – actresses, prostitutes, waiters, moneylenders, cab drivers, street vendors – many of them Jews. His views concerning how to represent the masses shift as the story progresses from a rational portrayal to something far more animalistic and in his estimation, primitive. He gets no further than writing the play's title on a blank sheet of paper, but manages to convince his work colleagues that it has already been completed and that he is corresponding with the Warsaw theatres about a production. Though at the opening of the story he is as economically deprived as many of the poor people he encounters outside his workplace – though clearly considerably richer in terms of opportunity – it never occurs to Szatkiewicz to align himself with them politically, emotionally or practically – he always keeps a distance and has a sharp eye for anyone with a 'hooked nose'. The central problem of the story, which tackles, as is so common in Zapolska's work, relationships between the personal and political, the private and the public sphere, is his close involvement with the actress Irena Pasantieri (her stage name), who is Jewish (Irma), a single mother, and who conceals her identity and her child – which he sees and responds to with distaste, having collated a 'Jewish look' with 'dirt and ugliness' – from him. Indeed, Szatkiewicz is shown benefitting, in various ways, from all the Jews he encounters and yet he is always determined to distance himself from them and able to numb any allegiance he has if it appears to threaten his career. Szatkewicz is drawn by Zapolska as a man of limited 'moral fibre', a man who will 'not look behind him' because he knows that if he does he will see a string of betrayals and repeated failures to connect.

Like Stefka in *Miss Maliczewska*, Irma is an actress who, at the beginning of the story, works in a theatre as a member of a chorus. Like Stefka, she must buy and sew her own costumes and in addition pay for her upkeep and the welfare of her child. As the narrative unfolds, we see her develop into a bit-part actress. Ironically, she is cast as a Sister of Mercy and Szatkiewicz, from whom she consistently conceals aspects of her identity, helps her with the role. Irma is very tender towards Szatkiewicz. They have a sexual relationship. In addition she helps to arrange a loan for him when he is in dire straits – in every sense she is his polar opposite and he treats her on the whole with contempt, seeing her as his inferior, since she is an actress and a woman. He refers to her consistently in the personal form, for example, whereas he must give her his permission not to address him formally. Irma is able to articulate her political views most clearly and simply and when she does so, Szatkiewicz frequently accuses her of stupidity, particularly since he is an impostor by comparison:

- I'd like to ask you something sir!
- Ask away!
- You must know better than anyone … is it true, that tomorrow they're going to launch a brutal attack on Jews?

Szatkiewicz shrugged his shoulders.

- I don't know, where did you get that from?
- That's … what they said …
- Perhaps … but what are the Jews to you?
- Nothing … I was just wondering.

They stepped out from beneath the arcade and turned in the direction of Szewska Street.

- And anyway – began Szatkiewicz again – where did you get the idea that I should know anything about when they're going to beat up Jews?

The woman was silent for a short while, then finally retorted, dropping her head low onto her breast:

- Because you work for that sort of publication, sir, in which they're constantly baiting the Jews.

Szatkiewicz shrugged his shoulders.

- Well, and what of it?
- Nothing... I was just thinking...

The snow began to fall again.

Szatkiewicz's attitude and loyalty towards Irma are tested when his superiors notice him stepping out with her and ask him to feed information to them, relating to scandals at the theatre where she works, in order to discredit that establishment. Szatkiewicz does this without much compunction. He is also represented as a habitual misogynist, objectifying the women he encounters. Irma realizes that information similar to that she is naively passing on to her lover regularly appears in an anti-Semitic publication, but has no idea that she is the source, such is her affection for and trust in Szatkiewicz. In a moving scene in Szatkiewicz's hotel room, where they make love for the first time, Irma tackles Szatkiewicz again about his job:

... She put her hand on Zygmunt's head with a dominant gesture, common only to those women, who sense that they are spiritually more resilient than their lovers.

She was silent for a long time – and her eyes were fixed on the window panes...

... at last she spoke slowly and clearly:

- And why do you hate Jews so much, sir?

But he at that moment didn't hate anyone. He felt calm, peaceful and well. Leaning with his cheek against Irena's knee, with his hands lowered towards the ground, he sat like a small, pitiful child, tired and sleepy.

And in a barely audible whisper he retorted:

- I don't hate them at all... where did you get that from?
- Oh... because you always write such things about them, sir!

He nodded mournfully.

- I write it... because I have to! – he replied almost humbly – you see, that's what they pay me for...
- Oh!...

The woman pondered for a while.

– And who pays them to invent such things about the Jews?
– Them? Who?
– Well, the editor … or the publisher …
– Them – nobody …

Irena raised her eyebrows, surprised.

– So they just do it, themselves? Huh … I don't believe that! It's clearly part of some geszeft!

She pronounced the final word deep in her throat, with a Jewish accent, and suddenly, as she remembered herself, added swiftly:

– Part of some deal they have!

Szatkiewicz did not want, or was not able, to offer a response.

What for? Why should he pick at someone's affairs – in any case what did he care about any of this.

– It must be part of some deal they've struck – repeated Irena – because surely, sir – all of the time they write that they're Christians and seem immensely proud of it. But the Christian religion is founded on love of one's neighbour … that's what the priests say … In which case why, at the National Courier, are they constantly inciting hatred against their neighbours? Surely if they're Christians they should be good to other people … and a Jew … is also a human being … well? Isn't that right sir?

He listened to these words with surprise and felt obliged to offer a response to her direct and logical argument.

– Yes … but Jews hate Christians too!

She smiled and replied with simplicity.

– What of it? So because a Jew does something wrong, a Christian has to do something worse? Surely if they're better they should set a good example.

She was silent for a while, then added:

– And you know don't you sir that with everyone, even a Jew, it's easier to get to the point through kindness rather than rage! And then – did God apportion each person a bit of land and say – this is for a Catholic, this is for a German, this for a Russian and this ... for someone else! Surely only God has that kind of right! And then if God created Jews then surely it was because they should also dwell on the earth ...

Szatkiewicz shrugged his shoulders.

– My sweet ... you don't know anything about it. These are economic, racial issues so you'd better avoid them.

She grew sadder and her eyes filled with tears.

– Perhaps ... she said – I know I'm stupid, but it seems to me that Christ did not throw stones at anyone, but rather that he forgave and spoke nicely to people!...

Now they were both silent ...[14]

Her co-workers at the theatre begin to eye Irma with suspicion because of her relationship with the 'right-wing' journalist. It becomes clear that her career will flounder. In the final test of his callousness and careerism, Szatkiewicz is asked by his editor, following his promotion to chief theatre critic at the press, to write an article discrediting the production Irma has her first bit-part in. He is instructed to report that the fact of her Jewishness renders her performance as a Sister of Mercy blasphemous. Szatkiewicz has never consciously considered the fact that Irma might be Jewish, and this is the first time it is brought to his attention. Following a very brief examination of his conscience, in the office where other editorial members of staff are present, he writes, in an act of violence against his better nature, a vitriolic, career-wrecking attack on her stage performance. He signs his name at the foot of the review, thus cutting all ties with her, very publicly.

... The role of a nun is played by the most unlikely Jewess, Irma Pasmantieri. Her Jewish background profanes the holiness of the habit and creates a sense of distaste and offence in a Christian audience ...

... Besides which this actress can't even speak Polish. The harsh sounds she emits are reminiscent rather of the jargon [Yiddish] used in Kazimierz [the Jewish district] than the sound of our mother tongue.

'The Anti-Semite' was printed in *Life* at the initiative of its editor Ludwik Szczepański, but this caused some consternation amongst the staff, two of whom threatened to leave if the story went further than the first issue. It did, however, and they did not carry out their threat.

Zapolska did not receive any money for the story and when it was published in book form in December 1898 it did not arouse much interest in the Kraków press. However, a journalist from the Warsaw publication *Izraelita* (*The Izraelite*), Kazimierz Sterling, wrote an extensive review, claiming that Zapolska had been, some years earlier, neither a philo-Semite nor an anti-Semite but rather that she had kept her distance from, as she had once reportedly called them in the presence of the reviewer himself, 'dirty Jews'. Sterling claimed that only on her return from Paris had she begun to objectively scrutinize the Jewish community and perceive that beneath the exterior of a 'dirty Jew' there frequently resided an unhappy, unjustly humiliated human being. He praised the writer's sharpness of observation and the realism of her story. Sterling underlined Zapolska's courage and boldness. Father Jan Pawełski, from a Kraków newspaper, on the other hand, accused Zapolska of having an 'over-active imagination' and of having produced a 'biased pamphlet' concerning the inter-personal relationships of Cracovians.

In 1898, Zapolska completed the sequel to *Małka Szwarcenkopf*, entitled *Jojne Firułkes*. This is a play about the breakdown of a community through inter-generational conflict. Like *Małka*, it is a five-act play written predominantly in Polish, with some Yiddish, but its form is expressionistic and episodic rather than naturalistic, which is a highly unusual departure for the playwright. She employed symbolist devices in some of her later plays, such as *Ich Czworo* (*Four of Them*), creating the mysteriously cloaked narrator figure Mandragora, whose speeches frame this essentially naturalistic tragic-comedy, as well as in a selection of one-act plays. However, in no other text does she represent environments so closely reminiscent in their aesthetic and spatial dimensions to Wedekind's, Strindberg's and Sorge's stagecraft (inevitably more familiar to an English-speaking reader) particularly as it is expressed in plays such as *Frühlings Erwachen* (*Spring Awakening*) (1891), *Et Dromspiel* (*A Dream Play*) (1901) and *Der Bettler* (*The Beggar*) (1912).

Zapolska's modernist settings for *Jojne* are highly stylized and a mixture of interior and exterior spaces. All the characters represented are Polish Jews living in Warsaw. Act 1 is set in the small shop Old Firułkes gave to Jojne and Małka when they married, as narrated in the play *Małka Szwarcenkopf*. However, rather than seeing the back room with an entrance door to the shop itself situated at the back of the stage, as in *Małka*, the spectator is presented with a vertical cross-section of the shop itself, situated to the right, and the back room, situated to the left, with a roughly central split. The entrance door is set in the back wall to the right of the shop space, where we also see a counter and various goods displayed in cabinets. The shop belongs to the increasingly wealthy Firułkes, who still thrives on exploiting his fellow men via various forms of double-dealing. The establishment is apparently managed by his son Jojne, who is hardly ever there, choosing to spend most of his time at the Jewish cemetery tending Małka's grave and lamenting her fate. In the room to the left we see five wooden beds and a table. This tiny space is home to fourteen people, including Jojne. Most of them are living in extreme poverty and unable to pay their rent. They include Jańcio, who leaves his wife Chana and their small children during this act, unable to cope with the constraints of his environment; Dawid, who sleeps all day because he works at a bakery producing unleavened bread during the night shift; the young and attractive woman Mozesa, who helps Jojne manage the shop; and her sister Gusta who is highly practical and pragmatic. This setting allows for the creation of a very dynamic space in which the tensions between public and private arenas are explored and where entrances and exits through and into 'compartments' are constant, evoking an atmosphere of intensive labour and restlessness. Indeed, everyone's actions and transactions are observed or overheard by another and there is clearly no such thing in this 'world' as seclusion. The split space also allows for mirroring effects and various visual and conceptual juxtapositions.

The relationships represented are complex given the number of characters in question. However, three of the most important aspects of this act are as follows. Firstly, Firułkes is most anxious to insure the shop and its contents against fire, seeming concerned that someone might attempt arson. Secondly – Dawid loves Mozesa; Mozesa loves Jojne; Jojne is unable to love anyone following Małka's death; Mozesa struggles with her jealousy towards the dead Małka, who is now strongly idealized by Jojne for what he perceives as her left-wing principles and compassion; Dawid is jealous of Mozesa's affection towards Jojne, who is still regarded as something of a pariah in this community, 'redeemed' only by the wealth of his father, which he himself scorns:

JOJNE   Yes, Mozesa, I was at the cemetery. There the snow had covered Małka's grave completely, snow as white as she was, when the undertakers carried her away from this place ... I stood by her grave today, Mozesa and I thought that she must of course be able to see me ... I heard her voice saying that I shouldn't love only myself ...

               If I loved only myself and not all of you, I would have left this place long ago ... Today Awrumel [a poet and teacher] told me that among us there is an aged Jew named Ahaswer; he wanders the world, wanders constantly. I'd like to wander like that too, Mozesa, so that I couldn't hear moaning, like Lajbele's moaning, so I didn't have to see Marjem hungry and her child crying, so that I could escape the poverty of others – because I'm too poor to help anyone myself ...

Thirdly, Chana's small son Lajbele, who has been attending a local school (cheder)[15] paid for by his mother since he was three years old, is finding lessons difficult, is clearly losing his good health and his will to live, and has to be forced to go to school. He is unable to hold information in his head and has to be rocked to sleep by Mozesa at night because his mother is too insistent that he should carry on learning.

Act 2 is set in the actual school he attends. On stage we see a small table and chairs and rows of desks. Through the open door at the back we can see another room, and through an open door in *that* room's back wall, we can see outside into the courtyard. The act opens with the children – Zapolska suggests 30 at the very least – sitting at their desks and reciting the alphabet in the presence of their teachers and teaching assistants, including the kindly aged Awrumel, and their mothers, who enter and leave the space, observe the proceedings, and sometimes bring new, tender young pupils with them. When the strict teacher asks for the recitation to stop, poor, ailing Lajbele continues. He is asked to be quiet repeatedly until the master realizes that he is actually reciting the alphabet in his sleep and has to be woken up. This takes place on the morning following the departure of Lajbele's father, Jańcio:

AWRUMEL   What are you thinking about Lajbele? Why aren't you looking at the text book?

LAJBELE   I'm weak … I'm choking, my chest feels tight … I'd like to get away from here into the fresh air …

AWRUMEL   (Sadly) You cannot, Lajbele, repeat after me …

MEŁAMED   Don't you understand, Awrumel, when I say that you talk to the children too much and needlessly; you just get on and teach, whatever is set down there, and no more discussion. The mothers pay for their children to learn. If I let you, you'd start chanting your own verses …

AWRUMEL   Lajbele is choking – he wants to go outside.

MEŁAMED   There's enough air in here for thirty children, so there's plenty for him too …

Later on in this act we hear a conversation between Jojne and Awrumel which is decidedly anti-capitalistic in its tone. The master accuses Jojne of being useless to his father, a withered branch, and then leaves the cheder.

JOJNE   I am a withered branch – I have to be cut away! I am a withered branch because I cannot go to the bank, because I cannot trade in the little shop! Oh Awrumel! Of course I know that the kind of business my father conducts is downright cheating; and I was there once, near the bank, with my Małka! We were passing and she said: Look, my good Jojne, how people here tremble at the sight of a grosz, how they turn into crows! I laughed then, because I didn't properly understand, but I've read it all now in the books she left behind, and then I started to think … when I met you, that's when I finally understood. Awrumel, I don't want to be a crow, because a crow can peck out a weaker person's heart and eyes …

In addition, in this act, revellers at the continuing Purim celebrations, who can at first be heard rejoicing outside, burst into the school in a flood of colour and vibrancy. A series of fascinating interactions between masked and disguised – including apparently cross-dressed – characters takes place. Dawid's jealousy towards Jojne is finally expressed publicly in the midst of this masquerade. He slights Mozesa, accusing her of illicit interactions with Jojne, thus ruining her reputation and then he assaults her alleged lover.

For Act 3 we return to the shop. The door onto the street is closed and in the left-hand space Lejbele's body is laid out on a table, covered in a sheet, and bathed in candlelight. The plot moves quickly, centring on the exploration of extreme emotions; the inhabitants of the shop mourn Lejbele, though Chana immediately decides to send her child Balcia to the cheder in his place; Mozesa tells Jojne that she is going to leave and do charitable work in Galicia, since she can no longer bear to be near him and remain unloved; Jojne tells his furious father that he can no longer remain in the shop, then leaves and returns almost immediately because he has forgotten to take Małka's books with him. In the interim, his father sets fire to the shop, hoping to claim the insurance, without realizing that Dawid is asleep in the back room; Jojne returns to see the fire, puts it out, is accused by Dawid of attempted murder and is cursed by his father who, in an apoplectic fit of rage, dramatically expires. Jojne now has a curse on his head and must live in a state of exile from his community. Reading through this catalogue of disasters, following swiftly on each other's heels, it is easy to forget how powerfully they might be expressed in performance.

Perhaps the most potentially atmospheric setting appears in Act 4. We are presented with a dark and dingy cellar housing a subterranean Jewish bakery for the production of unleavened bread. The space is filled with people who create a kind of production line for the forming bread, starting with a group of bare-footed women kneading dough at a table, surrounded by sacks of flour – passing men who further shape the bread and mark it with a knife – and ending with the bare-chested, sweating baker with his shovel standing before the red hot oven, which provides the only light in this oppressive place. Dawid and Awrumel are present in this environment. Dawid is the chief overseer of the proceedings and old Awrumel, having been thrown out of the cheder, is barely managing the work. We learn that Dawid has married Mozesa's sister Gusta, who has changed from a lusty woman to a thin, sickly mother and disillusioned wife and whose child is ill. We see various women bring their flour and dough to this place, since they have no ovens of their own, and the bakery owner complaining that business is not going well, since it will not be possible to start baking for profit until the needs of the poorer members of the community are satisfied. When Jojne, who has become a worker, arrives to visit Awrumel and is offered his job, Dawid falls into a rage, announcing that he has contaminated the flour and the bread because his father's curse lies on his head. Everyone except Awrumel bows to Dawid's authority and crowds around Jojne, taunting him. In an extreme collective act of violence he is viciously beaten and left for dead in a place that has come to resemble the pit of hell. It is little Balcia, who has been quietly minding a basket in a corner for her mother, who gives him a drink of water, in an interaction strongly reminiscent of Małka's scenes with Ryfka in Małka Szwarcenkopf.

Act 6 is comparatively short and set in the Jewish cemetery in Warsaw, with gravestones of the wealthy dead, including Firułkes, situated to the left and those of the nameless poor, including Małka, to the right. It is winter. In the stage directions Zapolska instructs that the snow should begin falling, then stop and that the moon should be seen to rise, illuminating the graves. In this location, she sets up an apparently dialectical interaction between (or within) Jojne (who is now a beggar dying of hunger, cold and thirst, because of his persistent good deeds) and the 'shades' of his father and Małka, which emerge respectively from a gravestone and the red brick wall stretching across the back of the space, bordering the cemetery. This spectral interaction was achieved with the help of electrical lighting in performance, an innovation for Zapolska. Małka informs Jojne that when she died, her soul entered him, in an act of what might only be described as 'ideological penetration':

MAŁKA'S GHOST   No Jojne! I'm very near, though you can't reach out and touch me. Not only was I close to you then, but I was you, Jojne. When I was dying, my soul went into you, and that is when you were spurred to action, Jojne, into battle, tears and suffering!

FIRUŁKES' GHOST	That is when you became disobedient and rebellious. That is when you became stupid and were deluded.
MAŁKA'S GHOST	That is when you saw clearly, Jojne, when you recognized where light and truth lie.
FIRUŁKES' GHOST	That is when you cast aside the money you had earned with the sweat of your brow.
MAŁKA'S GHOST	That is when you refused to sell your tears or sell your heart.
FIRUŁKES' GHOST	From that day on, I knew you were a failure at business because you denied yourself.
MAŁKA'S GHOST	From that day on you stopped thinking of yourself and began to think of other people – poorer people.
FIRUŁKES' GHOST	You ruined my business.
MAŁKA'S GHOST	You enriched your soul ...

An ancient guardian of the cemetery and his young, rosy granddaughter, Łaja – who has never been beyond its walls and asserts that she 'loves all the dead in this place' – discover Jojne, sleeping on Małka's grave. When he tells them he is cursed and can find no home, the guardian replies, in the closing lines of the play:

> Within these walls there is no curse – here God alone is the judge ... here they all sleep, just the same ... the cursed and the blessed ... and all turn to dust. Enter under my roof and may you feel at home. Łaja, take him by the hand and walk along with him ... I will light your way! (he lifts his lantern and goes on ahead, Łaja and Jojne follow him, with joined hands)

Prior to completing *Jojne* Zapolska reportedly conducted research, mainly by visiting the Jewish district of Kazimierz with the actor Ludwik Solski who was to play the title role. The playwright had received an advance from Dobrzański. As she predicted, there were initial problems getting approval from the Warsaw censor for performance of the play, apparently on the grounds that it had strong socialist tendencies. However, the premiere took place in Warsaw at the Vaudeville Theatre in July 1898. This year had also seen the completion of Zapolska's extremely successful, internationally performed play *Tamten* (*The Other*) written in Russian and Polish. Responses to the performance were on the whole negative and, as noted earlier in relation to Steinlauf's analysis, Jewish audiences kept their distance. It seems that Zapolska had made particular efforts to research the locations for the play and, for the Warsaw performances, a complete school with 'real' teachers and pupils was engaged. Czachowska records the largely negative responses of the press (far more negative than Steinlauf implies). The actors' performances and the direction were commended. However, the play itself was not on the whole seen as impartial, but biased, with a moralizing tone; its form read as broken-backed and faulty and the antagonism its protagonist felt in relation to his environment perceived as 'artificial' and irrational. These criticisms invariably have as much to do with the expressionistic devices employed by Zapolska – innovations in themselves – as well as the subject matter she chose to tackle. They may also have been intensified by the level of official censorship associated with this play, about which I have hitherto been unable to discover any concrete information.[16] Zapolska had nevertheless created an uneasy fusion of tendencies in a highly charged political climate. Interestingly, as Czachowska points out, at the Kraków premiere, anti-Semitic members of the audience were as opposed to the play as Orthodox Jews and Jewish intellectual circles. She quotes Zapolska, who asserted that several Jewish audience members came to see her, explaining that the performance was deeply offensive to them on religious grounds, and also on account of the cross-dressing, seen as profane, at a Purim[17] ball. When Zapolska went to see the performance, she subsequently described it as a distortion of her intentions and her own response as that of 'shaking with rage'. Interestingly, for the first time (since she had previously been ill) she worked on the realization of the Lwów performance herself and here some Polish critics suggested that the play was more significant in terms of its left-wing political and social agenda than *Małka*.[18]

Steinlauf is critical of the play once again in relation to issues of authenticity and representation that were just as pressing in 1896:

> Such efforts [by the playwright to achieve ethnographic accuracy via research] were in vain, however. Neither a *kheyder* [cheder] where Jewish children don't know the Hebrew alphabet, nor a 'Purim ball' featuring a can-can, nor a child's funeral at which a grieving mother reckons up burial costs, nor the use of a *kherem* [curse] (employed, and rarely, only by religious authorities) by a father to curse his son – none of this bears any resemblance to anything Jewish and, as the Polish-Jewish journalist Henryk Lew correctly noted, 'in fact stands in contradiction to the Jewish spirit.'[19]

Czachowska also records some of Lew's other comments – that the 'programme of reform' that Zapolska suggests in the play (which it is now perhaps more difficult to quantify, once one identifies the play's expressionistic form) is 'inaccurate'. Similar problems occur concerning Steinlauf's statement in relation to discerning what actually occurred as part of live performance. Once again Zapolska claimed that she left the sections involving Yiddish to be fashioned in more detail by the director, and complained about some interventions made by performers in Warsaw and Kraków. Consequently, what we have in printed and handwritten versions may not be a record of how some performances actually worked. Secondly, for example, there does not appear to be any reference to a can-can at the Purim ball in the text (which is a celebration that, like Małka's engagement, Zapolska represents as anti-spectacle, or an 'anti-ceremony' of sorts). This may therefore be a reference Steinlauf has located in a review to something that occurred during performance, rather than something Zapolska included in the stage directions or dialogue. From reading his article, I suspect Steinlauf would agree that Zapolska was attempting something extremely difficult and in many ways ground-breaking with both these plays and with her short story. She had the capabilities, relevant contacts and opportunities for reaching a mass audience, of changing opinion, of forging new modes of representation – particularly since she also stood in avid opposition to statements of the following kind, written about her literary and theatrical attempts in a review in the *Gazeta Narodowa* (*National Newspaper*) in Lwów:

> Occupying oneself with them [Jews], representing them on stage, arousing certain sympathies for them, those which arise in spite of us, we must consider extremely damaging – and even more unacceptable is the introduction onto our stage of plays written in Jewish jargon. This is perfectly acceptable for the Jewish theatre, but not for the national stage.[20]

Evidently, Zapolska's complex and provocative project had made a significant intervention in what remain highly charged debates about Polish-Jewish relations.

Notes

1. Where the title of a play text comprises of a person's name, I have adopted the convention, fairly consistently, of not translating it. Other titles have been translated.
2. Braun, K., *A Concise History of Polish Theater*, Lewiston: Edwin Mellen, 2003, p. 247.
3. See Rurawski, p. 191.
4. See Czachowska, p. 172.
5. See Czachowska, p. 173.
6. See Czachowska, pp. 171–83.
7. Orzeszkowa was twice nominated for the Nobel Prize for Literature.
8. Steinlauf, M., 'Cul-de-Sac: The "Inner Life of Jews" on the Fin-de-Siècle Polish stage', in Nathans, B. & Afran, G., *Culture Front*, Pennsylvania: University of Pennsylvania Press, 2008, p. 125.
9. Steinlauf, 'Cul-de-Sac', p. 125.
10. Lew, H., 'Ze sprawozdań o *Małce Szwarcenkopf*', Izraelita, 1897, nr. 29, s. 284.
11. In light of these factors, it is also worth considering more closely the issue of this play's censorship and how exactly it may have impacted on performance. This is an important qualifying factor when using theatre reviews for the purpose of understanding performance history, since reviewers were always responding to performances that had been censored at several points throughout the production process, including rehearsal. Precise and reliable information is extremely scarce, but nevertheless illuminating. Establishing a coherent narrative in relation to this is turning out to be a protracted process full of frustration and elimination. At the time of writing, I am still attempting, after several years, to gain more extensive information about the fortunes of this particular text in performance. A copy of *Małka* which was archived in Warsaw, for example, showed – according to Czachowska – clear evidence of censorship processes in this then Russian-controlled city. It was, however, destroyed during the Warsaw Uprising of 1944 when the city was razed to the ground. Research trails have a tendency to disappear and in addition, censorship functioned somewhat differently in each partition, adding other layers of complexity. In Galicia, between 1860–1918, texts being considered for performance were provisionally censored by local police officials, who then sent them, along with a report listing their various recommendations, to the Chief of Police, in Lwów. However, as time went on, censorship in Kraków, for example, became more localized. Theatres had

to submit, along with a copy of the play, a detailed description of the performance itself, including the planned mise-en-scene. Depending on what the decision was, texts would then be authorized for performance, cut or completely banned. Hauptmann's *The Weavers*, for example, was initially banned, and this is of interest in relation to Zapolska's story *The Anti-Semite*, which I consider later in this introduction (page 25). If a performance was authorized, copies were made for the cast and crew with cuts made in red and/or blue pencil. Red pencil typically illustrated cuts made by the censor(s), blue by the director(s). However, security officials would continue attending rehearsals and had the authority to terminate the performance as well as to censor it throughout its development into a live event. This complex process and the extent of the resulting cuts sometimes meant that texts did not reach the stage of public performance, or that a run could be terminated if performances were deemed controversial. A case I am currently investigating, and which may take some time to evaluate fully, is that of a handwritten copy of *Małka* held at the Słowacki Theatre archive in Kraków. Making handwritten, or typed, copies for performance was a regular practice for all theatres. It is difficult to exactly date this text. This is partly due to cataloguing errors; it is listed at the archive as a typed copy produced in 1903 and it has no date on it. A typed copy is in fact not lodged in the archive at all. The stamp on the text appears to indicate that it may have been used after 1918, since it specifies the Teatr Powszechny as a venue. This Kraków theatre existed between 1918–1921, after the First World War, when Poland had regained independence. The current theatre archivist, who is researching material for a book on Kraków theatres between the Wars, confirms that there was in fact no performance of the play at the Teatr Powszechny during this period. Czachowska, usually very precise, does not list a performance during this period either. The handwritten copy itself may have been made as early as, for example, 1903, which is the catalogued date, or even earlier, for the first Kraków performances of the play at the Teatr Miejski, as it was then called, between 1897–99. Additionally, it seems unlikely that a handwritten copy would have been produced after 1921, when typed copies were the norm; however, it is not impossible. Czachowska has dated the copy to 1909, produced for the Teatr Ludowy, though at the time of writing it appears possible that this too was an error; she does not follow the production up in her book, as occurs with all the others she mentions. The Teatr Ludowy typified a popular form of theatre practice being developed at the turn of the century, aimed at poorer, less educated audiences, and employing actors of a range of abilities, some of whom were appearing in public for the first time or had not been trained. As such it was regarded as less professionalized and particularly emphasized spectacle. This earlier date of 1909 is theoretically possible since theatres shared archives, and material was consequently transferred as venues changed names and locations. The stamp may merely indicate the fact of cataloguing at the archive of the Teatr Powszechny, earlier called the Teatr Ludowy. Czachowska claims to have reached her conclusion that the copy was made in 1909 on the basis of a cast list written by hand, with a fountain pen, next to the Dramatis Personae. This specifies surnames only. The entire text is copied in fountain pen but the script next to the character names indicates another hand. There is in fact an additional cast list of sorts, outlined to the right of characters' names, as opposed to that on the left, but this does not include an actor's name for each character and, since it is written lightly in ordinary pencil, it is now barely legible. It could be a speculative list, related to an entirely different performance or possibly indicating understudies. In Wosiek's book on the Teatr Ludowy, in an extensive, though not necessarily comprehensive list of actors appearing at that theatre during the relevant period, only one name listed in ink in the cast list is a possible match. Wosiek does indeed list a performance of *Małka* at the Teatr Ludowy in 1909, as well as earlier performances in 1901, 1902, 1903 and 1904. Czachowska mentions all these in detail *except* the performance in 1909. In online resources developed by the PAN archive in Warsaw, however, the names of two actresses sharing surnames mentioned in the cast list are indicated as performing at the Teatr Ludowy during this period, though not as having been involved in this play, which is not listed in the resource at all. In addition, Szydłowska's book on theatre censorship in Galicia contains an apparently comprehensive list of all texts censored in Galicia currently held in theatre archives, libraries and museums. *Małka Szwarcenkopf* is not listed – which seems to contradict the existence of the text lodged in the archive and other published information. As a result of these somewhat extreme and deeply frustrating inconsistencies, it is also difficult to determine the exact date of the censor's intervention as indicated in the copy in question, except to suggest that it occurred some time between the writing of the play and 1918: within a twenty year period. Information around the text is proving very difficult to find and I am currently exploring the possibility that the play was censored but that a performance did not take place, which, given what I subsequently describe, is not impossible. Most importantly, however, the text potentially reveals information that sheds light on attitudes towards early performances of the play in Galicia, where the play opened after its Warsaw premiere. It also suggests a new critical framework for the reading of the related press responses, through which information about performance can be accessed. The text evidences the extent to which it seems that the censor intervened and the manner in which the director responded, often with further remedial cuts, to these interventions. The text contains no police stamp and there is no accompanying document in which official changes have been suggested (the reasons for these were often very vaguely indicated). It may therefore be possible that this text is a copy of a copy that *did* have this accompanying information regarding censorship (made for the prompter or someone else working on the production) that has now been lost. The censor's cuts, if the usual conventions were followed, are demonstrated in red pencil and the director's in blue. The result can only be described as a shocking mutilation of Zapolska's play. Entire lengthy sections that develop questions relating to identity politics, particularly those articulated by Małka, which form the substance of the play, have been excised. References to the wealth of Małka's aunt are cut, as is any physical interaction or discussion of love or desire between Małka and Jakób. Any reference to Małka's internal struggle, relating to her 'bi-culturality', is cut severely or completely. In Act 3, scenes 7 and 8 are entirely crossed out with red pencil. Tellingly, the betrothal scene remains practically untouched (except for corrections, in ordinary pencil, of Yiddish terminology), as does the play's ending. What results is a text that appears simplistic and reductive in its development of questions relating to Jewish-Polish identity and gender roles; the plot is now inevitably underdeveloped, characterization over-simplified, relationships and interactions vastly under-motivated. The measures taken by the censor are extreme; the play is significantly deprived of thematic richness, ambiguity and complexity. This level of intervention by the Galician censor is, according to the archivist, not unusual. She insists that more extreme evidence of censorship exists in relation to other texts, which is in itself interesting information. What the cuts do imply is the sensitivity and inflammatory nature of the material Zapolska was exploring. In *The Man*, for example, as it exists in a hand written copy from 1901, lodged in the same theatre archive, censorship along the same lines is indicated. However, the cuts, made in red pencil, are very significantly smaller. Elka's expression of desire for Karol is cut, as are all Julka's speeches that develop socialist or feminist rhetoric. These cuts affect the play considerably, but they do not serve to distort it in the same way as the cuts inflicted on *Małka*. At present, it seems that the text in the archive is a handwritten copy – I know not how many times removed – of Zapolska's original. It may have been used to indicate censor's cuts, from a different censored 'original' – for a later planned performance, which did not in fact take place. Alternatively, the copy and the cuts may have been made in relation to the *same* performance. My exhausting but clearly not entirely exhaustive investigation continues. Very importantly, it is complicated by a long history of censorship in Poland that has also affected the evolution of theatre scholarship. This is making the interpretation of various sources used in my research challenging. This aspect of my research is most certainly a work in progress.

12. 'Minos', 'Z dnia na dzień', *Głos Narodu*, 1897, nr. 237, s. 5.
13. See footnote 11. This text was initially banned in Galicia. Zapolska is exploring issues relating to different levels and processes of censorship in this short story.
14. All translations in this introduction by T. Murjas, 2009.
15. A Cheder (meaning 'room' in Hebrew) is a traditional elementary school teaching the basics of Judaism and the Hebrew language.
16. See footnote 11. Szydlowska lists *Jojne* as a censored text. However, I have hitherto been unable to discover any copy that shows evidence of how the censor intervened.
17. A Jewish holiday that commemorates the deliverance of the Jewish people of the ancient Persian Empire from Haman's plot to annihilate them, as recorded in the Biblical Book of Esther.
18. Czachowska, p. 205.
19. Steinlauf, 'Cul-de-Sac', p. 125.
20. Barwiński, E., *Gazeta Narodowa*, 1899, nr. 141, s. 1.

Małka Szwarcenkopf (1897)

A Play in Five Acts

Dramatis Personae

Szwarcenkopf[1] (*pron. Schvortz-earn-kopf*) – a street trader
Małka[2] (*pron. Mah-wka*) – his daughter
Kolumna Wiedeński[3] (*pron. Cor-loom-nah Vyed-ain-skee*)
Maurycy Silbercweig[4] (*pron. Mau-ritz-ear Sil-ber-tzwayg*) – former counting house employee[5]
Jakób Lewi[6] (*pron. Ya-koob Le-vee*) – lawyer's assistant
Old Firułkes[7] (*pron. Fee-rue-wkez*) – shop owner
Jojne[8] Firułkes (*pron. Yoy-nair Fee-rue-wkez*) – his son
Bernard Kalhorn[9] – counting house employee
Mowsze Cytryna[10] (*pron. Mov-she Tsyt-rear-nah*) – young Jewish man
Izaak Pomeranz[11] (*pron. It-zak Pomerantz*) – young Jewish man
Mojsie Radosny[12] (*pron. Moy-share Ra-doss-nee*) – ninety-year-old elder
Marszelik[13] (*pron. Mar-share-leek*)
Doctor
Jenta[14] Tyszebuf[15] (*pron. Yen-tah Tish-er-boof*) – trader in second-hand goods
Ryfka[16] (*pron. Riff-kah*) – her eighty-year-old mother
Four children of Jenta
Glanzowa (*pron. Glan-zoh-vah*)
Pake Rozental (*pron. Pa-cker Roh-zen-tahl*) – matchmaker
Rózia[17] Hoen (*pron. Roo-dja Hern*)
Chanteuse 1
Chanteuse 2
Butler
Young and old Jewish men and women, girls dressed in white, children

ACT 1

(The setting represents a very expensively furnished drawing room. As the curtain rises, a card table is revealed, on which lighted candles, cards and money are set out. Champagne bottles also stand on this table, as well as empty bottles on other tables. Two CHANTEUSES[18] are on stage. One is sitting at the pianoforte playing 'Adèle, t'es belle'[19] and the other is singing out of key. On a sofa on the RH side lounge MAURYCY SILBERCWEIG, BERNARD KALHORN. By the table KOLUMNA WIEDEŃSKI sits shuffling and arranging cards)

SCENE 1

(Maurycy, Chanteuses, Wiedeński, Bernard)

MAURYCY	Louder! Sing louder if you please!
CHANTEUSE 1	My throat's gone dry – I cannot sing.
MAURYCY	Then wet it!
CHANTEUSE 1	All bottles are empty!
MAURYCY	Ring, Wiedeński! Let more champagne[20] be brought!
	(Wiedeński rings)
BERNARD	Remarkable! Bottomless well, is it, auntie's cellar?
MAURYCY	So it appears.
CHANTEUSE 1	Have you been down to the cellar yet, Moritz?[21]
MAURYCY	No – Wiedeński has made the descent in my stead.
CHANTEUSE 1	There must be heaps of bottles.
	(Wiedeński doesn't answer – occupied with the cards)
	Well, what's the matter, Kolumna – gone deaf? Won't answer to ladies?
WIEDEŃSKI	Don't disturb me – I'm practicing Kabbalah.[22]
MAURYCY	Kabbalah – I doubt it! You're devising a new majsterstück,[23] to flourish when you sit down to play, with me.

WIEDEŃSKI	Most decidedly not a majsterstück, only a chef d'oeuvre.[24] You've left the counting house now and aren't crouching behind safety bars[25] any longer, like some wild animal – you may as well learn to respond with clarity.
MAURYCY	My dear man, nothing satisfies me more than the crisp rustle of a banknote. Holding one of these, I can slur like a thousand fat drunkards,[26] no-one gives a damn...
WIEDEŃSKI	Huh! Besides money one should also possess social refinement.
MAURYCY	And you have social refinement but no money and that's why things aren't looking quite so rosy.
WIEDEŃSKI	Aren't looking rosy? Who told you that? I most decidedly do have money – it being temporarily... tied up in business affairs.
MAURYCY	Tied up! Hear that! Tied up!
	(all laugh)
WIEDEŃSKI	Laugh, go on! Rira mieu qui rira le dernier,[27] since pretty soon I'll show you a stack of banknotes this high!
CHANTEUSE 1	Ooh – do make every effort, Kolumna, to ensure this occurs without further delay.
MAURYCY	Spare your enthusiasm. It most certainly won't occur and even if it does, you'll soon discover that Kolumna Wiedeński evaporates like camphor[28] – that's the last we'll see of him!
WIEDEŃSKI	First of all, je m'acquit lerai[29] of my debt of honour...

SCENE 2

(The same and Glanzowa, an old Jewish woman dressed neatly and modestly)

GLANZOWA	You rang, gentlemen!
MAURYCY	We did, Mrs Glanzowa.
GLANZOWA	What is your request, sir?
MAURYCY	I would like... I'd like... (hesitates momentarily)

WIEDEŃSKI	Do please instruct 'em to bring more wine.
GLANZOWA	*(Remains still)*
WIEDEŃSKI	Well? What are you waiting for?
GLANZOWA	I await instructions from my master.
WIEDEŃSKI	Tu entens, Maurice.[30]
MAURYCY	Please tell them to give us some wine.
GLANZOWA	*(Slowly shaking her head)* You young masters have already drunk a very great deal.
WIEDEŃSKI	That, madam, is none of your concern. If Mr Maurycy has ordered more wine, then wine there should jolly well be.
GLANZOWA	I haven't the honour, most kind sir, of knowing you all that well and would request that you refrain from speaking to me, to Glanzowa, in such a manner. No-one has ever addressed me in that tone of voice and my mistress, the maternal aunt of Mr Maurycy here, God bless her memory, was used to call me 'My own Glanzowa'. And so I ask you with utmost politeness to respond in a more appropriate tone.
CHANTEUSE 1	Hear that, Kolumna, you're to refer to this lady as 'My own Glanzowa.'
	(Glanzowa regards Chanteuse 1 for a moment with an expression of contempt)
CHANTEUSE 1	*(Impertinently)* Why the look, Mrs G!
GLANZOWA	Because never in my poor, dear mistress's entire life did women like you, madam, ever cross our threshold.
	(To Maurycy)
	I will send up the wine in just one moment.
	(She exits, offended, shaking her head)

SCENE 3

(The same, without Glanzowa, then a Butler with two bottles of champagne in silver champagne buckets)

CHANTEUSE 1   The sheer impertinence...

CHANTEUSE 2   Crazy old bitch!

WIEDEŃSKI   To begin with, Maurycy, you should have that unfortunate old relic removed.

MAURYCY   When I arrived from Łódź[31] to claim my inheritance I found her already installed in the house. Apparently she'd been with my Aunt some twenty five years. Throwing her out would be difficult.

WIEDEŃSKI   Yet it must be accomplished. Pointless, all this – tarnishes your reputation. Old woman in charge of the house! Pointless!

BERNARD   Wiedeński is quite right you know – quite pointless.

MAURYCY   But really I...

WIEDEŃSKI   *(Rises and approaches him, holding the cards)* You put yourself under my protection, yes or no?

MAURYCY   I did.

WIEDEŃSKI   In that case, if you want to be like other people, get your priorities straight – listen to me. Dress like me, walk, sit, eat, in a word, do exactly as I tell you. Since our very first encounter in that train compartment you've had not a single dull moment, have you?

MAURYCY   Quite true...though I'll never forget how bravely you bled me dry in that compartment, when we played at cards.

WIEDEŃSKI   Luck is on my side, dear fellow, pure luck...

CHANTEUSE 1   Or else...pure deftness.

WIEDEŃSKI   Ça revient au même.[32] Now, come over here, I'll show you the sharpest little trick in the book...

    (Sits at the card table and lays out the cards in two rows – everyone approaches)

How many cards should I set down? Twenty? Fifteen? Tell me. It's all the same...

CHANTEUSE 2   In that case, twelve.

WIEDEŃSKI   Here they are. And the second row?

MAURYCY   Nine.

WIEDEŃSKI   All done. Now count up from here, choose any card for yourselves, pause on it, then come back, omitting the second row, count down through the same number of cards as before and I will tell you, at which card you made the pause.

MAURYCY   Never – impossible!

WIEDEŃSKI   Yes I will!

CHANTEUSE 1   You'll spy on us!

WIEDEŃSKI   Absolutely not! I'll absent myself! I'll sit over here at the pianoforte and play with the keys.

CHANTEUSE 1   Alright then – go!

WIEDEŃSKI   Now, who's ready for the game?

ALL   We all are, all of us!

WIEDEŃSKI   Merci... Maurycy then – on his own.

MAURYCY   Alright!

WIEDEŃSKI   How much!

MAURYCY   Ten.

WIEDEŃSKI   Huh – Maurycy – those counting house habits won't wash. Ten roubles![33] I won't do it for less than a hundred.

MAURYCY   Won't give a hundred.

CHANTEUSE 1	Go on, little Mitzi, hand it over, do![34] Where's the harm – he's bound to lose – it's quite impossible …
MAURYCY	In that case, make it one hundred.[35]
WIEDEŃSKI	Bene![36]
	(Moves across to the piano and plays the siciliana from The Light Cavalry[37] *singing in Italian – everyone else is quietly counting cards by the table, whispering, laughing and offering advice)*
MAURYCY	Finished, Kolumna! Cease your howling and get over here!
WIEDEŃSKI	Voilà!
ALL	*(Surprised)* He guessed!
WIEDEŃSKI	The one hundred?
MAURYCY	Here it is.
WIEDEŃSKI	*(He takes the money and covers up a number)*[38] Odd or even?
MAURYCY	Odd.
WIEDEŃSKI	Even! And another, thank you.
MAURYCY	*(Angrily)* Here!
WIEDEŃSKI	I've told you countless times – only parvenus[39] pay any debt of honour in a foul temper.
MAURYCY	Somewhat difficult to remain good tempered.
WIEDEŃSKI	When one is in possession of *such* an inheritance, why waste one's anger on two little hundreds.
MAURYCY	Quite true. You're right, Kolumna.[40] Let's drink your health.
WIEDEŃSKI	Ah – that's what I like to hear!
ALL	*(Drink)* Kolumna's health! Here's to Kolumna!

MAURYCY	And what, pray tell, is the latest news regarding my change of surname?
BERNARD	You're changing your surname!
MAURYCY	Indeed! I'd much prefer not to be some Silbercweig or other any more – shows I'm on 'the wrong side of the track'.[41] Wiedeński has assured me the matter will receive his personal attention and progress most smoothly. He even accepted forty roubles – expenses. Well, Wiedeński – how do matters stand?
WIEDEŃSKI	Already passing through the ministry for internal affairs – resolution expected any minute now. A certain excellent lady owing me numerous favours has lent her support, you understand ... (*Suddenly puts his hand in his waistcoat pocket*) Odd or even?
CHANTEUSE 1	I'll play. Even!
WIEDEŃSKI	Odd – all I had was a half-imperial![42] You're lost, my little beauty.
CHANTEUSE 1	Shame on you, bleeding us dry as well!
WIEDEŃSKI	Am I blushing – no! I introduced you to Moritz – you should be grateful.

SCENE 4

(*The same. Butler, then Jakób Lewi*)

BUTLER	A certain gentleman wishes to see you, sir.
WIEDEŃSKI	See whom.
BUTLER	Mr Maurycy.
WIEDEŃSKI	With respect, I told you to say 'the honourable gentleman', did I not, you stupid oaf?
MAURYCY	It's my lawyer's assistant. Show him in. Please excuse me while I take him through to my study.

WIEDEŃSKI   Go ahead, dear boy.

                 (The butler exits. Wiedeński sits at the pianoforte and begins singing extracts from The Beggar Student.[43] *A chanteuse sits on the piano with a glass in her hand, another on the sofa, Bernard beside her. Noise, laughter, squealing)*

MAURYCY   He'll go and bore me stupid with matters of business!

CHANTEUSE 1   In that case, evict him, post haste.

MAURYCY   Be certain I will do so, with pleasure.

                 (Enter JAKÓB LEWI, a young man, very handsome, distinguished gestures and speech)

JAKÓB   *(Pausing in the doorway)* Forgive me, I see I've come at a bad time.

MAURYCY   *(Offhand)* Not in the least – make your approach, sir. What have you brought me this time? If it's money, you're most welcome. Wiedeński, play us a march.

WIEDEŃSKI   A Turkish one?

MAURYCY   Hardly – all things Turkish are better savoured sweating and in the nude. Perhaps later.[44]

JAKÓB   It's not a matter of finance that brings me here today, sir.

MAURYCY   In which case?

JAKÓB   *(Indicating the rest of the party)* It's difficult to talk in the presence of such a sizeable gathering ... especially one ... so ... convivial ...

WIEDEŃSKI   Should I play the marche funèbre?[45]

                 (Begins to play Chopin's funeral march)

                 Glad to be of service![46]

MAURYCY   Do stop it Wiedeński – you're a glorified organ grinder. Let's go through to my study, sir.

WIEDEŃSKI	*(Leaps up from his place at the piano)* Know what, dear ladies – I propose a swift transfer to the dining room. Let's take ammunition – leaving Maurycy in the clutches of the son of... Themis.[47]
CHANTEUSE	Son of what?
WIEDEŃSKI	Beyond your scope, darling! Come, my own ladies...
	(Gathers bottles)
	May the goddess of law and justice go with you!
BERNARD	And keep her in there!
WIEDEŃSKI	We'll take the exotic birds – or cuckoos – with us...[48]
	(They exit laughing and jostling each other)

SCENE 5

(Maurycy, Jakób)

MAURYCY	What's the matter? I'm warning you, sir – I've very little time and they're waiting.
JAKÓB	Don't trouble yourself. Our meeting won't last long, sir.
MAURYCY	Please, be seated! Ah – before we begin, tell me, as a man of the law, how long formal proceedings concerning changes of surname tend on average to last.
JAKÓB	What do you mean, changes of surname? I don't understand.
MAURYCY	Here it is, sir – I want to be called something different – Silbercweig isn't particularly nice. I'd like to be called something noble, like Srebrnowski – rough translation[49] – works quite well, I think. Silbercweig does have a terribly Jewish ring to it.
JAKÓB	Are you ashamed, sir, of being a Jew!
MAURYCY	Well yes – in a way I am. At the counting house I could still get away with it – but now, after receiving such a sizeable inheritance, I'd like at once to change my skin and not be...

JAKÓB

A Jew? That's strange. You see, it is better to remain a Silbercweig. You can never really be a Srebrnowski - nor for that matter will you still be a Silbercweig. You'll sell your soul then hang like the man in the moon between heaven and earth.[50] Having parted ways with your own people, it'll be difficult to gain entry to the ranks of those others.

MAURYCY

Why should it be difficult? If I've money, it'll be quite straightforward. Let me tell you something. I know very well that Wiedeński there is just an ordinary Jew from Przemyśl[51] - but he has mingled with all sorts of people and always has some money and everywhere they accept him, even among the aristocracy.

JAKÓB

That's what he tells you, sir and you believe him.

MAURYCY

How can I not believe him! His cigar case is crammed full of cigars branded with the insignia of counts and barons, given to him by his friends, the counts and barons, and in his pockets he has big bundles of visiting cards, all from aristocrats. How did he manage that? Because Wiedeński had half a brain and added the noble soubriquet[52] 'Kolumna' to his surname - now it's practically double barreled. But I cannot add Kolumna, or Pillar,[53] or any other heraldic soubriquet, because my surname doesn't end in 'ski' only in 'cweig'. How ridiculous would that sound - Pillar-Silbercweig![54]

JAKÓB

I personally wouldn't change my surname for anything in the world.

MAURYCY

I would change it from Lewi to Lewiński.[55]

JAKÓB

Why so? Your primary concern is lineage. In my case, the ancient tree of Lewi[56] happens to be older than all those of the crested nobility, with their personalized family trees and genealogy records.[57]

MAURYCY

Wiedeński has told me that he will not provide introduction to any aristocratic household so long as my surname is Silbercweig.

JAKÓB

I know very little of Mr Wiedeński, but what I've heard has not been entirely flattering.[58] Besides, enough said. I'm not your mentor, sir - I've no intention of regulating your conduct. I do, however, note that your aunt - blessed be her memory - Silbercweig or no, did honourably imbue her surname with profuse goodness of heart and generosity towards the dispossessed. The shelter for orphans and cripples on Gęsia Street is good enough reason for her surname to be blessed through long years and down many generations.[59]

MAURYCY	My aunt was a philanthropist and a democrat. She wasted her money and was obsessed with cheering up crowds of no-hopers.[60]
JAKÓB	You call rescuing a few hundred human beings from moral and physical annihilation a waste of money?
MAURYCY	Huh, my dear man, was there ever any real need for my aunt to go mixing herself up in other people's affairs? If it wasn't for her philanthropy, the fortune I inherited would be twice as vast. I've only her sudden death to thank – and the lack of a will – for being able to drag myself out of poverty and breathe with a slightly more expansive chest. My aunt didn't like me, she behaved like a skinflint, never wanted to pay off my debts.
JAKÓB	You weren't in any state of poverty sir. You had a salary at the counting house and that could've been sufficient for your upkeep.
MAURYCY	Some upkeep!
JAKÓB	Ha! I've a modest salary and live decently – I don't complain about my lot.
MAURYCY	*(Puffed up)* Because you, sir, have more limited aesthetic requirements.
JAKÓB	Perhaps this pleases me. Let us, however, move finally to the matter that has brought me hither. Well then – you are aware, sir, that your aunt was for twelve years involved in raising a young girl, named Małka Szwarcenkopf, daughter of a poor Jew, who makes his living as a street seller of matches and cigarettes.
MAURYCY	Yes – I had heard.
JAKÓB	Miss Szwarcenkopf is currently eighteen years of age and having completed boarding school in Wrocław,[61] where she has dwelt these past eight years, returns now to Warszawa.[62] Her last year at the school was paid for in advance by your deceased aunt, sir, and so Miss Szwarcenkopf has continued to benefit from her philanthropy, going on to complete her education and formally receive her qualifications. Indeed, she must now make her return to Warszawa and to this end I received yesterday an urgent message informing me of her arrival, today, on the afternoon train. What, sir, shall you resolve with respect to your aunt's protégée?
MAURYCY	*(Lighting a cigar)* My own Mr Lewi – you surprise me. What is Miss Szwarcenkopf to me? Let her go where she pleases with her certificate,

since it's not in my mind to set up a shelter for young women who've just completed their education.

JAKÓB   (*Containing his distress*) This isn't about a shelter, only about assigning a certain sum, which would allow Miss Szwarcenkopf to continue living in a manner befitting her upbringing and education. In all likelihood she'll find some form of waged occupation on her own but in the meantime she mustn't be completely neglected. Indeed, she cannot go back to her father.

MAURYCY   I am wondering why not?

JAKÓB   Because old Szwarcenkopf is an ordinary Jew and Małka must be an educated and distinguished young woman. What form would her life take in surroundings so far below her station?

MAURYCY   Not my business. Once again sir I repeat – I will not waste money in as insane a fashion as my aunt.

JAKÓB   Then you'll do nothing for her?

MAURYCY   No. And may I suggest that if you've got plans to meet Miss Szwarcenkopf, do hurry up, because the train arrives at four fifteen and it's already five minutes past four.

JAKÓB   Do not distress yourself, I'll be there in time to familiarize her with the sad news. Poor child, what will happen to her now!

MAURYCY   She'll have no shortage of guardians.[63] I bid you farewell, sir.

JAKÓB   Fare you well.

         (*Exits*)

SCENE 6

(*Maurycy*)

MAURYCY   (*Alone*) Insufferable pedant! That's all I need – to extend my patronage to some Małka or other and lavish her with cash. She must be a regular looker, that Miss Szwarcenkopf from Nalewki.[64] Szwarcenkopf – black haired Małka![65] Black as ash and with a hooked nose to boot. Fine thing to waste money on.[66]

SCENE 7

(Wiedeński, Maurycy)

WIEDEŃSKI   (Through the door) Shot of him?

MAURYCY   The coast is clear.

WIEDEŃSKI   (Poking his head in) Odd or even?

MAURYCY   Odd.

WIEDEŃSKI   You lose, for in my pocket are two half-imperials.[67] Now, come join us. We've emptied the whole lot – we're in dire need of fresh ammunition.

MAURYCY   Without delay! Let's drain two more bottles then drive out to the races. I've an urge to throw my weight around. You'll never guess what that pompous oaf proposed … Glanzowa – hey – Glanzowa!

SCENE 8

(The same and Glanzowa. She carries two bottles of champagne. She is wearing her hat)

GLANZOWA   I know exactly what you're calling for, sir and have anticipated your desires. Here are the last two bottles. Sir.

                   (Passes the bottles to Maurycy)

MAURYCY   What do you mean, 'last two'?

GLANZOWA   I mean that this beverage was purchased only during the illness of our dear, blessed mistress.[68] The doctors instructed that nothing else should be administered in her final moments. We bought extra, little sensing that soon it would all be over. And now, sir, here are the keys to the whole house. There's nothing else for me to do here. I cannot and will not watch all these debased goings-on with a placid eye. I'd have to bear witness to everything later on before honest folk and my own conscience. Last thing I want is people saying that old Glanzowa looked on in silence while evil, sinful things took place in the house of her mistress. A lowly woman I may be but I know what's good and I know what's bad and Mr Maurycy is doing a bad thing and will surely go regretting it later. I'm leaving now but you, sir, should drive out evil counsellors and godless people too – reaching for your pockets, that's all. Good health to you, sir. Come to your senses, in her blessed memory – if this carries on you'll soon find yourself out in the haystack...

(Exits)

WIEDEŃSKI   Loosened her old tongue good and proper – off she goes, on her broomstick. Tomorrow I'll ask around and get you a proper caretaker...

MAURYCY   Much better idea. Evidently. Let's go.

(They exit left)

SCENE 9

(For a moment the stage is empty, then enter a Butler followed by Małka, who is a young, good looking, tall girl, dressed in mourning. There is much expressivity and distinctiveness in her speech and gestures)

BUTLER   If you'd be good enough to wait here, miss. I'll let the master know right away.

MAŁKA   No – first of all, please ask for Mrs Glanzowa.

BUTLER   I believe I'm right in thinking that Glanzowa left through the kitchen just now, but I'll check.

MAŁKA   *(Alone)*[69] So – here, again. I haven't seen this dear house since my holidays last year. My piano, my sheet music! And here – her photograph! Stained! On the ground? Oh! My beloved guardian, how mournfully you regard me from this broken frame.

(She moves further in and trips over bottles)

What's this? Bottles? And here a lady's hat? Glanzowa's? Impossible. Wouldn't be so many gaudy flowers – not her style...

(Pause) Strange impression it makes, this room – as though some wild, unruly savage had broken through the enchantment and trampled my spellbound memories into the sullied ground. Perhaps I should leave? I must see Glanzowa. Mr Jakób wasn't at the station... so then I wrote to father, that he should come to me here.

BUTLER   Mrs Glanzowa's gone out – why not wait here, miss. I've already informed Mr Maurycy.

MAŁKA	Whatever for? Take me to my old room. I'll wait there for Glanzowa and if an old Jew with grey hair should come calling himself Szwarcenkopf, then show him up, bring also my small English trunk usually kept in the attic. I'd like to arrange all my books and mementoes of the deceased lady.
BUTLER	That's going to be difficult because that room is now occupied by Mr Wiedeński … and … in any case … here is our master …
	(Exits)

SCENE 10

(Maurycy in a huff and Małka)

MAURYCY	(Without looking at Małka) Miss Szwarcenkopf?
MAŁKA	That's right.
MAURYCY	What can I do for you?
	(Pause)
MAURYCY	(Falls into a temper)
	If you think I'm going to behave like my aunt, miss, you're very much mistaken. Hadn't even crossed my mind … She was at liberty to throw away hundreds on you – I'm not a spendthrift.
MAŁKA	(With elevation) I don't understand, sir. What's your implication? Am I asking for anything?
MAURYCY	Any such request would come to nothing … Not a single thing will I do for you, miss.
MAŁKA	Firstly, may I say that I didn't come here to ask you for one single thing. Mr Lewi was supposed to be waiting for me at the station … He wasn't there … I'd nowhere to go. Mrs Silbercweig's home has been my only retreat. And so here I came and that is quite natural.
MAURYCY	You do have a father, miss, and – firstly – a daughter should go to her father.

MAŁKA	(Holding back her tears) My father doesn't live alone. I'm only too aware that he's only a corner to himself. I was afraid there'd be no room for me there. My father will be here shortly and he will take me away.
MAURYCY	He'll be doing the right thing.
	(Looks at her, fixes his gaze, momentarily, in surprise)
	What the deuce! How lovely ...
	(Suddenly)
	Sit down, won't you, miss.
MAŁKA	Thank you, sir. I'd prefer to look out for my father.
MAURYCY	(Suddenly pacified)
	I'll open the window for you.
MAŁKA	I can manage.
	(Goes to the window, leans against the frame and wipes away her tears)
MAURYCY	(Ashamed) You're cold, perhaps, or there's a draught?
MAŁKA	No – it's warm and there's no draught.
MAURYCY	(Suddenly) Would you like a drink?
MAŁKA	Thank you, sir! You've made it more than abundantly clear that I should feel no entitlement to anything in this house – not even a drop of water.
MAURYCY	I'm not offering you a glass of water, am I, only a glass of pure glitter.
MAŁKA	(Naively) What do you mean, pure glitter?
MAURYCY	It's champers!
MAŁKA	I do believe you're referring to a type of sweet sparkling wine from France?
MAURYCY	Indeed. You've a taste for that sort of wine, Miss?

MAŁKA	Never tried it.
MAURYCY	In that case, you'll take a glass with us. Why should you cry! Lovely eyes – shame to spoil them with tears…Upon my word – if I'd taken a good look at you before, I wouldn't have addressed you so impolitely. I thought you were ugly – that's why I was angry. But you're lovely – you are very lovely.
MAŁKA	(Frightened) Please let me through – it's time I was…
MAURYCY	(Increasingly intoxicated) Why leave, now you're here – stay. Hey, Wiedeński! Lady singers! Bernard! See what a choice little morsel has come to visit and bring some wine.
	(They enter – Wiedeński, Chanteuse 1 and Chanteuse 2, Bernard – all are drunk and carrying bottles)

SCENE 11

(Maurycy, Małka, Chanteuses, Wiedeński, Bernard)

MAURYCY	Direct your eyes this way and let your jaws drop.
WIEDEŃSKI	Pas mal! Pas mal![70]
BERNARD[71]	Mm, hm! Not bad at all!
CHANTEUSE 1	(Sings) Adèle! T'es belle T'es belle Adèle![72]
MAŁKA	My God! Who are you! What am I doing here! Let me go!
WIEDEŃSKI	(Blocking her path) Shan't, queen of my dreams, 'til you permit us to drink your health from that dainty shoe. Here, you see, we imbibe from the crack of dawn and you're still dry. Call that justice?
MAŁKA	I won't be doing any drinking – let me go – I'll cry for help!
MAURYCY	(Closing the window) Now, now! First things first, no scandal. Don't be so proud, miss – play along – then leave, if that's what you want.

MAŁKA	I'm begging you, let me go now!
WIEDEŃSKI	No! First things first – she should be required to drink one glass, at least.
CHANTEUSES 1 AND 2	Yes! She must drink at least one glass!
AND BERNARD	(*They fill a glass and press it hurriedly into Małka's hand – she is crying – then Wiedeński sits down at the piano and plays a polka; the Chanteuses, Bernard, Maurycy join hands and circle Małka, jump up and down with her, singing hoarsely)*[73]

Adèle!
T'es belle!
T'es belle!
Adèle!

SCENE 12

(*The same and Jakób Lewi*)

JAKÓB	Here you are, miss.
MAŁKA	(*Throws herself towards him*)
	Jakób, defend me!
JAKÓB	You vultures![74] Let the poor child go.
	(*He grasps Małka in an embrace*)
MAURYCY	Aha! Enter the sensitive guardian – well, almost – bursting into my house like this!? Under what pretext! You do know I could have you charged?
JAKÓB	If you were sober, I'd strike you across the face for this little prank. Not only do you lack the remotest inkling of how to honour the memory of a woman who's given you everything – you're so jaded, you want to spatter this innocent child with your own filthy muck. She has come to pray beneath this roof for your mutual benefactress, oh – the one who recently drew her last breath.
MAURYCY	Naturally. That's why she has come.

JAKÓB	Enough, you base creature!
MAURYCY	Spare the grand declarations. Nothing has happened to this young miss. We wanted her to join in, have a nice time, that's all!
WIEDEŃSKI	Naturally – that's all!
JAKÓB	These ladies here should be enough for present company. Keep your distance from people like Miss Szwarcenkopf. That's my sincere advice.
MAURYCY	How exactly would one describe, sir, your relationship to Miss Szwarcenkopf? Brother! Father? Fiancé – or what?

SCENE 13

(The same and old Szwarcenkopf)

(The aged Jew enters in a cloak. He has a long beard, is hunched and lacking in confidence. Around his neck he has a crate in which matchboxes are arranged)[75]

MAŁKA	Father!
	(Approaches her father slowly)
SZWARCENKOPF	Profuse apologies, entering like this, arrangements to meet my daughter Małka here – that is what she wrote.
	(Notices Małka)
	Is that you Małka?
MAŁKA	Yes father, it is.
SZWARCENKOPF	Profuse apologies to the present company! I have not seen my daughter for two whole years.[76] She has grown a great deal and is become a very tall young woman. What do you want, Małka?
MAŁKA	I want to come back, to you, father.
SZWARCENKOPF	What mean you, come back?
MAŁKA	Surely you know that Mrs Silbercweig has died suddenly and now I've got nowhere to go.

SZWARCENKOPF   Ay, ay! What will I do with you! I am an ordinary Jew and you, like a little countess. Where will I set you down, how will I feed you! Ay, ay![77]

MAŁKA   Nevertheless father, you must take me in, at least for the time being...

SZWARCENKOPF   Well then...well then...for the time being. I will find you a husband. He would do better taking you in.

MAŁKA   Save that for later – only now, father, let us leave this place!

JAKÓB   *(To Małka)* You're sure you want to go with your father, miss. It's just that...very harsh struggles await you, in those surroundings – material and moral.[78]

MAŁKA   Oh I know – but I'll never encounter that which wounds the most – an assault on my dignity.[79] Oh! I'm not a child any more – I know exactly what I'm talking about. Farewell, Mr Lewi. We've only met a very few times and yet you've always been uncommonly good to me. I won't forget! Ever! Let us go, father!

MAURYCY   Well...I might be persuaded to change my mind after all...if you were to calm down a bit, miss...I...

MAŁKA   Enough, sir! Now *I* may command *you*, because my father stands beside me and can act in my defense. Come![80]

SZWARCENKOPF   Very well, then, very well. Let us go.

    (Returns)

    Perhaps you gentlemen might consider buying some matches? Fine matches, good, strong, dry as a bone, Swedish – straight from the distributor, quality assured.[81]

MAŁKA   Let us go, father!

    (Pulls her father through the door, after him exits Jakób)

MAURYCY   *(Mocking Szwarcenkopf)*

    Matches – strong matches, dry as a bone!

WIEDEŃSKI   *(Goes to the piano and plays a polka)*

BERNARD	Beautiful Adèle she has gone away ...
CHANTEUSES 1 AND 2	Adèle! T'es belle!
MAURYCY	Matches, matches! (*shouting, shrieks, dancing*)

(*Curtain falls*)

ACT 2

(*A very small and cramped room is represented on the stage. Backstage, a door, to the left a stove,[82] two beds and a cot, bedclothes are scattered across the floor. All manner of vividly coloured clothing hangs on the wall – silk dresses, bodices, knitted stockings and underwear, ordinary old dresses. In the corner all sorts of oddments and objects are piled high – for example a samovar, hammers, pieces of metal, old hats and so on. To the right a type of giant tent made from old curtains and bedsheets, with a flap that can screen out the audience.[83] Behind the tent, a bed and a pile of clothes and objects. In the centre a table and a few chairs, each a different type. There are masses of objects on the ground; dusty and dirty, a lack of order. As the curtain rises aged, paralyzed Ryfka is sitting by the stove, on the ground Jenta Tyszebuf's four children are playing. Behind the tent on a bed to the right sleeps Old Szwarcenkopf. The door opens and Pake Rozental enters. She is an old woman, plump, wearing a scarf on her head. Her shoes are worn and she speaks slowly, half-shutting her eyes*)

SCENE 1

(*Pake Rozental, Children, Ryfka, Szwarcenkopf*)

PAKE ROZENTAL	(*To the children*) Nobody in?
CHILDREN	Grandma's here.
PAKE ROZENTAL	And Mr Szwarcenkopf? Aha ... yes ... yes ...! Comfortably installed in bed. Well – good health may it bring him ... I'll arrange myself just here, put up my own poor feet. Hush – little chickens,[84] less noise. Grandma is sleeping, see – Mr Szwarcenkopf too is having forty winks.
SZWARCENKOPF	(*Waking*) Who's there? Is that you, Małkie?[85]
PAKE ROZENTAL	No, Mr Szwarcenkopf, not your little daughter, only I, Pake Rozental, come to enquire after the health of your most worthy person and confer on our matter of mutual interest.

SZWARCENKOPF   (*Rising from the bed*) What news then, Mrs Pake?

PAKE ROZENTAL   The matter has been perfectly arranged down to the last detail. Young Jojne Firułkes is a worthy trader, in spite of his seventeen years. The small shop on Marszałkowska Street[86] belongs to him, opposite the railway itself – it's crystal clear that business on Marszałkowska runs not as it does here, on our street.[87] There the clientele are Counts and the profit, very nice indeed,[88] because people smoke, they write. His parents' only concern is that the youth should take a willing wife – of benefit to the shop and the husband.

SZWARCENKOPF   Małka is poor and owns nothing.[89] I've barely a breath left in me and though I earn little enough money to sustain us, yet still must I carefully count – then count over again – so that one or two kopeks[90] remain, for a fish on the Sabbath.

PAKE ROZENTAL   Jojne's parents are well aware that Małka is poor – but Jojne is somewhat dim-witted and in addition, though a ravishing man, tends towards the puny side.[91] They won't be setting his price too high.

SZWARCENKOPF   Małke is very educated. She finished her schooling over on the German side.[92] Her education cost … could be a thousand, maybe two thousand, even three thousand roubles. That is great, good money.

PAKE ROZENTAL   Old Firułkes also confers his fair share via the son – he wishes for Małka to take on the entire business. The old couple will trade in fruit and tallow candles in the shop on Świętojerska Street[93] and to the young couple will they give the small tobacco shop on Marszałkowska. Jojne cannot be left to fend for himself and must have an educated wife by his side.

SZWARCENKOPF   And what will become of me? If Firułkes profits from Małka's work then I will be making a loss.

PAKE ROZENTAL   Ay, ay! You old Szwarcenkopf want to lead me, Pake Rozental, off the beaten track! Your daughter's departure a loss! How? You profit from her! Well! What exactly do you need her for? Are you not an independent seller of matches and cigarettes who stands plying his trade outside the Eldorado theatre,[94] goods strung around your neck! For the running of such a business Małka is not essential. Here she clutters up corners and this way or that must be given something to eat … Jojne Firułkes as son-in-law would for you, Szwarcenkopf, be a great business opportunity and you, Szwarcenkopf, can only with the help of such a wise matchmaker as Pake Rozental seal a contract of this quality.[95] Stop in the name of reason screwing up your nose and shrug off this pretence that your daughter must stay here – you're practically trembling with joy that she'll finally be taken off your hands. Ah ha! Pake is wise, has lived a lot, knows many fathers who wanted to keep hold of their children and at the very same time give them away … find a son-in-law …

SZWARCENKOPF   Still it remains a great loss to my person …

PAKE ROZENTAL   And when your sight has failed completely – along with your hearing – and you're no longer able to stand outside the theatre by night, then you, Szwarcenkopf, shall take your place by the stove at your daughter's new house, like royalty, and in the winter season they will cover you with an eiderdown.[96]

SZWARCENKOPF   That will be later on, not now, and a loss is a loss if they take away my Małka. Let old Firułkes offer me at least something for such a learned daughter.

PAKE ROZENTAL   You should be grateful he accepts her in the dress she's wearing never mind be asking for payment.

SZWARCENKOPF   Let him at least provide me with a new robe for the wedding.

PAKE ROZENTAL   Ay, ay! What an indelicate person you, Szwarcenkopf, are … and what will I, the matchmaker, receive from you when the deal is closed.

SZWARCENKOPF   I've already told you that.

PAKE ROZENTAL   You call it telling! Words scattered to the four winds, I'd say! How can we describe such a sum – such a paltry sum … and Miss Małka, she already knows?

SZWARCENKOPF   No! When old Firułkes has settled up with me, then will I tell her. And now, Mrs Pake, I go to strike a bargain – dusk has fallen. Such a chill, my very knees are knocking.

PAKE ROZENTAL   At the back of the shop on Marszałkowska Street it'll be cosy and warm. I'm off to visit the Rozentals on Dzika Street[97] and to arrange for their daughter. What a son-in-law – a prince, not a son-in-law! Each of my eligible bachelors, without exception – a pearl – absolutely priceless!

SCENE 2

(The same and MAŁKA. Małka enters wearing a hat, as in the first act, only this time with a little black jacket. She is very pale and wan. Entering she kisses her father's hand and curtseys to Pake)

SZWARCENKOPF   It's good you're back. The street beckons me, while the children and Old Ryfka remain at home.

MAŁKA   *(removing her hat)* I won't be going anywhere else today – I'll stay in the house.

PAKE   *(Fondly)* Miss Małka grows more beautiful by the day.

MAŁKA   You jest, Mrs Pake. I look worse and worse.

PAKE   Because on your own you're sad and have reached the age at which every young woman looks about her for a husband.

MAŁKA   Not me – I've not even thought about a husband.

PAKE   That's bad! Young, ravishing men are countless as the stars and more than one is thinking about Miss Małka.

MAŁKA   *(Shrugs her shoulders and turns to her father)* Will you come back late, father?

SZWARCENKOPF   All depends on business.

MAŁKA   It's horrible outside today – terribly cold, windy, snowing … don't be too long.

SZWARCENKOPF   I'm two weeks behind with the rent … Caretaker passed it on, from the landlady, I'll be thrown out if I don't pay up.

MAŁKA   We've nothing left to pawn.

SZWARCENKOPF   No need – only as a last resort. I'll do some haggling, perhaps, and strike a bargain. Besides, things will soon change.

PAKE   Yes, Miss Małka, soon things will change.

MAŁKA   What will you eat this evening?

SZWARCENKOPF	Me? Nothing! Sabbath the day after tomorrow,[98] I'll eat enough to last me a week...Oy! How my legs do ache! You Małka stay here at home and don't go flitting away anywhere. I like it not at all when you Małka meander about the streets. Stay here, at home. Ah!

(Goes to leave and then turns back)

And don't you dare sweep up, you hear me! If you sweep up one more time, I'll teach you! Is that clear! Don't be wiser than your old father. They may have taught you from books on the German side but we here know more from living a godly life and honouring what has been passed down from our fathers.[99]

(Exits, Pake behind him)

SCENE 3

(Małka, Ryfka)

MAŁKA	Honouring what has been passed down from our fathers. Oh! All these moral and physical constraints will suffocate me. Wherever I look – ignorance and dirt. What's the point of my life in a world like this?[100]

(Goes to the tent and pushes aside the curtain so that a freshly-made bed can be seen behind it, and, lying across two chairs, a plank-cum-desk on which are arranged a few books, ink, the stub of a candle in a bottle. Małka sits on a small stool and leans her head on her hand)

Nothing! Not a thing! I can't find work, I can't give tuition. How terrible!

RYFKA	*(Moaning quietly)* Wa – ter, wa – ter![101]
MAŁKA	*(Reviving)* Oh! That poor paralyzed woman – she's moaning! I must go to her – nothing to be done![102]
RYFKA	Wa – ter.
MAŁKA	*(Approaching her)* Would you like something to drink?[103]
RYFKA	A! a! a!

MAŁKA	Wait – I'll give you some water – where is it? Ah! The pitcher is empty…what's to be done? Hah – the poor woman suffers terribly – give her a little water, that's all I can do.[104]

(After a while, taking the pitcher)

I'll fetch it myself![105]

(She goes to exit and encounters Kolumna Wiedeński in the doorway)

SCENE 4

(The same. Kolumna Wiedeński)

(Wiedeński stands with a hat on his head and an affronted expression)

WIEDEŃSKI	Does Szwarcenkopf live here?
MAŁKA	He does. He's not at home. What do you want, sir?
WIEDEŃSKI	My word, it does appear to be Miss Szwarcenkopf.
MAŁKA	That's right. Have you come on a matter of business?
WIEDEŃSKI	I've come only to you, miss – you alone. Has your father gone out?
MAŁKA	I suspect, sir, that upon entering, you'd already been informed my father isn't home. Come to think of it, you do seem extremely familiar. I see you milling about on our street and in such a backwater as this the appearance of an illustrious bachelor like you, sir, cannot pass unnoticed. If I remember rightly, you were at Mr Silbercweig's and belonged to that convivial throng who sought to undermine me precisely when I was petitioning for hospitality and in need of a safe haven.
WIEDEŃSKI	Would you please oblige me by putting down that pitcher, miss, and losing the tone of an offended princess, which really does precious little for your complexion. Let's have a talk, calmly and quietly, like two well-brought-up individuals about to strike a not altogether unattractive bargain.
MAŁKA	I don't understand – the two of us – some bargain? And as for this water pitcher, object of your mockery, it was intended to serve as a vessel to assuage that poor paralyzed woman's thirst. If you genuinely wish to offer your kind services, sir…please – you're more than welcome…

(She presses the pitcher into his hand)

WIEDEŃSKI	Err … Miss …
MAŁKA	When I was at Mr Silbercweig's you, sir, forced me to take a glass of champagne. I in turn can offer you a water pitcher and, to top it all, one that's quite empty.
WIEDEŃSKI	(Angry, not knowing what to do with the pitcher) Where on earth am I supposed to set this down? The place is crammed full of rubbish.
MAŁKA	Depends on your point of view. As they say in France, à chacun ses gouts …[106] You never know, perhaps your pitcher is half full, or even 'overfloweth' …
WIEDEŃSKI	How instructive.[107] (Puts down the pitcher and sits on it) As they say in France, ma foi, à la guerre comme à la guerre.[108] I sit, miss, though you do not invite me. The stairway, you see, is narrow and steep, besides which our discussion will last some time.
MAŁKA	Discussion?
WIEDEŃSKI	Quite so. Are you aware, miss, that you're a very beautiful woman?
MAŁKA	And so you do regard me as a woman, sir.
WIEDEŃSKI	I certainly hope so!
MAŁKA	How strange. Up until now everyone showing any respect for my womanhood has addressed me with his head uncovered … sir … there's something … not … quite …
WIEDEŃSKI	(In spite of himself removing his hat) Frightfully chilly and besides …
MAŁKA	Besides which I am destitute, I live in a corner, in a room full of rubbish and stench. My father is at this very moment out on the street, covered in snow and freezing cold – he is selling matches and so one may not only address me whilst wearing a hat but in addition take me unawares with some base proposition or other.
WIEDEŃSKI	You don't know that yet.

MAŁKA   I can guess. One needn't spend long in the school of life to learn all the privileges afforded to us, the poor young women.

WIEDEŃSKI   If you're poor – blame yourselves. Dear me! It's entirely unclear as to what you found so terribly offensive – we only desired to have you mingle with us. You missed countless opportunities. You might well have caught Maurice's eye and that's not to be sniffed at.[109] To be fancied by him equals escape from poverty – but it's not over yet. Luckily, Mitzi's[110] officially had his head turned by you and speaks of nothing else. Enfin – you may yet have another chance, if, that is, you're willing to take my advice. Goes without saying, that I'll receive, miss, from you, the requisite expression of gratitude, not without interest. Comprenez vous?[111] Why so quiet? Approve of my proposition?

MAŁKA   … because silence is the only viable response. If I rant and rave, you'll sneer at me ironically and mock me senseless. No choice but to remain silent and cover my ears, sir.

WIEDEŃSKI   Surely you've no intention of staying here all your life.

MAŁKA   My life may be shorter than you imagine!

WIEDEŃSKI   We all imagine we'll never die. And you should arrange your life like the rest of us, taking account of the longer view. Wit and intelligence, that's what I perceive in you, Miss Małka, though you're still extremely young! You shouldn't be wasting away here in poverty and neglect – come out on top and make your fortune. I'll give you a helping hand. I'm very well situated in a world that simply adores entertainment and have, for a long time, dreamed of finding an intelligent, educated, discerning, beautiful woman who is, above all, unknown in Warsaw and who could help in realizing my plans. If the right type of apartment were to be rented, we could hold soirées … have a little gamble … if you catch my drift …[112]

MAŁKA   (Goes across to her corner, lights a candle and sits reading a book)

WIEDEŃSKI   Aren't you listening? Shame! Nothing remotely Jewish about you – no-one would spot it. You look exactly like other people – like the rest of us.

MAŁKA   Aren't you a Jew, sir?

WIEDEŃSKI   Me? What a thought! I am Kolumna Wiedeński, of noble lineage. My family is very old indeed and was known right back in the time of King Łokietek.[113] One grandmother – née Czartoryska[114] – the other née Wiedeńska, married to Manueli,[115] Venetian Prince …

SCENE 5

(The same and Jenta. A Jewish woman, still young, a huge bundle of assorted clothing hangs from her shoulder. She enters, looks at Wiedeński, raises her hands and exclaims with joy)

JENTA   Mowsze![116] Is it really you!

WIEDEŃSKI   *(Falls off the pitcher, rises, drops his hat and cane)*

JENTA   Mowsze! Nice man about town[117] you've become but I did recognize you straight away. You and your brother, that rascal my husband, like two peas in a pod.

WIEDEŃSKI   What does this madwoman want from me?

JENTA   What's this, Mowsze? You don't remember? Jenta Wiedeńska – your blood brother's lawfully wedded wife. And those are his children – he himself has fled to America, devil take him![118] Perhaps you Mowsze have heard news? Left me with four children and sends not a grosz.[119] Children – come over here – nicely Bernard! Srulek! Gołde! Chaimek,[120] come and greet little uncle!

WIEDEŃSKI   My good woman – you appear to have taken leave of your senses. Once and for all detach yourself from my person. I am a nobleman and have never been a Jew. What a fiasco!

                         (Instead of his hat he seizes the pitcher, wants in the confusion to put it on his head, water drips from it, wets him, he puts on his hat, puts down the pitcher and approaches Małka)[121]

                         What should I tell Maurycy? Are you determined to be cruel? He's even ready to offer an apology.

MAŁKA   I'd leave right now, Mowsze, if I were you, in case another sister-in-law emerges from the woodwork.

WIEDEŃSKI   Very funny![122] I'm going – just think about it...

                         (Leaves, knocking one of the children)

                         Ouch! Pardon! Mille[123] pardon!

                         (Exits)

SCENE 6

(The same, except Wiedeński)

JENTA   On my life, that was Mowsze, never mind – he's a gentleman now – wants nothing to do with our sort, the destitute. Quiet children! Quiet children! I've brought a bagel[124] each. Ay, ay, Chaimek, how greedy you are, don't take your little sister's food.

(To Ryfka) What about mother? Asleep, mother, are you? Want a little milk, mother? I'll bring it now. Today I made as much as twenty seven kopecks on an old lamp I'd bought and two pairs of trousers. And you Miss Małka, reading again! You'll ruin your eyes!

MAŁKA   No, honest Jenta, I'm used to reading in the evenings.

JENTA   Yes, but Miss Małka once read in a different way, next to a big, bright lamp, not a candle like there is here – ptt, ptt, ptt...!

(Approaches slowly) Is Miss Małka sad?

MAŁKA   Not exactly cheerful.

JENTA   I understand! We are stupid, poor Jews and Miss Małka is a learned young lady.

MAŁKA   You, Jenta, with your lack of education, are worth more than me. You work hard all day and earn bread for your mother and four children. And me – what do I do? I look for work and can't find any.

JENTA   Work, like this, for a delicate child – impossible! Miss Małka received an education and should simply sit on a couch drinking honey from a little glass and eating challah.[125] Well? An ordinary Jewish woman like me can run up and down flights of stairs looking for cast-offs and bartering second-hand goods. Let me tell you – all sorts of people, I visit their houses. Rich, poor, Jews, actresses – I've got my regulars – they sell me old dresses. Listen here, miss. Nowhere have I seen such an open, such a lovely young woman. Ay, ay! It's a crying shame – a gilded bird stuck in a pit like this. Ay, ay!

MAŁKA   What's to be done, Jenta. You can run headfirst at a wall again and again but it won't fall down.

JENTA	One other thing, miss. Your father doesn't invite Pake Rozental here for company. You don't know, but she's the most notorious matchmaker on the whole of Gęsia, Nalewki, Franciszkańska[126] and even now and again Długa Street.[127] She's got her eye out for you.
MAŁKA	*(Fearfully)* A husband? For me?
JENTA	Well, pardon the expression, but she must have some crooked youth, that nobody wants him, lined up just for you. I heard a rumour – his name is Jojne Firułkes, son of old Firułkes – owns a small tobacco shop on Marszałkowska Street. He's short, he limps and he's got these enormous, enormous great eyes.
MAŁKA	But father told me nothing.
JENTA	Miss Małka doesn't know our customs. Here no-one consults young people. When a deal's been struck, Mr Szwarcenkopf will tell Miss Małka. No-one asked me either, did I want to marry Wiedeński. There – they settled it – gave me away. I was seventeen, he was eighteen, a pair of asses the two of us – simply the custom. Matchmakers and parents arrange everything. They'll lead Miss Małka the same way to her wedding – the same for centuries. That's how they gave my mother away … it'll be the same for my daughter. It's just a custom. I'll go for some milk.

(She takes a cup and turns to the children)

	You be good, now – mother will be back before you know it, oy, oy! How my legs do ache! How my legs do ache!

SCENE 7

(Ryfka, Children, Małka)

MAŁKA	Can it be possible, what she said! They could marry me off? Give me away! Is a father's rule so utterly boundless? It's simply impossible; I too have a soul, free will and can say 'I don't want this'. What destitution! What terrible moral destitution!

(Jenta returns with milk, goes to the stove, pours a little in a cup and brings it to Małka)

JENTA	*(Tentatively)* Have a drink of milk, Miss … you've eaten nothing since morning.

MAŁKA   *(Weeping)* Thank you, kind Jenta.

JENTA   Miss, don't you cry – my eyes well up at the sight. I already wept buckets when that rascal of a husband threw me over – wandered off to stupid America – it's a miracle these eyes weren't corroded by tears. More unhappiness there is in this world than happiness, that's so. Ay, ay!

                       (Goes to the stove, pause, then the quiet singing of children is heard offstage)

JENTA   *(To the children)* Hush! Listen all! How children in the cheder downstairs learn to sing so beautifully.[128]

SCENE 8

                       (The same and Jakób Lewi)

JAKÓB   Is Miss Szwarcenkopf at home?

JENTA   Miss Małka is sitting in her little corner, just there. Go to her, sir, if you don't mind, since she's very sad and weeps! You did well to come by and see us today…

JAKÓB   The snow's falling thick and fast. I wanted to come earlier – not a sleigh in sight.

JENTA   You did well in any case, sir. Your good mother's health? Your father's? And Miss Flora? I was at the Schranne family home on business today and saw her through the door. A very worthy young lady. The wedding will be when?

JAKÓB   I know not, my own Jenta!

                       (Approaches Małka who has been sitting in her tent with her head in her hands)

                       Good evening, Miss Małka!

MAŁKA   *(Joyfully, lifting up her head)* Oh, it's you, sir.

                       (Gives him both her hands)

JAKÓB   Were you waiting for me?

MAŁKA	To be honest, sir, I'd have to say, yes!
JAKÓB	And you were sure I'd come?
MAŁKA	I was sure you'd come.
	(During this conversation Jenta slowly puts her mother and the children to bed)
JAKÓB	What have you been doing all day long?
MAŁKA	What I do every day. I rushed around the town looking for someone who needs tuition.
JAKÓB	Any luck?
MAŁKA	No! The certificate from Wrocław gives me no right to teach in Warszawa. I don't know what else to do. I've already been to two warehouses. Seeing me decently dressed and speaking correctly, they did agree I could get some practical experience – if I paid them. I left saying I'd think about it. You see, sir, so much false pride! I was ashamed to admit that I'm hungry and ready to thread needles all day long and run errands for a pittance.[129]
JAKÓB	I'm thinking of you constantly and longing to find you a decent occupation. Yet even I, wherever I apply, am met with rejection. There are moments when I completely lose hope!
MAŁKA	I lost it already long ago.
JAKÓB	Things cannot remain like this. You cannot waste away in these surroundings! An atmosphere so lethal to your soul!
MAŁKA	Everyone, beginning with honest Jenta, keeps saying so, but who'll succeed in extricating me from this misery! It's not my fault, my error, that's locked me in this vicious circle – no escape! Light, learning, revealed new perspectives! I was plucked from a stifling pit of superstition – allowed to breathe freely – then, when I'd just begun to savour the fruits of my preparatory labour…I was shoved back into the darkness from which I'd emerged. Oh! Mr Lewi, if you only knew, sir, how very much I suffer. In double measure do I suffer because above all I feel that these people are good, honest, that my father has every right to expect my obedience and respect yet I'm in no fit state to give them anything! Not even love,

not even attachment. I feel so unhappy being with them and I no longer have the courage to go on living.

(Weeps)

JAKÓB   *(Moved)* Miss Małka! In your sadness, take sustenance from the fact that, albeit from afar, a friend's heart watches over you.

MAŁKA   From afar!

JAKÓB   *(Taking her hand)* Though no less intently or sincerely for it... Who knows, what the future holds for you. Do you think anyone is free from anxiety and bitterness? If you only knew...

MAŁKA   Is something worrying you?

JAKÓB   A heavy burden! Your whole life is ahead of you – mine is in bonds forever.

MAŁKA   Tell me, sir, the root of these worries.

JAKÓB   Not now – not today. You'll surely find out before too long – just remember that what to others may seem like happiness is misery and bitterness to me.

(Children singing outside the window)

How mournful, those childish voices, lamenting the loss of the Promised Land.[130]

MAŁKA   Their song echoes in your heart, sir, as in mine?

JAKÓB   Today more than ever. My heart weeps because it will never know happiness or peace.

(They both listen to the children's singing in silence. The candle has gone out, through the window the moon outside Małka's window illuminates them with its beams)

JAKÓB   *(Taking Małka's hand)* You're crying?

MAŁKA   With you I'm not ashamed of tears.

JAKÓB   Why not? You trust me?

MAŁKA	More than that…I believe in you blindly and completely. I think if you said 'die' – I would die this minute. I shed tears not for myself – only for your sorrow.
JAKÓB	(Passionately) My sweetest child! How dear you are! How dear to me, how close! (Stopping himself) If only you knew the true extent of my friendship.
MAŁKA	I'm very dear to you – that's what you said.
JAKÓB	Oh yes! Because like me you're weary and discontented! Good health to you, Małka.
MAŁKA	You're going already?
JAKÓB	It's getting late. Go I must.
MAŁKA	Oh – of course – I see you're wearing an evening suit. Are you going to a dance?
JAKÓB	Yes.
MAŁKA	Have a good time…Go to the dance and have a good time!
JAKÓB	(Grasping her hands) Look, I've already told you once – I'm miserable – I'm not one to waste words. Leaving this place, I'll be a hundred times more miserable…
MAŁKA	Is there no remedy for your unhappiness? Can…I…not…
JAKÓB	You, Małka, less than anyone else. I wish you well!
MAŁKA	When will you come again sir?
JAKÓB	Better for me and for you, if we never see each other again.
MAŁKA	(Paling with emotion) So, this is our farewell?
JAKÓB	Yes, Małka, it is.
MAŁKA	(With effort) May God guide your steps, sir!

JAKÓB

I thank you, Małka.

(When he is already at the doorstep, he turns suddenly, as though wishing to rush back in Małka's direction, but after a thought exits rapidly, closing the door)

MAŁKA

(Stands as though turned to stone, then bursts into tears and falls on her knees by the bed) He doesn't love me! He doesn't! Oh, madness! Madness! Madness!

(Weeps)

JENTA

(Approaches Małka slowly) Miss Małka! Miss Małka? What is this? Why are you crying? Remember yourself! Whoever saw such a thing! Ay, ay, a lovely young lady ruining her eyes!

MAŁKA

(Coiling up with pain) Oh, my own Jenta! Now it's all over!

JENTA

Why?

MAŁKA

I can't tell you! But if you only knew!

JENTA

I know, I know – I've watched carefully, whenever that Mr Lewi's been here – he's stolen Miss Małka's heart, it's clear. And I've known it'll come to nothing as well. All in vain, his to-ing and fro-ing. He's already promised, to a rich young lady, no less, hand-picked by his parents.

MAŁKA

(Leaping up) Him? Promised to someone?

JENTA

Of course! Only today I was at the home of his young lady's parents. Their surname is Schranne and they're rich people ... They're giving ten thousand at the very least for their daughter and a trousseau. Only today I bought two pairs of shoes from this young lady. She has quite big feet. I'll sell the shoes on to one of our own and they'll look so fine walking along ...

MAŁKA

(To herself) Now I understand it! What he said! Yet he didn't have the courage to sever those ties and preferred to bid me farewell and leave me with a bloodied heart.

JENTA

I thought it best to tell Miss Małka the whole truth, for why should she trouble her head with him. They're having a dinner dance today and that's where he's gone. He'll dance with her the whole night long. You should've seen all the mayonnaise prepared by their cook! Ay, ay! A mound as big as a house and all slippery yellow! Some dance that will be!

MAŁKA   Yes, some dance!

JENTA   Why don't you lie down Miss Małka and get some sleep – it's late. I'm going to bed. I have to be up at the crack of dawn, get over to Gęsia and deliver a samovar someone wants selling on. Fell off the back of a cart, but Jenta must close her eyes – four children and a sick mother – money must be earnt…

                 (Goes breathing heavily to her corner and lies down to sleep)

MAŁKA   (Sits alone on her bed) He's at the dance right now! Why didn't he just say so! Seems to me I've been buried alive! I've lost my sense of self, any urge to live, my will – everything! The thought that I must live here year after year without end, oh, it torments me!

SCENE 9

                 (The same and Szwarcenkopf)

SZWARCENKOPF   How very cold I am! hu! hu! My hands are frozen stiff! Małka! Małka! Where are you?

MAŁKA   Here I am, my father.

SZWARCENKOPF   Don't you have a candle stub, light it – and here's an orange. Given by Maurycy Silbercweig who said, take this for your daughter.

                 (Małka takes the orange and places it in the cot of one of Jenta's children)

                 Mr Maurycy was leaving the theatre today – very jolly too… Ay! ay! I made very little… snow falling thick and fast, no-one wanted to stop and buy cigarettes!

                 (He removes the strap of his street vendor's crate from around his neck, goes towards the stove)

                 The stove is cold! Jenta didn't light it!

MAŁKA   No, she probably didn't have the money.

SZWARCENKOPF	If only my enemies led this kind of life! Wandering from place to place in my old age and not a grosz can I earn.
MAŁKA	Yes – and in addition I am like a mill stone around your neck and sit here doing nothing instead of helping you, my poor father.
SZWARCENKOPF	You can help if really you want to. I've a piece of good news, wonderful news! You'll leap for joy like a little lamb when I tell you.
MAŁKA	You want to give me away, my father!
SZWARCENKOPF	How did you find out, Małka?
MAŁKA	(Feverishly) Never mind that – if you judge that my marriage can be of help to you, then, of course, I agree, I will marry.
SZWARCENKOPF	Małka! You are a good, honest child!
MAŁKA	Only let everything happen quickly, my father – my strength may fail me, or the bridegroom change his mind! No beating about the bush! If it's good business – it must be concluded swiftly, isn't that right, my father?
SZWARCENKOPF	That's right. But you, Małka, are trembling all over…you're ill, what's the matter?
MAŁKA	With me? Nothing? I'm alright! I'm cold! Oh!
	(She suddenly slides to the ground in a faint)
SZWARCENKOPF	Małka! Is she dead? Jenta! Jenta! Ryfka! Małka is dead!
JENTA	(Leaping up from her bed) Ay vay! What's wrong with her?
	(Rushes to Małka)
	Nothing! She's in a faint, that's all. Ladies' troubles, you understand.
	(Curtain falls)

ACT 3

(The same room as in the previous act, only cleaner and tidier. Fixed to the tables and the stove are tallow candles. Everywhere candle stubs in bottles, even on the floor. Małka's little tent has been put away. By the stove Ryfka dressed in clean clothes. Jenta's children dressed in varied brightly coloured theatrical clothing, all slightly too big. Jenta finishes dressing Ryfka and throws a blanket on her back)

SCENE 1

(Ryfka, Jenta, Children, Szwarcenkopf)

JENTA	*(Singing)*[131] Now mother – she shouldn't move, only sit nice and still – because mother looks like some princess or a countess on her throne. Trejne,[132] you bad girl,[133] don't tear at your dress... That is a beautiful gown – in it a rich lady dances at a ball and mother has lent it to you for today's celebration, the furszpil,[134] so that you can dance around the bride with the other girls.
	(Knocking at the door)
	Who's there?
SZWARCENKOPF	*(Dressed for the celebration)* I can still come in?
JENTA	You can, you can! The girls will gather in an hour or so, the furszpil will begin in two. Ay! ay! Look how you, Szwarcenkopf, are dressed today! Tut, tut! You didn't even have a robe[135] like that at your own wedding.
SZWARCENKOPF	*(Pleased)* A fine robe indeed! Old Firułkes kept his word – a trustworthy and precise personage. And where are the gifts?
JENTA	I hid them in Małka's pocket. Not a single cupboard, they could get lost.
SZWARCENKOPF	At the signing the gifts will have to be shown.
JENTA	And so they shall be. Gifts both worthy and wonderful! A brooch and earrings and a ring with a green stone, worth roughly seven roubles by my reckoning. Miss Małka will be satisfied.
SZWARCENKOPF	My time to delight in her has come and where is she?

JENTA   I don't know! Miserable the whole morning, then dressed and out she
                    went...

SZWARCENKOPF   She's a maiden and shy, that's all. She grieves and she rejoices, that she
                    will have a husband.

JENTA   I'm curious to see this Jojne!

SZWARCENKOPF   By yesterday Gabite had already collected no less than two hundred
                    roubles for the wedding! Though only a street seller, the local Jews do
                    respect me. Everyone gave generously, so that I had something to offer
                    Jojne alongside Malka.[136] I will set down in the document, the tenaim,[137]
                    one hundred roubles for her dowry and to Pake Rozental will give the
                    appropriate fifth for matchmaking. The rest must be spent on the wedding
                    itself and on Małka's clothes.

JENTA   And now you must go, or you'll give the girls a fright. Wait, until the young
                    man arrives with the marszelik and neighbours.

SZWARCENKOPF   Alright, then so be it. I will enter in their company.

JENTA   So be it!

                    (Szwarcenkopf exits)

SCENE 2

(Ryfka, Jenta then Maurycy, Wiedeński)

JENTA   (Walks from corner to corner lighting candles, securing and arranging
                    them) Darkness has fallen. The candles must be lit. Ay! ay! So beautiful,
                    it brings back memories. And that rascal Wiedeński, devil take him for a
                    husband! I wish him as much joy as my worst enemies! Ay! ay!

                    (Knocking)

                    Why the knocking? Straight away enter! Who's there?

WIEDEŃSKI   (Standing in the doorway) It is I, Kolumna.

JENTA   Ay! ay! What do I see! Mowsze? Is it you, Mowsze? Kolumna you're
                    called now, is it? How is that possible - Ko-lum-na - that's how we refer
                    to a big cylindrical block, not a person...

WIEDEŃSKI   (Sharply) My good woman, you are profoundly stupid! I don't know you nor have I ever known you, understood? Well?

(Approaching her and threatening with his cane)

If you don't stop calling me Mowsze and trying to persuade me you're one of my relations, I'll bring down the power of the court on your head so hard, you'll be thrown into prison.

JENTA   (Shocked) My most humble and profuse apologies to the illustrious Mr Mow...so sorry, sir, but I was convinced that the illustrious gentleman used once to be that wastrel Mowsze, whom we were wont to call Tyszebuf[138] on Krochmalna street. ['Ty-sze-buf' – that surname means 'bad tempered', I believe]

WIEDEŃSKI   (Livid) Me? Named Tyszebuf? ['Bad tempered'?] Did you ever hear the like?

(Forgetting himself, begins to speak in Yiddish[139] then suddenly remembering himself changes his tone and ends in French)[140]

JENTA   And what a great delight to hear the most illustrious gentleman speak in the Yiddish tongue...

SCENE 3

(The same and Maurycy Silbercweig)

MAURYCY   (Poking his head around the door) May I come in?

WIEDEŃSKI   Come in! Come in!

JENTA   My most sincere apologies, good sirs. Men, as yet, are not permitted. The ceremony must begin with the dancing of girls – only later the young man arrives with his friends.[141]

MAURYCY   And I am here to prevent this young man from arriving.

JENTA   With your permission sirs, why should Jojna[142] Firułkes not be admitted?

MAURYCY   I'm not going to divulge my plans to you. Where's Miss Małka?

JENTA   Gone out.

MAURYCY	When will she come back?
JENTA	Whenever it is she does.
MAURYCY	But when exactly!
WIEDEŃSKI	Don't talk to her – she's an idiot.
JENTA	If only I had as much luck in business as I have good and sound sense. Ay! You Mow – er hmm, you, most illustrious gentleman have a very quick tongue. If only your hand were as quick to reach out to poor, needy relations.
WIEDEŃSKI	Be silent, we deplore all forms of answering back.
JENTA	I'll go and see if Małka's on her way.
WIEDEŃSKI	Why did we come here in any case? You instruct me to dress with unreasonable rapidity, climb into a carriage and follow you. It beggars belief – I've no inclination to ascend or rather drag myself up those filthy stairs into this even more filthy hole and yet you send me in just the same – very 'avant-garde' of you, I'm sure. C'est trop fort, monsieur![143]
MAURYCY	Lucky we're not too late. Downstairs the women told me that today's Sabbath will include a celebration in the bridal home and that the wedding itself will take place on Tuesday.
WIEDEŃSKI	So what if we had come too late, what of any great magnitude could've happened! The transformation of Miss Małka Szwarcenkopf into Mrs Jojne Firułkes!
MAURYCY	I'm a long way from having a developed conscience – but I must admit – I couldn't sleep peacefully thinking that a lovely and distinguished young girl was going to become – because of me – the wife of some common, stupid little Jew.
WIEDEŃSKI	Because of you? Can't be my doing, all this. I bet that Mrs Glanzowa's turned your head and Małka's beautiful eyes and svelte figure have accomplished the rest.
MAURYCY	Yes, Glanzowa may have explained Małka's predicament from a woman's perspective – I may gradually have come to realize how a girl raised and educated differently won't be able to cope in this kind of environment. The matter may yet have to be postponed – but I know about the marriage now and judge it to be my responsibility ...

WIEDEŃSKI	I would judge, that it's your responsibility to depose Mr Jojne Firułkes as potential husband and in the remaining vacuum advance your own suit – as lover.
MAURYCY	No, Maks,[144] that's not what I'm thinking. I've no designs on this girl except to improve her situation and give her leave not to become Mrs Jojne Firułkes.
WIEDEŃSKI	(With irony) You justify your actions on humanitarian grounds.
MAURYCY	Even if I could find the words, any effort to explain what's guiding me now would be in vain – you wouldn't understand. Listen carefully. There's one thing we're not going to do, and that is, offend this young girl yet again. On the contrary, I'd like her to pardon my transgression and try to understand that, then, I behaved like a stupid, drunken fool. I'm asking you Maks – reserve your irony for another occasion – dropping in to see a cute little Florcia or a neat little Melania[145] perhaps – and here instead behave as you would towards your own sister.
WIEDEŃSKI	Mitzi! Little Mitzi![146] Barely recognizable! For a couple of weeks now you've had no inclination for drink, you've not surrendered a single banknote…what's going on! Have you not perchance fallen in love with Małka. If so, I give you my lowest bow and take flight for other spheres. I can pander to your fantasies, but to your madness, jamais![147]
MAURYCY	I am not in love with Małka, of that you can be sure. In the beginning I did expect her to yield and would gladly have squandered a little money. Today, I've a completely different feeling towards her and I prefer not to discuss it with you.

SCENE 5

(The same, Małka, Rózia, Jenta)

(Małka in a white dress, over which she has a long coat, Rózia, a young girl dressed tastefully in a promenade suit)[148]

JENTA	These gentlemen are present!
MAŁKA	(To Jenta) What do they want?
JENTA	Who knows – for Miss Małka not to marry Jojne, looks like to me.
MAŁKA	What are you saying Jenta!

JENTA	Upon my life!
MAŁKA	(To Rózia) Dear Rózia, allow me to first of all dispatch these gentlemen. They are uninvited guests and should remove themselves post haste.
RÓZIA	Take no pains on my part, I beg you, dear. I'm the one who insisted on seeing you to the door. I don't want to cause you any embarrassment – I'll leave ...
MAŁKA	Whatever for, no – please, stay. I've nothing to hide from you.
MAURYCY	(To Wiedeński) Please, move aside, let me speak with her alone.
WIEDEŃSKI	Why on earth did you drag me here, then? Look closely at the other. What a lovely girl.
MAURYCY	(Looking with admiration at Rózia) Quite true – a picture! Something else requires my attention ... how strange, I feel like a coward ...
MAŁKA	(Approaches) The gentlemen wish to speak with me. I can be nothing other than surprised, seeing them here, but judge that some extraordinary occurrence has induced them to come such a long way. I am on a temporary basis able to put aside ...
MAURYCY	No, miss – forever! That's exactly why I've come to see you.
MAŁKA	Is that right? Mr Silbercweig, does this signal a renewed desire to offend me? You must, sir, remember that then I was defenseless and surrounded. Presently, I'm here – in my own home – and however close this home may be to a mere hovel, providing shelter for several families, it will nevertheless always remain the roof over my head, my dwelling place, a corner of my own and in it I will not allow myself to be insulted.
	(Rózia approaches and stands beside Małka)
MAURYCY	You are severe, I endure obediently – I feel that I've treated you very badly. My transgression was not however so great – there was much vacuity and stupidity involved. It was a joke.
MAŁKA	That joke opened my eyes at once – it gave me to understand my current position in society very clearly. Enough has been said. Why exactly are you here, sir?

MAURYCY	Though not remotely unprepared for your question, miss, I hesitate with my response.
MAŁKA	If it's calculated to offend me, then do withhold it, please.
RÓZIA	(Quietly to Małka) Don't be completely merciless. He's a very pleasant, good-looking boy.
MAŁKA	(To Rózia) What a child you are!
MAURYCY	I've been told you're getting married?
MAŁKA	That's right. My betrothal is today – my wedding will take place on Tuesday.
MAURYCY	That wedding cannot take place.
MAŁKA	That wedding must take place.
MAURYCY	I'm able to prevent it.
MAŁKA	How exactly?
MAURYCY	Listen to me miss, for just one moment, only without anger and superiority. My aunt took charge of your upbringing. It was she – when you were still a child and denied any say in the matter – who took you away from here and schooled you, setting your life on another course. After her death that... responsibility falls to me... and for this reason I do not want – cannot allow – you... to rot in destitution... in the midst of poverty, filth and ignorance... Miss Małka, you mustn't think I'm a completely bad person... I...
WIEDEŃSKI	(Who has been listening with irony) Next step – flourish and apply handkerchief to nose... wipe away tears of emotion and fall to knees.
MAURYCY	If you don't leave me alone I'll be forced to sever all contact.
	(To Małka)
	You're surprised, miss, by my speech – perhaps one day, when I explain the strange effect your presence exerted in my aunt's house, you'll understand that I too can be sober – maybe even just.

MAŁKA	Hearing these words does please me greatly, sir. You do seem completely different from the man who spoke to me in such a drunken and offensive manner.
MAURYCY	So I may have hope?
MAŁKA	Of what?
MAURYCY	That you'll continue to accept assistance, as administered by our aunt[149] – that you'll cancel your wedding and arrange your life in a manner befitting your upbringing and education?
MAŁKA	No, Mr Maurycy.
MAURYCY	But why not?
MAŁKA	Ah! So many reasons! You want me to forgive you? That I can, sir! But forget – never. To accept anything – whatever it may be – from you! I cannot. Your words of greeting at your house would always echo in my ears. In any case, I accept nothing from strangers.
MAURYCY	You accepted something from my aunt.
MAŁKA	She was my mother, my guardian – all that and more – whereas you sir are a stranger to me.
MAURYCY	And now you're about to accept something from your husband who is also a stranger to you.
MAŁKA	That won't be charity. We'll work together and in actual fact I'm the one who'll be managing the entire business, earning our bread. I've made exhaustive enquiries, Mr Silbercweig, as to whether I'm likely to be sitting with my hands folded in my lap, taking account of what husband sets down ...
MAURYCY	You will be running a business?
MAŁKA	Yes indeed sir! A small shop on Marszałkowska Street – nor will I die of it, I'm sure. An independent position such as this is superior to reliance on the favour and good humour of strangers. I'll try to create a new life. I judge, that I will succeed.
MAURYCY	And I judge the opposite.

RÓZIA	If permitted to say a few words regarding this matter, I too would suggest Małka that this existence you intend for yourself can never be enough.
MAŁKA	It must be enough.
RÓZIA	It's easy to say that, but to actually ...
MAŁKA	My dear Rózia, you are still a child – you cannot yet conceive that he who must, is capable of much.
MAURYCY	(To Rózia) I am gratified, miss, to have found an ally. Desire then to persuade Miss Szwarcenkopf that, in casting aside my request and marrying in absolute opposition to her conviction and desire, she'll be doing herself considerable damage.
MAŁKA	All this is useless and you, Rózia, don't even try to persuade me or change my mind. I bid you farewell now, Mr Maurycy, my guests will at any moment begin to congregate.
MAURYCY	You will be unhappy.
MAŁKA	But no-one will ever know. In actual fact my misery does have one positive aspect. It has served to alter some of your convictions and your life ... That means a lot ...
MAURYCY	But not quite everything. Will you allow me miss to count myself among your friends? I would like at least occasionally to speak with you.
MAŁKA	That I cannot deny ... of course, whenever you've some free time and I am relieved of my duties, do come here and stay as long as boredom doesn't set in. And now, fare you well, sir.
MAURYCY	Farewell, Miss Małka!
	(To Rózia)
	Miss!
RÓZIA	(Curtseying) Sir!
WIEDEŃSKI	(To Maurycy, exiting) Don't despair! She won't be so harsh once married life rubs her up the wrong way.
MAURYCY	(Rapidly) Silence! Right now I could strangle you!

WIEDEŃSKI	Gone insane or something.
MAURYCY	(Turning back) Tell me, miss, to what cause I should put the monies left you by my aunt?
WIEDEŃSKI	Complete lunacy.
MAŁKA	There's so much destitution in the world – especially in the poorest class of Jews. Even here – see – in this corner, there lives and suffers a woman abandoned by her husband and she works hard, so that in poverty she can feed four vulnerable children and her paralyzed mother. This here is destitution more grievous than mine and worthier of your pity.
MAURYCY	I've not the courage to make an offer myself. If you, miss would care to …
MAŁKA	Very well! Rózia and I will occupy ourselves with ensuring that any money offered by you sir doesn't go to waste. We'll set up a shop or small business for Jenta which will enable her to raise her children and care for her mother. Well Rózia? Do I have your agreement?
RÓZIA	Most decidedly.
MAURYCY	And thus you have, miss, to some degree appeased the disappointment I felt on hearing you deny my request.
MAŁKA	Further arrangements will be made by letter, then in person, after my wedding. Now leave us sir. Later on I will tell Jenta all about her good fortune.
MAURYCY	Yes! Yes! That, miss, is something you alone can accomplish, for this is your work not mine! Good bye for now!

SCENE 6

(The same except for Wiedeński, Maurycy)

RÓZIA	Do you know, Małka, I've got tears in my eyes. This has genuinely moved me.
MAŁKA	I should no longer be moved by anything. I must forget that I'm a living being and have a heart. Otherwise … my strength may fail me. Today's only happiness will be an unexpected meeting with you in the street. If it weren't for that, I wouldn't be wearing this happy smile.
RÓZIA	My poor Małka! Just think – we'd been at boarding school for a full three years when I received my mother's telegram and rushed to attend

at father's death-bed. Thank God his health returned – but I, alas, was left unable to get back across the border and so completed my education here in Warszawa...

MAŁKA   You call that completion of our education! We hadn't even begun! You needn't look far. I've had to overcome so many obstacles – am I adequately equipped? I know nothing about the practical side of things – it's a struggle – I'm being torn apart. From now on I'll put up a fight, but I've a sense I won't survive it – that I'll perish!

RÓZIA   This is your conviction!

MAŁKA   Yes. To you alone I say this. No-one else. I don't want to play the role of victim – I'm moving on with my head held high. I don't know how long my strength will last.

RÓZIA   My own Małka! Why can't I do anything! Why didn't you allow that young man to...

MAŁKA   No more about that, please.

RÓZIA   To me he seemed very sympathetic – in essence an honest person. That other one, with the monocle – I didn't much like him. He must be an evil spirit. Don't you think?

MAŁKA   I think so.

RÓZIA   It would be necessary to remove the evil spirit in order to save that young man from demise. And now, let me embrace you, wish you... (quietly)... happiness – and bid you farewell. I must go home. My parents will be getting anxious.

MAŁKA   Good health to you, my dear Rózia. If you'd like to, come and see me from time to time. I won't be able to visit you – you're rich people, whereas I will be Mrs Jojne Firułkes and... earning my keep.

RÓZIA   But surely...

MAŁKA   No, no, my dear, I know what I'm talking about. Ah! After my wedding we will all three occupy ourselves with setting up Jenta in her little shop.

RÓZIA   Have you at least seen your future husband?

MAŁKA   No, I will see him today.

RÓZIA   Good bye, Małka! Be happy, if that is possible.

               (Exits)

MAŁKA   (To Jenta) My good Jenta, will the guests be here soon?

JENTA   The young girls alone will come. The bridegroom entertains his neighbours
               and friends. Miss Małka is not aware of our customs?

MAŁKA   No, Jenta.

JENTA   She doesn't know then that during today's ceremony the pledge will be
               made and the bridegroom will promise in writing[150] no less than four
               hundred roubles for Miss Małka.

MAŁKA   I know not and care very little.

JENTA   I'll go downstairs once more and see if the guests are coming. Miss
               Małka will laugh and joke with the young girls. That will make me happy.
               Though for her even they aren't the right kind of company. Ay, ay! Poor
               Miss Małka!

               (Exits, the children have left during the previous scene. Only Małka
               remains with the paralyzed Ryfka)

MAŁKA   (Alone) Poor Małka, they say! Poor Małka and yet my destiny must be
               fulfilled. I move, as though driven by some unseen, unstoppable force.
               When I learnt that, morally, he isn't free – that's when I realized how I've
               loved him for a long, long time, since our first meeting, when my guardian
               was still alive.

               (Looks around)

               I am at this moment alone[151] and yet in spite of all these lights seem to fall
               into darkness. Who's that, so pale among the shadows? Ah – it's poor
               Ryfka, gazing with adoration at the meagre little flames...

RYFKA   (Mouthing joyfully) Light! Light!...[152]

MAŁKA   Yes, to you it is light, to me it is darkness, it is a tomb! What a terrible
               tomb!

               (She leans against the wall and covers her eyes)

               Will I ever see him again!

SCENE 7

(Ryfka, Małka, Jakób Lewi)

(Jakób Lewi enters quickly without taking off his coat)

JAKÓB	*(Approaches Małka and grasps her hand)* Miss Małka!
MAŁKA	*(Suddenly cheered rushes quickly, then holding back)* Is it you sir? What can you want from me?
JAKÓB	Miss Małka, I've come to ask whether it's true – you're to be married?
MAŁKA	And to a common shopkeeper at that!
JAKÓB	To a common shopkeeper! Why are you doing this? Why!
MAŁKA	I must have my reasons. I don't ask you sir why you're getting married.
JAKÓB	This is not about my wedding.
MAŁKA	Of course not – this is about our weddings. You, sir, are taking a wife and I a husband. You're marrying a young educated woman with a dowry whereas I am marrying an ordinary, poor little Jew from the same class as my parents, these people around us and myself.
JAKÓB	But your soul has come to know the light.
MAŁKA	What of it? In any case, it's faint – faint as the light from these candles, arranged to cast a warm glow over my betrothal. Any illumination I've experienced serves only to render me incapable of feeling happiness or pleasing others. Leave me, sir, to my fate and go your way.
JAKÓB	One thing only can justify your actions. Do you love your intended?
MAŁKA	That may well be the case, Mr Jakób.
JAKÓB	Małka, is this possible?
MAŁKA	Don't you love your intended, sir? You see – you remain silent, you love her. I would never presume to think you'd want to marry without love in your heart.
	(A chorus of women's voices is heard from afar)

JAKÓB	And so with a clear mind and in all good conscience you are taking a husband?
MAŁKA	Yes. With a clear mind and in all good conscience!
JAKÓB	Your father didn't press you into making this marriage.
MAŁKA	No, I alone embrace it eagerly and of my own free will.
JAKÓB	But a set of circumstances has... emerged and acts to... force your step.
MAŁKA	(After a pause) That may be so... God steers our fates. We must each tread our own path.
JAKÓB	Małka, if you wanted to...
MAŁKA	No, I don't, I cannot, Jakób, I'm not permitted to want anything. Wish me luck sir and go. The girls approach, to help make merry and await the bridegroom's arrival. So custom dictates... and this must be respected.[153]
JAKÓB	One word only, please...

SCENE 8

(Jenta's Children burst skipping onto the stage and Jenta rushes on after them)

JENTA	Here they come, they're coming!
	(Notices Jakób)
	Is it you, sir? Mr Lewi! You must leave – the girls are coming... not permitted!
JAKÓB	I'm going! May you be happy, Miss Małka, with your husband and in your home!
MAŁKA	(Swallowing her tears) And may you, sir, be happy with your wife and in your home!
JAKÓB	Some time will pass before your wish is fulfilled – of that you may be sure!
	(Exits quickly)
MAŁKA	(Alone) Time will pass? But it will be fulfilled! Ha! It's all over now! Only death remains... only death!...

SCENE 9[154]

(Małka and the girls, then Jojne, Marszelik, the matchmaker, Mowsze,[155] old Firułkes, Szwarcenkopf, Jewish men and women. First enter the young girls, singing, bearing flowers in their arms – they surround Małka and singing quietly they dance nimbly and gracefully, dressed brightly, poorly, in white dresses and coloured little shoes. Małka stands in the centre unmoved, she takes flowers from the girls and kisses each individually)

MAŁKA	Thank you, thanks to all most sincerely.
GIRLS	(Clapping their hands) The bridegroom approaches!
JENTA	He doesn't quite approach – he's being led.
GIRLS	Why so?
JENTA	Because he weeps profusely!
GIRLS	Weeps?
JENTA	In great sobs – it's true!
	(Pake bursts in, perfectly turned out)
PAKE	The Marszelik approaches! The Marszelik approaches!
GIRLS	(Clapping their hands) The Marszelik is coming! Here he comes at last…
MARSZELIK	(An elegant, ceremoniously dressed Jew, with a fair beard, a pocket watch, in his hand he holds a red kerchief. He bursts in waving the kerchief)[156]
	Greetings! Greetings to all![157]
GIRLS	(Clapping their hands) Greetings! Greetings to you!
MARSZELIK	The bridegroom is coming! Here, he approaches![158]
GIRLS	The bridegroom approaches!
MARSZELIK	Where is his intended?[159]
GIRLS	Here is his intended![160]

MARSZELIK	Ah! How beautiful she is...how beautiful his intended! Greetings Miss Małka![161]

(Małka bows to him in silence)

MARSZELIK	Your bridegroom approaches.[162]

(Runs to the door)

MAŁKA	*(To herself)* Will I have enough courage!

MARSZELIK	Enter here all you who are old, young, rich, poor, blind, lame, bald, hunchbacked, upright and broken, to see the young bride, who like an anxious dove sits in a little chair, waiting patiently for her mate...

(From behind the entrance door, bundling together, burst the Jewish men, who have among them the weeping Jojne. Old Firułkes and Jósek Pomeranc lead him in, he tears himself away from their grip and escapes to the right side of the stage. The Jewish men lead in old, grey Mowsze Radosny and seat him on a chair. The men occupy the right hand side of the stage, the women the left. Old Szwarcenkopf also enters with them)

MARSZELIK	Aha! Here comes the host. With a large, vibrant throng of people![163]
JENTA	A! Szwarcenkopf, how you advance! You have managed to get Jukicel Krikus[164] himself for Marszelik.
SZWARCENKOPF	With the help of good people...
MARSZELIK	*(To Jojne)* What, are you stupid, Jojne. Are you crying? Nonsense![165] If your intended was quaking with fear, then that would be quite the fashionable thing, for a young girl must drench ten handkerchiefs before she gets married. But you, Jojne, you are a dolt...you are not an upright bridegroom,[166] you are practically dissolving – you've been smearing yourself all morning like a calf with a big tongue.[167] Aj! Jojne, how I long to be in your shoes, after seeing what a rare beauty[168] you will have as a wife.
JOJNE	I don't want to.
MARSZELIK	Because you are stupid. If I were you I'd take one giant leap and land right by her side.
JOJNE	I'm frightened!

OLD FIRUŁKES	*(Strong, apoplectic Jewish man with a stick and a top hat over his skullcap)* Makes no difference[169] now whether he wants to or not as the gifts[170] have been sent, so no more discussion.
MEN	Yes, yes. No more discussion!
MARSZELIK	And when you are finally led in[171] to your bride, under the chuppah,[172] you'll be jumping for joy, like a young rabbit at the sight of fresh lettuce. What now?[173] Crying again? Enough! A, Jojne Jojninke![174] What a fool you are![175] Wait, I will give you a treat for good luck![176]
	(Gives him a hazelnut)
	Don't gobble it all at once, I know what a greedy boy you are!
FIRUŁKES	Prepare the document.[177]
SZWARCENKOPF	Here everything is written down and should be signed according to our agreement.
FIRUŁKES	Mowsze here wishes to assume a role of importance – put the red kerchief in his hand.
MARSZELIK	And what a kerchief, elegant and fine, the kerchief of a true bachelor.[178]
	(He gives his kerchief, Mowsze takes it in his hand and led by the Marszelik goes to Jojne, followed by two men as witnesses)
FIRUŁKES	*(To Jojne)* Take Jojne this kerchief…
JOJNE	I'm frightened!
MARSZELIK	You are stupid – this is not fire or a red hot iron – see? If I was holding a box of sweets you'd be trembling with joy. Do as you must.[179]
	(Jojne takes the red kerchief)
MARSZELIK	Good, good…[180]
WITNESSES	Good, good…
	(All approach Małka)
SZWARCENKOPF	Małka! Take this kerchief!
	(Małka takes the kerchief)

WITNESSES	Good, good![181]

JOJNE

(Suddenly) I don't want to! I'm going home! My hat's too big! Father, get this hat off my head.

MARSZELIK

Your hat is too big? What nonsense![182] You'll grow into it. If you don't, it can be adapted to make smaller hats for your children, for little Jojniszkes, who will have eyes as lovely as Miss Małka, Małkele, Małgorzateczke[183] and ears as big as you, Jojne, Jojnełe, Jojniszke![184] Well – now find me a table, quick as you like!

ALL

A table! A table![185]

(The young men fall to it with a shout and set up in the centre a table, paper, ink, pens)

MARSZELIK

(Standing at the table) Now be still! And don't interrupt me![186] Where's Jojne gone? Disappeared? Perhaps he's dissolved in a river of tears and we cannot say to him Mazel Tov?[187] Jojne! There you are! Well! We all understand the purpose and terms of this document – the tenaim[188] – may it bring health to you both, Jojniszke and Małkełe Malgorzateczke[189] – a sweet-tempered young woman. And evil spirits and ailments of every kind may they flee this place for all eternity.[190]

(A little boy smashes plates)[191]

ALL

(Joyfully) Mazel Tov! Mazel Tov!

MARSZELIK

Now I ask for your signatures here. The young couple first and then the witnesses. Write boldly and clearly…[192]

(Goes to fetch Jojne and leads him to the table)

Jojne! Come here and sign the tenaim![193]

(Jojne signs and runs away)

MARSZELIK

Now Miss Małke!

SZWARCENKOPF

Come, Małke!

(Małke goes to the table and, resigned, signs the document and returns to her place)

MARSZELIK

And now the witnesses! Jósek Pomeranc! Mowsze Cytryna!

(They sign)

Josełe Zucker!

(He laughs)

Cytryna – literally, a lemon[194] – zucker – literally, some sugar[195] – mix them up and you'll get lemonade! Lejbuś Pantofel … get along with you![196] Only the main witnesses here!

(The witnesses sign as they are called)

MARSZELIK   *(After a pause)* Jojne take the young bride by the hand and lead her over here nicely!

(Jojne takes Małka clumsily by the hand and pulls her towards the table)

MARSZELIK   Where is the vodka and honey cake?[197]

(Jenta passes vodka and a glass, Pake the honey cake sliced on a plate)

MARSZELIK   *(Giving the papers to Jojne and Małka)* Keep them safe – they will prove useful. And now Mazel Tov to the young couple! I wish you joy and many children! Miss Małka, six boys – but not all at once!

(Passing her a nut with gallantry)

Here's a treat for good luck![198]

(He drinks)

All good health to you Jojne![199] All good health to you Malke!

ALL   Good health![200]

(They drink one by one and eat the honey cake)

MOWSZE   *(His voice shaking)* All have seen the terms handsomely and justly agreed. Firułkes has already committed payment to my hands. Szwarcenkopf likewise. Here is proof of monies received.[201] If either party should choose to break the agreement, then all monies and gifts must be equally split.

ALL   Agreed!

MOWSZE   You Jojne need no lesson in how to love and respect your wife. Your pious father took you last Sabbath to the most worthy rabbi and he explained what is required. Now will I go hence leaving the young people to their dancing and celebrations.

(The elders leave)

MARSZELIK   Keep the document safe – the rabbi will need it for the wedding rites. Well! Now you can celebrate. Miss Małka! I will recite some verses of my own composition ... if I may ...[202]

No, they have escaped me. Let Mazel Tov be enough then! And you Jojne must also dance ... Don't just stand there! Who will stand in the middle?

(He arranges everyone in a circle and counts in Yiddish, quietly, pointing with his finger, ends up at Jenta)

I have landed on Jenta.

(Everyone laughs)

MARSZELIK   Ej Jente! Jentysze, Jentyszulu. Luck is on your side![203]

(Loud laughter. Marszelik counts again, lands on himself, he lifts the edge of his robe and in one stride moves to the centre and begins to sing Jewish wedding couplets, which the choir repeat after him. Next after each verse the men alone with wild leaps traverse the stage. The women clap and are merry, the candles in corners gradually go out, the atmosphere becomes sad and dark. In the corner, sick paralyzed Ryfka. A little group of children squealing tussle on their beds. Małka sits on a chair completely motionless, deathly pale, with her eyes fixed into space)

(Curtain slowly falls)

ACT 4

(The interior of a room behind the shop belonging to Jojne Firułkes; two beds made up high, with white, clean bedclothes. A samovar on the wardrobe, a table, a threadbare couch. Near the stove sits old Szwarcenkopf warming himself, on the couch sits Jojne)

SCENE 1

(Szwarcenkopf, Jojne)

SZWARCENKOPF   Why do you not, Jojne, go through to the shop?

JOJNE   Why should I, when Małka is there.

SZWARCENKOPF   Why not try your hand at business?

JOJNE   Why should I, when Małka works for two!

SZWARCENKOPF   She is a woman – better for her to stay in the house and for you Jojne to address the customers.

JOJNE   But my head always hurts. Why in any case did I get married? What is a wife for? Let her trouble herself and not me.

SZWARCENKOPF   You Jojne have become mighty hard headed and sharp tongued. Once you sat quietly but now you're very clever and talk a lot.

JOJNE   What of it! Am I not a trader, like other Jews? And I have a wife and a robe and a little shop.

    (Silence)

SZWARCENKOPF   Jojne? Are you asleep?

JOJNE   I am not!

SZWARCENKOPF   You know, Jojne, that the day after tomorrow is the Sabbath?

JOJNE   Yes – my mind also dwells on it, Szwarcenkopf.

SZWARCENKOPF   And what else does your mind dwell on, Jojne?

JOJNE   I'm thinking, there will be a tasty fish, which we, Szwarcenkopf, will eat with relish.

SZWARCENKOPF	You are a prankster Jojne … you think about eating a fish, but how best to earn one doesn't even enter your head …
JOJNE	And why do you, Szwarcenkopf, do nothing?
SZWARCENKOPF	You are stupid Jojne! See, how grey my beard is. What age am I? When you can count this many years and so much toil, then will you have the right to sit by the stove contemplating the eating of fish on the Sabbath.
JOJNE	You toiled, Szwarcenkopf, because you didn't have parents able to give you a small shop – I do have parents, who've given me a small shop, so why should I work? I prefer to sit on the couch and let my mind dwell on all good things.
SZWARCENKOPF	If you toiled a little, Jojne, you'd have more.
JOJNE	To what purpose? I'm not a Kronenberg, nor will I ever be a Bloch[204] – why, then, should I exert myself?

SCENE 2

(The same and Małka)

(Małka enters from the shop, she is dressed almost in the garb of poverty, in a big blue apron. On her head she has a blue kerchief, tied at the back. She is very pale and transformed)

MAŁKA	Jojne! Go, please, through to the shop. I am sick and tired.[205] Besides, I have seen Rózia on her way to visit me.
JOJNE	I have a headache.
MAŁKA	Please, go, only for a while.
SZWARCENKOPF	You really do look pale, Małka. Are you very sick? Perhaps you should visit a proper doctor?
MAŁKA	No my father! All I need is to be alone with Rózia. Why don't you take a short stroll, it might even do your health some good.
SZWARCENKOPF	I'll go and keep Jojne company in the shop so he doesn't get sad and then I'll go for a stroll.
MAŁKA	In the shop there is no time for sadness, there is always some occupation.

JOJNE	*(To Małka, approaching her tentatively)* I will go Małka into the shop ... only ... let me kiss your neck.
MAŁKA	Leave me in peace, I have a headache.
JOJNE	What a bad wife you are to me ... a bad wife!
MAŁKA	I cannot be any different. I do what I can. Go through to the shop.
JOJNE	Ay, ay! You Małka, what a princess, what a princess you are!
	(Bell is heard offstage)
MAŁKA	Someone has entered the shop. Go on then – or they will steal something.
SZWARCENKOPF	*(Rushing out, dragging Jojne)* Come on Jojne, hurry up!

SCENE 3

(Małka, Rózia, Maurycy)

(Rózia enters through the side door)

RÓZIA	Good day to you Małka. How are you feeling?
MAŁKA	I am alright. My head hurts a little.
RÓZIA	You're not being honest. You look very pale, wretched. You've lost weight since your wedding – a shadow of your former self.
MAŁKA	It's just your imagination.
RÓZIA	It is not. I observe you closely. This work is killing you.
MAŁKA	This work keeps me alive. If I didn't immerse myself in constant toil I think I'd go mad. I'm just a mannequin, adept at the mechanical execution of all tasks. I don't think about anything, at least I try not to ... Let's not talk about me. What news of Jenta? Have the two of you found her something suitable?
RÓZIA	I have my eye on a shop, near the corner of Frańciszkańska Street, but I wouldn't like to do anything without your advice or the opinion of Mr Maurycy.

MAŁKA	*(With a smile)* Ah…Mr Maurycy?
RÓZIA	*(Animated)* Why the ironic smile? It is he, after all, who's given the money and you yourself…
MAŁKA	*(Kissing her)* Alright then, it's alright, no need for energetic explanations…
RÓZIA	Well, as I love my grandmamma, I think you've made a faulty assumption…
MAŁKA	I have assumed nothing but – but I do see, that Maurycy is a brave young man and that your influence could make a great deal of difference.
RÓZIA	Not my influence, Małka – yours. He speaks of you with such adoration all the time, he calls you a superior woman, extraordinary, whereas I…You know what? Sometimes, when I hear Maurycy, speaking like that, I am angry with myself, angry…
MAŁKA	Why?
RÓZIA	Because I am – I am me and not you!
MAŁKA	Dear Rózia, you are who you are – no need for self-reproach. My influence is just the sort any sober friend might have. Yours will be the beguiling sort that remains with Maurycy through good times and bad.
RÓZIA	*(Embracing Małka tightly)* Oh Małka! Do you really think he'll come to love me!
MAŁKA	He already does, though perhaps he doesn't know it just yet.
	(Maurycy has already entered a few moments ago through the side door and been listening to the women's conversation, suddenly he rushes over to Rózia)
MAURYCY	On the contrary, he knows it very well…I have from the moment I came to see Miss Małka…
RÓZIA	You, here, sir.
MAŁKA	My own Rózia – spare the comic performance. Did not the two of you arrange a meeting here today…
MAURYCY	Yes – we planned to look at the little shop on Franciszkańska.

MAŁKA   You see, Rózia, he's more honest than you.

RÓZIA   He can afford to be, he is a man – I have to lie.

MAŁKA   You do not – there's nothing standing in your way. Your parents, as far as you've told me, have eagerly extended their hospitality to Mr Maurycy.

RÓZIA   Most eagerly. Especially since he and Mr Kolumna Wiedeński went their separate ways.

MAŁKA   At long last? Oh, that's good, that's very good!

MAURYCY   A minor sacrifice on my part, ladies – to be perfectly honest, that gentleman's company had become an irritation – more – it filled me with disgust. Truly I cannot comprehend how I managed to put up with that kind of influence and when I recall it now, the very thought appalls me.

MAŁKA   Now I do have hope that Rózia will be completely happy.

RÓZIA   It's all thanks to you, dear Małka!

MAURYCY   Yes, no question. This is your work and yours alone. Firstly, I met Rózia in your home – secondly, you raised my awareness of the value of this treasure – I love her with my whole heart.

MAŁKA   Sir – I'd only seen you twice in my entire life!

MAURYCY   Yes, but you were always there with me, in my aunt's house, once your home – you left countless mementoes. Servants would refer to you as 'our young miss' – I came across your childhood toys in cupboards – later on, exercise books, dresses. Wiedeński set up home in your room – even his presence failed to erase the charm emanating from those papered blue walls, that delicate white furniture, porcelain figures arranged on little shelves. These may be minor details but their constant presence provoked thoughts of you – I wondered, might it be possible, by looking in a different way, to discover the truest source of beauty in a woman – that is, to see at her core this graceful and bewitching girl...

               (Małka suddenly leans her head on her arm and begins to weep silently)

RÓZIA   Małka! What's the matter?

MAŁKA   There's nothing the matter! Today I feel strangely aggravated, that's all. I've never felt like this before...

RÓZIA   It's Mr Maurycy's fault – recalling the past, his aunt's home.

MAŁKA   Oh no! Something else ...

RÓZIA   May we know what?

MAŁKA   No Rózia, no-one may know – only God.

RÓZIA   You're suffering, my poor Małka. Regard, sir, her appearance. She's grown paler, more fragile ...

MAŁKA   Physically I feel perfectly well. Depression – from the work – it will pass.

                  Jojne's voice is heard offstage: Małka, come through here for a minute![206]

MAŁKA   Apologies to you both, I'll be back shortly, my husband is calling me into the shop.

                  (She exits into the shop)

MAURYCY   *(Gripping Rózia's hand)* Oh, Miss Rózia, we'll be so happy!

RÓZIA   Yes, we will – this is hardly the time to be selfish about it. Let's consider poor Małka, to whom we owe our happiness. You saw how she's changed. Look around you. Would you call this a fitting environment? For Małka, who at our boarding school was treated with kid gloves? And have you seen her husband? Not two words could I exchange with him. And she, would you believe it, she speaks to him gently, as though to a child – in the evening she reads him children's stories, until he falls asleep on the couch. I cannot understand that woman!

MAURYCY   Nor can I – only admire her.

RÓZIA   Do you know that on the day of her engagement she said to me 'I am afraid lest my strength should fail' – today, as I watched her weeping, that moment seemed finally to have arrived.

MAURYCY   Moral – physical exhaustion aside – there must be another cause. Małka must have been in love, before her wedding. The embers of this emotion smoulder away in her heart – her anguish is doubled. I could even hazard a guess as to his identity.

RÓZIA   Małka never told me any of this.

MAURYCY	Małka is proud and secretive. This man can't have returned her love – that's why our love, our happiness, is for her a well-spring of suffering.
MAŁKA	(Returns) Here I am – I can stay a little longer now. Honest Jenta is here, she'll take my place in the shop beside my husband.
RÓZIA	Yes! But it's only a momentary respite. Mr Maurycy and I have been...
MAŁKA	Mr Maurycy and your good self would be better off going to view the shop on Frańciszkańska Street. Poor Jenta is dying of impatience to finally see herself settled.
RÓZIA	Since you're throwing us out – we'll make haste. Come, Mr Maurycy!
MAURYCY	Good day to you, Miss Małka!
MAŁKA	You keep on calling me Miss Małka!
MAURYCY	In spite of myself. I can't accept, that it's any other way.
	(They exit)

SCENE 4

(Małka alone, then Jojne)

MAŁKA	(Goes towards the window and looks out, without moving aside the curtains) Jakób isn't there any more. Today he walked past the shop twice. Yesterday, in the late evening, closing the window, I noticed him standing across the street, smoking a cigarette. Why does he come here? Why won't he leave me alone! Even without this I feel so bitter – so ready to rebel – one drop more and my cup will overflow...
JOJNE	(Poking his head in) Małka, may I come in?
MAŁKA	Come in, Jojne. Why have you left the shop? Jenta might need you.
JOJNE	(Shyly) Because I'm so sad without you, Małke!
MAŁKA	We'll see each other in the evening – you'll be with me then, my poor Jojne!
JOJNE	I can't do without you for one single moment, Małke.

(He crouches before her and takes her by the hand) How delicate your hand is Małka...like my best, most beautiful kerchief...to kiss it is like drinking honey, or eating sweet almond biscuits...[207]

(He kisses her hand)

You, Małka, I would not – not for ten thousand, not for twenty five thousand roubles – give away to anyone, because I'm very happy with you and I love you very much.

MAŁKA	You, Jojne, are happy with me! That might be true. You do forget, Jojne, so quickly, all that I tell you.
JOJNE	I try to remember everything you say to me Małke!
MAŁKA	No, because once I spent a whole Saturday explaining, that you don't love me – only yourself. If you want to have me near you, it's not so that I can be happy, but so that you can be jolly and cheerful. And so it's yourself – not me – that you love, Jojne and that is egotistical and selfish.
JOJNE	(Saddened) Is that a sin, Małke?
MAŁKA	No, Jojne! But such selfish love can often cause someone else great unhappiness and make that person suffer.
JOJNE	I too was unhappy when instructed to marry you – I cried till the guests and the marszelik made me a laughing stock. Now even I am happy and like my marriage very well. I have my own house and wife, my own Sabbath celebrations – that's everything I need.
MAŁKA	Yes, Jojne, that's everything you need.
JOJNE	And I wouldn't give you up to anyone, anyone!
MAŁKA	Calm down, my poor Jojne, no-one wants to take me away from you.
JENTA	(Pokes her head round the door leading to the shop) Jojne! Jojne! Come here – quickly now![208]
MAŁKA	Go Jojne, Jenta is calling.
JOJNE	(Dragging his heels) I don't much feel like going, Małka.
MAŁKA	(More severely) You have to go, Jojne!

JOJNE	Alright, Małka … but I'll be back in a minute.
MAŁKA	I'll go through again shortly – father's gone out?
JOJNE	For a walk.
	(Goes into the shop)
MAŁKA	*(Alone)* If I could only rouse that snail of a soul to life and stir some nobler instinct. I fear my efforts are in vain!

SCENE 5

(Glanzowa, Małka)

GLANZOWA	*(Enters through the central door)* Good day to you, Małka!
MAŁKA	*(Joyfully)* Glanzowa!
	(She rushes to her and kisses her)
GLANZOWA	Yes, here I am, my dear Miss Małka – for this is no marriage.
MAŁKA	It goes without saying – Glanzowa was dead set against my marriage. You weren't even at the wedding, I wanted you, no-one else, to cut my hair, since it did have to be cut …
GLANZOWA	I didn't want to come – I couldn't look on in silence while you gave yourself up to such a common, ugly Jojne. Ay! Małka, Małka, what a grave sin lies on your conscience!
MAŁKA	Mine?
GLANZOWA	Yes, yours! You married Jojne with love for another man in your heart.
MAŁKA	How do you know?
GLANZOWA	Nothing escapes Glanzowa's watchful eye. You've forgotten, I was there – in our blessed mistress's house – when Miss Małka's father brought her and left her with us. You grew under my care like a flower, from child to maid, always fond of Glanzowa, with no secrets from her. Though you may – through pride – have kept certain things from me, I would always guess what they were and could read Miss Małka's heart like an open book.

MAŁKA	My good Glanzowa.
GLANZOWA	Isn't that so, Miss Małka? Even the mistress herself was wont to say 'tell me Glanzunia,[209] what is Małka thinking?' Even she knew less of Małka's thoughts, her heart, than I did. That's why I understood, long ago, that your heart had answered a summons – to love a good, honest man. That's why I'm here today – on his behalf.
MAŁKA	*(Startled)* His behalf?
GLANZOWA	Yes. And though at first glance my actions appear dishonest, since one should not approach a married woman giving voice to another man's love, I've no sense of sin – I can state my purpose boldly. Yes, Miss Małka, I assume Jakób Lewi's voice – I ask you to be his wife.
MAŁKA	Glanzowa! I'm already married.
GLANZOWA	For us, there is a word that has great weight and importance, when someone endures an unhappy marriage and that is, divorce!
MAŁKA	*(Paling with emotion)* Divorce![210]
GLANZOWA	Yes! It didn't cross your mind that escape from the tomb, release from such profound unhappiness, is possible. To others, go ahead, pretend you're happy, you can't fool old Glanzowa – gazing on your sad face, your sad eyes – she knows everything. Divorce! Małka, divorce! Just think – you'll divorce Jojne and marry Mr Jakób. You've loved him a long time, perhaps longer than he's loved you, but now he knows it, he will not live without you.
MAŁKA	But Mr Lewi was betrothed.
GLANZOWA	Mr Lewi broke off the agreement and now is free.
MAŁKA	*(Joyfully)* Free!
GLANZOWA	As a bird! As you, Małka, will be free when, with Jojne's agreement, your divorce is granted. Today our blessed mistress appeared to me in a dream, 'Go you, Glanzowa, to Małka' she said, 'tell her this suffering must cease – let her divorce and be happy at last'.
MAŁKA	And I will at last be happy!
GLANZOWA	So said our mistress. All scruples – I cast them aside, saying to Mr Jakób – I will go, I will tell her, you want to see her … that you …

MAŁKA   He wants to come here!

GLANZOWA   He's waiting just beyond the threshold; he can enter boldly – not like a thief to become your lover, but to take you for a wife, to prevent your death, for you will die, Małka, if you stay here any longer and torment yourself like this.

MAŁKA   (*In a sudden outburst, weeping*) Yes, Glanzowa! Yes, I will be lost, I will die! Save me! I can live here no longer! I did everything to endure it, but I've no strength left and today, when I know, that he's free, that he wants me for a wife…I want to, and must be free as well…

GLANZOWA   Tell him so yourself – may this be an end to your suffering.

                 (*Goes towards the door*)

                 Come in Mr Jakób, sir.

SCENE 6

(*Jakób, Małka, Glanzowa*)

JAKÓB   (*Stands in the doorway and holds out his hands to Małka*) Małka, my own Małka!

MAŁKA   (*Also holding out her hands*) Jakób!

                 (*He grasps her hands and kisses her*)

JAKÓB   At last! At long last. Will you agree to a divorce? Do you want to be mine?

MAŁKA   Do what you want with me. The balance has tipped. At last even I long to be happy!

JAKÓB   I swear it – you will be! When I lost you I came to see, how dear you are, how long I've loved you – my life's purpose. When you were home from school, remember, I made up excuses to visit your aunt, I fooled even myself – to see you, hear your sweet voice – it bewitched me. Betrothal to my cousin meant a parting of ways – nothing remained to bind us, occupy each other's thoughts. Then you returned and my misery began. A hundred times dearer you became – I loved you with my entire soul. But my word was my bond, it stopped my mouth, my heart. Yet at last I determined to sever those ties and drag you from this mire. Learning of your marriage, I ran to you, eager to explain – yet from your own lips heard that you loved your betrothed, what else could I do? What?

MAŁKA	Why didn't you tell me this sooner?
JAKÓB	Why? My word had shackled me to another woman. I'd no right to speak of love. Today I'm free Małka and ask if you'll be my wife! Ah! Don't even think about that child – he'll grant a divorce without a second thought – little does he care what kind of woman he marries.
MAŁKA	You may be mistaken, sir... That man appears to be in love with me.
JAKÓB	That is not love.
MAŁKA	I didn't say he loves me – he is in love with his own reflection. That kind of love tends to be the strongest – it's built on egotism. Little do I care! Desire for life – for happiness awakens in me today! I refuse to deny myself joy, since at long last it has smiled on me! I'll fight for it with my last drop of strength and must achieve it, even it costs me my life!
JAKÓB	Oh Małka! My dearest love! Remember – I belong to you completely... you're crying.
MAŁKA	(Weeping with joy) Permit me! These are sweet tears, they bring relief. Just think how many bitter tears I've shed... my heart is overflowing.
JAKÓB	An end to bitter tears.
MAŁKA	Who can say for sure! But I can't struggle any more. I loved you too, Jakób, when I was still a child – at school I dreamt of you constantly. Even my darkest moments of grief I could endure, for the sight of you, your words, gave me courage. One evening, remember? You said we should stop meeting. You left... father came home... hungry and chilled to the bone – I consented to this marriage – wouldn't it be better, for the price of my freedom, to guarantee sustenance and warmth to an old man, since I no longer cherished any expectations of life? That is the history of my marriage.
JAKÓB	We have been the victims of a misunderstanding, but today...
GLANZOWA	I see I must involve myself – people who love each other always chatter on until daybreak – not a single intelligent word is ever uttered. Małka should by the end of today inform her husband of their separation and her desire for a divorce. Later she should let us know his answer and how we should proceed. Agreed?

MAŁKA	Rest assured – I'll tell him at once – or I'll feel like a bad, wayward wife. Good health to you, Jakób, thank you for my good fortune, dear Glanzunia![211] You've acted in my best interests. May God reward you.
GLANZOWA	*(Leaving)* The two of you, happy – that will be my greatest reward. Come, Mr Jakób!
	(Exits)
JAKÓB	*(To Małka)* Małka … today I can by right bid my future wife farewell? Can I not?
MAŁKA	Oh, yes! Yes! How different – how happy I feel! This is sunlight! This is redemption! A new life has come into view!
JAKÓB	I see it, my love!
	(Clasps her in his embrace, kisses her and exits swiftly – at this moment Jojne enters from the shop, sees how Jakób kisses Małka and runs to the front of the stage)

SCENE 7

(Małka, Jojne, Jenta then Szwarcenkopf)

JOJNE	Małke! What did I see? Who was that? That man?
MAŁKA	My future husband!
JOJNE	What do you mean, Małka? You want to dig me a grave? I'm alive!
MAŁKA	No, Jojne. I don't desire your death – not in the least – nor should you be given permission to desire mine. We must get divorced, Jojne.
JOJNE	Divorced? You and me? Why? Why?
MAŁKA	Because I don't love you, Jojne.
JOJNE	But I love you and I need you very much, for the shop and as a wife.
MAŁKA	That may be so, but it doesn't make any difference. I'll marry someone else, a husband I've chosen.
JOJNE	This means nothing! I won't agree to a divorce! I will not agree! You must live with me and carry on being my wife because I will not go near a divorce…

SCENE 8

(The same, Jenta, Szwarcenkopf, Old Firułkes)

SZWARCENKOPF   Mr Firułkes and I met up in the street – I asked him to come in for a while.

JOJNE   Ay ay! What has happened here! What a terrible worry has happened here!

ALL   *(Except for Małka)* What's the matter?

JOJNE   Ay ay! Here Małke, my wife, stood kissing a strange man and when I asked her, who is he, she said, her future husband.

FIRUŁKES   What are you talking about? You mischievous creature![212] You're telling lies.[213]

JOJNE   Not lies – the truth. Let *her* tell you! Let *her* say it! She wants a divorce.

ALL   *(Except for Małka)* A divorce?

SZWARCENKOPF   *(To Małka)* You want a divorce? Why do you want a divorce?

MAŁKA   Because every human being has the right to live – to be happy. Because I've given you well nigh an entire year of my life while you, father, have sat by the stove, my husband on the couch and it hasn't even occurred to you to notice, that moment by moment I have been dying, in chains, like a galley slave, or a horse harnessed to a plough.

SZWARCENKOPF   What else did you need? You had everything, you had a business, you had a husband!

FIRUŁKES   Everything necessary for the housekeeping, from the brass to the bed-sheets, we gave it!

JOJNE   *(Weeping)* And such a lovely samovar...

MAŁKA   Take everything away, then – the business and the bed sheets and the samovar and let me out of here with my soul intact, for you do not have any right to my soul. No document, no law allows you to imprison the soul of a woman, who understands life differently from you and requires something else from it.

FIRUŁKES | *(With a shout)* Divorce? And who will recompense me for my loss? Who will pay back the expenses we laid out for the ceremony and for the gifts and for Jojne's clothes? Her management of the shop has brought only loss – no profit. You must pay it all back!

JOJNE | I will not go near a divorce.

FIRUŁKES | Pay up.

SZWARCENKOPF | *(Shaking all over with anger)* Wait Firułkes! Wait Jojne! I'll have it out with her! Disobedient child! Despicable child![214] So you want a divorce!? You want to throw your old father out into the gutter again with his matches and cigarettes? You will not – for uttering such a word as divorce – escape my hands alive! You hear me!

MAŁKA | Father of mine – you can be certain I will!

SZWARCENKOPF | Silence! Once you vowed to be Jojne's wife. You have no shame – you, discovered under your husband's roof kissing a stranger... you – fall on your knees before Jojne, accept his forgiveness – he will take you in once more.

FIRUŁKES | Not like this he won't. You, Szwarcenkopf, must compensate me for damages.

SZWARCENKOPF | You hear, what you've done!

(Seizing Małka by the scruff of the neck)

You fall at Jojne's feet and don't even think of divorce, you...

(He throws Małka to her knees before Jojne. Małka tears herself from his grip and lunges towards the door)

SZWARCENKOPF | I will disown you if you cross the threshold of this house!

MAŁKA | Disown me! Only let me out of here alive.

SZWARCENKOPF | *(Pushes her away from the door and locks it)* You will remain – disobedient, disgraceful child! This is your home! You will not take a step beyond it! Everyone else come into the shop, leave her here to come to her senses!

(Curtain falls)

ACT 5

(The same room as in the previous act, on the table burns a candle. One of the beds is surrounded by a screen. Jojne is sitting on the couch dozing. Jenta is sitting in a chair and also dozing. After a while knocking is heard at the door. Old Szwarcenkopf enters, approaches Jenta and wakes her)

SCENE 1

(Jenta, Szwarcenkopf, Jojne, behind the screen Małka)

SZWARCENKOPF   Jenta! Wake up … The doctor will be here soon.

JENTA   *(Waking with difficulty)* The doctor … what for?

SZWARCENKOPF   What for? To see … her!

JENTA   Ah! Yes – Małka.

(Rising)

I was having a nap.

SZWARCENKOPF   Has she said nothing at all?

JENTA   No! Perhaps she's finally fallen asleep.

SZWARCENKOPF   Go and see what she's doing?

JENTA   *(Goes to look behind the screen)* She's sitting in a corner by the bed with her eyes open.

SZWARCENKOPF   She hasn't slept for four nights.

(After a while) Jenta – is the shop door locked and bolted?

JENTA   Fear not, Szwarcenkopf, no thief will enter.

SZWARCENKOPF   Not thieves, Jenta – only … that other one might creep in – conspire with Małka. Yesterday that Glanzowa tried to force herself in but I, Jenta, realized that she must be an accomplice and didn't let her into my house.

JENTA   That was wrong, Szwarcenkopf. Perhaps she had something important to say …

SZWARCENKOPF	What, for instance? I don't want her to see Małka.
JENTA	Meet with her, Szwarcenkopf. This is most important. Let her explain.
SZWARCENKOPF	I don't want to hear explanations. Małka is possessed by an evil spirit, I went to the rabbi, he'll pray for her, if that doesn't work, he'll come in person. For now he's instructed me to call the doctor – lest she fall into a terrible sickness … The rabbi told me to have faith in a good outcome … that she will return to her senses and all will be as before. A, Jenta! Jenta! How good it was – and quiet, here … so obediently did Szwarcenkopf sit by the stove – comfortable – warm … Disobedient! Disgraceful, disgraceful child! Jojne! Jojne!
JOJNE	*(Lifting his head)* I'm not asleep, Szwarcenkopf.
SZWARCENKOPF	If you're not asleep Jojne then why not come here and listen to what the rabbi said.
JOJNE	*(Shaking his head sadly)* To you, Szwarcenkopf, the rabbi said one thing – I to myself have said – another.
SZWARCENKOPF	You are stupid, Jojne – what the rabbi says is worth more than what you make up in your thick head.
JOJNE	The Rabbi doesn't know my thoughts, my soul. I do – and for four whole days now I've been thinking – a lot has passed between me and myself, Szwarcenkopf.
SZWARCENKOPF	While you're at it, arrange your clothes and get up – shortly the doctor will arrive. Oh! Here he comes now. *(Jojne does not get up from the couch only leans his head in his hands and loses himself in his thoughts)*
DOCTOR	*(From the doorstep)* Does Firułkes live here?
SZWARCENKOPF	He does! He does! Please! Come in, doctor.
DOCTOR	*(Entering)* Who requires my services?

SCENE 2

(The same and the Doctor)

(The doctor is not a young man, he is affluently dressed, looks down his nose at everyone and treats them carelessly)

DOCTOR   Who is the sick person here?

SZWARCENKOPF   My daughter, doctor.

DOCTOR   What ails her?

SZWARCENKOPF   Jenta, go and fetch Małka.

DOCTOR   Give me another candle – dark as a tomb in here.

SZWARCENKOPF   At once, doctor.

                (He goes to light another candle, Jenta leads Małka out from behind the screen, pale and very changed)

JENTA   Here is the sick woman, doctor!

                (Małka stands before the doctor not looking at him)

DOCTOR   (To Szwarcenkopf who has brought the candle)

                Put the candle down. Yes!

                (To Małka)

                Now, respond clearly and quickly – I don't have much time. What ails you? What is wrong? Head! Lungs, stomach?

                (Małka does not reply)

SZWARCENKOPF   Apologies, good doctor, sir, but I...

DOCTOR   Silence! Let the sick woman speak. Cat got your tongue? Sore throat?

SZWARCENKOPF   She will not reply...

DOCTOR   Why not? Deaf, is she? Dumb? Lost her tongue?

SZWARCENKOPF   No, doctor, she has a worry, from thence her sickness. She won't eat, or talk, or sleep, she just sits in a corner and thinks.

DOCTOR   You must have hurt her.

                (To Małka)

Can you tell me what happened?

(Takes her pulse)

Hm! Severe exhaustion and immense nervous exertion!

MAŁKA	I've a great favour to ask, doctor!
DOCTOR	Talking at last! How fortunate.
MAŁKA	Four days I have not slept. It's wearing me out... I'd so like to fall asleep and sleeping, rest a little... Perhaps you doctor could give me some medicine to help me sleep...
DOCTOR	Of course, I can prescribe a small dose of morphine. Sleep will be peaceful. But excepting lack of sleep – what ails you?
MAŁKA	Nothing!
DOCTOR	Concern of a moral nature – most likely – quite common among your sort. Married? Yes! There we are then. Set-to with the husband! Something to calm the nerves – I'll prescribe it. An attack of nerves is better avoided at your age – become a regular old battleaxe before you know it. Husband will throw himself to the four winds trying to escape. Well then, go to bed, sip thickened chicken broth, dose yourself with the powders and give me some peace and quiet. You and your ailments! Pen and paper?
SZWARCENKOPF	Everything is prepared, doctor.

(Doctor sits at the table and writes a prescription)

SZWARCENKOPF	(To Jenta) How much should we give him?
JENTA	Perhaps thirty, perhaps fifty kopeks.
SZWARCENKOPF	I'll give him thirty and wrapped in paper, then he won't notice.
JENTA	And when he unwraps it?
SZWARCENKOPF	I'll say I've made a mistake.
DOCTOR	(Writing the prescription) Take this to the apothecary – then, administer with care – too large a dose can be harmful.

(Jenta takes the prescription)

JENTA

I'll go and wait – it'll be ready quicker.

DOCTOR

(Noticing Jojne) And this one? Toothache, is it?

SZWARCENKOPF

No, doctor – he has a worry – he just sits and thinks; that's the husband.

DOCTOR

(Laughing) That! A husband! He should still be going to cheder[215] not getting married…Good health to all. Don't tax me again with such nonsense. When one of you really is at death's door, I won't believe it, I shan't attend.

SZWARCENKOPF

Here? Dying? What a thought!

DOCTOR

In that case, live!

(Szwarcenkopf hands him the money in the paper. The Doctor takes it, unwraps the paper, at this moment Szwarcenkopf begins)

SZWARCENKOPF

I made a mis…

(Seeing that the doctor puts the paper away without counting)

Goodnight, doctor.

(Doctor exits, Szwarcenkopf lights his way out with a candle)

JOJNE

(Lifts his head and looks at Małka)

Małka!

(Małka does not reply, only approaches the table and feverishly writes a few words on the remaining sheets of paper)

JOJNE

Who's that for, Małka? You won't speak to me, Małka – I so badly want to say…that…

SZWARCENKOPF

(Returns, Małka hides the paper she has written on in her bodice)

Go and lie down, Małka, soon Jenta will bring the medicine. Tomorrow, after you've slept, I'll repeat the rabbi's words. I had to visit him and speak my shame – all because of you. So – let him judge between us and tell you a thing or two.

MAŁKA   Your visit was futile, my father! One judge only – most high, most just! I will go to him – appeal for our case to be heard and a verdict reached in our dispute.

SZWARCENKOPF   Summon me to court, would you? You shall not leave this place, I have said so!

MAŁKA   No, father, I will not leave this place. You may rest easy. A summons to court will not arrive today, nor tomorrow, though – who knows – sooner, perhaps, than you expect. Good health to you, my father! Good health to you, poor Jojne!

(Goes behind the screen)

SZWARCENKOPF   Perhaps she has come to her senses.

SCENE 3

(The same, Old Firułkes, then Jojne)

FIRUŁKES   *(Enters rapidly)* What's happened?

SZWARCENKOPF   Nothing has happened! What should've happened!

FIRUŁKES   Where's Małka? She hasn't escaped?

SZWARCENKOPF   Why should she escape! She's a little sick – she's lying behind the screen. Why are you, Firułkes, dashing about making so much noise?

FIRUŁKES   How can I not make noise when me and my son have nothing but loss and shame on account of your daughter.

SZWARCENKOPF   You can't have lost anything yet, because no-one knows the outcome ... Jenta stayed in the shop today – trade was good. What exactly do you want, Firułkes?

FIRUŁKES   And Jojne's worry? The food Jenta eats?

SZWARCENKOPF   To compensate, Małka eats nothing.

FIRUŁKES   Not this way ... it cannot be! Gabide, who collected for your daughter's wedding – let him gather extra. Give it to us, if you want my Jojne to keep your daughter in this house ...

SZWARCENKOPF	By no means; Gabide can help give a daughter away, yes – but not get mixed up in something like this.
FIRUŁKES	(Shouting) Do what you like … as I live and breathe I'll make sure I don't lose out!

SCENE 4

(The same and Jenta)

JENTA	Here's the medicine!
	(To Szwarcenkopf)
	I must have a word, Szwarcenkopf.
SZWARCENKOPF	Go, give – let her take it.
JENTA	(Approaching the screen) Here, Małka – take the phial.
	(To Szwarcenkopf)
	Glanzowa is here. She wants to talk. She comes with a good, honest, golden proposition. Well now! Where's the harm? It's only conversation. Costs nothing! A word from her and things may start looking up!
SZWARCENKOPF	A proposition – you say. For us!
JENTA	Upon my life!
	(Speaks in an undertone)
FIRUŁKES	You, Jojne – no making up until we get what we deserve.
JOJNE	I won't make it up with her at all.
FIRUŁKES	Listen you – when they pay up, that's when you make up …
JOJNE	Don't you shout at me father – I won't wince … I know what I have to do and I will do it.
FIRUŁKES	You rascal![216] You know what to do? Idiot! Turnip head![217] No need to think – I'll do that for you and more!

SZWARCENKOPF	*(To Jenta)* Go, tell her to come in. See first whether Małka's fallen asleep.
JENTA	*(Goes behind the screen and returns)* She's asleep. I shook her, but she didn't wake.
SZWARCENKOPF	Conceal her carefully behind the screen and fetch that woman.
	(Jenta exits)
FIRUŁKES	What kind of woman is this?
SZWARCENKOPF	One who says she has a golden proposition from which we can all make a lot of money.
FIRUŁKES	Make haste, then, let her enter.

SCENE 5

(The same and Glanzowa)

GLANZOWA	Good evening! Why so slow to admit me, Szwarcenkopf?
SZWARCENKOPF	Because you, Glanzowa, must be an accomplice of the man who wants to marry Małka!
FIRUŁKES	*(With a shout)* Who has made me and my son Jojne endure so many losses.
SZWARCENKOPF	Quiet. Firułkes! Małka will awaken. Isn't that so, Glanzowa, am I right, was he the one who sent you?
GLANZOWA	*(Quietly)* Yes, Szwarcenkopf, he sent me then, as he sends me now.
SZWARCENKOPF	And you've no shame, Glanzowa? No shame in approaching a married woman like this?
GLANZOWA	No, because to me Małka isn't a married woman. She's beautiful, delicate, wise – like a princess – and you gave her away to a common, ugly, ignorant Jojne, who could barely get some Ryfka or Sura from a village to be his wife.[218]
FIRUŁKES	My son owns a small shop.

GLANZOWA   And he's all broken and crooked.[219] I'm not the one who should be ashamed but you – you planted a lovely flower in a heap of rubbish to watch it wither away – but, as long as Glanzowa lives, her poor, dear mistress's charge will not be allowed to perish. You, Szwarcenkopf, gave Małka away, so that you wouldn't any longer have to walk the streets selling matches and could sit peacefully by the stove. Mr Lewi, who wants to marry Małka, offers you two hundred roubles cash today, followed by twelve roubles on a monthly basis for your upkeep. Tell me, is that not superior to waiting for Jojne's favour with ne'er a kopek in your pocket?[220]

SZWARCENKOPF   I wouldn't say it's worse. But what assurance do I have?

GLANZOWA   He will inscribe it in his tenaim[221] and two hundred roubles will be given today or tomorrow.

SZWARCENKOPF   Who knows, whether he's that kind of gentleman?

GLANZOWA   He is Mr Jakób Lewi, lawyer, shortly to set up his own chambers.

FIRUŁKES   Really![222] A lawyer!

SZWARCENKOPF   Well…that may have silenced me, and Jojne – but Old Firułkes…

FIRUŁKES   No! No! We have endured many losses…we do not wish it.

GLANZOWA   Tell us the extent of your losses?…

FIRUŁKES   Do I know? Could be as much as five hundred roubles…maybe more – not counting Jojne's worry.

GLANZOWA   Have you no shame, Firułkes, saying such things to me, an intelligent woman. The betrothal and wedding were paid in half by Szwarcenkopf with money Gabide collected from good people. I know how much everything cost – the hall, the marszelik, the furniture – down to the last detail…

FIRUŁKES   (Riled) You know nothing. What can you know? And how? That couch alone cost me seven and a half roubles on Krasiński Square![223] If only I were lucky in business, if only I hadn't been blinded, if only Jojne hadn't broken his arms and legs!

GLANZOWA   I can see no agreement will be reached with you. So I'm leaving…

SZWARCENKOPF	Why leave now? What a hot-head you are, Mrs Glanzowa…There should be no anger in matters of business, agreement can be reached.
GLANZOWA	I can't bring myself to listen to him… Five hundred roubles for such a Jojne, no, no! Even were he made of gold he wouldn't be that expensive.
FIRUŁKES	In this day and age a young Jewish man owning a small shop is worth his weight in gold.
GLANZOWA	He is worth at most one hundred and fifty roubles.
FIRUŁKES	Ridiculous![224] One hundred and fifty roubles! A horse is worth more and doesn't even own a shop!
GLANZOWA	You want two hundred, like Szwarcenkopf.
FIRUŁKES	Impossible – at the best of times. I lay out as much before selling a single item.
SZWARCENKOPF	Three hundred, then and let us call it an agreement…
FIRUŁKES	Look! What a clever man he is! Got two hundred himself with added interest of twelve percent a month – tells me to take three hundred.

SCENE 6

(The same and Jakób)

GLANZOWA	Here we have Mr Jakób, now you can draw up plans together.
JAKÓB	I couldn't bear the uncertainty any longer. What's going on here? Have you reached an agreement? Where's Małka?
	(Jojne rises and very moved looks at Jakób)
JOJNE	*(Aside)* It's him! He's the one Małka loves!
GLANZOWA	Old Szwarcenkopf has agreed, but Jojne's father drives a hard bargain.
JAKÓB	*(To Szwarcenkopf)* I thank you – be assured, you won't regret the exchange. I'll do my level best to see that for the rest of your life you want for nothing. By giving permission, you contribute to our happiness – Małka and I will repay you in kind.

FIRUŁKES	Whereas I am unable to give my permission …
JAKÓB	How much do you want?
FIRUŁKES	For myself – five hundred roubles.
JAKÓB	Though a bold request – I agree. You shall have it …
FIRUŁKES	As for my son … Jojne … you've been the cause of his great worry … He too must receive compensation …
JOJNE	(Suddenly in an assertive tone with a remnant of shyness and battling with his tears) I require no compensation, father!
FIRUŁKES	You fool, do not interrupt proceedings …
JOJNE	(Approaching Jakób) The two of them, sir, have sold you Małka but Jojne will not sell his wife, his tears or his worry. No man possesses a sum sufficiently vast to serve as payment for a wife, for tears, for sadness.
FIRUŁKES	You fool, do not spoil the business – you must proceed with a divorce.
JOJNE	I won't sell Małka, sir, but I will give her to you. Take her as your wife – you're a better match than simple, stupid, ugly Jojne. She's been so good – and kind – but I understand that with me her life has been difficult and wretched. At least now only I will have sadness and regret and she will be well and live in contentment with you sir … I'll proceed with arrangements for the divorce only don't give me any money … Jojne may be stupid, but he won't exchange his heart for money.
JAKÓB	(Holding out his hand) Poor, kind heart – it beats honestly and nobly against its oppressive surroundings!
JOJNE	(Moving his hand away and steering himself towards the door) I'll go out for a breath of air! One thing only, I ask you! When I return, let Małka be gone! I wouldn't be able to look at her.
	(With loud weeping exits and bids them farewell)
	I wouldn't be able to look.
JAKÓB	Tomorrow we'll go together, formalize the agreement, and then the money will be paid. Now, where is Małka? She should get ready to leave. Would you, Mrs Glanzowa, take her in for the time being?

SZWARCENKOPF   Małka is a little unwell – she's asleep after her medicine.

JAKÓB   Then wake her. She should come with us. Jojne's request must be respected – we must do, as he asks.

SZWARCENKOPF   (*Goes behind the screen*) Małka! Małka! Get up – the best possible conclusion … you are to divorce … hear me?[225] Divorce!

(*Silence*)

JAKÓB   Glanzowa, you go and wake Małka, my own Glanzowa.

(*Glanzowa goes behind the screen, moves it so that the bed is visible to the spectator. On the bed lies Małka, clothed, dead. In her hand she holds an empty phial of morphine. To her breast is pinned a piece of paper and on the table burns a candle*)

GLANZOWA   Miss Małka! Miss Małka! Get up! I am here – so is Mr Jakób – we have come to get you …

(*Suddenly moves away in fear*)

Mr Jakób! Look you, sir!

JAKÓB   What's the matter?

(*He runs to the bed, looks at Małka, leans over her, grasps her around the waist, the phial falls from the hand of the corpse, he tears the piece of paper from her breast*)

JAKÓB   She has poisoned herself! She's dead!

SZWARCENKOPF   Dead?

JAKÓB   (*Reading the note*) 'Do not weep – grant me your forgiveness. At this moment, at last, I am completely happy'.

(*Falls to his knees by the bed*)

Małka! Małka! I was the one bringing you happiness – but I arrived too late!

(*Curtain slowly falls*)

Notes

1. Szwarcenkopf translates from Yiddish and German ('shvarts'/'schwartz' and 'kop'/'kopf') as 'black-headed' or 'black-haired'.

2. This is the Polish form of the Hebrew girl's name Malka (Romanized spelling). The Yiddish version would be Malke. The meaning of Malke or Malkeh is 'queen'.

3. See footnotes 40, 52 and 53.

4. See footnotes 21 and 49. Maurycy is the Polish version of the name Maurice, which is of Latin origin and means 'dark-skinned' or 'Moorish'. The Germanized and Yiddish version of this name is 'Moritz' or, as it is spelt using the Polish alphabet to attain phonetic equivalence, 'Moryc'. Indeed, Maurycy's full name implies a connection with Prussia/the Prussian partition.

5. A counting house was the building or room in which a firm carried on operations, particularly accounting. The term is primarily used in the context of the nineteenth century or earlier periods.

6. See footnotes 55 and 56.

7. I believe Zapolska has polonized the Yiddish word 'ruekh' or 'ruakh' (rukhes) in order to develop this surname. There is a phonetic similarity. The word means 'ghost, devil or demon', which seems to correspond with the character developed by the playwright. The first part of the surname 'fi' is not dissimilar from the exclamation 'fe', meaning 'ugh!' or 'yuck!' It might therefore be argued that the surname has connotations of 'horrible ghost' – an influence that both Jojne and Małka must work hard to exorcise – a set of influences associated with the past.

8. 'Jojne' is derived from the names 'Jonas' and 'Jonah', which are connected. In this context, the significant origins of the names are Hebrew and biblical. The Hebrew version of 'Jonas' means 'dove', a symbol of peace. The biblical version of the name includes the Hebrew connotations but additionally means 'he who destroys or oppresses'. As a variation of 'Jonah', 'Jonas' can also mean 'gift from God' or 'accomplishing'. The biblical character Jonah entered the whale's gape but was spared by God and managed to leave the gape whole and unscathed. Zapolska's choice of name might be a clue to her thinking about this character – an indication of the extent of his self-exploration throughout the play and his changing attitude towards Małka. It is also important to bear in mind the play Zapolska wrote following *Małka*, entitled *Jojne Firułkes*, which features Jojne as central protagonist.

9. Bernard is of Old French and Old German origin. It means 'strong brave bear'.

10. Mowsze is the polonized version of the vernacular Yiddish name Mojsie (see footnote 12). Cytryna means, in Polish, 'lemon'. This becomes the subject of a joke during the betrothal ceremony in Act 3.

11. Izaak is a variant of the Hebrew name, Isaac/Yitzhak, which means 'laughter'. Pomeranz sounds like the Polish word for 'orange', which is 'pomarańcza'. This becomes the subject of a joke during the betrothal ceremony (Act 3).

12. Mojsie is the vernacular Yiddish version of the Hebrew name Moshe, or Moses. Radosny, in Polish, means literally 'joyful' or 'joyous'.

13. The 'master of ceremonies', who entertains the guests at a betrothal ceremony/wedding.

14. This name sounds like the Yiddish word 'yente' or 'yenta' or 'old-fashioned woman'. It can also mean a 'busybody' and usually refers to an older woman. It is the polonized version of the Yiddish name Yentl, for which 'Yente' is also the 'pet form'. Yentl is the Yiddish form of the French word *gentille* meaning 'noble, or good-hearted'.

15. See footnote 138.

16. Ryfka is the polonized form of Rifka. Rifka is the Yiddish form of Rivka. Rivka or Rivqah is the Hebrew form of Rebecca, and means 'a snare'. The name is biblical. Rivka or Rebecca was the wife of Abraham and the mother of Jacob and Esau.

17. This name means 'little Rose' in Polish.

18. In this case, 'chanteuse' refers to a woman who works as a 'nightclub singer', synonymous with prostitution. At least one of the women sings very badly ...

19. It is likely that these lyrics are associated with Johann Strauss II's operetta *Die Fledermaus* (1874). The libretto for this opera was originally written in German. The original source for *Die Fledermaus* is a farce by German playwright Julius Benedix (1811–73), *Das Gefängnis* (*The Prison*). Another source is a French vaudeville play, *Le Réveillon* (1872), by Henri Meilhac and Ludovic Halévy. These texts feature a character called Adèle, a serving maid.

20. Characters sometimes refer to champagne as 'szampańskie wino', or 'wine from Champagne' throughout this scene. This drink would have been much sweeter in the 1800s than what we now refer to as 'champagne' and as such would also have been known for its curative properties. This becomes relevant later in this act, when Glanzowa the housekeeper explains that during the illness of Maurycy's aunt the doctor instructed that she should sip the wine (see footnote 68).

21. 'Czy schodziłeś już do piwnicy, Morycu?' The Chanteuse alludes phonetically to what would have been Silbercweig's identifiably Yiddish first name, Moritz (which is also the German translation of 'Maurice' – significant given the relationship between the German and Yiddish languages). Maurycy is the Polish version, whereas Maurice is the French. Wiedeński uses the French version, perhaps pandering to Silbercweig's aristocratic pretensions. French was the language traditionally associated with and spoken by the Polish aristocracy.

22. Kabbalah (in Hebrew, literally 'receiving') is a discipline and school of thought discussing the mystical aspect of Judaism. Wiedeński may be performing his contempt for a type of Jewish religious practice for the benefit of the gathered company. It is our first clue of his complex attitude to his roots.

23. The polonized spelling of the German word 'meisterstück', or 'masterpiece'. Here, Silbercweig means a card trick of genius.

24. Wiedeński, in spite of having mentioned cabbalistic practice, becomes annoyed when Silbercweig uses a German word. This has associations with the Germanic roots of the Yiddish language. That is why Wiedeński offers the aristocratically imbued French translation and instructs Silbercweig not to speak like someone who works in a counting house – that is, by his calculation, most likely a Jew – but rather like an aristocratic gentile – in this case, a Pole.

25. Presumably bars intended to keep intruders away from certain parts of the counting house rather than to keep wild counting house employees in! A health and safety measure!

26. The word used is 'grojseszyki'. I believe this derives from two Yiddish words, 'groy' meaning big or large and 'shiker' meaning drunkard. The polonized version implies, in its ending, the plural. This translation seems most likely given the context for the scene, the drinking etc.

27. The saying goes 'rira bien qui rira le dernier' – 'well laughs he who laughs last'. It seems that Wiedeński's French is not so good after all – or else these are printer's errors (for ease of access I have used the version of the play published in 1923) – or examples of late nineteenth-century polonized French expressions. His 'correctness' or not in speaking French could work either way. Either he slips up and is not as 'socially mobile' as he likes to think, or he does speak fluently, which would have different though equally plausible implications. There is also his drunkenness to take

into account, which might affect his speech. However, there are further issues relating to accuracy (this also applies to the use of Yiddish throughout) which should be considered (see p. 15).

28. Camphor is an active ingredient (along with menthol) in vapour-steam products. The fact that Maurycy is not completely taken in by Wiedeński, as revealed here, becomes significant later.

29. This should presumably read 'je m'acquiterai' – 'I will acquit myself of my debt of honour'. The printed French is incorrect. See footnote 27.

30. It seems that Wiedeński is trying to suggest that Silbercweig should resolve something with Glanzowa by trying to use the verb 'entendre' – to come to an agreement with someone. See footnotes 27 and 29. Notice the French version of 'Maurycy' used in Glanzowa's presence.

31. Łódź is a city now in central Poland, about 135 km from Warsaw. During the nineteenth century it was part of Russian Poland and was nicknamed 'ziemia obiecana' or 'the promised land'. Rapid immigration (from countries including England, Ireland and Portugal) accompanied swift industrialization – indeed, the city has also been referred to as 'the Polish Manchester', given its proliferation of mills and factories. The population was dominated by three main groups – Jews, Germans and Poles. Much of the industry was managed by Jews. In the late nineteenth century the city was an important centre of the socialist movement and large-scale strikes took place there. Between about 1820 and 1870 the size of the population doubled every ten years.

32. 'It comes to the same thing'. This is correctly expressed.

33. The Russian rouble was the world's hardest currency during the nineteenth century. The gold rouble was introduced by decree of the Russian Emperor Nicholas II in 1897.

34. She calls him 'Morek', which I have translated as 'Mitzi', a kind of cute fusion of French, Polish and Yiddish versions of his first name.

35. This could be a 100 rouble banknote, which was then in circulation, or the total sum made up in smaller notes and/or coins. The latter is most likely, given what Wiedeński does with the money later in this scene.

36. It seems that Wiedeński can also speak Italian – 'good'!

37. It seems most likely that this could be Franz von Suppé's operetta *Leichte Kavallerie* (*Light Cavalry*) from 1876. The libretto was written in German – Wiedeński sings in Italian.

38. Wiedeński is covering up the number on one of the banknotes Maurycy has counted out for him. If this had been a 100 rouble banknote his trick would not work, since Maurycy would know that the number was even!

39. This word comes from the French language. It refers to a person who is a newcomer to a socio-economic class.

40. 'Kolumna' does literally translate into English as 'column'. This is a somewhat pompous-sounding assumed name and Jenta, Kolumna's sister-in-law, does make a joke of it in Act 2, when he arrives at her residence. See also footnote 138.

41. Maurycy actually says 'too close to the wrong side of that Iron Gate we all know'. He is referring to the Iron Gate located at the entrance to the Ogród Saski, or Saxon Garden, in Warsaw during the nineteenth century. It served as both a literal and symbolic divide between rich and poor Varsovians. The Saxon Garden was a fashionable place of elegance where wealthy Varsovians could promenade and take mineral waters. On the other side of the Iron Gate was a market, largely for street vendors, the largest in Warsaw, on Plac Żelaznej Bramy, or Iron Gate Square, where the Yiddish and Polish languages mingled. A sign hanging on the gate informed passers-by that anyone 'badly dressed or carrying packages' would not be admitted to the garden, and this rule was

enforced for some years by a guard. Since I have judged the reference too obscure in a contemporary performance context, I have found a parallel expression. Whether and how the actor playing Maurycy 'uses' the inverted commas I have added is a significant performance decision. I have added them to frame the phrase textually in a particular way – in order to indicate that this is potentially an expression and concept recognizable in everyday conversation and thus ideologically significant within the 'world of the play' (and the 'world' it is naturalistically representing), rather than entirely subjective and particular to Maurycy. These implications create parallels with the socio-cultural connotations and practices actually associated with the Iron Gate. In performance Maurycy might assume that, as a Jew, Jakób will recognize the expression and the issues in question.

42. The imperial – Russia's new gold coin minted in 1897 – was worth fifteen roubles between 1897 and 1917. A half-imperial was, as its name implies, worth seven roubles and 50 kopecks.

43. An operetta in three acts first performed in 1882. It was written by Karl Millöcker (score), Friedrich Zell and Richard Genée (German libretto). The action is set in Kraków in 1704.

44. Maurycy says literally, 'Whatever next; if I was naked, you could play a Turkish march, but since the opposite is true...' My interpretation is that he is referring to being in a Turkish baths, so I have made this more explicit in my translation.

45. The funeral march for piano written by Fryderyk Chopin in 1837. It became the third movement of his *Piano Sonata in B flat minor, Op. 35* and the theme for his *Marche funèbre in C minor, Op. 71 no. 2*.

46. This is something of a bad joke that has emerged in the English translation. I think it serves to highlight Wiedeński's mischievous frame of mind and so I am leaving it in.

47. In Greek mythology, Themis was the first wife of Zeus and his advisor on the precepts of divine law and the rules of fate. Justice appearing as a divine personage.

48. Wiedeński says 'Wdówka z nami!' before he leaves. I have chosen to extend his joke about Themis in the previous line in order to clarify fully for a modern audience what the reference signifies. I have then added an extra line for the actor to speak after Bernard's line. A 'wdówka' is an indigo bird or whydah. These are small passerine birds – that is, song birds or perching birds. My understanding is that he is referring to one (or both – though he uses the singular) of the two women in the room, who are, of course, 'singers' and may be wearing feathers in their hair, hats or on their costumes. The birds in question are also brood parasites, that is, birds that lay their eggs in other birds' nests. Unlike cuckoos, however, they do not destroy the host bird's eggs. A mention of indigo birds and whydahs here would probably be lost on a contemporary audience, so I have tried to find a translation that combines all the different qualities of these birds and of the situation in question. The women are probably costumed in an 'exotic' way, we know that one of them sings out of key (a cuckoo's song is not particularly tuneful) and they are 'laying their eggs in another bird's nest' (exploiting Maurycy's generosity, probably at Wiedeński's behest).

49. I have added this comment in order to clarify. The root of both surnames means the same; it is the word meaning 'silver' – 'srebro' in Polish and 'silber' in German.

50. Jakób tells Maurycy that he will be like 'Pan Twardowski' or 'Mr Twardowski'. My attempt to clarify this via translation draws on details about this well-known character from Polish folklore. According to ancient tales, Twardowski was a Faustian figure, a nobleman and sorcerer who entered into a pact with the devil and sold his soul in exchange for special powers. His fame and fortune grew until eventually he was abducted by the devil, who carried him to hell. En route, Twardowski began

to pray to the Virgin Mary and the devil dropped him. He fell on the moon, which is where he resides to this day.

51. Przemyśl is now a town in South Eastern Poland, near the border with Ukraine. During the 19th century it was part of Polish Galicia.

52. This is a familiar name, like a nickname or fancy name, by which a person is identified. Often applied to famous people, especially politicians or the generally notorious. Columns frequently feature within heraldic design; therefore this soubriquet both personalizes and confirms Wiedeński's so-called aristocratic credentials. The root of his surname, 'Wiedeń' is the Polish word for 'Vienna'. Combined with the soubriquet, his full 'surname' might therefore translate as something like 'Austrian Column'. Maurycy has just indeed revealed that Wiedeński is from Austrian Galicia. Using this literal translation, however, would be inappropriate. It would sound excessively eccentric and lose the Polish sound of the names, which locates the action geographically and historically. As it is, the pomposity of the name might be easily conveyed by the actors via pronunciation.

53. Maurycy uses the word 'Filar', jokingly finding a tautological equivalent for 'Kolumna'. I have translated this literally – I think the joke still works because 'Kolumna' is close enough phonetically to its English translation 'column' to still be recognisable in the context of the translated 'Filar' (which is not phonetically close enough to 'pillar' to be recognisable to an English audience in this context). 'Pillar-Silbercweig' does sound vaguely ridiculous, as it should. An alternative might be to substitute 'filar' with a reference to another heraldic symbol but the context would not, I believe, be strong enough for an audience to register the point and the humour.

54. Maurycy is exploring the relationship between name, class and ethnicity. This combination is, for him, a complete anomaly – the mock-Polish noble soubriquet and the apparently identifiably Jewish/Yiddish surname.

55. Jakób's surname is Lewi, pronounced Levi/Levy. Maurycy polonizes it by adding the ending 'ski'.

56. Levi or Levy was, according to the Old Testament, the third son of Jacob and Leah and the founder of the Israelite tribe of Levi (the levites).

57. Jakób partly refers to the fact that titles can be bought – though he is not being entirely cynical. His comment is also a statement of fact!

58. It is likely that he has heard, among other things, of Wiedeński's particular association with 'nightclub singers'. One of the ways he earns his money is by playing the pimp.

59. The majority of Warsaw Jews resided in an overcrowded, run-down district in the city's north section. On its streets – Nalewki, Gęsia, Zamenhofa, Miła, Pawia, Ostrowska, and many others – hundreds dwelt in houses with a multiplicity of courtyards. Gęsia Street has been renamed M. Anielewicza Street, after Mordechaj Anielewicz (1919–43), the leader of the Warsaw Ghetto Uprising. The new street is laid out along old Gęsia Street, which was one of the most important streets in Jewish Warsaw, the road that all the funeral processions took on their way to the Jewish Cemetery. I have translated the following excerpt – written by Isaac Bashevis Singer in 1944 (when Jewish Warsaw had been razed to the ground) and quoted in www.um.warszawa.pl/zmh/wstep. htm, in which he remembers and describes the streets of Warsaw – in order to give a sense of the geography and culture of the area and potentially indicate a series of related practices and ideologies.

'Warsaw Jews divided the capital's streets into two categories, roughly speaking the northern and southern parts. Those regarded as "good" streets were situated in the southern part of Jewish

Warsaw: Śliska, Pańska, Grzybowska, Twarda, Grzybowski Square, Gnojna, Krochmalna, Mariańska. Here lived the most devout and conservative members of the Warsaw Jewish community. Large firms did not tend to situate themselves here, most frequently seen were small grocers shops selling spices, milk, confectionaries, as well as small shops selling coal. The majority of inhabitants lived a poor existence, but if someone was rich, he was steadily rich, without any bankruptcies, debts, mortgages. On these "good" streets in nearly every open space could be found a Chasidic shtibl [prayer house/room] and every few houses or so was situated a ritual washroom. Boys and young men studying the Torah [the first three sections in the Tanakh, the Hebrew Bible] rarely hid their peyos [long side locks of hair] by twisting them around their ears – here there was no need for this. On Friday evening, before the onset of Sabbath, a group of monitors would walk around the whole area making sure, that all the shops were closed earlier than on other weekdays. It never happened that a shop or storeroom remained open on the Sabbath. On Saturday morning the streets filled with the aroma of cholent [a traditional Jewish stew simmered overnight] and kugel [traditional puddings and desserts]. Through all the windows echoed sounds of Sabbath hymns. Here was the land of Israel.

To the 'other' streets belonged: Dzielna, Pawia, Gęsia, Miła, Niska, Stawki, Muranowski Square, and above all Nalewki and Franciszkańska. Constant hustle and bustle reigned there. Before the First World War the Jews of this area would trade with Vladivostock [a large commercial Russian port], Petropavl [a Russian trading city], and even with China. Their shops were crammed full of items right to the very ceiling. In that area rent was high because every house was a small business. Truly, no-one would be able to count the small industries that could be found there. The hullabaloo of unforgettable voices bargaining and trading did not ease throughout the day for one moment. Houses of learning and Chasidic shtibls also stood there, but they were invisible amongst the shops, warehouses and factories, that surrounded them. On "those" streets people moved with a quickened step and even to make a short journey got on a tramcar. Thousands of travellers left this place with goods for the farthest flung locations. Almost every house on "those" streets also served as a little shop or was let overnight. The unloading of imported goods was perpetual. On Gęsia enormous warehouses of blue silk could be found, that supplied clients from all over Poland. It was here that the rise and fall of markets was discussed, the progress of foreign currency was speculated upon, it was here that it entered people's heads whether the pound would rise or fall. Here Chasidic Jews donned stiff collars and ties, because this helped with business. In this area people dreamed of building Israel and a socialist revolution...'

During the 19th century, wealthier figures of Warsaw's Jewish community supported many culture and sports clubs, as well as charitable institutions, including orphanages. Małka's guardian and Maurycy's aunt is an 'absent presence' throughout the play. She is referred to regularly as a replacement mother figure for Małka, whose biological mother is never discussed. We learn nothing about her background or her actual relationship with Małka or her father. In addition, she appears to have died relatively young, since the death has come as a shock and no will securing Małka's future has been produced. Maurycy, her nephew, inherits her wealth. We know nothing of how she acquired her wealth, though it seems that she married into the Silbercweig family, from a comment later made by Jakób. Her decision to send Małka away to school implies a move away from orthodox traditions – Małka returns knowing very little about the cultural and religious practices associated with her background. She also seems to have spent much of her time at her guardian's house (she has her own room there and comes back for her holidays, for example) without acquiring any of this information. It seems therefore likely that Zapolska alludes via the figure of the guardian (and her housekeeper Glanzowa) to questions concerning assimilation and acculturation – the playwright invites us to speculate on differences between the household established by the absent guardian and the contexts in which Małka is featured during the rest of the play. The guardian's philanthropy and social activism provides a sort of 'moral focal point' for the play, establishing the sense of a less orthodox matriarchal system acting in tension with the conservative patriarchal system represented by Szwarcenkopf and Old Firułkes, who arguably do not have enough money to be philanthropists. This is particularly significant given the importance of the mother figure in relation to beliefs and practices within the Jewish tradition relating to ethnic and religious identity and authenticity.

60. It is interesting that Maurycy refers to his aunt's political leanings, particularly since, in 1897, the year in which the play was written, the Bund, a Jewish socialist secular party, was founded in Wilno. It sought to bring together all Jewish workers in the Russian Empire into a united socialist party. The Russian Empire then included Lithuania, Latvia, Belarus, Ukraine and most of Poland, countries where the majority of the world's Jews lived. The Bund sought to ally itself with the wider Russian social democratic movement to achieve a democratic and socialist Russia. Within such a Russia, they hoped to see the Jews achieve recognition as a nation with a legal minority status. However the actor playing Maurycy decides to inflect this statement in a live performance, it is interesting to note that Zapolska sets up this idea in relation to Małka's guardian. Throughout the play she is an absent figure whose memory is used to justify various attitudes, choices and decisions. Other characters 'project' onto the 'space' she has left 'unoccupied'.

61. During the partitions, Wrocław (pron. 'Vrotz-wav') or Breslau, was part of Prussia. German Unification in 1871 left Breslau the sixth largest city of the German Empire. Its population more than tripled to over half a million between 1860 and 1910. The 1905 census lists 470,904 residents, including 20,536 Jews and 6,020 Poles.

62. Pron. 'Var-sha-va'. Since I have used Polish place names throughout, it would be unsystematic to employ the English name of the city, Warsaw.

63. Maurycy is probably implying that she will either become someone's mistress or a prostitute. As we see later from her interaction with Wiedeński, this is considered one of the only ways in which she can earn a living and remain 'single', given her new position.

64. A street in the Jewish district in the northern part of the city. There was a reformed Polish-language synagogue on this street, established in 1850 by Zelig Natanson. 'Nalewki' refers to receptacles used to collect water. The name dates from the period when there was no direct water supply to each property. It comes from the verbs 'nalać'/'nalewać', which means 'to pour into/onto'. The fact that Małka is from Nalewki is interesting given the business with the water pitcher in Act 2.

65. I have added this clause. This is the literal translation of the surname Szwarcenkopf, which she has inherited from her father – 'black-headed' or 'black-haired'.

66. How a director actually casts Małka and Maurycy in terms of appearance is very interesting in relation to Maurycy's racist statement – particularly since Maurycy's hatred is turned at least partially against himself.

67. See footnote 42.

68. See footnote 20.

69. This is the first time Małka offers what appears to be a short soliloquy. This is extremely interesting given the naturalistic form of the play. I also think it is important that she is constructed by Zapolska

as essentially solitary; there appears to be no-one with whom she can communicate with absolute directness. It is also crucial to note that the device of the photograph helps to establish the aunt as very much 'present' throughout the play – she is someone who is addressed and re-called repeatedly by various characters. Małka's other apparent 'asides' take place in the presence of characters who are also, on some level, constructed as 'absent' (from her point of view); the paralyzed woman, Ryfka, Jenta's small children. With reference to the play's ending, (when Małka is concealed from the audience and the other characters in the room behind a screen and herself acts as an 'absent presence') this series of 'asides' or short 'soliloquies' – depending on how one reads them – and their relationship to each other, is significant.

70. 'Not bad!' (French).

71. Bernard is a man of very few words. However, given the drunken scenario, having another character present who is largely silent allows for the development of much interesting stage business. His presence might be used to construct Wiedeński's authority in a particular way as well as explore the nature of 'economies of sexuality', through his relationship with the Chanteuses, in the play.

72. See footnote 19.

73. My reading of the play is that this behaviour has to be extreme, aggressive and overtly malicious in its lecherous intent. The scene must be shocking enough to provoke the events that follow – the play will not make sense otherwise. What was considered shocking in theatrical terms in the late nineteenth century clearly differs from our own standards. However, as in Miss Maliczewska, the sense of sexual threat, the breaking of boundaries without consent, should, I believe, be palpable. Małka's subsequent behaviour should not seem out of proportion to the events that take place at her aunt's house. I suspect that, theatrically, Bernard might play a significant role here.

74. He says 'nikczemnicy', or 'scoundrels/villains/wretches'. I have opted to use 'vultures' here because it seems stronger in a contemporary translation – the other options have, I believe, slightly comic overtones which are not entirely appropriate here. I use 'base creature' later on in the scene, in the same context, which perhaps retains a late nineteenth-century 'tone'.

75. He is a street trader.

76. It is therefore a long time since Małka has seen her father. However, she mentions earlier in the scene that she was at her aunt's house the previous year during her holidays.

77. I use the exclamation 'ay, ay!' (aj, aj! (Yid/Pol.)) and 'ay vay!' (aj, waj! (Yid/Pol)) throughout the translation, to match Zapolska's use throughout the play. Using it, I am aware of the complex problems it may cause in contemporary performance. In a Polish context it is an identifiably Jewish exclamation, now somewhat hackneyed. However, I believe it should be retained in the translated printed text and importantly, considered in its original context. I have thought about substituting it with another exclamation more rooted in a British linguistic/performance context. This has been difficult, especially given the other conventions relating to Yiddish/Polish names, place names, expressions that I have set up. I would suggest that anyone staging the play can make an appropriate substitution or cut it out altogether. If retained, it should be used sensitively.

78. My interpretation is that Jakób here refers to the situation Małka indeed later finds herself in – being approached by someone who is seeking a mistress, or a pimp seeking a prostitute-in-the-making. Given her extreme poverty and the fact that she is now over-qualified for her new environment, the possibility that she will accept such an offer has potentially increased. Lewi finds a relatively tactful way of putting this.

79. It is likely that she does not quite understand Lewi's full implication at this point. That is exactly what she encounters, as Lewi predicts, in the figure of Wiedeński. Perhaps she is currently thinking about her father's environment in different terms. From her point of view, she is 'stepping down' or 'taking a step backwards' given her acute sense of her own level of education and 'enlightenment'. If she does not understand the full import of Lewi's words, this renders her attempt to subsequently adapt to and dignify her 'new' environment, by attempting to dwell in and understand it, more complex.

80. It is unlikely that anyone really believes Szwarcenkopf to be capable of this, given his frailty. This perhaps makes my reading of the preceding interaction plausible. Małka's pride is being highlighted, as is her strong sense of what she is entitled to as a woman. This connects with her aunt's influence, strongly associated with the environment she is in (remember that her aunt's photograph in its broken frame is in the room) but is framed visually by the presence of several men and two apparent nightclub singers. It is also ironic that, ultimately, her father's attempt to 'protect' her, combined with other factors, leads her to despair.

81. Two points are particularly being highlighted here; firstly, Szwarcenkopf's extreme poverty; secondly, the prevalent attitude towards a young, unmarried woman.

82. 'Komin'. This implies that the stove is cast iron rather than tiled.

83. It is interesting to dwell on this 'tent' for a while. It is clearly an attempt to create a private space for a young woman. Inside, we later learn, is a plank laid across two chairs to form a desk, with an ink bottle, a few books and a candle stub. Zapolska never shows Małka working. However, the sense of a room within a room, or an attempt to create a 'room of one's own', is strongly signified, and signs of education and intellectual activity are present. It is also worth mentioning that Jewish wedding ceremonies take place under a huppah or chuppah (mentioned later in the play) or canopy, rather like a tent, held up on four poles. This represents the presence of God, as well as the couple's future home. It also signifies a sanctified space where wedding vows are exchanged. Theatrically, particularly to an audience conversant with this tradition, this helps to construct the space and the young woman in a particular way. It is significant that when Jakób visits Małka in Act 2, she has been sitting inside the tent with her head in her hands. The suggestion being that he enters the tent and converses with her there. This is highly significant. The tent can therefore be read on a number of levels. It is also very interesting that its interior is not revealed until later on in this scene.

84. 'Bube'. A friendly Yiddish term for people you like. Also close to 'bubele' which is usually applied to children and means something close to 'love' or 'darling'. I have tried to find a fond term that expresses the children's chatter and helps to give Pake Rozental 'character'.

85. This is a polonized diminutive of the name 'Malka' (Hebrew) or 'Malke' (Yiddish). If the director of a production thinks it sounds out of context, then it could be substituted with 'little Małka'. My sense here is that Zapolska is trying to convey Szwarcenkopf's affection for his daughter.

86. One of Warsaw's main streets. The Saxon Garden (see footnote 41) can be found on the corner of Marszałkowska and Królewska streets. Pake says 'półsklepik' or 'half shop'. This refers to the fact that Jojne owns a house of which the street-facing part is used as a shop and the back as a living space. This becomes clear during later acts, when the theatrical space is constructed in this way. The best way I have found of expressing this at this juncture is 'small shop'.

87. She is partly referring to the fact that Szwarcenkopf is a street trader and has no fixed place of trade. He might therefore be considered working class as opposed to middle class like the Firułkes family.

88. The word used is 'fain' or 'fayn' (Yiddish). I have translated it as 'nice' rather than 'fine'.

89. 'I nic mieć nie będzie' – literally, 'and she will have nothing'. He means that she will have no dowry.

90. The kopek, or copeck, is a unit of Russian currency. It is a division of the rouble. The rouble is divided into 100 kopeks (see footnote 33).

91. Pake says 'zdechławy'. This adjective derives from the verb 'zdechnąć'. It is difficult to translate into English. It is a verb used to describe the death of an animal (often a dog, a mongrel – the lowest of the low). When the death of a person is being described, the verb 'umrzeć' is used. This has a far more respectful tone. If one were to suggest an ideology of death implied by the existence of these two terms, one might explore the fact that that they separate – and therefore associate particular values to – the demise of base creatures, or animals (more precisely, of beings, in nineteenth-century religious terms, with no soul) and noble creatures, or humans (those higher beings 'above' animals and possessed of a soul). Pake uses the word to describe Jojne's physical appearance, rather bluntly. He looks thin, perhaps rather emaciated, like a corpse. He does not look manly – he is slight, even weak, she suggests, for his seventeen years. I have contrasted 'ravishing' with 'puny' in order to help express Pake's rather florid and yet direct bargaining style. If he were more muscular, she implies, and potentially better breeding material, then his parents would be entitled to expect a girl with a dowry.

92. Szwarcenkopf means the Prussian partition. There are some clues in the text as to the kind of school education Małka may have received in Breslau, or Wrocław, which at that time had a powerful university and polytechnic. By the 1890s Breslau's reputation as a seat of learning had begun to grow. It attracted artists and academics with national reputations and the arts. This is presumably why Szwarcenkopf values it as he does. Małka would not, of course, have been able to enter a university in Prussia, since Prussia delayed female matriculation until 1908. It is clear that she has been at boarding school from Act 1. We know that her education has been predominantly secular and private; she cannot speak Yiddish or Hebrew, knows nothing of the customs of her community and her aunt paid for her education. We do not know what she has studied but it seems clear that she has been taught in Polish. It was very unusual to consider sending a Jewish girl from Małka's background to school, which hints again at the political/social activism of her aunt as well as her potentially feminist leanings. Małka therefore represents the tendency towards assimilation and/ or acculturation and all the benefits and pitfalls associated with it. In addition she moves from one partition to another, then one community to another. Her journey maps fractures in geography and concepts of identity.

93. Świętojerska street took its name from a medieval church, Św. Jerzego or St George's in whose grounds it originated. It developed rapidly during the nineteenth century. During the eighteenth century three palaces were built on this street by the aristocracy. At the turn of the nineteenth century the inhabitants of the street were varied. Of the 859 inhabitants, many were dignitaries and tradesmen. However, prostitutes and beggars also populated this area of town. From 1824 the Evans brothers' factory was situated on this street (heavy manufacture). From 1864 the reconstituted firm was known as Lilpop, Rau and Loewenstein. After the 1880s, when the firm had moved, a business for the manufacture of fabrics and lace was established and this thrived for many years. In 1830, stone tenement buildings constituted 70 per cent of habitations. During the late nineteenth century, Jewish traders began to dominate the street, dealing in, among other items and goods, wine, writing materials and fabrics. On the corner with Nowiniarska Street the

headquarters and press of an important newspaper, Gazeta Warszawska, or Warsaw Post, was located. This publication represented the voice of the middle classes. In 1862 the road was widened. During the inter-war years it was a vibrant trading locale for Jews. During World War II a section of the street was part of the Warsaw Ghetto. In 1943 its inhabitants were murdered and the street was destroyed. It was never rebuilt.

94. The Eldorado Theatre was a 'garden' or outdoor theatre. It was located on Dzielna Street and during World War II was active as a theatre in the ghetto. Nineteenth/early twentieth-century 'garden theatres' existed in Warsaw between 1868 and the start of World War I. 80 Polish plays were premiered in these theatres, which were often owned by restaurants. They included the Eldorado (known as a Jewish theatre), Alhambra, Tivoli, U Giersza, Pod Mostem, Pod Lipka. They were regarded as sites of entertainment and subversion. They were subject to censorship, though it was easier to introduce notes of resistance into work performed in these spaces, since they were regarded as 'popular' rather than 'state' theatres. The theatres provided a forum for all those artists who could not or would not perform in state-run (Imperial) theatres and were a step along the road to the establishment of privately run or independent theatres. Artists from the provinces would arrive in Warsaw when those from the Warsaw State Theatres were taking their summer break. Zapolska herself performed at garden theatres. The first performance of *Małka Szwarcenkopf* took place at the Eldorado Theatre. Dzielna Street, where the theatre was located and Zapolska's Szwarcenkopf sells matches and cigarettes, was lit by gaslight from 1864. The first factories began to open, producing carbonated water, curtains and lace, in the late nineteenth century. Before 1908, a synagogue was built there, not long after a hospice for Christian elders recovering from medical treatment. During World War II the street lay on the border of the ghetto and was largely destroyed during the Warsaw Uprising. It was re-built following the war, but did not retain its pre-war appearance.

95. The Yiddish word 'geszeft' or 'gesheft' is used, meaning 'business' or 'deal'. In Kabbalah, a gesheft involves more than just a material exchange – any exchange of something more for something less valuable is seen to have consequences in higher realms.

96. A duvet filled with feathers from the eider duck.

97. During the late nineteenth century Dzika Street was developing rapidly. New tenement buildings were constructed in the neo-baroque style. The first horse drawn trams, later replaced by electric trams in 1908, ran the length of the street. It was also known for masonry production. In 1895 the Albertine Brothers established a shelter on the street for the homeless. During World War II the first odd-numbered section of the street was part of the ghetto. Dzika Street was destroyed during the war and only one building, constructed in 1939, has survived.

98. If Sabbath is on Saturday, then we can assume that today is Thursday evening.

99. This is in some ways a puzzling statement but I would suggest the following interpretation. Initially I thought that Szwarcenkopf might be referring to one of the prohibited Sabbath activities mentioned in the Talmud. With her secular education (on the German side, as Szwarcenkopf suggests) Małka seems to be unaware of religious custom. Sweeping is not mentioned in the Talmud as prohibited, though what might be seen as related domestic activities are; sewing, kindling a fire etc., the key here being the prohibition of any activity that 'creates' or exercises control or dominion over one's environment. It is therefore not unimaginable that, within specific cultural contexts, housework of different kinds might be customarily included under this 'umbrella'. It appears, however, to be Thursday evening and not the beginning of the Sabbath, that is, Friday

evening. It may be that Zapolska is trying to demonstrate that Szwarcenkopf's daughter has previously swept up on the Sabbath – that, in his desire to control her, stemming from his affection for her, Szwarcenkopf, a weak, aged man, remembers this transgression and, under Pake's watchful eye, reminds her that this is not an activity she should engage in. He has just been speaking about the Sabbath and it is on his mind, so this connection seems plausible. So when he says 'stay here at home' he actually means that she should stay in generally, but specifically the following day – and not sweep up on that day but show the relevant respect for tradition. The way in which Zapolska traces the arc of Szwarcenkopf's thoughts here possibly allows the actor to express his age and explore what influence Pake's presence exerts on the interaction. The disciplining of Małka might become a performance for Pake's benefit. He is demonstrating that he still has influence over his daughter, perhaps, and that she is biddable. We also know from the stage directions that the environment is cluttered and dusty. Jenta works hard, is extremely poor, is often away, has many dependents, collects clothes and objects to trade with and stores everything in the small space where all these people live, with a distinct lack of privacy. Małka is not much help around the house. Szwarcenkopf's sight is also poor and he cannot presumably see his environment clearly. There is therefore potentially an added poignancy to his words. In addition, the word I have translated as 'fathers' is 'dziady'. A more accurate translation would be 'ancestors', but 'dziady' suggests the masculine and I consider a sense of the patriarchal to be important to the gender politics at this point; hence my choice of 'fathers', which implies both lineage and patriarchy. This may need clarifying in performance, or a director may choose to make a cut at this point.

100. This comment possibly demonstrates the sense of cultural disjunction that she feels – her inability to reconcile herself to her new environment, which seems to her to be full of constraints and whose logic and custom she cannot contextualize, given her aunt's influence. It may be that she also has a strong sense of her father's failing health and his inability to perceive his environment in the way she does – they are looking, reading what is around them differently. It is extremely important, however, that the comment is read as subjective. It is also made in the presence of the paralyzed woman and the children, who frame Małka, though it reads as the beginning of a soliloquy because it is easy to forget about these characters when reading the text. Theatrically, this would not be the case. In order for the actor to effectively trace the young woman's development, it is essential to explore fully what motivates this comment and how events that follow humble her, or prompt her to punish/take revenge on – herself/her environment/fate etc. If this play were a melodrama, the protagonist's motivation would not have this rich complexity. What do we need to see at this moment? Her anger? Despair? Frustration? Do the children look up? Is she trying to assert control? Perform her frustration?

101. Ryfka says 'vaser' (Yiddish) – printed 'wasser' (German), from which the Yiddish word derives.

102. Note the tone of this comment in relation to footnote 100. No name is used for the woman. It seems that Zapolska is portraying Małka overcoming some sort of resistance in herself.

103. She says 'chcecie pić' – she uses the plural, formal 'you', which indicates some respect for – or a distancing of herself from – Ryfka. The actor's tone here is likely to be highly significant. Indeed, this is potentially one of the most fascinating interactions in the play. Zapolska's 1906 text, *The Morality of Mrs. Dulska*, features a character that is silent, yet active, throughout the whole play, except for one line. Ryfka prefigures Dulski in many ways – she is constructed as 'inactive' in terms of her paralysis and yet in some ways potentially incredibly 'active' as a theatrical sign. In

performance, her attitude towards the young woman would be crucial and the extent to which they are somehow mirroring each other is an area for exploration.

104. There are a number of significant references to bear in mind here. Firstly, her father has asked her not to go out. Secondly, she seems to find making contact with Ryfka problematic. She thinks she can offer her water, literally, but nothing else. Thirdly, the concept of Ryfka's thirst is very important, as is the image of Małka with the pitcher going, presumably, to the pump – the equivalent of a well. In biblical terms, thirst as a metaphor is highly significant, as are images of women at wells.

105. In the mid-nineteenth century in the Russian Empire, sewerage systems were considered a luxury. Only four cities – Warsaw, Odessa, Kiev and Yalta – had one. Warsaw's waterworks were founded in the nineteenth century. In the mid/late 1800s economic and demographic expansion took place. Tsar Nikolai I issued a decree for the construction of a main waterpipe network supplying the entire city. It was designed by English engineer William Lindley. The design was the subject of a lengthy and heated debate among many Polish engineers, property owners and representatives of the intelligentsia. Lindley designed for a city of 350,000, assuming that by the end of the century the number of residents would not exceed 500,000. However, at the beginning of the twentieth century, Warsaw already had nearly 800,000 residents. Fortunately, the designer had assumed considerably larger water consumption per capita than was actually the case, so the network served the city adequately much longer into the twentieth century. At the end of the nineteenth century sewage still flowed straight into the Vistula River from open gutters or covered drains, causing the usual public health problems. Given the part of the city in which Jenta lives, there was probably no direct water supply to the house.

106. Finding a translation for what Małka might mean here has been a challenge. She says literally – 'that's not rubbish, it is good luck/happiness – would you care for some ça vous portera bonne chance ...' She presumably ends the sentence in French for two reasons. Firstly, to demonstrate to Wiedeński that she is educated; secondly, to mock his aristocratic pretensions. The first part of her sentence is about perspective, hence my translation. She is possibly affronted by his criticism of her home, though it is likely that a hint of irony in relation to her own position might be involved, given her recent interactions with her father and with Ryfka. 'To nie śmiecie a szczęście' – the first part of the sentence – may indicate a saying current in Warsaw of 1897 – there is a phonetic similarity between the words 'rubbish/litter' and 'luck/happiness' in Polish. It is also possible that Małka is being spontaneously witty. I have been unable to discover the roots of this saying, if it is/was one. It is also difficult to see how the French part of the sentence relates to the Polish. 'This will carry/bring you good luck' might also be a witticism/stock French phrase used by Poles at the time. She is clearly alluding to the weight of the pitcher and the fact that she asked him to carry it (he also puts it down subsequently). So a closer translation could be something like 'it might be a vessel of good luck for you' or 'if you're looking for a vessel to bring you good luck, look no further'. I have decided to try and find a way for the actor playing Małka to convey all these different semiotic levels – the implied criticism of her visitor's tone, the sense of irony, the use of French (I have chosen 'to each his own tastes', which relates to her opening comment); the tone of stock phrases/platitudes. I hope this translation is more 'performable'.

107. He says 'sufiniment obligé'. The word 'sufiniment' does not appear to exist in the French language, whereas 'obliger' does. This is either an instance when he speaks poor French, or there is a textual error. The closest word might be 'suffissament', 'sufficiently'. 'Sufficiently obliged', an ironic sort of 'thank you very much' is probably the closest I can get to in this context. 'How instructive' is a

translation that attempts to capture/convey his potentially ironic tone. I have taken out the French here, though a director might choose to put the badly pronounced or incorrect French back in. I have retained the French for his following comment. In an English language performance, Kolumna's French-speaking ability relative to Małka's could effectively be conveyed through a juxtaposition of varying levels of effective/poor pronunciation/accent.

108. 'By Jove, war is war'. This appears to be accurate.
109. 'Et c'est beaucoup par le temps qui court'. Intended I think to mean something like 'and this means much when the season/time is short', which perhaps has connotations akin to the English saying 'make hay while the sun shines'.
110. He repeatedly uses the diminutive 'Moryś', so I have translated with the French version of his name and the fanciful diminutive one of the chanteuses uses in Act 1.
111. I have added the French here to make up for my earlier omissions. 'You understand?'
112. It seems he is thinking of setting her up as a mistress or high-class prostitute or both.
113. King Władysław Łokietek I (1260–1333). Buried in Wawel Cathedral in Kraków.
114. The surname Czartoryski has been associated with Princesses, for example, Izabela Czartoryska, (1746–1835). She was the founder of the first Polish museum, in Kraków, the Czartoryski Museum.
115. It has been very difficult to find any information about this person …
116. Literally translated into English, this name would be 'Moses'. The name Jenta uses is the polonized version of the Yiddish name Moishe, which derives from the Hebrew name Moshe. This name is usually translated as 'one who is saved (from the water)', as the biblical Moses was, in his basket, by the daughter of Pharaoh. There is an interesting irony here, given this character's interaction with Małka about the pitcher and the water.
117. Jenta calls Mowsze a 'fain puryc'. 'Fain' is a Yiddish word meaning 'nice'. 'Puryc' is a Polish word, somewhat archaic, which used to refer specifically to a wealthy Jew, and was subsequently used to refer to a person who had 'made it good'. The word has connotations of 'new money' and bourgeois social advancement.
118. Emigration was a common feature of nineteenth-century life in partitioned Poland. Following the November Uprising in 1831, until a few years after the January Uprising of 1863/4, waves of what is known as the Great Emigration of the Polish political and intellectual elites depleted the numbers of these classes. However, many working-class Poles also migrated, particularly to America, in order to find work. This was particularly prevalent in Galicia, where unemployment was very high. We are given no reason for the 'emigration' of Jenta's husband. It may be that he has not, in fact, emigrated but has used this as an excuse for having left her. She has certainly lost track of his exact whereabouts. This may contribute to Wiedeński's discomfort in this scene. There are, however, other possibilities.
119. Polish currency – its smallest denominator.
120. Srulek is the polonized diminutive version of the Yiddish name Sroel, which derives from the Hebrew name Israel, meaning 'equal power'. Gołde is the polonized version of the Yiddish girl's name Golda or Golde, meaning 'gold'. Chaimek is the polonized diminutive for the Hebrew boy's name Chaim, meaning 'life'.
121. This is an interesting stage direction, given that we may have been led to believe up to this point that the pitcher is completely empty.
122. He uses the French expression 'quelle blague!'

123. The French word for 'one thousand' – 'a thousand pardons/apologies'.
124. The Polish word is 'obarzanek' or 'obwarzanek'.
125. A special braided bread. It is customary to begin the Friday night meal and the two meals eaten during the Sabbath day with a blessing over two loaves of challah, to commemorate events in the biblical Book of Exodus when manna fell from the heavens during the 40 years when the Israelites wandered in the desert, following their exile from Egypt. Challah has great symbolic significance in Jewish religious ritual.
126. During the nineteenth century the Jewish community predominantly inhabited this street. It was a very important street for trading.
127. This street is one of the oldest in Warsaw. During the second half of the seventeenth century palaces and tenement buildings were constructed there, making it a wealthy part of the city.
128. A Cheder (alternatively, Cheider, meaning 'room' in Hebrew) is a traditional elementary school teaching the basics of Judaism and the Hebrew language. Cheders were founded in Europe before the end of the eighteenth century. It was usual for only boys to attend the cheder – girls were educated by their mothers at home.
129. It is likely therefore that the warehouses she has been visiting are part of Warsaw's developing textile industry.
130. The Promised Land, according to the Hebrew Bible, is a term used to describe the land promised by God to the Israelites. The term has also been used at times for the Land of Israel as well as Palestine. The theme of loss expressed in the children's song parallels theatrically the emotion associated with a romantic relationship between Małka and Jakób that appears unrealizable. Note also that in order to have this conversation with Małka, Jakób has entered her tent (see footnote 83).
131. The macaronic song, in a combination of Yiddish and Polish, goes:
    Hajde, łajde mame, tate,
    Djabeł skacze na łopate,
    Sam a szwarce jur!
    It is a sort of nonsense song and translates literally something like:
    Come, come, mother, father,
    The devil jumps onto a spade,
    Poisons the year ahead with bad luck
    I have not provided a formalized translation – a director might develop this song as required in performance.
132. Pronounced 'Trayne'. This is not the name previously given to the female child in Act Two, which was Gołde.
133. She says 'szlechtes kind' (schlechtes kind – Yiddish), or 'bad child'.
134. 'Furszpil' or 'forshpil' which means 'prelude' – my understanding is that this was the Saturday night before the wedding (see bcrfj.revues.org/document2862.html).
135. Jenta says 'chałat' or 'chalat' (Yiddish), meaning a Jewish man's robe, especially one in the style worn by the Chassidim.
136. Szwarcenkopf means the equivalent of a dowry. He has no savings, nor does his daughter, therefore the local community clubs together and makes a contribution.
137. Szwarcenkopf says 'tuchim' – I believe this is a misspelling of 'tenaim' or 't'naim'. The celebration Zapolska is attempting to represent has its modern-day equivalents, which are presumably derived

from such Ashkenazic engagement traditions. An L'Chaim or a Vort is an engagement party. An L'Chaim (lit. 'To life!') is less formal, with friends and family gathering in the bride's or groom's home to wish the couple good fortune, or 'Mazel Tov!' For some couples, a Vort party (lit. 'word') will follow, at which, in some communities, a 'tenaim' will be signed. 'Tenaim' literally means 'conditions' – a statement of the groom's acceptance of his obligations towards his betrothed. The signing of the document is followed by the 'breaking the plate' ritual (see footnote 191) www. mazornet.com/jewishcl/Celebrations/Wedding/Orthodox/Engagement.htm.

138. We know this is his original surname from the Dramatis Personae. It is listed as Jenta's surname and she is married to Wiedeński's brother. This surname (in its polonized spelling) is very close to the Yiddish word 'tishebov'. This means 'gloomy/bad mood'. Jenta plays on this meaning since she says 'we nicknamed you Tyszebuf'. She uses the word on two different levels. It is difficult to convey this in translation given the conventions I have been using regarding names. That's why I have added the explicatory phrase in square brackets, in case it is of use in performance. It does tie in with various other issues relating to the meaning of names in the play.

139. He says 'a harst man, a jetwa, a głupia?'

140. He concludes 'je vous ai dit – comprener?' – 'I told you – understand?'

141. Note the rules relating to gender segregation, as Zapolska expresses them.

142. This is not a misspelling, but another version of the name 'Jojne'.

143. 'It's too strong, sir!' (i.e. 'it's too much!')

144. This is the first time Wiedeński's first name is alluded to.

145. A diminutive of Małka – 'Malcia' – is used here, but I have changed it in order to avoid confusion.

146. Wiedeński uses the diminutive 'Moryś'. I have opted for this translation with reference back to the Chanteuse's naming of Maurycy in Act 1 Scene 1 (see p. 50).

147. 'Never' (French).

148. A suit designed specifically for 'walking'.

149. Rurawski suggests that Maurycy and Małka are related by blood. This probably arises as a result of this comment – the use of the words 'our aunt'. My contention is that there is nothing else in the play to suggest this. In my opinion, what motivates Maurycy to choose these words is his desire to find a basis for expressing an equality and 'kinship' with Małka, so that she will go on to accept his offer of support. This impression can only be conveyed through the manner in which the actor speaks the line, with a particular emphasis on the word 'our', as well as the response of those in the room to this emphasis. This interpretation appears logical, given the conversation that ensues, in which Małka expresses her attitude and feelings towards her guardian quite clearly.

150. She says 'spisze się szyliszes'.

151. She is not alone in the room.

152. She says 'Licht! Licht!' (Yid.)

153. See p. 30.

154. This is the scene in which attempts to use Yiddish occur most frequently. There are disputes about the accuracy of its usage (see p. 28). In addition it is often 'Polonized', in the sense that the Polish alphabet is used in an attempt to convey phonetic equivalence. Thus, linguistic and semantic frameworks collide. I have attempted a translation but have included a footnote to accompany each instance of Yiddish usage, detailing the original form (from the hand written text now archived at the Slowacki Theatre, Krakow and the 1923 printed edition), should this be useful to directors

when deciding to what degree my translation might be followed or whether Yiddish might in fact be re-introduced throughout.

155. Mowsze Cytryna (see footnote 10).
156. Meaning.
157. 'Gitwoch! Gitwoch!'
158. 'Der Hussen geht!'
159. 'Wo ist die kałe?'
160. 'Die ist die kałe!'
161. 'A! Wi schön…a wi schön…ziker sis schön kałe! Gitwoch Panna Małka!'
162. 'Der Hussen kimt'.
163. 'Hej hu! Der Belbues sołkimen du. Er verbette a groise ojlem! Si essen is wist du!'
164. Pronounced 'you-kee-tsel kree-kus'.
165. 'Waj nisz!'
166. 'Hussen'.
167. 'Ty jesteś szmendrykowater, ślimakowater, mazgajowater…'
168. '…rarytne cackies…'
169. 'Freig im nisz…'
170. '…as die prezenten…'
171. '…interferer…'
172. See footnote 83.
173. 'Wu ist?'
174. A diminutive.
175. 'Was haste für a minke!'
176. '….na mazeł'
177. 'Gebt her zwei bogen papier.'
178. 'I du a roite sznupftucheł, szain-eleganckie'.
179. 'Na nim a tücheł'.
180. 'Schön, schön…'
181. Ibid.
182. 'Szad nichts!'
183. These are diminutives that reduce the name 'in scale' each time. 'Małgorzateczke' is pronounced 'ma-wgo-zhat-etch-keh'.
184. In the same way as footnote 174, these are diminutives of the name Jojne.
185. 'A tisz! A tisz!'
186. 'I mach mir nicht nacieciwko!'
187. 'Mazeł toff'.
188. I have added this. In the printed version the spelling is 'tuchim', which I believe is incorrect.
189. 'Zucker sis'.
190. Literally, 'may they enter that cockerel, that sings cock-a-doodle-doo, cock-a-doodle-doo, cock-a-doodle-doo'.
191. Plate-smashing is still part of this ceremony. Often it is carried out by the mothers-in-law, symbolizing a breaking with the past.
192. The Polish word for 'Jew' was also used to describe an ink splodge on a piece of paper. The Marszelik actually says 'and don't make any blots on the paper [using the word for Jew as the word for 'ink blot'] because there are enough of us [Jews] here already'.

193. Again, the word 'tuchim' is used.
194. 'Cytryna' is a Polish word.
195. In Yiddish, though the Polish word is also very close to this – 'cukier'.
196. 'Lay-buoosh Pan-toe-fel'. There is no mention of this character in the dramatis personae. He may be a comic character trying to get 'in on the action'. The Marszelik says to him 'sza! Mach mir nicht nacieciwko!'
197. 'Wie ist die wódke in piernik?'
198. 'A zwilling na mazeł'.
199. 'Al haim die bare habe Jojne!'
200. 'Al hajm!'
201. Szylines – the document of agreement.
202. 'Tego tuchim ist git, tego tuchim ist schön, tego życzenie dobre jest … i … ja … też …' He begins to recite. However, the sentence structure suggests that he breaks off, perhaps he tries to address Malka and is met with little response. This moment can be staged in a number of ways but it does seem important that Malka's silence and problematic demeanour should motivate aspects of his behaviour, determine the atmosphere in the room and also affect the spirit in which the subsequent celebrations take place.
203. 'Du kanst gehn lulu!'
204. Leopold Kronenberg and Jan Gotlib Bloch were two eminent, successful, ambitious and rival Varsovians and businessmen, both from Jewish backgrounds. They were associated with banking, the railways and industry. They were also related through marriage. In addition, Bloch was a philanthropist.
205. The audience may be wondering at this point whether she is pregnant. There are a number of ways of reading what ensues. There are also questions around whether the marriage with Jojne has been consummated. Again, various readings are possible.
206. 'Małke a kim na minutkes!'
207. 'Makagigenkuchen'.
208. 'Kim her – a schucler'.
209. A diminutive of the surname 'Glanzowa'.
210. In terms of convention, Jojne would have to divorce Małka, not the other way around. In this case, Jojne is in any case at the mercy of the older men, which in this context is disempowering.
211. A diminutive.
212. 'Myszygene'
213. 'Bombiny'
214. 'A schlechtes kind! A verflochtes kind!'
215. See footnote 128.
216. 'Myszygene'.
217. 'Dumer kerl'.
218. This comment reveals Glanzowa's snobbery. Sura and Ryfka appear to be names with connotations of a rural environment, perhaps a shtetl [Eastern European Jewish small town/village].
219. There are numerous indications that Jojne might be represented as disabled throughout the play. His father wishes that he 'hadn't broken his arms and legs' later in this scene. We do not learn how this happened. Though both fathers might in contemporary terms be considered somewhat tyrannical, I believe that Zapolska gives us the 'back story' in each case as to why this might be

so, and in a sense patriarchal traditions, conventions and economies render these characters more able to exert their power. Firułkes is protecting his weakly son's interests fiercely and Szwarcenkopf is attempting to assure his future and his daughter's. All this takes place in a context where extreme poverty and difficult circumstances determine people's lives and this context and complex motivation is expressed by the playwright. In fact, I would argue that it is strongly critiqued by her, though never polemically but rather, dialectically, via a series of textual and visual juxtapositions.

220. It is interesting to speculate when exactly Małka takes the morphine behind the screen – how much of the conversation she actually chooses to listen to, hears etc.

221. See footnote 137.

222. 'Sicht!'

223. There is now a monument on this square commemorating those who took part in the 1944 Warsaw Uprising.

224. 'Kikste!'

225. 'Herst du?'

'CONDEMNED TO DESIRE WHAT WE CANNOT POSSESS'

The Man (1901)

In deteriorating health, which prompted her to have to undertake short curative visits to Switzerland, Zapolska could yet be found, in the late 1890s, working as an actor in Kraków. Her roles included Gina and Nora in, respectively, Ibsen's *Vildanden* (*The Wild Duck*) (1884) and *Et dukkehjem* (*A Doll's House*) (1879). However, her professional relationship with director Tadeusz Pawlikowski was becoming increasingly strained. Dismissed, then suddenly re-instated to the ensemble in 1898, she was subsequently cast less frequently in his productions. Finally, their Kraków working partnership disintegrated completely in a context of considerable animosity. It seems that Pawlikowski was in a severe dilemma regarding Zapolska; he reacted sharply and negatively to her demands as an actor but was acutely aware of the benefits – both economic and artistic – that could be derived from staging her plays.

At the same time, the playwright's ties with the publication *Life* (which had announced her arrival in Kraków and had published 'Antysemitnik' ('The Anti-Semite') (1897))[1] grew increasingly problematic. This situation was fuelled by complaints from the journalistic team of her excessive influence over the editor Szczepański, with whom she had become personally involved. Links were finally broken when the editorship changed hands.

Additionally, Zapolska's interactions with the Cracovian group of self-proclaimed modernist writers and artists, Młoda Polska (Young Poland), led by playwright and novelist Stanisław Przybyszewski, were also full of professionally driven animosity. Zapolska objected to Przybyszewski's preoccupation with occult practices and mysticism and what she perceived as

Figure 12: Should they become lovers? Research performance of Zapolska's *The Man*. University of Reading and POSK Theatre, London, 2004/5. Sam Milsom as Karol, Sophie Green as Elka. Photo by Lib Taylor.

the group's elitist attitudes and snobbish literary concerns. Czachowska wryly comments that Zapolska's intellectual contempt for the group was returned in equal measure.[2]

In 1899 she established closer contact with the Lwów theatre via several guest appearances. These provided contacts that eventually facilitated her signing of a contract with Ludwik Heller, the director, at whose request she also wrote the play *Sybir* (*Siberia*) and to whose productions she contributed her knowledge of stagecraft and breadth of expertise as a practitioner. Her first performance as a member of his ensemble took place on 2 September 1899. Her roles during this season included Regan in Shakespeare's *King Lear*. However, it was around this time, in her early forties, that Zapolska began to shift her focus towards more intensive concentration on literary activity and comparatively less on performance. This may partly have had something to do with her age and a reduction in the number and status of roles available to her, at the same time that her persona and reputation as a writer were becoming very securely established. The sense that she had to fight harder to sustain her position as an actor and work harder to, for example, provide more elaborate and impressive costumes, comes across very strongly during this period. In addition, she also became more selective about the sources for, and recipients of, her work. Lucjan Dobrzański, who had directed *Małka Szwarcenkopf* in Warsaw, arrived in Lwów in 1900 in order to ask her to write a play for his 'garden theatres'. Perhaps surprisingly, Zapolska refused.

During the same year, in a twist of fate, the Lwów Town Council elected Tadeusz Pawlikowski as the new director of their theatre. This was clearly problematic for Zapolska, who subsequently attempted to regenerate contact with the theatre in Kraków, where Pawlikowski had worked previously, without success. Consequently, she had little choice but to swallow her pride and approach Pawlikowski himself about signing a new contract with him in Lwów. However, he turned her down.

Deprived, not for the first time, of a regular income, Zapolska applied herself to seeking employment. The time-consuming work she did find took her away to a certain extent – though by no means completely – from the theatre and playwriting. She did still manage to write in prose and dramatic form. She sent manuscripts to various theatres throughout partitioned Poland and remained closely involved with both the professional and amateur theatre scenes in Lwów. What created a conflict of interests for Zapolska was the type of work she found it necessary to do in order to earn her bread; namely, journalism. She was successful, in 1900, in reaching an agreement with the editor of the liberal newspaper with the highest distribution in Galicia (11,000 in 1900), *Słowo Polskie* (*Polish Word*). Stanisław Szczepanowski, who in fact died later that year, accepted her onto his editorial team and two of her diverse responsibilities were to act as theatre critic and social commentator. Zapolska wrote, for example, a series of articles focusing on contemporary life in Lwów, entitled 'Przez moje okno' ('Through my window'). It also appears that she treated her journalistic work as a mode of, and means to, social activism. She was, during her period with the *Word*, castigated and praised with equal fervour by both co-workers and journalists from rival publications, for example the conservative *Dziennik Polski* (*Polish Daily*). Rumours circulated, not for the first time, about her apparent close connections with the Russian military police and she was also criticized for starting a campaign to provide financial aid for the unemployed. It was in addition suggested, in an ironic tone, that she had become 'not only the chief editor of the *Polish Word* but also the mentor and leader of Polish women'.[3]

Towards the end of 1901, on account of her marriage to the painter Stanisław Janowski, her second husband, who was ten years her junior, Zapolska gave up her job at the *Word*. They moved to Kraków, where she made efforts to take over the directorship of the People's Theatre. This proved problematic. Instead, in order to have at her disposal an ensemble of actors, she decided to set up a theatre school, drawing on her experience of training and performing in Paris. A complex and comprehensive programme of actor training classes was offered, alongside lectures on dramatic history and forms, dance and fencing lessons. Publicizing the school, which opened at her house in September 1902 with a student body of about 30, she asserted:

> ... above all I would like to develop my students' vocal range ... work on their breathing ... their diction ... three times a week each student will take one-to-one lessons with me ... the

scenes they have rehearsed will be played to each other in group sessions on Fridays...
during which time I will talk to them extensively about performance style...I will also
teach pantomime, since this is excellent in aiding the development of movement, gesture
and facial expression...[4]

The high point for the first troupe of actors to be coached in Zapolska's school was a series of
extensive and fully realized public performances that were reviewed very positively. However,
there is again a strong sense during this period that Zapolska was, perhaps unsurprisingly,
exhausted. There was no substantial profit to be made from a theatre school, in spite of the
assistance of her husband with the teaching of scenography and costume design, and realizing
the settings for the final 'showcase'. Zapolska had contracted malaria at the start of the year
and had been to the mountains near Zakopane, in southern Galicia, to recuperate. By the end
of 1903 she had resigned herself to the fact that she felt well enough to write – which she
continued to do, prolifically – but not to work in any capacity as a theatre practitioner, certainly
not with the same energy as she had managed to muster in the past.

To add to these concerns, in the autumn of 1904, on his return from a trip to Florence, Janowski
wrote to her requesting a separation. She agreed. Having subsequently attempted three times,
as was required by law, to make the marriage work, both parties admitted defeat and the
divorce was finalized in the winter.

During 1901, the year of her marriage to Janowski, Zapolska had produced three plays: *Panna
Józia* (*Miss Józia*), which has been lost, then, at Pawlikowski's request, *Życie na żart* (*Life is a
Joke*) and, in December, *Mężczyzna* (*The Man*). The latter, which is the next play to appear
in this volume in translation, consists of three acts. It was first titled *Ahaswer* (*Ahasuerus*), the
name of a legendary character, a wandering Jew, who is said to have cursed Christ on his
way to the crucifixion.[5] Pawlikowski persuaded her to change it prior to the first performance in
Lwów. The translation of the revised title *Mężczyzna* is problematic, since in a literal version it
would read simply *Man*, potentially a descriptor of the male sex in general. However, the word
'man' in English can also act as a generic term for 'humanity', whereas in Polish this meaning
is not implied. Hence my choice of *The Man*, which allows for greater specificity in relation to
the central male character, Karol, a specificity which Zapolska actually felt was lacking in her
revised Polish title.[6] In addition, the new title points clearly towards her exploration of issues
relating to gender roles in the text. Julka, for example, certainly has what might be described
as 'masculine' qualities.

The narrative centres on the relationship between two sisters, Julka and Elka. Julka is a socialist
and teacher who will inevitably have to give up her job – following the conventions of the
period – if she ever gets married. Elka, the younger of the two, works in an administrative role
for an agency, but must resign when she becomes pregnant. Linking the two sisters is Karol, a
married man, who fathers a child with Elka. He is a somewhat politically vague journalist, who
seems reluctant to divorce his neurotic wife, Nina, a character created in the vein of Zapolska's
Little Frog, mentioned in my introduction to *Małka*. Elka loses her baby. Subsequently, Karol
expresses his undying love for Julka, who rejects him. Nina finds a new husband and Karol is

Figure 13: Research performance of Zapolska's *The Man*. University of Reading and POSK Theatre, London, 2004/5. Sam Milsom as Karol, Sophie Green as Elka, Francesca Clark as Julka. Elka's frustration with Karol increases. Photo by Lib Taylor.

forced to leave. The play ends with an apparent – in fact highly problematic – strengthening of the relationship between the two sisters, who are left alone in their apartment, which is the setting for the action.

Up until this point in her career Zapolska had maintained her reputation as a dramatist capable of writing very effectively for large casts and creating visually spectacular effects via the medium of crowd scenes. In this text she attempts something quite different. The sharp focus of *The Man* is the developing set of relationships between these four figures and Zapolska's exploration of their psychologies. It might in this respect be described as Strindbergian. It certainly has the thematic flavour and brooding tone of one of the Swede's chamber plays, though the dialogue still works chiefly through a gradual exposition of motivation through direct verbal communication rather than an interest in its concealment or obfuscation. The humour is less dark and more overt, emerging through characterization, verbal idiosyncrasies and, very importantly, costume – particularly Nina's ever-changing toilette. It is interesting to note that during this year, Strindberg himself wrote *Et Dromspiel* (*A Dream Play*), a text that contrasts starkly with Zapolska's naturalistic approach in *The Man*, which took her only three days to complete.

The play was staged in Kraków, Lwów (where Zapolska also acted as director) and Warsaw and was revived with some regularity up until the 1960s, though it has never attained the popularity of, for example, *The Morality of Mrs. Dulska* (1906), which remains Zapolska's best-known text in Poland. *The Man* was translated into Czech, Croatian, Latvian, German, Russian and Italian. Some extreme and unusual critical responses emerged in relation to the early Galician productions. On the one hand, the construction of a naturalist play around four contrasting psychological 'types' was classed by some critics, for example Wilhelm Feldman, as distinctly modernist, though they also considered the character of Julka to be rather one-dimensional, having reductively read her as Zapolska's 'mouth-piece'. Kazimierz Ehrenberg, editor of the anti-Semitic daily *Our Voice*, on the other hand, accused Zapolska of immorality, on account of her interest in representing the erotic. In connection with this opinion, when the play was published in 1903, the editor also censored it on the grounds of immorality, cutting certain phrases relating to the expression of passion between the lovers in Act 1 and, further on, excising lengthy passages on account of certain 'socialist ideals' and 'social responsibilities' articulated by Julka.[7] The handwritten copy of the play, now lodged in the Slowacki Theatre archive and produced for the 1901/2 Krakow production, contains identical cuts in red pencil, indicating the censor's intervention.

In Lwów, Stanislaw Womela argued that the play represented 'Strindbergian and Przybyszewskian tendencies in reverse' and contended that Zapolska had used the expression

Figure 14: The sisters try to find out whether servant girl Hanka has ever been to an 'all-night café'. Research performance of Zapolska's *The Morality of Mrs. Dulska*. University of Reading and POSK Theatre, London, 2003/4. Rose Walton as Mela, Zoe Gamon as Hanka, Laura Farrell as Hesia. Photo by Lib Taylor.

of left-wing ideals to conceal, 'like a lipstick stain', the 'sexual absurdities' on which the narrative dwells.[8] In response to reservations expressed by critics on account of precisely these 'ideals', the directors of the Lwów theatre introduced certain changes, without the playwright's knowledge, but continued the run. Julka's final speech, for example, was cut. Zapolska did not find out about the cuts until later that year.

It was probably as a direct result of these events that an infuriated Zapolska kept a closer eye on the Warsaw production, focusing on detail in performance and the realization of the naturalistic environment. It appears she took pains to ensure that mise-en-scene and performance style was fully rooted in realistic conventions, stressing that diegetic sound and lighting effects specified in the stage directions for Act 2 – such as falling rain, the town 'waking', the intensification of street lighting towards evening – should be perceptible to the audience. This rigorous attention to detail enabled her to fulfil her need to ground her work in the contemporary. This approach clearly bore fruit, since a lengthy run of 33 performances (when most plays would receive three or four) followed, and extensive reviews appeared in the press. These were overwhelmingly positive, stressing as effective the play's psychological

Figure 15: Hesia, with plaits, tries to explain the facts of life. And fails. Research performance of Zapolska's *The Morality of Mrs. Dulska*. University of Reading and POSK Theatre, London, 2003/4. Laura Farrell as Hesia, Rose Walton as Mela. Photo by Lib Taylor.

'veracity', its tragi-comic tone, its realism – as an exercise in 'psychological vivisection'[9] – and its contemporary resonance. Reservations were also expressed. It was suggested that the change of title had been effected in order to 'tone down the rather vivid feminist agenda'.[10] Discomfort was expressed at Julka's political views and Władysław Rabski of the *Warsaw Courier* suggested that the ending, in which she expresses her opinions about the suffering of the masses, should simply be cut.[11] Czachowska suggests that this opinion must have been widely felt, since the ending was indeed cut.[12]

My translation of this play is the one that has altered most since its first draft. This has been largely to do with the challenge of balancing the play's fundamentally realistic setting and dialogue with the symbolic constraints of its dramatic construction, specifically in relation to character. Zapolska vividly moulds each character around an idea – her own concept of 'stock' or 'type'; Nina is governed by her nerves, Karol by his lust, Elka by her heart and Julka by her mind. Elka and Julka own the environment represented. Their names both echo and contrast with each other – they express difference within likeness. This creates an effect of polarity *and* mirroring, oscillating around the play's central problem; a series of questions around the pathology of extremes and the desire for resolution and integration. This is expressed most overtly in the play's closing lines.

Here, Zapolska explores the possibility of reconciling, in an attempt at psychic and intra-psychic stabilization, those impulses associated with emotion and reason. This is strongly allied with the political and social, in the sense that, in order to be able to explore the possibility of this union, and in order for it to be problematized dramatically, the sisters must reject both Karol and Nina, whom they have associated with disruption, vacillation, lack of clarity, lack of respect for personal boundaries and the exploitative penetration of physical and bodily spaces. In this play, the personal most certainly is political. The language in which each character is expressed and expresses him/herself reveals patterns of imagery associated with their governing 'humour' and yet it is used in realistic contexts, for naturalistic purposes. Balancing the naturalistic *and* symbolic linguistically, and simultaneously creating rhythms and register that resonate both with the historical *and* within the contemporary, results in a challenge that has driven me to persistently re-draft my translation.

When I staged the play in an earlier draft in 2005, I enjoyed expressing its symmetrical composition visually (see Fig. 13). A partial box set was created along a rough line of symmetry. A pair of structurally identical, functional shelves stood against the walls, one on the left, belonging to Elka, and one on the right, belonging to Julka. This device was aimed at expressing the similarities between the sisters. However, the objects on the shelves were personalized by each actress as her characterization evolved. Julka's shelves were used practically and almost exclusively contained books, but also a money box with a key (on the top shelf) and a display of stuffed small birds behind glass. Elka's shelves were more decorative, with a family photograph, a comb, hairbrush, small box and various fragile glass ornaments. Spatially, the area around each set of shelves also constituted a territory. Stage left and right were constantly used as areas which the sisters could own, infiltrate and defend and so on.

Centrally – in-between the two sets of shelves – I located a large battered trunk, which characters used to sit on (see Fig. 5), store things in, hide things in and to pull things from. Karol and Julka's prelude to sex at the end of Act 1 took place on the closed trunk (see Fig. 12) and Act 2 opened with Karol actually sleeping inside the trunk, having fully infiltrated the centre of the space and Elka's body. Nina, on the other hand, always managed to leave a trace of her presence behind her in the form of an item of costume or an accessory – for example, her muffler, which at one point ended up inside the trunk. Such visual devices allowed me to explore the symbolic properties of Zapolska's brand of naturalism – I explored the notion of 'sisterhood', as it relates in the text to both biological and political bonding and bondage!

The Man is a play about feminism and love. It explores how fin-de-siècle Polish socio-political 'reality' can be read and explained, taking account of questions relating to gender construction, biological sex and patterns of sexuality. These concerns are brought into sharp focus by the play's naturalism, which would have highlighted the significance of the contemporary world in its early performances. Throughout the text, Zapolska explores the nature and purpose of sexuality and pleasure, and the contradictions that existed between professional and personal life. She investigates what kind of socio-political context might facilitate the definition and realisation of equality between the sexes. Julka, for example, voices concerns that imperialist

Figure 16: The sisters consider their future. Research performance of Zapolska's *Miss Maliczewska*. University of Reading, POSK Theatre, London, 2007/8. Sam Tye as Michasiowa, Phoebe Garrett as Stefka. Photo by Matt Ager.

oppression – in terms of a quotidian reality – is undergoing a process of normalization and that political trauma is being internalized to such a degree that disempowerment, inequality and dissociation find their further distorted expression on a psychosexual level. The play gives expression to the energy of Julka's determined political drive and messianic fervour as well as her chilling and consciously chosen sexual repression. In fact, it does so without de-eroticizing her. The viability of her political and socio-sexual impulses, as expressed in terms of a behavioural and ideological programme, is nevertheless profoundly de-stabilized by the playwright, as she explores Julka's problematic relationship with her sister and her sister's lover. Here, certain underlying despotic tendencies and a tyrannical pragmatism emerge. These begin to verge on the fascistic. This tension both within Julka and between the sisters is expressed as emanating from a wounded place located within a broader political disempowerment. This itself is inscribed as a feature of the play's imperialist mise-en-scene, also powerfully represented, both audibly and visually, by the city outside the room, accessed through the two windows specified in the stage directions.

Julka deploys religious imagery to describe a vision of a revolutionary future, which would be the necessary public manifestation of her conversion to left-wing politics and feminism. She uses the image of an unfettered 'soul', protected by its 'casement', the body, and connects this with a state of autonomous national identity – an authentic 'core'. Julka's sexuality, desire and fertility are suspended, however, in a state of potentiality, to be reserved and preserved for an appropriate context and set of conditions and awaiting an appropriate person – whether a man or a woman – with whom they can be entrusted. The result is that, for Julka, work – specifically teaching – acquires erotic potency, since it represents autonomous action, creativity and self-expression. Zapolska evokes a present in which non-familial, particularly heterosexual, relationships are highly problematic, a time of stress, change and anxiety, combined with a sense that beneath the surface of everyday interaction resides trauma, dispossession and a lack of hope for the future. The play is thus framed by Julka's understanding of the contemporary national milieu as being in extreme crisis and emergency – a time in which it is difficult to 'really love'. This connects with historical debates about how to resist the partitioning powers. It gives voice to a suggestion that arousal and pleasure are misleading and procreation redundant when explored in such circumstances, as echoed symbolically in Elka's miscarriage. It explores Julka's assertion that conduct in everyday life should be disciplined, ascetic, 'sharpened up' and intellectualized for the national cause, and that unfocused, unfettered sexual energy and expression within the economies of imperialism signifies the fact that the 'oppression of the natives' has been normalized and has reached its destructive nadir. The relationship between concepts of religion, politics, spirituality and feminism is explored within all of these parameters.

Julka struggles urgently against, and is frustrated by, the fact that her traditionally masculine virtues and political drive are more evident than Karol's, particularly since Karol has greater possibilities in the public sphere, because he is literally *The Man*. Karol is torn between three women, as Poland is torn between three occupying powers; he can find no home – he is dispossessed. As Julka intimates, he cannot possibly be loyal to all three of them at the same time. Questions concerning whether he can *love* all three of them at the same time and what this might imply in terms of *conduct* linger throughout. Julka links Karol's objectification and idealization of women with his de-politicization, disempowerment and lack of emotional intelligence and 'authenticity'. He is described as existing in a liminal – in this case a highly unfocused – state. Rather than perceiving him as virile – a 'knave of hearts' – Julka re-constructs his inability to be alone and produce 'fertile journalism' as signs of political impotence, pointing out his tendency to overcompensate for this in his sexual life, where his inability to *connect* is also very evident. Karol's inability to see the women as 'complete' appears to complement their own inability to 'feel complete' or 'integrated'. In addition, though Julka's political 'voice' clearly drives the play, Zapolska simultaneously problematizes the manner in which she apparently determines her sister's future. She appears oppressive. Elka's vulnerability and passivity when faced with her sister's visionary zeal produce a balancing tension at the end of the play. We are left asking whether Julka's attitude is a symptom of imperialist oppression, a viable solution to it, admirable self-possession or simply the 'sour grapes' – as Karol would describe it – of a so-called 'frigid spinster' or 'control freak'. Her certainty, as it evolves, is both exhilarating and terrifying. For her, desperate times demand desperate measures – even 'spinsters' must join in. Julka compulsively examines her political conscience in relation to these issues. What she learns about in the closing stages of the play is that she remains incomplete. However, she refuses to consider that any contemporary man would be able to 'complete' her. It is to her sister that she assigns this function. As a consequence, the play's ending vacillates between an anxiety about co-dependency on the one hand and an appreciation of the potential benefits of a separatist feminism on the other.

The text resonates boldly within the Polish feminist discourse, too complex to explore fully in a short essay such as this. However, I have selected three figures to express the development of 19th century Polish feminist thought and practice, against which the construction of Julka can be considered.

Klementyna Hoffman (1820s/30s) encouraged women to take an active part in public life and emphasized the benefits of education for women. She was not a proselytizing figure and did not engage in a discussion about revising gender roles. However, she did treat writing as a profession and in this way entered the public arena.

Narcyza Żmichowska (1840s/50s) was also a writer and Polish patriot. She led a group of women who called themselves the Enthusiasts. They were predominantly members of the landed gentry and intelligentsia. They expressed their support for women's education as a means of bringing about equality and shaping citizens who would be socially valued in the same ways as men. They encouraged women to be financially independent and to take an active part in public life. This was the period between the November and January uprisings (1832 and 1863) and these women supported the cause of national independence. Indeed, Żmichowska was regarded as something of a role model for Polish women, combining an awareness of political matters with sensitivity to women's issues, without causing controversy.

Eliza Orzeszkowa (1870s/80s), a prose writer, is associated with the period following the 1863 insurrection. She emphasized the need for emancipation. She broke away from a failed marriage and had an affair with a married man in a provincial town. She protested against discrimination against women at all levels and objected to the traditional assignment of gender roles.

In order to contextualize further the lives of these women, and Zapolska's female characters, it is highly significant that finally, in 1870, the first Polish woman entered Zurich University – the first European University to open doors to women – as a medical student. Yet when she returned to Poland she was barred from becoming a member of the Medical Association. In the 1880s the first women successfully qualified as doctors at the University of St Petersburg. This gave them the right to practice throughout the Empire, including the Polish territories. In Warsaw, by 1911, there were 37 legally practicing female doctors and 600 female teachers. In 1910 a Warsaw bank took on its first female employee. In 1894/5 the Jagiellonian University in Kraków admitted three women for the first time and by 1905 women constituted 11.4% of this university's student population. In 1906, the first of them completed her PhD. The partition that took longest to admit women to higher education – in 1900 – was Prussia. There, in 1903, women made up only 2.8% of students, in 1914, 6.7%.[13]

It is also evident that during the 1890s, the decade before The Man was written, women like Julka were active feminists and participating in Polish politics, most notably in the Socialist party. Feminism existed in its most organized form in Galicia and there the agenda for reform focused on five main areas: the dismantling of strict gender roles; the de-stabilization of repressive domestic norms; the abolishment of the practice of chaperoning; legal reform relating to property, inheritance and political participation and the right to higher education, professional life and financial equality. The nationalist and Catholic press came out decidedly against the increasingly vocal feminists. They were perceived as a threat to religious morality and the religious establishment, which was, perhaps ironically, already heavily dependent for its day-to-day functioning on women. In particular it was feared that feminists would discuss women's rights within completely secular parameters and that this would disrupt the preservation of national identity, which was and is regarded as one of the key achievements of the Polish Catholic church alone. The question of how to develop and where to locate feminist discourse – a 'language of sisterhood' – in relation to the language of the church and the language of political struggle, is therefore of great significance with regard to the choices made by Zapolska when forging Julka's rhetoric and its patterns of imagery throughout the play.

Zapolska's interest in the notion of sisterhood and what was, for her, a persistent tension at its heart remained throughout her life. She explored it in many plays. In Little Frog she questioned whether the urbane, middle-class protagonist Little Frog and her sister-in-law Maria, who had felt more at home on her parents' farm with her brother than in town, can manage on any level to be sisters, or mothers to Little Frog's daughter. In The Morality of Mrs. Dulska, she created Hesia and Mela, the adolescent daughters of the household. Note once again the affinity between their names, which is in tension with their differences of temperament; Hesia is bold, sexually aware and physically robust, Mela, neurotic, repressed and sickly. In Miss Maliczewska, the last translation to be included in this volume, Zapolska created the actress Stefka and her sister Michasiowa – another pairing. Towards the end of the play, Michasiowa asks Stefka which role she should assume now that the latter is to become the mistress of a different man; that of sister or servant. Related concerns had already been raised ten years earlier, in *The Man* – namely, is the condition of sisterhood characterized by a state of equality or a state of hierarchy? Does biological sisterhood guarantee connection? Is sisterhood a real possibility without biological connection? Zapolska's dialectical approach to this issue, central to feminist debate then and since, theatricalises the pleasures and pains engendered by the search for inter-personal 'complementarity', both physical and metaphysical:

JULKA   I haven't been a sister to you – I felt... contempt... for your passion, your desire.

ELKA   You were perfectly right, Julka! You should indeed have held me in contempt.

JULKA   No, Elka! I saw with what suffering you paid for that elusive shadow of happiness. Then I came to understand that I was fleeing blindly from my own fulfillment, cowering behind perfect restraint. Next to you, Elka, I perceived my own nothingness. So radiant, you seemed, as you waited for the baby to come... then later, so beautiful in your bitter grief. Please, try to forget my coldness and forgive me. Allow me to still be – your sister.

ELKA   Night stretches before me. I fear the darkness. Sometimes it seems I stand gazing into my freshly dug grave.

JULKA   Will you take my hand? Allow me to be your guide. Now my conscience is clear. You have paid a woman's debt. You did give birth at the edge of a grave. Now you must turn away. Your wounded desires, your injured heart, allow them to kindle your thoughts! Emerge like a phoenix from the flames, into a new morality! I'll lead you towards the things I hold most dear, my ideals, to my world!

     (As she speaks she takes Elka's hand, rises, and slowly moves towards the window leading Elka behind her, who follows her slowly. Julka should speak simply and straightforwardly, but with conviction)

     It is a very different place! No cultivation of personal impressions or intimate little gardens of suffering! There one must work not for oneself, but for new generations. One must unearth and uproot, when required, and subject one's own life to the very same process!

     (She opens the window, a gust of wind blows in, in the distance she can see the city, its houses brightly lit)

     There it is Elka – the new world! All that illumination and yet the contours of tragedy and suffering must still be made visible! I will teach you to hear the voice, which emanates from the depths of that city. I will teach you to understand the force of its reproach and then you will see outlined before you a series of great responsibilities.

How your own suffering will seem next to the suffering of the masses! Just like a grain of sand!

ELKA   Is it possible for me, Julka? Is it possible?

JULKA   It is. Your pain will render you robust, like steel, yet faced with the poverty and suffering of others, you'll learn when and how to soften, like wax. I can't experience or understand suffering as you can, Elka. And so, we will go together- into that world filled with reproach. Together we will step into the sea of poverty and injustice. To light our way, let us bear aloft all that we have to offer – your tormented senses, your injured heart...

ELKA   ...and to send the shadows flying, your keen, clear mind.

(They remain like this by the window, gazing intently at the city)

(Curtain falls)

Notes

1. See p. 33.
2. See Czachowska, p. 186.
3. S.R, 'Pani Gabriela na czele kobiet polskich', *Dziennik Polski*, 1901, nr. 148, str. 2.
4. See Czachowska, p. 282.
5. There are various versions of this tale, which appears to have emerged during the 13th century.
6. See Czachowska, p. 253
7. See Czachowska, p. 253. The sections in question are: Act 2, Scene 2 – three pages of text; Act 3 towards the end of the play – one page. These are marked in the translated text.
8. Womela, S., *Kurier Lwowski*, 1902, nr. 30, str. 6–7.
9. See Czachowska, p. 256.
10. S.K., 'Erotyzm na scenie i w Życiu', *Niwa Polska*, 1902, nr. 1, str. 5.
11. Rabski, W., 'Z Warszawy', *Kurier Warszawski*, 1902, nr. 269, str. 1–3.
12. See Czachowska, p. 256.
13. These statistics are taken from Chwalba, A., *Historia Polski 1795-1918*, Kraków: Wydawnictwo Literackie, 2000.

THE MAN (1901)

A Play in Three Acts

Dramatis Personae

Julka[1] (pron. Yool-ka)
Elka[2]
Nina
Karol[3]
The play is set in city[4]

ACT 1

(Quite a small room, very tidily arranged. Doors situated to the left and right. Two windows at the back – clean muslin curtains, tied back. A bureau, shelves with books, a sofa by the wall – in front of it a table, two armchairs, a chair – a lamp on the table, a piano, screen, stove. All in all, the furnishings indicate a domestic haven. When the curtain rises the stage is in darkness – only the stove is lit. In front of it sits Julka, wrapped in a shawl, observing the flames which illuminate her with their red glow. Long pause. The clock strikes six. Julka is disturbed from her reverie)

SCENE 1

(Julka, Karol)

(The bell rings.[5] Julka rises, goes right, opens door to hallway. Enter Karol, covered in snow, pops his head round from the hall. Julka re-enters ahead of him and looks for matches)

Figure 17: Julka disapproves of her sister's relationship. Research performance of Zapolska's *The Man*. University of Reading and POSK Theatre, London, 2004/5. Francesca Clark as Julka. Photo by Lib Taylor.

KAROL   What's this, Julka? All alone ... in the dark?

JULKA   I'm searching for the matches.

KAROL   No need! I have some right here.

            (*He hands her the matches through the doorway, Julka takes them and lights the lamp*)

KAROL   (*Changing in the hallway*) It's bitterly cold outside.

JULKA   Yes, I can see, frost on the windowpanes ... look ... they're glittering, like jewels!

KAROL   (*Entering*) Ah ... jewels! If only! We could make our fortune.

JULKA   A curious thing, human nature – condemned to desire what we cannot possess.

KAROL   Indeed.

         (Extends his hand)

         How are you, my good sister?

JULKA   Very well, thank you, and you? How's everything at the daily press?[6]

KAROL   Same as ever, always the same! Such pointless work, a burden, grinds me down, that's all. Complete waste of...

JULKA   No such thing as pointless work.[7]

KAROL   Oh clap-trap! You do sometimes talk a fine lot of clap-trap, Julka.

JULKA   That does depend on what one means by 'clap-trap'.

KAROL   And, you take a strange delight in contradicting me – constantly.

JULKA   Learn to live with it! You won't find me falling at your feet. You must accept the fact that I, a woman, also possess an opinion.

KAROL   *(Warming himself by the fire)* You're quite the modern miss. A feminist – isn't that what they call it?[8]

JULKA   *(Quietly)* Oh please, don't you talk about things you can't understand.

KAROL   Pardon me, do. Not so long ago, I wrote a whole article on the subject of feminism.

JULKA   *(Shrugging her shoulders)* One can of course write a whole article and still know nothing about its subject.

KAROL   Prefer it, would you, if I got my hat and left?

JULKA   Perish the thought. Elka would never forgive me.

         (Pause, Karol approaches Julka and stands facing her)

KAROL   Julka!

JULKA   *(As though distracted from her thoughts)* I'm listening.

KAROL   You don't like me, do you?

JULKA   You are mistaken.

KAROL   You do like me?

JULKA   Not exactly.

KAROL   In that case?

JULKA   I am indifferent.

KAROL   I think I'd prefer it if you didn't like me.

JULKA   *(Smiling)* You could always add that to your agenda.

KAROL   I've got this strange feeling it would never get ticked off. You don't know how to love or hate anyone. You're too restrained, Julka – you lack…fire.

JULKA   Personally, I'm absolutely satisfied. Do you know – when I look at you, at Elka, at how your lack of restraint torments you, I infinitely prefer my own cold fish's blood.

KAROL   If ever you get married – I pity your husband.

JULKA   I'll never get married, that's for sure.[9]

KAROL   Feminism!

JULKA   *(Sharply)* I've asked you once already not to talk about things you can't understand.

KAROL   Do you have any idea why you don't want to get married?

JULKA   It's quite simple really. For me, marriage isn't the apex of joy. I have a carefully developed opinion about it.

KAROL   A theory!

JULKA   Concrete examples! It's enough to look at you.

KAROL   Ah…

             (Pause)

JULKA   Pardon me. I honestly didn't mean to upset you.

KAROL   No … you're quite right. I'm bound and gagged and I don't even notice any more. Marriage can be something of a straightjacket. But I do still …

JULKA   *(Adopting a certain tone)* You want to marry Elka.

KAROL   Oh! Don't you see? That will be completely different.

JULKA   You really think so?

          (Pause)

          How do matters stand?

KAROL   Not so rosy.

JULKA   She's been questioned again?

KAROL   Yes … again … and my lawyer's been informed that, in its current state, her version of events is perfectly useless! And without her, without her help, we'll never reach our goal. No divorce! Neither of us can really be held accountable for what's happened … I've nothing against her moral conduct – no reason – same goes for her, with me.[10] *(Julka raises her head and looks at him stubbornly)* Why the look? My relationship with your sister, right! I am completely innocent. However much it costs us, we haven't crossed the line. We're still engaged, so to speak.[11] You don't doubt that, Julka – surely?

JULKA   *(Dryly)* In future, spare me the details, would you.

KAROL   Ooh – pardon me! Slipped my mind entirely, with what ceremony you sport your vestal virgin's robe. I did think I was talking to a woman – now I see I'm dealing with a block of marble.

JULKA   You're mistaken, Karol. I do not sport my vestal virgin's robe with ceremony. But what I do think is that neither you nor my sister should try to justify your actions, in front of anyone – me or the rest of the world. Do I ever unburden myself in your presence?

KAROL   Oh! You dwell among abstractions. Your whole world ends in ism – feminism, socialism …

JULKA   *(Rising)* I take it you still wish to wait for Elka?

KAROL   I simply wanted to … suggest … that you shouldn't be … the way you are. Nothing good will come of it. You'll become addicted to activism and that will be absolutely excruciating …

JULKA   It's absolutely excruciating to be – nothing … even worse – to be average.

KAROL   And which of the above am I?

JULKA   *(Nonchalantly)* Decidedly average.

KAROL   Because I don't share your red persuasions?[12]

JULKA   Because you are … colourless.[13]

KAROL   I can live with that.

JULKA   Oh, of course. Remarkably convenient position – every editor in the land will happily take you on. You'll never be compromised.

KAROL   Don't you try and deny it – that crowd of yours would love to have me in the party – I'm quick witted, very clever…

JULKA   *(Coldly)* Not much use to us, I'm afraid. Membership of our party relies on rather more than that.

KAROL   I plead ignorance.

JULKA   Above all, strength of character – moral consistency – vacillation is most certainly not permitted.

KAROL   I don't think I vacillate.

JULKA   I have clear evidence to the contrary.

KAROL   My separation from my wife, you mean? Purely emotional matter! Social conviction's got nothing to do with that.

JULKA   You're mistaken – a person must be complete. All his or her actions, whether they occur in the sphere of sentiment, or on a broader social scale, are connected.

KAROL   *(Leaps up and paces the room uncomfortably – after a while stands before Julka)* So what you're in fact accusing me of is that, whilst being married, I fell in love with your sister?

JULKA   No – merely that you didn't have the strength of character to suppress your love.

KAROL   You're like a blind man passing judgement about colour. You haven't the faintest idea what emotional warmth or kindness is.[14]

JULKA   Everyone cultivates his own repertoire of emotions.

KAROL   Cultivates? Clap-trap. Our emotions are roused before we even have a chance to think. And so the impulses of the heart shape the way in which we reason.

JULKA   If we're supposed to be talking logically here, then consider whether our senses are first awakened. These, according to your theory, govern our emotions – which, fuelled by our senses, ultimately determine how we think.[15]

KAROL   (Bursts out) Must you always turn things back to front! Your reason has been awakened…

JULKA   And it has shaped what you would call my heart. That is why, in all my emotional dealings, I govern with my reason.

KAROL   (Bursts out) And I suppose I am governed by my senses.

JULKA   (Coldly and gravely) And you indeed are governed by your senses. Remember this. All these emotions, you think they're so sincere but what you feel is lust – nothing more.

KAROL   And so, according to you, I'm still in the first stages of development? A severely limited repertoire of emotions? No reason to speak of? Nothing – only my senses?

JULKA   That is my conviction.

KAROL   (Rapidly) It is flawed.

JULKA   Possible but highly unlikely.

            (Julka goes to the window, rests her forehead against the pane and remains thus, motionless)

KAROL   (Paces the room, stops by the table and looks through papers)

            What's this?

JULKA   (By the window) Where?

KAROL   Here, on the table.

JULKA   Today's lecture.

KAROL Where?

JULKA At the reading room, in town.

KAROL May I look?

   (Goes to sit and takes out his notebook)

JULKA Don't say you've run out of things to write about! Ink well's dried up, has it? Is there a drought at your newspaper, that you're digging for sources in *this* little backwater?

KAROL *(Closes his notebook and returns it to his pocket)* Perhaps – I have thought about quoting you.

JULKA That would cause me great offence.

KAROL I know! I know! And I understand perfectly. Your modesty does render you uncommonly proud.

   (Approaches her and stands by the window)

   One of these days, Julka, I will catch you out...I'll publish my exclusive interview with you.

JULKA *(Turns towards him rapidly and stares angrily)*

   You will not.

KAROL And why not?

JULKA *(In a low voice)* Because I'll hate you for it.[16]

KAROL Knowing how to rouse your hatred could prove extremely useful.

JULKA *(Leaning on one side of the window, he on the other)*

   Best not try and provoke me, Karol. It'll be much safer that way.

   (Key is heard in the lock)

   Elka!

SCENE 2

(Julka, Elka, Karol)

KAROL   At last!

ELKA   *(Runs into the room, she is a young blonde, modestly dressed in dark colours and covered in snow – she rushes in and throws her arms around Karol's neck)*

            Has he missed her?

KAROL   *(Kissing her passionately)* Has she missed him?

ELKA   You're mine! All mine!

            (They kiss – in Karol's embrace)

            Why that look, Julka?

KAROL   The eminent pedagogue measures, rather clinically perhaps, the rising temperature of our aching hearts.

JULKA   Too long, badly constructed and downright false. In fact the mercury seems rather low. In my considered opinion, coronary activity has sunk to its lowest point.

ELKA   *(With accusation)* Not all this again?

JULKA   I am extremely persistent.

            (Sits at the table and begins to assemble the pages of her lecture. Karol and Elka move to the other side of the stage. Elka removes her jacket, hat – Karol takes all this into the hall)

ELKA   Do you love me?

KAROL   *(Kisses her)* I do.

ELKA   How much?

KAROL   *(Kisses her)* With all my heart!

ELKA   *(Nearly fainting beneath his kisses)* I am the same!

            (Looks in Julka's direction laughing)

Psst! ... Quiet ... older sister has a serious look about her.

KAROL   *(With irony)* Pondering some topic of acute social relevance, no doubt, let's not disturb her.

ELKA   Kiss me!

(Julka looks at them)

We're not disturbing you, are we! Poor old thing!

(Runs towards her and kisses her)

Ugh! Your lips are so cold!

(Julka doesn't reply – simply looks at her)

ELKA   You look at me with such reproach! Julka, let me be happy!

KAROL   Come over here, Elka, to me – don't disturb Julka's work.

ELKA   Wait ... I have a brilliant solution ...

(She seizes the screen[17] and conceals Julka behind it)

Now, dearest sister, you'll have no interruptions!

JULKA   *(With irony)* Ah! Such heartfelt displays of concern!

ELKA   Intolerable, that's what you are!

(She runs to Karol, sits on the sofa and pulls him towards her – fervently)

Sit here, next to me. And if you've got bad news, keep it to yourself for now. Wait – let me be happy ...

(She cuddles up to him passionately)

Oh! I love you ... so much!

KAROL   Elka – how pale you are!

ELKA   *(Feverishly, half-naively)* Oh, but no ... no ... I can endure the pain most willingly. Because it's mixed up with pleasure. I'm trembling all over, my whole body cries out...ah...here...just look...my teeth, they're chattering so hard and my lip's bleeding, just from trying to bite all this down...something I long for...something I want...I can't say...ahh...[18]

(Pause)

Why aren't you kissing me?

KAROL   (Pushes her away gently) Elka! Dear Elka!...I find...I have some bad news...

ELKA   (Paling) Oh...I can guess...another delay.

KAROL   (Quickly) Yes...that's right...but only a delay...

ELKA   (Bursting out) Oh, she's a base, evil woman! To torment us like this – to keep us in bonds. What does she mean by it? Can't she understand you won't go back to her! She has no heart!

KAROL   That's very true. She has no heart. That is her fatal flaw. That is why I've stopped loving her. Instead of a heart, that woman had a fashionable hat, a fashionable dress – her whole life was one long tea party.[19]

ELKA   (After a pause) In that case, why did you marry her?

KAROL   (Reluctantly) I've explained it to you so many times.

ELKA   But I don't understand. You're so intelligent...so...important...and to marry such a...doll.

KAROL   Aesthetic impression...my artistic sensibility got the better of me.

ELKA   I don't understand.

KAROL   (With irony) Nina...she was 'the woman for me'...she was always so lovely, so shapely, so coiffeured...and what a face...I kept going back for more. She was a work of art...bit like Botticelli's Primavera, only in modern dress...I was a hardened primitivist back then...anything tenuously pre-Raphaelite and that was it! I stumbled upon a living Primavera and I married her. Quite ridiculous? Alright?

ELKA   (Saddened) Some of the things you say confuse me...but...there's one thing I do know. She was beautiful and she had beautiful clothes...

KAROL Yes, she was simply beautiful and dressed simply beautifully - tra, la, la! That's not *quite* enough...

ELKA *(Sadly)* But it was enough to make you fall in love with her.

KAROL No - it was enough to make me stop loving her... what's the matter now?

ELKA I feel sad.

(In tears)

That other woman was beautiful and had perfect frocks. I am practically ugly - my dresses are plain and threadbare...

KAROL *(Bursts out)* But you're different! Don't you see - your modest simplicity attracted me at once! I saw straight to your heart... remember? You materialized before me like a small white statue, covered in snow - you had tiny white stars in your hair, you were powdered like a French marquise... no... you were a small angel, descended straight from the clouds. That evening, I was weighed down by worries - I was longing for someone to open her heart - I could have howled and pleaded for warmth and kindness... well... and you of all people didn't reject me... you showed great discrimination...

ELKA Yes... but how I must seem to you after that other woman. And this place... is so... poor.

KAROL *(Looks around)* This is a palace to me! Unlike my own 'home'! Whenever it strikes six, I can barely contain myself... here it's quiet and warm - this room appears before me like an oasis and I hurry towards it.

(He begins pacing about the room, hands in pockets - approaches Elka)

Here, I would like to settle down, here a woman's heart burns like a sanctuary lamp...[20]

(Approaches Elka)

... you've got to understand, Elka - kindness, that's all I want from you! Open your heart! Then I'll have peace and stay calm. There, huh, with her - everything was too new, too pleasant, everything was fashionably arranged and it was always cold - moral chill, physical chill - or else those endless neurotic displays! 'I'll just faint... over here... darling... fetch me my smelling salts!'[21] And what about my needs!? Well... nothing more to be said is there - I'm a man! When I'm at home, I need to be surrounded by warmth... there, what was I? A guest... nothing more...taken for granted – me, my work, my mind – everything. Does it still surprise you that I left? Does it?

JULKA   *(Who has been scrutinizing him for some time, moves the screen aside)* How much time elapsed between your first meeting with your wife and your wedding?

KAROL   Three months.

JULKA   You tell me you're quick witted, in which case you must also have keen powers of observation – you should have observed her.

KAROL   I was dazzled by...artifice.

JULKA   In that case, you are to blame.

KAROL   Oh no! You go too far...now it's my fault she was a...mannequin! I blame the whole thing on Botticelli!

JULKA   Did Nina ever show signs of an extensive emotional repertoire? Did you ever ask her to prove that she has a kind heart?

KAROL   She did marry me!

JULKA   Then perhaps she too was dazzled...oh!...not by your appearance – because you can hardly be described as a Botticelli – but perhaps, Mr Editor, your professional status took her breath away – you have a certain effortless charm, do you not?

ELKA   You're defending her, aren't you?

JULKA   Saints preserve us! I'm simply defending a woman against the accusations of a man. I am generalizing.

(She gathers together her papers)

I'm going out. Shall I be seeing you here again, Karol?

KAROL   I've got to get back to the office – though I might just call in later on.

JULKA   And so...until later!

(Exits left)

SCENE 3

(Karol, Elka)

KAROL   *(Watching her leave)* What a relief!

ELKA   Because Julka's gone out?

KAROL   *(Bored)* I find her terribly wearing.

ELKA   Me too. In a different way. She's so very intelligent. She's always reading at night. Our parents had her educated. They said I was rather slow and they were loath to spend the money. Mother, God rest her soul, said I would get married without too much effort – she thought I was pretty. She always said I was made to be a wife and mother. After that, I lost my looks.

KAROL   But you are lovely!

ELKA   Oh – I'm so rosy – I have such a round face.[22] At the agency, they're always making fun of me.

KAROL   Well to me you're beautiful and wise and good and everything else that really matters – you're my little girl.

   (With growing, suppressed passion – they speak more quietly, almost in a whisper, the words catch in their throats)

ELKA   *(Coyly)* Really?

KAROL   Really.

ELKA   *(Naively)* Give me your word of honour – because when a man gives his word of honour, he never lies, does he?

KAROL   Never! And so I give you my word of honour that I love you more than life itself and that you seem to me the most beautiful, beautiful creature in all the world.

ELKA   I provide a good ... what's that word you use ... *Prima* ... anaesthetic ...[23] oh ... I can't even repeat it ... I'm so stupid ...

KAROL   *(Caressing her)* Aesthetic impression ... only it's much more than that – you are a work of art made flesh. Heat seems to emanate from you ... like springtime, *Primavera* ... you ... are ... so, so lovely and warm, you bring me straight back to life ...

(He kisses her passionately, she swoons, he wipes the sweat from his brow and paces the room)

I think I should probably leave now, alright, Elka?

ELKA   *(Quietly)* Where will you go?

KAROL   *(Confused)* To the office, to do some writing – something for tomorrow's column. I have to proof read Saturday's edition more carefully. Well ... goodbye for now ... my dearest love ... perhaps I'll drop in later on.

ELKA   Oh please – you must! Julka won't be back 'til quite late today ...

KAROL   What's the use, Elka! There's little sense in coming here after ten anyway, is there. I still have so much work to do.

(Bursts out)

If I had a divorce and was your husband, I'd write at home. I'd have my desk – positioned here – and here, an armchair – and I'd sit beside you calmly and quietly.[24] In such an honest, unaffected atmosphere I'd be more creative and more efficient. Then I could offer you more. It's so empty at the office, regimented, lonely – and I'm a man of heart, understand, Elka? Above all else, a kind, open heart. Well ... take good care of yourself! Kiss me goodbye!

(With an outburst of frustrated passion)

You kiss with such ... intuition ... oh, you ... let me go!

(He rushes out)

SCENE 4

(Julka, Elka)

(Elka stands as though semi-conscious for a while then slowly tries to regain her composure – she undoes her collar, goes to the window and tries to open the casement)

JULKA   *(Enters, her jacket and hat in her hand)* What are you doing by the window?

ELKA   It's stuffy – I'm hot ... I need some air.

JULKA   *(With irony)* That won't cool you down – you'll catch a chill, that's all.

ELKA   *(Moves about the room, adjusts lamp briefly, then falls into a chair and bursts into tears)*

            I think my heart must be melting! It can't go on like this...

JULKA   *(Quietly)* That's up to the two of you.

ELKA   Did you hear nothing? His wife refuses to agree to a divorce! She's frozen his efforts
            yet again with all her ridiculous protestations.

JULKA   *(Coldly)* In that case, separate.

ELKA   *(Leaping up)* Julka! Julka, what are you saying? That we should part? Is it possible
            that we could live without each other?

JULKA   Without him – I don't know. But it's more than certain he can live without you.

ELKA   You're always putting me off – you do everything to convince me that he doesn't
            love me.

JULKA   *(Quietly)* Because he doesn't love you!

ELKA   *(Angrily)* You're evil – evil! You saw, how he kissed me – how much he admires
            my kindness, craves my warmth...

JULKA   *(Nonchalantly)* That is not love.

ELKA   *(Quickly)* You're jealous – that's all.

JULKA   *(Accusatively)* Elka! Elka!

ELKA   *(Pause)* Why do you push me this far? You see what's happening to me, don't you?
            That I'm ill, with the fever! Look! How my face is burning! That's how it is all day!
            When he's not here I feel as though I've been overcome – all I do is wait 'til he
            arrives... oh... I'm so unhappy!

JULKA   I do believe you're unhappy.

ELKA   And I don't, I really cannot go back to the way things were. It seems to me that
            then I slept and that now I've awoken – only now am I truly alive.

            (Looks at the clock)

            What's the time?

JULKA   Occupy yourself. You have books – read them!

ELKA   I can't! I just can't!

                (Paces about the room)

                Besides...I did something definite today. Who can tell, perhaps things will change...

JULKA   Oh! Elka, what have you done?

ELKA   Nothing all that stupid! Oh, you think I'm terribly stupid and could never concoct anything clever. And yet, in defence of our happiness, who knows what I'm capable of...

JULKA   I've some anxiety that you may, in defending your happiness, inadvertently destroy it.

ELKA   Of course I won't. Today I suddenly had a thought...oh, very well...I'll tell you everything. Right from the beginning. All this secrecy is choking me.

                (Pause)

                Alright...I...wrote to her...

JULKA   (Alarmed) To his wife?

ELKA   (Rapidly) Yes. I wrote everything down. That we love one another that we're very unhappy that he'll never go back to her and that she'd be much better off admitting all this formally. I didn't beg or plead, because of course I do have some ambition – but I did write it rather well. My friend at the agency thoroughly admired it.

JULKA   I would have advised you against such a letter.

ELKA   Yes...very likely...that's why I preferred not to tell you. What do you want from me? I'm a simple, sincere girl and I follow my heart. That's what Karol says and that is what he loves me for.

JULKA   (Soberly and ironically) In due course you'll find out exactly what Karol loves you for. As for your letter, I've no idea of the effect it will produce.

ELKA   My feminine intuition tells me all will be well.

JULKA   And my powers of logic tell me it will not.

                (Doorbell is heard)

ELKA   Who could that be? Do you suppose it's Karol?

JULKA	Karol is at the office – it's someone else.
ELKA	(Concerned) You go – open it! I'm afraid of something.
JULKA	If it's your own unhappiness you fear, that will seek you out anyway.
	(Takes candle, lights it, goes through to the hall, opens the door; after a while, enters and says with a slightly altered voice)
	Please, madam, do come in.

SCENE 5

(Julka, Elka, Nina)

(Enter Nina, dressed with outstanding ceremony and beauty, blonde, nervous, with hair arranged à la Botticelli)[25]

NINA	(Nervously) Are you the Misses Korecki?[26]
JULKA	We are indeed.
ELKA	(Confused, to Julka) It's her.
JULKA	(Quietly, calmly) I know that.
NINA	(Rather impertinently) Which of you is … the younger?[27]
JULKA	Pardon me – my sister must leave us. She's not well. I'll speak with you myself.
NINA	Ah … so that is … 'the other woman'?
JULKA	Yes … precisely … the other woman.
	(To Elka)
	Go through, Elka, to the bedroom. You have a temperature. I'll call if I need you.
	(Elka exits obediently, swallowing her tears)
NINA	(With irony) Your sister, madam, is braver in writing than she is in the flesh.
JULKA	(Always calm) My sister is still an anxious child. She finds herself unable to cope. Fate has positioned her in the midst of a tragedy.

NINA   *(Still mocking and angry)* A child you say? Strange, then, that she should know how to conduct affairs with married people.

JULKA   *(Sharply)* Be quiet, madam! Did you come here to insult us?

NINA   *(Nervously tugging at her boa)* I came here, in person, to deliver my response to the second-rate essay I was handed this morning, by the messenger. I certainly don't play at compromising scribbling – especially when I know into whose hands my letter might ultimately fall.[28] I came here...

JULKA   Pardon me for interrupting. You came here simply because you were hoping to encounter your husband and, for his sole benefit, to make...let us use that rather hackneyed phrase...make a scene. Am I wrong?

NINA   What right do you have to cross-examine me?

JULKA   *(Quietly)* Am I wrong?

NINA   *(Confused, changes her tone)* You are a very peculiar woman...

JULKA   *(After a while, meets Nina's gaze)* Would you still be capable of loving your husband?

     (Nina nervously opens her mouth a few times, as if to reply – eventually draws her hand across her brow and looks about her for a chair)

     Please, sit down...yes...have a drink of water...

     (Draws up a chair, Nina sits, Julka passes her the water)

     Now we can talk.

     (Sits on the other side of the table, lamplight falls across Nina's face)

     As far as I can see, you, Madam, are a bundle of nerves...

NINA   *(Her lips tremble, her eyelids droop in spite of her efforts)* It's true – I am a highly strung individual.

JULKA   Is it so surprising, then, that your behaviour lacks...forethought...is full of agitation? You came here driven onward by your shattered nerves – not accounting for the consequences.

NINA   *(Increasingly agitated)* I've been patient now for quite some time...You must admit I've had every reason to feel extremely affected by your conduct, and your sister's.

I soothed, as much as I could, my very raw nerves and said to myself, 'Oh! It's a passing fancy, that's all – what harm can she do…'

(Restraining herself)

I am sorry.

JULKA   *(Quietly and politely)* Please, go on – I am capable of putting myself in your position and can appreciate how excitable this must have made you. I'm listening.

NINA   *(Increasingly losing the impertinent tone she had on arrival, but with growing nervousness)* I meant to say…wait…it's all confused…your sister put me in a state of such agitation with that letter! My doctor had to call in twice and even he remained unable to calm me down. Where was I? Judging it to be a passing fancy…I waited. Whereas now, from your sister's letter, well – it's plain as day there's something else going on. She's making certain claims…demands that I agree to the divorce…quite simply beyond the pale!

(Fresh burst of nervous energy)

I'll *never* condone it. I've a *right* to Karol, a *right* conferred on me by our marriage. I won't step aside, ever!

JULKA   *(Coldly)* Stay calm. Otherwise we'll never reach an understanding. You refer constantly to your husband…but…Karol no longer is your husband.

NINA   *(Violently)* What are you talking about? A divorce hasn't been granted, alright, nor shall it ever be!

JULKA   Yes…a formal divorce…and yet, in reality, the moment your husband left you, spiritually and physically you ceased to be his wife. And that's when your husband met my sister and began spending time in our house.[29]

NINA   If it wasn't for her, he would have…come back to me.

JULKA   You're mistaken. Karol would never have gone back to you.

NINA   How can you know anything about it?

JULKA   That's none of your business – but I do know. Now listen carefully. Perhaps this is the first time in your life that someone, some other woman, has had the mettle to tell you – quite brutally – the whole truth. You're used to having a small coterie of sycophants around you to make you feel better. You've been gravely misled. I won't do that. And so – remember this. You whipped your husband's nervous system into a state of permanent arousal. Arousing people must be your strong point. It's perfectly clear, everything about you is calculated to arouse and agitate practically everybody, particularly men – your figure, voice, gestures, glance, attire – your way of being – titillates and tantalizes. Simply put – it's nervous arousal. And a man takes this to be love.

NINA   (Listening, in spite of herself) Please, do go on...

JULKA   On this occasion, you might have...overplayed it. Because now, at last, your husband's own over-stimulated nervous system has grown acclimatized to you – you've ceased to exert an impression. Beyond titillation, agitation and a tantalizing array of swoons, it seems you've nothing left to offer...

NINA   (Rapidly) Why must I always exert myself? He should've made more effort to love me...

JULKA   On the grounds that one is an egotist, it's best to refrain from starting anything with men. Advisable to keep your distance! I am an egotist and hence will remain an old maid. But I digress. You need to realize that life at home was...disappointing for your husband. You stirred him up with your charms and your attire – you should've found an alternative strategy. From his point of view, it was...cold...at home...he said so himself.

NINA   (Stupidly) Over-heating plays havoc with my complexion. They light the stoves only once a day in our house – that's that.

JULKA   (With a smile of pity) If you're still intent on being perverse...both he and I were thinking of a different kind of warmth...

NINA   (Who with shame perceives her own foolishness) Aha.

              (Pause) But it's all so melodramatic. Does very well in books, I'm sure. You don't seriously mean to imply that your sister can cater for the refined sensibilities you've described! Huh! It's enough to read her letter...

              (She throws the letter on the table)

JULKA   It's something else that draws him towards my sister.

NINA   Well I wonder what that could be.[30]

              (Julka is silent, Nina bites her lip)

              Ugly...common...

(Nervous excitement)

Oh yes – she's frightfully ugly...

JULKA   Refrain from hysteria, Madam.

NINA   *(Stamps her foot)* She's downright ugly, I tell you...and besides...what gives you the right to address me with such impertinence? To read me my penance! I come here to lay the blame on you – to judge you – and you, madam, call me the guilty party, stand me in the dock! That's quite enough! That's the limit! Not so clever now, are you...been wasting your time. Your sister's hiding – she's petrified! What a surprise! Well, you can tell her I won't back down, I'll never agree to a divorce...never...ever!

JULKA   *(Quietly)* The word 'never' should be eliminated from our vocabulary.

NINA   *(In a fit of passion)* You dare to mock me?

JULKA   Heaven forfend! Only I am calm, hence my superior position.

NINA   *(As before)* Your superior position? How dare you! I've no idea why I'm talking to you!

JULKA   *(With a smile)* To relieve your shattered nerves.

NINA   *(Shaking nervously)* You can't hurt me. I'm perfectly capable of telling your sister's fortune with some accuracy. She'll never receive my consent – I'll defend myself to the bitter end. As for you, do whatever you like.

JULKA   *(Calmly)* We shan't be doing anything. We'll just wait.

NINA   You'll never wait long enough! Listen to me, you...

JULKA   Hush now, madam! You might say some despicable, common things. That would be entirely out of harmony with your persona.

NINA   *(Choking with passion)* You, madam – the sheer impertinence! I bid you farewell!

JULKA   *(Politely)* Goodbye, madam.

(Takes the candle)

Allow me – it's very dark out there...

NINA   I can see myself out.

(Runs out, door is heard slamming)

SCENE 6

(Julka, Elka)

ELKA *(Runs in flustered and embraces Julka)*[31] I heard everything! Julka, she's an evil woman.

JULKA *(Coldly)* No – she's unhappy, like you. You have to be fair, Elka.

ELKA *(Quietly)* Julka! Did you hear? She loves him still.

JULKA *(Calmly)* She loves him – with her whole nervous disposition – but she does love him.

ELKA Clearly less than I do! Isn't that right, Julka?

JULKA *(As before)* It's difficult to judge.

ELKA She called me ugly, common. She made fun of my letter. I cried so much when I was writing it.

JULKA That's precisely why it was amusing. What we give to the world in tears generally arouses laughter ... if you wanted to put someone in a black mood, you should've laughed while you were writing. That's worth remembering.

ELKA How could I laugh? My whole life is falling apart! What shall I do now? What shall I do? Today one of the girls at the agency told me something.[32] It made me very uneasy. She had a sort of fiancé too – like mine – they couldn't get married because he had too many debts and the moneylenders were always hounding him. And so they waited. He used to come to her – a bit like Karol does to us. But it was all taking too long. He got bored beyond belief, he found someone else. And then he dropped her! Is that possible, Julka?

JULKA *(Slowly gets ready to go)* It's entirely possible, Elka.

ELKA He could drop me as well! He could get bored, just like that – couldn't he?

JULKA He could.

ELKA *(Paces avidly, wringing her hands)* What's to be done? What can I do?

(Pause)

I can't bear to watch him. He longs for a peaceful life – to be calm, quiet, safe, in a family home. He stood there, today, he said, 'if I only had an armchair, here and here, a desk, I'd write away without a care in the world'. Yes! That's what irks me most. I'm desperate to bind him to me. What's to be done?

JULKA   (Dressed to go out – looks at Elka with pity and says) Poor child!

ELKA   (Suddenly dissolves in tears) Yes! Yes! Poor me ... poor him! Julka! Advise me!

JULKA   (Sadly and quietly) No, Elka ... I can't.

ELKA   (Seizing her by the hands) Why not? But you are my sister!

JULKA   (Even more quietly) Precisely.[33]

ELKA   (Collapses into a chair by the table weeping) What! I want to die!

SCENE 7

(Julka, Elka, Karol)

KAROL   (Peers around the door to the hall) The door was open – your door is always open.[34]

JULKA   Elka! Karol is here.

         (Elka swallows violently)

KAROL   (Enters the room) It's cold at the office, radiators aren't working, I can't write ...

         (Approaches Elka)

         What's all this, Elka?

ELKA   (With a tearful outburst throws her arms around his neck) Karol! She was here!

KAROL   (Confused, detaches from Elka) Who was?

JULKA   (Quietly) Your wife ...

KAROL   Here? What on earth for? What did she want? How dare she! The sheer nerve of the woman?

ELKA   It's all my fault! I wrote her a letter. Oh! Don't be angry! I thought I might be able
          to bring her round ... she came here and ... and ...

          (Bursts into tears)

          So pretty – such lovely clothes! What am I next to her? How can I measure up!

KAROL   *(To Julka)* What did she say?

JULKA   She emitted a stream of nervous and chaotic clap-trap, punctuated by a few
          impertinent comments ...

KAROL   She offended you?

JULKA   *(Quickly)* Not at all! She aroused our pity. Sometimes even bird-brained creatures[35]
          are capable of suffering, Karol ...

KAROL   And the outcome?

JULKA   She put her foot firmly down. Of course ... when there's something missing ...
          (indicates her forehead) ... here – stubbornness runs riot, like a weed.[36]

ELKA   She said – never!

KAROL   I saw it coming.

          (Paces, eventually sits on the sofa and covers his face with his hands)

          Oh – she's as pinched as they come. It's not as though she even loves me.

          (With a rapid gesture Elka places her finger on Julka's lips)

ELKA   *(Quietly, to Julka)* Don't say a word!

KAROL   *(As if to himself)* All this sadness! Not the remotest hope of an end to my rootless
          existence, my homelessness, my little stint as envious voyeur of domestic lamp-lit
          bliss.[37] The doors are barred against me. It's all out of reach. I am a wanderer,[38]
          day in, day out, stumbling from one heart to another, my own desires ... my
          needs ... abandoned, buried, forgotten![39] *(Bursting out)*

          Because that is the way of the world!

          (Pause)

Huh! Well! If this is it...

(Looks around and puts his head in his hands once more)

Ladies, an eternal guest, so shall I remain, in your home! A guest – nothing more!

(Pause)

I'm so worn out...

ELKA   (Quietly to Julka) You'll see...he'll drop me! He's ready to go back to her. Advise me, sister! Give me some advice!

JULKA   I can't.

SCENE 8

(Elka, Karol)

(Long pause. Karol sits with his face concealed. Elka slowly approaches him and kneels at his feet, she takes his hands from his face and says, moved)

ELKA   Lolek?[40] What is this...tears?

KAROL   (Wiping his eyes) Don't take it to heart...all this has...built up inside me. You see...since childhood, I've been shunted from pillar to post, from the arms of one stranger to another. I've never had any peace.[41] Just now I had the firmest grasp on you, like a drowning man. Surely, I thought, I'll sink, if I carry on squandering my life away in bars and the homes of strangers. With you, finally, I felt able to breathe! I felt safe! Everything could be so good for us...together...you, me, Julka. Not possible! Who forbids it? The law! The world! The same law applies, equally, to everyone...and here each person is different, each soul is different, each and every tragedy of each and every soul is different...and now, there's nothing left. Nothing for me, for us, Elka – nothing...

ELKA   (In a sudden, passionate outburst) It's a lie that there's nothing left! Everything is for us, do you hear me! Everything!

KAROL   Elka! What do you mean!

ELKA   (Passionate and fevered) Yes! Yes! Enough of tears...quite enough! They've all taken against us! Her, the law, the world! They've tied us down; they're tormenting, oppressing us. Why? You have chosen me and I you! This poor little corner, so dear to you, stay here! I can't describe what's happening inside me. Something, here, has rebelled – it's terrifying, I can hardly breathe...

KAROL *(Eyeing her intently)* Elka, at this precise moment, you are quite lovely, more and more lovely.

ELKA *(Kneeling, in Karol's embrace)* Stay here, with us, in this little place you love! It'll be good for you! This can be your home...

KAROL Your eyes are shining! Your lips! Like spring petals bathed in sparkling dew! Look at me – look straight at me!

ELKA I will be everything, all that I can be, to you, only never cry again!

KAROL *(Passionately)* A haunted twilight! The witching hour! Elka! You're being transformed in my arms! You dazzle me... so lovely... my hands burn on your skin...

ELKA My heart has never been more open. Before God, I long to love you, to be faithful to you for the rest of my life...

KAROL *(Passionately)* Elka – you're perfect! A work of art! Your lips... your eyes... moist with tears...!

ELKA *(More or less fainting in his arms)* I am your servant!

KAROL No! You are my wife!

  (They kiss passionately and at great length)[42]

  (Curtain falls)

Figure 18: Elka, now pregnant, wants Karol to give her some attention. Research performance of Zapolska's *The Man*. University of Reading and POSK Theatre, London, 2004/5. Sophie Green as Elka, Sam Milsom as Karol. Photo by Lib Taylor.

ACT 2

(The same setting as in Act 1, only the bureau is standing by the window; next to it a wastepaper basket. On it burns a lamp. Dawn light is seeping through the drawn curtains. Karol sleeps on the sofa fully clothed. Julka sits at the bureau, in her dressing gown, covered with a shawl; she is writing)

SCENE 1

(Julka, Elka, Karol)

JULKA   All done!

(The bell rings)

Karol! Probably the boy from the printer's needing the draft.

KAROL   *(Mumbling in his sleep)* On the desk... the meeting... then the proceedings... Town Council on its way...

JULKA   Alright, alright!

(Arranges draft on the desk, takes it through to the hall, returns, extinguishes lamp, raises blinds, pushes window ajar and breathes in the morning air)

ELKA   *(Pushes door ajar, left, is in her dressing gown)*

Who rang?

JULKA   The boy for the draft.

ELKA   And Karol is sleeping!

JULKA   I already made the finishing touches using his notes and passed it on – he was so tired when he came back, he couldn't work.

ELKA   Did he get back late?

JULKA   *(Evasively)* I didn't notice the time.

ELKA   You know very well – you don't want to tell me the truth, that's all.

(Pause)

Figure 19: Julka tells Elka that she has what she deserves. Research performance of Zapolska's *The Man*. University of Reading and POSK Theatre, London, 2004/5. Sophie Green as Elka, Sam Milsom as Karol, Francesca Clark as Julka. Photo by Lib Taylor.

He was probably playing cards again.

(Enters wearing soiled dressing gown, worn shoes, her hair is falling tousled over her shoulders, she is pale)[43]

JULKA   As far as I know, he had an appointment, something to do with proceedings at the chamber of commerce and after that there was still the Town Council meeting.

ELKA   *(Pointing)* Yes…for sure…his own personal council of friends in the town, no doubt…

JULKA   *(Looking at her with furrowed brow)* Elka! Go and get dressed, cover yourself…what an appearance…

ELKA   *(Shrugs)* Oh! What do I care!

(Goes over to Karol)

JULKA   Leave him in peace, don't wake him!

ELKA   (*Angrily*) Well I never! Leave him! I've hardly seen him at all these past two days. He comes home in the early hours and then apparently dashes away to the office … Karol! Karol! Stop sleeping!

            (*Karol mutters incoherently, pushing her hand away*)

            Kiss me!

KAROL   (*In his sleep, wrapping the blanket around him*) Let me sleep!

ELKA   (*Pulling the blanket away*) Stop sleeping! Well then – greet me properly!

KAROL   (*Leaps up angrily, pulls the blanket away from her, wraps it around himself and lies down*) Leave me alone!

ELKA   (*To Julka, who is sitting by the bureau, writing*) Look, how he conducts himself in my presence! No – it's quite beyond the pale. He comes here to steal forty winks between one night of cavorting and the next … You saw, did you?

JULKA   Yes, I did. And I find that you have what you deserve. Let him sleep.

ELKA   And, should I place a cushion beneath his head? One moment …

            (*Pulls the cushion from under his head and throws it to the ground – he sleeps like a dead man*)

JULKA   Elka! Elka! Remember yourself. You'll alienate him completely with this behaviour …

            (*Pause*)

            Do go and get dressed.

ELKA   I don't know what to wear.

JULKA   Well at the very least arrange your hair. Look – even I'm wearing a dressing gown. I didn't get a wink of sleep all night but it doesn't look that way.

ELKA   At least you're pretty. I am ugly. You have a nice new dressing gown but because I've had to leave my job, I have nothing.

JULKA   Not so long ago I gave you ten zlotys.[44]

ELKA   All gone … and anyway, I've got other expenses now. I've had to buy a lot of things.

JULKA   I know.

(Elka traipses around the room and eventually looks in the pocket of the coat draped across the chair)

Elka! What are you doing?

ELKA   Once, in this manner precisely, I found letters from his friends – letters inviting him out to play at cards.

JULKA   Please, don't do this. If Karol sees you ... he'll most certainly be angry.

ELKA   But you, when I came in, were likewise rifling through his coat pockets.

JULKA   I was obtaining the notes from the Council sitting – I need them for the article.

ELKA   What? You're writing articles for him yet again?

JULKA   That's right and please I ask you do get along now because you're disturbing me and any minute the boy will burst in demanding the draft.

ELKA   *(Spreading her arms)* Well I never! Do you know, ladies and gentlemen, this really is the edge of the world if you're hunched over his article so that he can get the best of forty winks!

(Sudden fury)

I'll rouse him and relay some home truths.

JULKA   *(Leaps up and seizes her hands)* Elka! Leave him alone! Stop needling him! He'll pack his bags and leave.

ELKA   Let the four winds take him!

JULKA   *(Meaningfully)* You can't say things like that *now*.

ELKA   *(Bursts into tears suddenly – moves to an armchair)* That's true – it's quite true.

JULKA   *(Returns to window and tries to decipher notes)* It's difficult to make any sense of this.

(Goes to Karol and bends over him with tact)

Karol? Karol?

KAROL   *(In his sleep)* What's the matter?

JULKA   It's only me, if you'd oblige, I just need some information for the article…

KAROL   *(Sleepy)* What article?

JULKA   About yesterday's Council sitting? Tell me – what's that Councillor's surname – the one who mediated in the matter concerning the abattoir? I can't read your handwriting.

KAROL   Bombecki, Trąbecki, Dąbrecki – I haven't the foggiest idea…[45]

JULKA   Well, I don't know either.

KAROL   *(Leaps up, suddenly sits on the sofa, rubbing his eyes)* What's the time?

ELKA   *(Sulkily)* The time when all decent people rise and shine and eat their breakfasts!

KAROL   Hell and damnation! Hell and damnation!

        (Goes to the desk – returns – rummages through his coat pockets)

Figure 20: Julka is tactful. Research performance of Zapolska's *The Man*. University of Reading and POSK Theatre, London, 2004/5. Sam Milsom as Karol, Francesca Clark as Julka. Photo by Lib Taylor.

ELKA   Won't you wish me a good morning?

KAROL   I had notes…I had notes…

ELKA   *(Playfully submissive)* Kiss me, at least.

KAROL   Leave me alone…you can see I'm looking for some important notes, can't you?

JULKA   If you mean the Council ones – I have them here on the desk.

            (Karol sits by the desk. He is unwashed, pale, unattractive – his shirt is creased, his collar has become unfastened, he turns the papers over nervously, he cannot hold them properly in his hands)

ELKA   *(Tearfully)* Well I never! Do you know what ladies and gentlemen, it's quite beyond the pale! You find yourself incapable of even greeting me?!

JULKA   *(Taking Elka by the hand)* Elka! Go through to the kitchen – take charge of breakfast.

KAROL   Just give me a cup of tea and quickly because I have to get to the office.

ELKA   Oho…coming up!

JULKA   Quietly! Please! Go on – bring the tea.

SCENE 2

(Karol, Julka)

KAROL   I was supposed to write about the Spójna meeting as well. Damnation! I haven't a clue what went on there.[46]

JULKA   I penned a thirty line column myself. Nothing out of the ordinary – it was short and sweet because the commissary disbanded the meeting. I found out at Binder's[47] lecture, at the University.

KAROL   Thank you so much, Julka…wait…something else happened yesterday…Chamber of Commerce, I think it was…

JULKA   Yes – you jotted a few things down when you came in. I gave it some finishing touches based on what I saw on my way back from the lecture. There's only the Town Council left to go…make haste…the boy will rush by any minute…just here…I've made a start – go ahead, add a conclusion.

KAROL   Julka! Julka! I really must suggest to the editorial team that you're offered some form of employment.

JULKA   Thank you so much – I have enough work to keep me going.

KAROL   After the Council meeting we went here, there and everywhere ... well ... and somehow ...

         (Outburst of gratitude)

         Julka! I owe you for this!

JULKA   You'd better put pen to paper. You can thank me later.

KAROL   Wait! Wait! I must have a cigarette.

         (Lights a cigarette, looks towards the door)

         What's happened to that tea?

JULKA   Elka! Elka!

ELKA   *(From behind the door)* What is it?

JULKA   The tea?

ELKA   *(As before)* Wait a minute! Only the samovar's gone out.

KAROL   Dear God! That one – when she gets started ... brr! I can't write a thing ... it won't budge! The letters are actually leaping about in front of my eyes.

         (Writes, throws down pen)

         I can't work without tea! Well, I simply can't!

JULKA   *(Gently)* Allow me ... I began it, so I may as well complete it too.

KAROL   Go ahead, write! I am categorically unable to hold a pen in my hand.

         (Goes to sofa, lies down smoking, doesn't fall asleep, Julka sits at the desk and writes, the rising sun illuminates her with its purplish-golden glow, Karol regards her with curiosity – outside someone is heard practising scales, also rugs being beaten[48] – after a pause)

         Julka!

JULKA   *(Still writing)* What is it Karol?

KAROL   You are an extraordinary woman.

JULKA   *(As before)* You are mistaken. I am a most ordinary human being.

KAROL   Why do you correct me? I said 'woman' – you say 'human being'.

JULKA   Firstly, to re-state the obvious yet again, there's very little about me that is womanly – womanly in your sense of the word – and, secondly, for the most part, I feel like a human being, since I'm capable of assessing my own worth, hence my eagerness to locate myself within this category.

KAROL   You're wrong, Julka.

JULKA   In describing my humanity?

KAROL   No, in negating your womanly attributes – womanly in *our* sense of the word! Oh yes! I've a jolly good grasp of what you've been driving at. The kind of femininity that acts like a magnet, keeps us spellbound. Well – you've got more than your fair share of that ...

JULKA   What are you talking about? All men consider me just another friendly fellow and nothing more.

KAROL   Undoubtedly so and it's the 'friendly fellow' who's dominant in you ... but you have a peculiar charm ... all your own ... something ... quite indescribable. If you could only see yourself now, illuminated by the rising sun, in that light dress with its gathered skirts ... there's something very spiritual about you.

JULKA   *(With irony)* *Primavera?* Botticelli?

KAROL   Do you know ... there really is something about you ...

JULKA   *(Laughing)* Any minute now you'll start pinning on my wings ...

KAROL   No need for that – you might fly away and then it would be rather empty in this house.[49]

JULKA   *(Puts the pen aside, looks through the window for a while)* The city is waking. Its brisk song of toil begins, only to end in a nightly howl of blame and degradation. Haven't you, Karol, ever noticed how within that voice, emanating from the depths of the city, tragedy resounds in all its fullness?

Figure 21: Elka makes tea. Research performance of Zapolska's *The Man*. University of Reading and POSK Theatre, London, 2004/5. Sophie Green as Elka, who tries to serve tea. Photo by Lib Taylor.

KAROL   You want me to answer as an artist or someone whose social convictions differ from yours?

JULKA   (*After a pause, picking up the pen*) Ah! Best if you don't reply, I suppose. I forgot. I apologize.

KAROL   (*Aggravated*) That's right! Of course! Not worth talking to me, is it? (*Pause*) You know what, Julka? You've got a real gift for expressing your superiority.

JULKA   (*Writing*) Superiority? You're quite mistaken. We're on opposite ends of the political spectrum, that's all, so discussion between us, of any sort, is utterly pointless.

KAROL   Oh stop it! I can feel you perfectly well, bearing down with your superiority.

JULKA   If that really is how you feel, whilst sensing *at the same time* the superiority of my convictions – why bother to sustain your own *position* of inferiority?

KAROL   Convince me then, why don't you!

JULKA   You can't go implanting a sense of justice just by reasoning. It awakens of its own accord, that's how it awoke in me.

KAROL   Oh do stop it! Someone or other must have converted you!

JULKA   (*With irony*) Some beautiful and young man, for sure!

(*After a pause, forcefully*)

How was I converted? Simply – by a voice, crying out at sunrise and in the dead of night, from the city. Intently, I listened and beyond the glorious trumpeting of cultural progress, the gushing admiration of sensitive artists, the pealing of gothic bells, I picked out the groans and accusations of the oppressed, the hungry. I listened intently – to that – and here indeed was the activist who roused me.[50]

(*Moved, she leans against the window; she is at this moment very beautiful, glowing in the sun's rays. The city awakens with growing insistence and tram bells and a factory siren are heard*)

KAROL   (*Has raised himself on the sofa – whilst watching Julka his cigarette has gone out and he holds it mechanically, speaking slowly and soberly*) For that you need a sensitive soul, Julka! A highly attuned and sensitive soul!

JULKA   (*Impassioned*) No – our souls all begin the same. Only later, as we live, we either leave their casement crystal clear, so they can look out with ease at the world and observe its movements, or else, enslaved by our baser instincts, we cake it with a layer of filth so thick that nothing at all can ever reach them again...not a thing...not the groans of the exploited, not their accusations, not even the rasping breath of some poor innocent being choked to death...

KAROL   Oh Julka! Mud dries up...it crumbles off on its own!

JULKA   (*Hotly*) Not true! When moral filth dries rock hard, *nothing* will clear it. Just think...today there you were, coming back half drunk...oh don't deny it! Elka's not here, I can speak the truth! You were drunk and you practically reeked of the gutter! I can say it because (*Sadly*) unfortunately life holds very few mysteries for me now! On you pressed, all your faculties dimmed, hauling your soul through ditches and quagmires of one sort or another. And so how, when dawn was breaking, were you supposed to concentrate on listening...to properly distinguish the cries and groans yielded up by yet another tragic night! Your own muddled soul was keening with pain, beating against those crystal walls, caked with their fresh layer of filth! If that's what you're like, you've no one to blame but yourself!

KAROL   (*Lost in thought*) Who knows! Who knows!

Figure 22: Elka gives in to despair. Research performance of Zapolska's *The Man*. University of Reading and POSK Theatre, London, 2004/5. Sophie Green as Elka. Photo by Lib Taylor.

SCENE 3

(Elka, Karol, Julka)

(Elka enters with glasses[51] on a tray and says in a tearful voice)

ELKA   The samovar doesn't want to boil ... I don't know what's happened to it. I've gone and burnt my fingers all for nothing ... oh ... I'm going to get blisters ...

           (Goes to Karol)

           ... let him take a good look – she's burnt her fingers, she's in pain.

           (She cuddles up to him, he moves her aside unwillingly)

KAROL   What about that tea?

ELKA   It hasn't boiled yet. We'll have to buy a new samovar. Our old one's completely ruined.

KAROL   *(Combing his hair)*

              So buy one!

ELKA   And then you'll be so amazed, about what happened to all that money! And that's precisely why, from this moment on, I shan't purchase one single item without your agreement. Should I purchase a samovar?

KAROL   *(Impatiently)* Purchase one – don't purchase one – do whatever the hell you like!

ELKA   *(Offended)* I'm so terribly sorry, dearest love – but some thought and attention does need to go into our home.

KAROL   Our home, home, home – I keep on hearing that word.

ELKA   Apparently not quite often enough, since it always tends to slip your mind.

              (Exits left to the kitchen)

SCENE 4

(Karol, Julka)

KAROL   *(Approaches the desk)* What now? Still writing?

JULKA   Finished. Care to proof read?

KAROL   What for? I know you've been more precise than I ever would be. I can feel myself becoming a feminist.

JULKA   *(With irony)* Having come to experience the blissful results of so-called feminism.[52]

KAROL   Julka!

JULKA   *(Tidying the desk)* What do you want, Karol?

KAROL   Give me your hand.

JULKA   What for?

KAROL   In reconciliation.

JULKA	Are we not reconciled?
KAROL	Doesn't seem like it to me. Either you've an ironic smile, whenever you look at me, or else there's something slighting in your manner...
JULKA	Completely involuntary, I assure you.
KAROL	So you do treat me like this because of unshakeable principles?
JULKA	(Evasively) What do you care about my opinion?
KAROL	Seems I do care, since I'm keen to reform your cast-iron convictions.
JULKA	(With irony) You think that'll happen if I shake your hand.
KAROL	Foiled, Julka, yet again, it seems.

SCENE 5

(Elka, Karol, Julka)

ELKA	(Enters breathless with the tea) Tea is served!
KAROL	(Collects the draft from the desk and puts on his coat) If the boy from the printer's should come, tell him I've already gone to the office.
ELKA	Do drink your tea!
	(Julka exits to kitchen, left)
KAROL	Not a minute to spare. I'll drink some later on, at the tea rooms.
ELKA	(Tearfully) You could just for once drink it at home.
KAROL	Too late! In this house, no-one pays much attention to getting me what I need in good time.
ELKA	I am ill – I can't work.
KAROL	If you're so ill, then lie down. I don't make any demands...I usually eat at the restaurant in any case.
ELKA	Naturally – everything tastes better at the inn. And a wolf's nature beckons him onward! To the woods!

KAROL   No – only at the inn they give me whatever I need in very good time and most of all no-one makes a blasted scene.

ELKA   Oh! My darling! These are all excuses really. Such grave concern you once expressed about having a home – ah, you said – if I could only stay here, have a desk here, have an armchair here, how well I would write! Well then, you now have a desk, you now have a home, what more do you want? Why aren't you writing? Why aren't you ever here?

KAROL   (Evasively) Let me go!

ELKA   (Stubbornly) No! Answer me – why don't you stay in the house. You have a desk, don't you; you have an armchair, alright...

KAROL   (After a pause, quite violently) Want to know why? I have a desk, I have an armchair, I have a house – but I also have you!

ELKA   (Misunderstanding) Well...I did have something to do with it, I'm sure...

KAROL   Ah.

        (Pause)

        Come over here, into the light. Let's take a long hard look at you.

        (Takes her by the shoulders)

ELKA   Huh! Best avoided I think! I look a fright!

KAROL   But I really would love to take a closer look, you're such a peculiar specimen.

ELKA   (Offended, upset) Leave me alone!

KAROL   God bless!

        (Goes through to the hall)

ELKA   (Running after him) Listen, you!

KAROL   (Impatiently) What now?

ELKA   Will you be back for dinner?[53]

KAROL   I will, I will.

ELKA   You'll march off and impale some smoked sausage or other onto a fork and that's
            how much I'll be seeing of you!

KAROL   If I've said I'll be here, then I shall be here.

ELKA   Kiss me.

KAROL   I'm in a hurry. I have to be in court – very special case. Let go of me!

ELKA   I'll let go after you've kissed me.

            (Karol kisses her carelessly and exits. Elka alone, she shakes her head, sighs,
            moving through the room loses her shoe, regards it, surprised that it has holes in it,
            then sits down to the tea left by Karol. Outside the window, the sound of the organ
            grinder – Elka listens for a moment then runs left)

ELKA   Julka! My precious Julka! Give me two grosze![54]

JULKA   (Offstage) What for?

ELKA   The organ grinder! I must give him something. He plays the Miserere so
            beautifully.[55]

JULKA   (As before) There's change on the desk in an ashtray.

ELKA   Thank you.

            (Runs to the desk, wraps money in paper, leans out of the window and throws the
            money down into the street, waits a moment then shouts through the window)

            Hello, up here! Over here! On the pavement, they can't see it, well, further to the
            left, yes, at last!

            (Stands by the window and listens as the organ grinder plays – slowly, however,
            her expression changes; childish delight is replaced by great sorrow, her eyes
            fill with tears, which stream down her cheeks – Elka slides into a chair and sobs
            despairingly)

Figure 23: Julka attempts to comfort her sister. Research performance of Zapolska's *The Man*. University of Reading and POSK Theatre, London, 2004/5. Sophie Green as Elka, Francesca Clark as Julka. Photo by Lib Taylor.

SCENE 6

(Elka, Julka)

(Enter Julka in a dark-coloured dress, holding a bundle of exercise books – she approaches the desk and sees the sobbing Elka)

JULKA   Elka, what is wrong with you?

ELKA   *(Crying)* Oh God – oh my dear Lord.

JULKA   Don't cry like that. You know it's bad for you.

ELKA   Oh God!

JULKA   Have you and Karol been quarrelling again?

ELKA   No.

JULKA   Is it because he's gone out? You've got to understand he has work to do at the office.

ELKA   It's all because of that organ grinder.

JULKA   But you like listening to the organ grinder. You're always pleased – you throw money down.

ELKA   Yes! But I don't know what's wrong with me. Now, whenever I hear it, I feel pleased, and then I feel sad … so very sad … Julka! Julka! I think I'd rather be dead.

JULKA   Be quiet! Calm down! There – he's stopped playing. He'll go somewhere else.

ELKA   *(With despair)* Oh! What have I done!

JULKA   This is no time for despair. You should be looking at life differently now, trying to keep Karol beside you.

ELKA   *(Wiping her eyes again)* Oh it's not that. He's got to stay with me now. It's his responsibility.

JULKA   You're talking like a child. When it comes to relationships, it tends to be women who think in terms of responsibility. And in any case, legally, Karol isn't remotely responsible for you. It's simply a question of moral duty and that depends entirely on how you inflect his feelings towards you.

(Sits at the desk and arranges the books – Elka gets dressed slowly, combs her hair carelessly and pins it up, removes her dressing gown, puts on her skirt and jacket, speaking all the while)

ELKA   Oh … my dear … you understand the whole situation … I'm quite incapable … I simply take things as they come. Karol has told me he loves me, that he'll marry me when he gets his blasted divorce. I have believed him, now he must stay with me forever …

JULKA   Even if he stops loving you?

ELKA   *(Surprised)* And why should he stop loving me?

JULKA   Why did he stop loving his wife?

ELKA   Because … because … do I know … maybe she didn't love him.

JULKA   No, you know very well she did. I'll tell you what it was, alright. She, like you, has no idea how to express her love for him sensibly.

ELKA   Oh, not something else to worry about. Why can't he make an effort to be liked by me and not the other way around!

JULKA   *(Puts down her pen and looks at Elka for a while)* You say that too? You as well?

               (Rises, goes towards her)

               Listen to me, carefully. When you made this an open house for Karol and said to him 'Stay with us', who did you do that for, yourself, or him?

ELKA   For him, of course. He was so unhappy, he complained, about being knocked from pillar to post, he wept. What have I gained? Well – misery – that's all. Plain as day, I did it for him.

JULKA   If that's true, why don't you cultivate that thought? Try to control your egotism, put yourself to one side and give him precedence in all things?

ELKA   I do whatever I can – I'm still the same, as I was before.

JULKA   That's not true. Anyway, even that's not enough for a man. He'll always crave novelty – in view of which, ensure that you provide it and not somebody else.

ELKA   But he told me he doesn't want anyone else.

JULKA   When? Last winter – and now it's already summer.

ELKA   *(Saddened)* So what should I do, Julka?

JULKA   I can't give you specific advice. I've been speaking generally. Just try to make sure that in this house – which you both seem so concerned about – besides a cup of tea, he can still smell the flowers … is that clear enough?

ELKA   Oh! If that's what you mean … I'll buy a whole armful of roses today …

JULKA   *(Regards her with pity)* You take what I say too literally. Never mind.

               (Sits down to work)

ELKA   I'll go into town. I need to make a purchase. Karol will be back for dinner. How about you?

JULKA   No, I'll eat at the canteen. I'll finish marking these exercise books. I have to teach a class at ten, at the day school.[56]

ELKA   (Pause) I always feel so awkward going out. I'm afraid of meeting someone from work – or an acquaintance.

JULKA   What's to be done!

ELKA   You know, I... met... her yesterday. I felt myself go white as a sheet. My knees buckled. I wanted to step back inside the gate but it was too late. She came closer and looked at me. Only in such a strange way... her eyes weren't angry – she only seemed very surprised. And do you know, although she looked terribly smart, she seemed unwell... and pale as wax, maybe even paler than me. I thought she might speak, but she didn't, just stood there staring... I saw because I turned to look at her as well.

            (Approaches the desk and stands fully dressed, with her hat on her head)

            Julka! Perhaps God will have mercy after all and her conscience will be pricked – what do you think?

JULKA   I really don't know, Elka! If she's genuinely capable of love, then she'll step aside.

ELKA   What are you talking about? If she really loves him, she'll want to get him back!

JULKA   No, Elka... real love isn't selfish. Women who genuinely love, have no desire to keep anyone captive.

ELKA   Oh, it's all the same to me, how and when, so long as it happens. I don't know how to pray any more and I dare not.

JULKA   Oh – you should always pray.

ELKA   (Sadly) I'm too scared.

JULKA   (Coldly) Why? God is mercy itself.

ELKA   (Tentatively) In that case I'll call into church when I'm out.

JULKA   Yes, do, Elka.

ELKA   (In tears) Kiss me, Julka! No-one kisses me and means it any more.

            (Julka embraces her nonchalantly, Elka suppressing her tears exits to the hall)

SCENE 7

(Julka then Karol)

(Julka sits for a long while lost in thought and sad, then she lowers the blinds because the sun is in her eyes, she looks through the notebooks, enter Karol)

KAROL   You're still at home. Good.

JULKA   Did you forget something?

KAROL   No – I've come to make you an offer. There's a vacancy in our administration section. Not a bad position. There's lots of competition – I heard them, talking about all the women who've applied. You'll have a desk of your own and the work is altogether quite straightforward. I immediately thought of you, because I feel so sorry, to see you rushing about from lesson to lesson, that is, spoiling your lungs.[57]

JULKA   Thank you so much, but that's not my kind of job.

KAROL   You prefer to teach children.

JULKA   I do. At least I've the very great pleasure of seeing how, under my influence, their intellects are awakened. There, in your administration section, well, figures and numbers, repetition, rather dry, absolutely no appeal.

KAROL   But you'll ruin your health completely.

JULKA   Yet I must surely give something of myself to society.

KAROL   A pointless sacrifice! Society doesn't care about you.

JULKA   That's not true. Perhaps we've lost our sense of this, but care nevertheless is, and must be, expressed. That's how it was, is and will always be – the individual gaining from the work and effort of others. So it's logical that in return I should offer my own work and effort.

KAROL   I thought I'd be making things easier for you.

JULKA   Thank you – why aren't you in court?

KAROL   They're reading out the verdict. We'll be printing the whole thing anyway. There's plenty of time.[58]

.   *(Pause)*

Figure 24: Nina tells Elka she agrees to the divorce. Research performance of Zapolska's *The Man*. University of Reading and POSK Theatre, London, 2004/5. Victoria Brown as Nina. Photo by Lib Taylor.

JULKA   Karol.

KAROL   Yes, Julka?

JULKA   Tell me, what will happen to Elka?

KAROL   What do you mean, what'll happen to Elka – I don't understand.

JULKA   Have you edged any closer to divorce?

KAROL   *(Confused)* I've had no time for all that recently.

JULKA   *(Gravely)* You really must find the time – without delay. Elka feels more than you suppose...

KAROL   I doubt it! I'd no idea such a thoughtless, thick-skinned creature could even exist. God only knows what's happened to her. How different she was in the winter. Ha!

Ha! Well, tell me yourself Julka, wasn't she more subtle then? Very perceptive, don't you think? It was a real pleasure spending my evenings here … and now …

JULKA   Has she really changed all that much?

KAROL   (Paces the room smoking) Terribly – terribly, beyond recognition.

JULKA   And let me tell you Karol, that this Elka is still the very same Elka – just as Nina was the same Nina before and after the wedding. Only your repeated disappointments, they're partly your own fault. I told you once that you're an average human being and that's the way things are. I must admit I'm exactly the same. However, you look at every single woman with whom you're intimate through either an artistic or sensual lens … or else … I don't know … you stick some halo on their heads. And when you've finally got what you want … it goes a bit crooked – can't have been stuck there very securely in the first place. You lay the blame for your own lack of spiritual resilience on women and cry 'Ha! She has changed!'

KAROL   Take my word for it – that could never happen with you. The halo would stay firmly in place.

JULKA   (Surprised) Me? Who was talking about me?

KAROL   (Somewhat confused) We're talking about women.

JULKA   I don't count.

KAROL   (Passionately) Oh excuse me, but you do! Oho! Listen – I've known you since the winter, just like Elka and I always have something to talk about with you. I always find you engaging, indeed, one might say, increasingly engaging. Every day I discover a new attribute. And so you see, there are women who do improve on closer acquaintance.

JULKA   What on earth are you talking about, closer? Put me in the same position as Nina or Elka, I'd soon seem rather lacklustre.

KAROL   (Fervently) Upon my word you would not!

JULKA   Clap-trap!

KAROL   (With enthusiasm) I mean it – I give you my word!

(Pause, after a while Karol begins to pace the room again, Julka writes)

JULKA   (Not lifting her eyes from the books) Time to go back to the courthouse, perhaps?

KAROL   Are you trying to get rid of me? Am I disturbing you?

JULKA   Hardly!

KAROL   *(Irritated)* Oh, I know, what am I to you? Fluff, dust! I can't even manage to disturb you.

JULKA   *(Putting aside her pen)* I can see you're very upset. But since you do want my attention, allow me to once again raise the subject of Elka.

KAROL   Elka? Mm, what on earth can we say about Elka? What's to be said about *her*? When she's at home she talks about herself so much it's more than enough for three.

JULKA   I'll summarize briefly.

          (Turns to him and looks him in the eye)

          If you're no longer in love with that woman either, then at least have the strength to not let her sense it... have you understood me?

KAROL   *(Confused)* How do you know I don't love Elka?

JULKA   I don't know anything! All I'm saying is, 'if'.

KAROL   Given that you consider me to be an average man, why insist on heroism?

JULKA   Heroism? Who said anything about heroism?

KAROL   I did. Because living with Elka, without loving her, 'til death us do part, would be an act of sheer heroism on my part.

JULKA   My dear man, average men have a certain average dose of strength, sometimes referred to by them as adherence to one's responsibilities. That's the strength I'm asking you to demonstrate – until her time comes, naturally – because, in your case, the 'unto death' scenario lacks plausibility.

KAROL   You don't know me! I long for nothing more than a soul-mate – someone to understand me. Can there be greater joy than securing as a long-term companion, a woman with whom one can talk! That is the apex of joy!

JULKA   You can't have everything at once. Who knows whether Nina and Elka didn't also dream of something rather different when they joined with you.

KAROL   *(Obstreperously)* Oh! They love me just the way I am!

JULKA   That is proof of their strength of heart and the sincere and beautiful directness of their untrammelled commitment to you.

KAROL   I too would have the same strength of heart and ability to commit if I came across the right sort of woman for me.

JULKA   A few months ago, Elka was the right sort of woman for you. Today, things have progressed to such a degree that she must remain your woman forever.

(Karol sits morbidly in an armchair)

The divorce proceedings need to be speeded up. I ask that you accomplish this.

KAROL   I will not get down on my knees and beg Nina to give her consent nor to appear in person with her own version of events.

JULKA   Nina is currently otherwise disposed towards Elka. I have concrete proof. I know she's curious about us and aware of our living arrangements. Who knows, it might just be an auspicious moment.

KAROL   *(Bored)* I'll think about it.

(Pause)

Listen Julka, must you always take me for a complete idiot?

JULKA   Heaven forfend!

KAROL   No, no, I can see, I can feel it, you're always twittering on about average human beings...

(Outburst)

How can I be extraordinary? Gunpowder's been discovered, our great classics have been written,[59] Gibraltar's been conquered...what's to be done? Well? What?

JULKA   *(Arranging her exercise books)* Shallow and trivial.

KAROL   *(Leaps up and seizes her hands)* Julka! Julka!

JULKA   *(Surprised, looks at him for a while, disengages her hands)* What now?

KAROL (Confused) I don't know – I just don't know...

(Moves away from her, goes to the window and leans his forehead against the windowpane – Julka arranges the exercise books and wants to exit left, he turns at the rustle of her skirts and saying nothing reaches out his hands to her, she looks at him with growing amazement)

JULKA Release me. I have to get changed...I'm going...to take the lesson.

(Exits left, Karol remains alone, stands leaning against the window ledge for a while, then begins whistling, breaks off, paces, smokes a cigarette, eventually sits in the armchair and looks at the door through which Julka has exited)

SCENE 8

(Karol, Elka)

(Elka enters right, holding a basket filled with provisions and a bunch of roses, seeing Karol she stops, delighted, puts the roses on the desk, runs towards him, flings her arms around his neck and inclines her cheek)

KAROL (Irritated) You've gone mad.

ELKA Kiss me.

KAROL Let go!

ELKA I'll let go when you've kissed me.

(Karol kisses her)

ELKA (Flirtatiously) Why has he come? Could it, perchance, be for his breakfast? No time to prepare it just yet, but she will make haste.

KAROL I have in fact been meaning to ask you for quite some time to refrain from addressing me in that tone of voice. It's silly, it's pathetic, there's no sense in this pretending to be a child that you do.

ELKA (Aggrieved) Once upon a time, you said you liked that about me, because it was an integral part of my charm.

KAROL I don't recall saying anything to that effect.

ELKA You always used to refer to yourself as 'he' – or 'Lolo'.⁶⁰

KAROL What? Pardon me, what? Don't tell me such trivial nonsense ever took place. Can't you just be … a woman?

ELKA I do think I in fact am – a woman.

KAROL But a woman-person – a woman-person!

ELKA And are there women-animals?

KAROL Oh there are! Yes there are! Women-ducks, women-geese! Women … oh you wouldn't understand …

ELKA For sure – you understand far more than I do. But I'm not completely stupid. You said yourself that the thing you look for most in a woman is a warm, kind heart.

KAROL Well yes. That goes without saying. You have heart. A heart and nothing more.

(Goes to desk and in looking for notes knocks flowers to the ground)

What is this mess.

ELKA Oh.

(Regards the flowers for a while then purses her lips, as though engaged in some internal conflict and says in an altered tone) Should I prepare something for your mid-morning snack?

KAROL Thank you – once preparations have commenced the proceedings could take more than a little time. I'm going to the office.

ELKA *(Feigning happiness)* I can see you want to make a scene. But you won't succeed. I've decided to endure everything patiently.

KAROL One would think you were being tortured or executed.

ELKA Well, you're not physically chopping my head off, that's for sure, but you can't very well tell me my life is a bed of roses.

KAROL A bed of roses! What an expression! Like one of those sickly poems in greeting cards or the sentiments of a washerwoman … or a seamstress … a bed of roses![61]

ELKA *(Sadly)* I speak in the only way I know. I speak just as I used to.

KAROL	You must nevertheless admit, my dear, that having listened to such turns of phrase it subsequently becomes difficult to extricate oneself and write in the style of an intelligent person.[62]
ELKA	I speak with you so rarely.
KAROL	Whatever could it be that you wish to discuss?
ELKA	(Quietly) You always find something to talk about with Julka.
KAROL	(Suddenly) I should think so too! You know why? Because she is a woman-person – a woman person!
ELKA	Once upon a time, you found her irritating, you made fun of her, called her an old maid, a socialist…
KAROL	(Livid) Oh did I? When was that? Refrain from spouting such nonsense or I shall go to the office immediately.
ELKA	(Bursting out) And so ladies and gentlemen, this really is quite beyond the pale, at every single step you accuse me of lying, you latch on to the tiniest thing, I daren't utter a single word any more, and what have I done to deserve it? Been unhappy? Been good! Been loyal, like some sort of dog…
	(Pause)
	…and you could speed up the divorce.
KAROL	I will speed it up, alright. Just leave me alone.
	(Sits at desk and puts his head in his hands, Elka looks at him for a while, approaches him and stands at the opposite side of the desk)
ELKA	Karol!
KAROL	What do you want?
ELKA	Don't be angry!
KAROL	I'm not angry.
ELKA	(Comes closer) Do you love me forever?
KAROL	Why must you keep on asking me?

ELKA   But do say it...

KAROL   You know very well...

ELKA   In that case, kiss me, only for a long, long time, like we used to...

KAROL   No, no, leave me alone, I've got a sore throat, you'll catch your death and then what...

ELKA   You've probably picked something up from scavenging about all over the place, do stay at home this evening, we'll sit down together, just the three of us, Julka won't be going anywhere today, will you stay?

KAROL   I'll stay.

ELKA   *(Pleased)* That's good. That is very good. She says thank...that is – no...I'm sorry...I thank him – no...you – oh, anyway, what's the harm, she thanks him nicely and then exits to prepare a late breakfast, breakfast, breakfast!!

            (Runs off left bumping into Julka, who is wearing a hat)

            Julka! You stay too! I'll make both of you a late breakfast.

JULKA   I can't. I suppose I could come back in an hour or two, for dinner, if it matters that much.

ELKA   Hurrah! It will be a momentous occasion. Karol will also be dining at home! I can be found in the kitchen.

            (She runs out)

SCENE 9

(Julka, Karol)

JULKA   Thank you, Karol.

KAROL   What for, Julka?

JULKA   You must have been good to Elka – that helps to wipe the slate clean.

KAROL   Oh, it was nothing. But I treated you atrociously just now. I've been trying to work out why I did that. I've cross-examined myself. And come to the conclusion that it's all your fault. Why must you maltreat me?

JULKA	Chasing your own tail again, aren't you? And you want me to join in. I wouldn't say I maltreat you exactly.
KAROL	But why do you refuse to acknowledge my worth?
JULKA	Do I try to force you to acknowledge my worth?
KAROL	Can't you at least tell me which of my character traits, in your eyes, primarily renders me a so-called average man?
JULKA	Certainly I can – easily explained. In your life, the love question is pre-eminent. You're one of those people who measure their lives by the number of dramatic love affairs they conduct. You harness and surrender everything to your pursuit of love. If you were a writer, sensuality would be your theme – if a painter, amorous scenes would sprawl across your canvas.
KAROL	What's to be done! In every pack of cards there must be a knave of hearts.[63]
JULKA	Some societies find whole legions of knaves indispensible in sustaining their superlative erotic activities. [However, societies also exist in which your constant Konrad is far more necessary than your greedy Gustave.[64]
KAROL	I quote: "Have a heart and look to your heart!"
JULKA	I complete: "A heart for the millions!"] In your position, you could do so much! This very day! You see your work at the press as hard labour! You see yourself as some galley slave. If you could only move beyond your blinkered 'sexual-artistic collisions',[65] you might appreciate the wide vista opening up before you! That flimsy little paper rag gets through to places books will simply never reach! And the words you choose really do live – they have immediacy! They're not dead! You rouse people to action! You shape people's thoughts! People's thoughts!
KAROL	Delusions!
JULKA	No, Karol, now let me go – I really must be going. I'm needed at the school.
KAROL	Stay a while. It's so good, such a pleasure, to talk with you.
JULKA	Just now you accused me of maltreating you.
KAROL	Then go ahead and maltreat me – I much prefer that to your indifference and silence.
JULKA	Why does my opinion matter so much?

KAROL   (Quietly) I don't know. I really don't know ...

          (Pause, Julka bends down, picks up the flowers, puts them in a vase on the desk)

          Julka, do accept the job in administration. When you're near me I'll work more
          efficiently, I'll change my habits. I can sense it.

JULKA   No.

KAROL   You are an egotist!

JULKA   In this particular instance, yes – I am. Having weighed the potential fruits of your
          labour, conducted under my influence, against the yield of my present occupation,
          I'm fully convinced that society will reap greater benefit from the latter; hence my
          heartfelt response – no!

KAROL   Why is it so hard to believe that I could also make a more substantial contribution,
          give more of myself – create something great, with your assistance!

JULKA   (Wearied) Because only those people who work hard at transforming themselves,
          who grow in spirit, who accomplish all this with a clear conscience, can perform
          pure and great things and you ...[66]

KAROL   (Passionately) And me?

JULKA   (Looking him in the eye) And you are still passionately chasing your own tail.

KAROL   Julka!

JULKA   Let me go. I've always considered you to be an average man, make sure I don't
          discover that you are ...

KAROL   That I am?

JULKA   Something far worse ...

          (Exits quickly, Karol remains alone, thinks, goes to kitchen and says to Elka)

KAROL   I'm going to the courthouse. At the very least try to ensure that breakfast is ready
          by the time I get back.

          (Deep in thought takes his hat and exits to the hall, on his way meets Nina
          entering)

SCENE 10

(Nina, Karol)

(Nina is dressed elaborately in a summer dress, she is in fact very pale; entering, she sees Karol, pales even more momentarily, closes her eyes, then revives and moves forward without looking at him)

NINA   *(Nervously, in a broken voice)* Is...the younger Miss Korecka in? The door was ajar...

KAROL   *(Confused, turns his hat over and over in his hands)* Yes, they've a peculiar habit here, they never close the door – I've told them so many times...

NINA   *(Slowly turns her head towards him and regards him with a certain superiority)* May I speak with the younger Miss Korecka?

KAROL   Certainly, Miss Korecka is in. I would, incidentally, be curious to know why you, madam, are here.

NINA   That is a matter for Miss Korecka and myself! Oh! No call for anxiety, sir, I'm not planning to make a scene.

KAROL   And yet, knowing your nervous disposition, madam...

NINA   *(With a sad smile)* I've been seriously ill, sir – a breakdown – I wouldn't have the strength to make a scene. I thought you'd be at the office.

                (Weakens)

KAROL   *(Forgetting himself)* May I offer you a chair?

NINA   No, thank you – one thing only – do go outside, I cannot...look at you...it's all too taxing...

KAROL   *(Surprised and irritated)* You hate me that much?

NINA   *(Quietly)* No, only I'd managed to forget what you look like and now it's all come flooding back...

ELKA   *(Offstage)* Karol! Who are you talking to?

NINA   *(Passes her hand across her body)* That's her!

(Karol agitated, doesn't know what to do, grabs his hat and says quickly)

KAROL   Well, there we have it – I simply must...be going...

(Exits rapidly)[67]

SCENE 11

(Elka, Nina)

(Nina stands looking indecisive, eventually she makes a gesture as if to say 'oh well, never mind', goes towards the door behind which Elka is standing)

NINA   *(Opening the door)* Do accept my apologies, madam...but I need to speak to you.

         (Elka runs in, she is wearing an apron, her hands are covered in flour, seeing Nina she stands stock still)

ELKA   It's you?

NINA   Yes it is...

         (Pause)

ELKA   *(Distressed)* What can I do for you, madam?

NINA   *(With some effort)* To begin with, I need to sit down, I've been ill, I'm still very weak.

ELKA   Please.

         (Indicates a chair)

         I am so sorry...I have you all covered in flour...

NINA   Where?

         (Perfunctorily checks her dress)

         There's no harm done.

ELKA   Saints be praised!

         (Pause)

NINA   I've come to tell you I consent to the divorce.

ELKA   *(With great joy)* Oh! Dear, dear madam! Thank you – thank you – thank you ... but – perhaps you don't really mean it ...?

NINA   No – I've decided. I know the whole story. I have a heart as well, you see and now, I pity you. You must feel so ashamed, I know and your shame can only increase. I've thought about it long and hard. And of course, in addition, you're not the one to blame because he wasn't living with me any more when you met him. That is my conclusion.

ELKA   You're very good. I thought all you cared about was fashion ...

NINA   Don't think I'm doing this chiefly for your benefit. I'm doing it for your child. Because it must of course have a surname, since that is the custom. Children without surnames are subject to vicious abuse.

ELKA   *(Starts crying)* But that's ridiculous – it's not their fault that their mother was a bad woman.

NINA   *(Holding back her tears)* Dear madam, you really mustn't cry. It does me no end of harm. I simply can't watch – my nervous disorder. All that time before ... this ... happened to you ... I wanted to get Karol back, because I was utterly convinced that I meant more to him than you do ...

ELKA   *(Humbly)* Of course ... because you were ... his wife.

NINA   Indeed. But you'll be the mother of his child. I saw it straight away, this was something so important, something that bound him to you very strongly and I told myself ... it's all over ... that you'd better be his wife. So I wanted to inform you personally that I'm giving my consent, because I've been causing you a great deal of anxiety and really all I want to do is make you happy. I must tell you that I've always imagined motherhood to be something extraordinary ... and then it occurred to me that when I have a baby, I won't think about frocks or anything else ... only I'll be able to ... dress my child ...

            (Pause)

            Besides, you've caused me untold suffering and I remain in a state of nervous exertion ...

ELKA   *(Humbly)* I am ... so terribly sorry, madam.

NINA   *(Pause, examines herself)* In that case, I'll take my leave ... tell him I'll testify after
            all, as he wishes, let him send my lawyer the script for the consistory[68] and I'll learn
            off by heart all the required responses. And let that be an end to the matter ...

            (Rises)

            I wish you joy!

ELKA   *(Crying)* On behalf of me ... and my child ... may God reward you!

NINA   I hope you're very happy, madam.

            *(Exits swiftly, choking on her own tears, Elka accompanies her to the hallway and
            returns, she throws herself onto the chair near the desk and dissolves into spasms
            of weeping)*

ELKA   Oh God! Oh my dear Lord! What good fortune! What good fortune!

SCENE 12

(Elka, Karol)

KAROL   *(Enters swiftly, approaches Elka)* I've been waiting for her to leave, under the stairs,
            she refuses, doesn't she? I was sure of it! Well – the usual story. Don't cry – it really
            makes no difference! We'll just have to persuade ourselves out of marriage.

ELKA   *(Joyfully)* But ... no ... no ... on the contrary!

KAROL   What do you mean, on the contrary?

ELKA   I'm weeping with joy! Do you hear me! With joy! What a good, kind-hearted – a
            saintly woman! She gives her consent – it's quite alright, she said! That you should
            send to her lawyer, whatever she needs to say for the consistory and she'll say it
            exactly so, word for word.

KAROL   *(Shocked)* She said that?

ELKA   Yes ... yes, she did ... and she was very good to me and polite ... and friendly ...

            (Kneels before Karol)

            We're going to be married ... do you hear me ... at last we'll be husband and
            wife ... for the rest of our lives ... we'll really be ... together! But when will it happen?
            When?

(*Karol is in a state of shock, he slides into a chair and stares at the ground, mortified*)

ELKA   (*Unsettled*) Karol! Karol! I'm talking to you and you're not listening! Loluś! Loluś![69] Aren't you pleased? Lolek…

(*Karol suddenly emits a nervous, muffled cry of disgust, leaps up and goes towards the window, leans against the pane and remains thus; Elka rises, taking a few steps towards him*)

ELKA   (*Choked*) Karol… Karol… surely you… will marry me?

KAROL   (*Without turning from the window – through his teeth*) I'm not sure.

ELKA   (*Breathlessly*) What? What did you say? But you have to…

(*Karol, turning suddenly in his place by the window, his expression has altered – he is pale, his lips are firmly set, he holds his hands behind his back*)

KAROL   I have to? And who says so? I do not have to! No! No! I do not!

ELKA   (*Her voice faltering*) Oh! Oh!

(*She collapses on the ground in a faint*)

(*Curtain falls*)

ACT 3

(*The room is the same as in the previous acts. Only the bureau and the armchair stand in their former positions. It is dusk. The stove is lit. In front of the stove, wrapped in a shawl, sits Julka. On the couch, also wrapped in a shawl, sits Elka. She is propped up with a pillow in a white pillowcase. Elka is pale, she has deteriorated dramatically during her illness. She is wearing a colourful morning kaftan and a skirt. Her face is much paler and her hair is combed smoothly into a middle parting, so that it covers her ears. A great transformation is evident in Elka's countenance. She is more beautiful and graceful. Her behaviour and manner have acquired more grace. Julka is also somehow different. Her manner towards Elka is warmer – more sincere and maternal*)

SCENE 1

(*Julka, Elka*)

JULKA   Elka, are you asleep?

ELKA   No, I'm not.

JULKA   Are you crying?

ELKA   No, I haven't cried for the past few days.

JULKA   That's good. You'll make a speedier recovery.

            (Pause)

ELKA   Julka, will they take me back at the agency?

JULKA   I can't say. So many women apply when vacancies come up…Elka…I have my doubts.

ELKA   If they don't take me back, it'll be all because…well, because…of this. The news must've spread abroad by now…

JULKA   Don't think like that Elka! If they don't take you back, it's simply proof that there's too little employment to go around and too many poor women in the world.

ELKA   *(Bursts out)* Remember the saying – each of God's creatures has its own place under the sun? What do we live for? Tell me? Ha! Even you, so much wiser than I am, there's nothing but destitution in return for your work. Now I too have fallen like a weight on your shoulders! Your own sister! What my illness must have cost you!

JULKA   Please don't think of it like that.

ELKA   *(After a pause)* Julka!

JULKA   What's the matter?

ELKA   You…didn't accept anything from him, did you?

JULKA   Not a thing – I can swear to that.

ELKA   If I found out he'd paid for one single spoonful of my medicine, I think I'd die…or… for a little coffin. Julka!

JULKA   *(Approaches her and strokes her hair)* Elka…please…

ELKA   That little coffin…

            (After a pause, takes Julka's hand)

            Tell me – was there a priest at the cemetery?

JULKA   Of course, Elka, yes – a kind, grey-haired priest, he made the sign of the cross, he didn't ask any questions...he...[70]

ELKA   Autumn is upon us so suddenly! When I became sick, it was still the summer. It seemed to last forever...why couldn't I have died as well?

JULKA   I'll light the lamp, it'll be more cheerful.

ELKA   *(Wrapping the shawl around her more tightly)*

        No! Please don't. It's twilight...a good time to talk. Are you listening Julka?

JULKA   *(Sitting by the stove)* Yes.

ELKA   You must tell me if I bore you. And you won't mock me?

JULKA   No, Elka – I won't.

ELKA   *(Tentatively)* I've changed so much Julka. I lay there without moving for days on end but I wasn't asleep, I was thinking. I can't find the words to tell you exactly how I've changed, but I feel it – for the better...

JULKA   Pain, suffering – they transform everyone...

ELKA   In the beginning, whenever I remembered it...and...him...what he did to me...I despised him. The more I cried, the more my heart softened and the anger passed. Now, whenever I think of him, I haven't the strength for rage. It's hard to remember what he looks like.

JULKA   *(Softly)* Too many tears in the way!

ELKA   One thought keeps coming back to me – it just won't leave me alone. Today is the day, Julka, I've resolved to tell you. I mustn't delay a moment longer.

JULKA   I'm listening.

ELKA   Thank you.

        (Pause)

        Does he...come here?

JULKA   In the beginning, he enquired at the caretaker's every single day. Now, I meet him on occasion, by the gate.

ELKA Does he...talk to you? Oh! You mustn't think I'm interested for my own sake...it's all over. There are other reasons.

JULKA We have exchanged a few words. I told him about you...that...it...is not alive any more...that you have been...so ill. I'd no desire to speak with him at greater length.

ELKA That's good! If you should ever meet him again, don't talk to him, Julka.

JULKA (Approaches the couch) Stay calm. I'll do anything within my power. What do you want me to do?

ELKA I've been thinking...of her.

JULKA Who?

ELKA Of her...his wife! I dream about her all the time. She's always so sad, so terribly sad – so kind. It was clear to me then – she loved him and probably loves him still. As she was leaving, she could barely hold back her tears. I felt immediately that she would bring me no happiness...and I was right...

JULKA What is this, Elka?

ELKA I want...her...to know that I'll never marry him. That's why she need not divorce him.

JULKA But they won't be reconciled...

ELKA Who knows – he vowed he'd marry me...it's just the same. I want God to stop punishing me for her tears and to let me stop dreaming about her all the time. There's something else as well.

JULKA (Patiently) Yes, Elka?

ELKA Don't be angry! Yesterday I read my fortune, with cards, on the counterpane. Are you angry?[71]

JULKA (Patiently, with a smile) No – no, I'm not.

ELKA An ace of clubs[72]...came up...and whenever the rain starts beating against the windowpanes, I become so afraid that she...that she...may try to...

(Buries her face in the cushions)

JULKA	Don't be afraid, don't be afraid, please – Elka!
ELKA	*(Avidly)* She must be informed immediately … immediately.
JULKA	Perhaps you could write her a …
ELKA	Oh no! It's quite impossible to write something like this down. Besides, she mocked me, remember. She needs to be told. To have it explained. Listen to me! You! You must go and see her …
JULKA	Elka!
ELKA	*(Kissing her hands)* Please go! For me! If you don't, when you're out I'll go there myself and tell her I apologize. That's all I want. You'll see! I will do it!
JULKA	Don't you dare! You don't have permission to go out.
ELKA	Then go … immediately. I will be able to sleep peacefully and she will be happy. Julka! Please, go now.
JULKA	This minute?
ELKA	Yes. It's already dark. No-one will see you. After this, it'll all be over. Go, Julka. She was so anxious! At the very least, put an end to her tears.
JULKA	Alright, calm yourself, I will see her. But they'll never be reconciled.
ELKA	It doesn't matter. Our duty will be done.
JULKA	I'll light the lamp.
ELKA	*(Picks up Julka's jacket and hat)* I'll light it myself.
JULKA	Here's your sweet wine,[73] here are your biscuits, have a bite to eat …
ELKA	*(Rises from the sofa)* Yes, yes! My heart feels lighter.
JULKA	*(Dressed)* I won't be long. Please try to keep calm. It's not that far. Where's my key …
ELKA	*(Stopping her)* Tomorrow we should ask for the locks to be changed.
JULKA	What for?

ELKA   Because he... has a key...

JULKA   *(Stopping her)* Don't you trust yourself Elka? If that's the case, I won't leave.

ELKA   I do, Julka, I do trust myself... only I... don't trust him.

              (They are both standing centre stage)

JULKA   Elka. I'm not sure about this.

ELKA   I've changed, older sister – I have changed.

SCENE 2

(Elka, Karol)

(When Elka is alone, she approaches the table and lights the lamp, she drinks a glass of malaga, in which she dips a small biscuit. Her movements are heavy, uncertain – she coughs. She wraps herself in a shawl and sits on the couch once more. The scrape of a key in the lock – Elka raises her head. Footsteps are heard in the hallway. Karol appears in the doorway. Elka, shocked, kneels on the couch and with outstretched hands, as though shielding herself from an apparition – she cries out...)

ELKA   No! No!

KAROL   *(In his coat, hat in hand, pale)* No, don't be afraid... is Julka not here?

ELKA   *(Regaining her composure)* She's gone out – why... are you... why?

KAROL   *(Confused)* I wanted to ask her how you are. I assumed you'd be asleep, that I'd find Julka here and ask her...

ELKA   *(Still on the couch)* I'm alright. I have been ill.

KAROL   *(As before)* I know and I am very, very sorry... though of course...

ELKA   Never mind, it's nothing, it's over, I had a good doctor and medicine... Julka was with me...

KAROL   Ah, it's all for the best. All for the best...

              (Pause, the rain is heard beating against the window)

              Will Julka not be coming back today?

ELKA   She'll be back, she hasn't gone far. Do you wish to speak with her, sir?

KAROL   Yes, she's always in a great hurry to get away from me.

ELKA   What about? Perhaps you'd better tell me directly.

            (Karol is silent)

            If it's about our marriage, sir, then I'd prefer to discuss it straight away.

KAROL   *(Rapidly)* Another time, perhaps – you're still weak, madam, you don't have the
            strength.

ELKA   No – no. Better to deal with things promptly. I think you must have come here
            because your conscience has been pricked and you want to marry me. But I was
            close to death. Everything seems clearer to me now. If it were all to come around
            a second time, things would be very different. No need for anxiety – no need to
            propose marriage. I am not for you – you are not for me. Do go away and leave
            us alone. May God forgive you, sir. We'll manage.

            (With great simplicity)

            I will also try to forgive you!

KAROL   *(Coming to his senses)* The fault was not exactly mine.

ELKA   One day God will decide which one of us is most at fault. I have paid dearly for
            my sins…

            (Softly)

            … most dearly … I was so ill I couldn't complain, I couldn't cry … I was so frightened,
            when they carried out that little coffin. They carried it out of the house quietly, they
            thought, I was asleep. Something tugged at my heart … whispered 'I've gone away
            now – I'll never come back to you … ever …' I think I have paid the Lord everything
            I owe him for my sins.

            (Pause, the wind is heard rattling the window, Elka wipes her eyes)

            Never mind. It's over and done with now. I'll never marry you, sir. Never! Between
            me and you, that little coffin, always. And if you don't want to be the object of yet
            another person's resentment, you could at least … go back to your wife. I didn't say
            anything then, but it's perfectly clear. She still loves you, very much …

KAROL   *(Energetically)* That is completely out of the question.

ELKA   You're wrong. She could forgive you more easily. Not like me.

KAROL   I, however, cannot bring myself to forgive her. This has got nothing to do with you any more.

ELKA   No – you'll do whatever you think is best.

          (Pause, Elka observes Karol tentatively)

          You don't look very well, sir.

KAROL   I'm not.

ELKA   Perhaps it's … all that restaurant food, again.

KAROL   It could be.

ELKA   *(With great generosity)* You should turn your life around. Will you?

KAROL   *(Impatiently, turning to look at the door)* Will Miss Julka be here soon?

ELKA   She said she wouldn't be too long …

          (She leans against the arm of the couch and sits like this for a long while, tears begin to flow from beneath her closed eyelids. Karol looks at her and, noticing that she is weeping, bites his lip impatiently – Elka, quietly and coldly)

          Now I remember everything.

KAROL   You've distressed yourself. I'll leave.

ELKA   *(As before)* No. You're here, but I can't see you properly. You're like a ghost – do you understand? That other man was different. You're a complete stranger to me, sir.

          (The scrape of the key in the lock)

          Julka!

          (Karol, confused, retreats towards the window, enter Julka, quickly)

SCENE 3

(Julka, Karol, Elka)

JULKA   *(Approaches Elka – doesn't see Karol)* She's not in. I left a calling card. What's the matter? Elka! You're white as a sheet!

ELKA   *(Indicating Karol)* He's here – over there.

JULKA   *(Turns swiftly)* You, here, sir! To what end?

KAROL   I thought I might see you. I want to talk.

JULKA   To me?

ELKA   I've already told him. My decision! I will never be your wife. Never! You may go free, sir.

JULKA   Do you hear, sir?

KAROL   I hear.

JULKA   And in spite of this, you do not leave?

KAROL   No, because I've come here to speak with you. I have wished to do so on several occasions, in the street. You have avoided prolonged contact every time.

JULKA   I've got nothing to say to you, sir.

KAROL   But I have – to you, madam.

ELKA   Julka! Don't. It's quite alright. If he wants to talk, I'll go through to my room … I'm really very sleepy and I'm cold.

JULKA   Yes – you're still too weak to be unsettled like this. Come and lie down.

                (To Karol)

                Wait here.

SCENE 4

(Karol then Julka)

(Karol paces the room for a while then sits down, suddenly remembers that he is not in his own home, leaps up, goes to the bureau, seizes the double photo frame, notices Julka's photograph, takes it out of the frame and puts it in his pocket – at this moment enter Julka, who, seeing the movement, approaches him with threat in her eyes)

JULKA   Why do you need my photograph?

KAROL   *(Quickly and quietly)* Because I love you to distraction...I cannot live without you.

                (Julka moves away from him and looks at him wide-eyed)

                What a wretched description of my feelings...too abrupt, probably too brutal, repressed for too long...I...love...I love you...and now it seems that...I am certain it was...you I loved from the moment I crossed this threshold.

JULKA   Is that what you wanted to tell me?

KAROL   That and one thing more.

                (Approaches her)

JULKA   *(Moving away with superiority)* Keep your distance.

KAROL   You needn't worry. I hold you in the highest regard – rather like a statue. I will worship from a distance, if I must.

JULKA   Why should I listen to this?

KAROL   And why not? Only an average woman would fail to understand what's happening inside me. At the very least have the decency to hear me out! You are responsible for this.

JULKA   I am?

KAROL   You cannot deny it. Alongside your sister, you seemed such a spiritual being. Your every word, the subtlest movement, the smallest gesture, was imbued with some kind of...superiority. Gradually, you bound me to you. Again and again I've heard you repeat 'you are average'. Now I see that's not precisely what you mean. You are different from every other woman. You go about things – in a different way. You have bewitched me.

JULKA (*Rapidly*) Ah! That's what I've been waiting for! I am different! Therein resides my great power. You tell me you love me because I'm whiter than white, distant, spiritually potent, rather like a statue. Turn your gaze on yourself. Had you met *me* on the same evening that you met poor Elka, now you'd be losing your mind for *her* in exactly the same way – *she'd* be the one who seems ... different.

KAROL (*Fervently*) No, that's not true. You've overpowered me, not because you're different but because you simply are – yourself, a woman-person, a complete woman, fit to be a man's lifelong companion, his friend, adviser ...

JULKA ... though not, presumably, his lover. I could never satisfy you. The enemy of each woman – her perilous enemy – is every other woman. The one that possesses a kind heart, may fail to exert an aesthetic impression, the one that exerts an aesthetic impression, may ultimately fail to arouse, and the one that arouses – a woman more spiritual vanquishes her. And so on. Quite the vicious circle!

KAROL You appear to rationalize coldly – with distance and indifference. I need you to steady me, to still a mind that wrestles constantly with thoughts of you! You could turn me into a man of work and action.

JULKA (*With irony and greater seriousness*) For how long? Until your desire to be aroused, your artistic sensibility, or your need for kindness and comfort cry out for satisfaction?

KAROL You speak very plainly. And so I must tell you that the very thought of you ...

JULKA Sensuality, spirit, intelligence – how are they connected? You've got no idea what has possessed you. Believe me – it's just a passing fancy to catch what has slipped through the net.

KAROL I'll waste away without you, I can feel that now.

JULKA Impossible! You'll leave in pursuit of another woman. Your unquenchable thirst! You've created a miniature world of intrigue, desire, romantic adventure – Gullliver in the Land of Lilliput – there are thousands like you. You drive yourself to insanity, yes, you like it that way, and so it goes on – deaf to everything, dumb about everything that bears no relation to your egotistical, erotic affairs. The tragedy of social struggle, the glorious reign of death in our times – it's quite impossible to achieve some perspective, isn't that right? Can't you see? It's too late now.[74]

KAROL You're cold as ice. Yet still you beckon me on. Peace, repose – I can find all that in you, my stability depends on you! Believe this – you have changed me. I no longer recognize myself.

JULKA   In what respect?

KAROL   *(Confused pause)* Well, I...

JULKA   Do you not, more than is usual, seek to engage others in conversation about yourself, about your affairs? When the child died, I went to look for you. I wanted to tell you all about it. I went to your home, to your office – I was told you were out on business. I saw you, eating, drinking, throwing tit bits from your table...

         (Pause)

KAROL   I went there to drown my sorrows – I was looking for a distraction...

JULKA   *(With irony and sadness)* Nowhere to rest your head![75]

KAROL   *(Livid)* Julka! Julka! How to convince? How to plead?

         (Pause)

         Have mercy! At least try to understand me...

JULKA   I'm here. I've been listening, for how long? That's mercy. Now leave us alone. Your persistence is most impressive but we cannot see you any more.

KAROL   Julka...Julka...your company...our conversations...your voice...I've got used to all this ... must I deny myself? I cannot bear it! What's to become of me now?

JULKA   Your wife had also got used to you and she had to deny herself everything...Elka...

KAROL   That is completely different.

JULKA   How?

KAROL   It's easier for them, they are women – I am a man.

JULKA   Your powers of logic astound me – perhaps you'd care to leave.

KAROL   Are you trying to get rid of me?

JULKA   Oh no, I indicate the same route by which the coffin of your child was carried out of our home. We grieved, we mourned, where were you?

KAROL   *(Livid)* Julka! Julka! Be still – don't enrage me!

JULKA   (*Coldly and quietly*) Your rage doesn't frighten me. It resolves very little, I'm sure, in these epic affairs of the heart. I trust that you'll respect my sister's peace of mind. She's ill as a direct result of your romantic blunders. She will remain so for a very long time to come.

KAROL   It seems you'll never be... my wife?

JULKA   Nor your companion, your lover or your soul-mate!

KAROL   Must I... let you go?

JULKA   In each of my manifold forms!

KAROL   This wall of ice, this barricade you construct between us and bolster with irony, I will breach it.

JULKA   It is impregnable!

KAROL   I'll show you that this has absolutely nothing to do with lust and everything to do with lifelong commitment. Understand? I will present you with evidence of my love.

JULKA   How? I won't accept your evidence.

KAROL   You won't have much choice! I will marry your sister!

JULKA   (*With a muffled cry*) Elka? Marry Elka so that you don't lose me?

KAROL   Yes – to keep you.

JULKA   This is impossible.

KAROL   It will happen, you watch me – it will!

JULKA   My sister doesn't love you any more...

KAROL   What? You're quite mistaken. I've spoken to her. I've got a keen eye. It wouldn't take much.

JULKA   What you say sir is utterly base!

KAROL   No – my motives are of a higher kind. Like this, I'll once more find myself in closer proximity to you.

JULKA   You're wrong – I will escape you both. No! I'll never let Elka fall into your clutches.

KAROL   You can try. We'll see who is the stronger. And so, until she recovers and we meet again, just by chance…then will you know how deeply, how passionately I have loved you. Until then!

           (Exits)

SCENE 5

(Julka, Elka)

(After Karol's exit, Julka's gaze remains fixed in its direction – she appears frozen to the spot – in the doorway, left, appears Elka)

ELKA   Julka!

JULKA   *(Jolted into consciousness)* I thought you were asleep.

ELKA   I tried, but I could hear raised voices. What did he say? Did you explain? Did you tell him to go back to his wife?

JULKA   *(Confused)* Yes – yes…

ELKA   What did he say?

JULKA   *(As before)* Nothing – he nodded and gave single-word answers.

ELKA   You're lying. Don't hide your face. That's not the whole truth, is it?

           (The bell rings)

SCENE 6

(Julka, Elka, Nina)

(Enter Nina, dressed with exceptional ceremony, a different toilette, chains and pendants are jangling, skirts rustle, she is in a choice humour and very jolly – it is evident that this is one of her excitable phases)

NINA   *(Politely)* A short while ago I returned home only to encounter your card. Which of you ladies came to the house?

JULKA   It was me, my sister is indisposed.

NINA   I know, I know, a frightful tale! Well, well, I'm hardly the one to blame – I spared you every possible anxiety. Upon encountering your card, I deduced that something quite remarkable must have occurred. Without further ado, without even changing my outfit, here I am. Whatever can the matter be?

JULKA   My sister wishes to speak with you.

NINA   *(Smiling politely)* I am listening.

(Sits)

ELKA   Julka – you say it.

NINA   Might it perhaps relate to the divorce? I must assure you ladies that everything has taken the best possible course. They've accepted my version of events. The reasons for the divorce will be entirely correct and respectable. It's all a terrible drag I know but I expect the whole matter to be settled amicably.

JULKA   My sister no longer depends on the divorce.

NINA   *(Surprised)* Ah! Really? Is that because ... how to express it ... he stays away? Don't be so surprised. I know a great deal, almost in spite of myself.

(Smiles)

At first I had to find things out, now they simply reach me. Everything will surely fall into place. Never fear, Karol will come to his senses.

ELKA   I don't want him back. I'll never be his wife, whether or not he wants it and no matter how much ... I know you love him and that you suffer a great deal, this is my only concern ...

NINA   *(Somewhat confused)* I must unburden you of your misconception. I don't love him at all – I've come to the conclusion that this divorce is my salvation, even were he to change his mind, I'd still go ahead ...

ELKA   You no longer love him? How can that be? Only two months ago, here, you were so sad ...

NINA   *(Bursts out laughing)* Two months! But my dear madam, in two months one may ponder, deliberate, come to one's senses and – become engaged!

ELKA   Engaged?

NINA   *(Merrily)* Why yes! Yes! Oh dear me! My little secret is out! Ah! Never mind! My relationship with you ladies is decidedly unique. I came bursting into your home in order to make a scene, that was my first visit – then I came with sentiment and mourning, such was my second – and finally I appear a third time and inform you that – I am engaged!

JULKA   *(Quietly)* You are a nervous wreck.

NINA   Quite so! That is why I do masses of silly things. Perhaps my marriage won't turn out to be so silly after all – a very good person, with regards to position, social standing, financial credentials – completely appropriate for me. In a word, today I absolutely do not regret that Karol and I have separated. I'm even grateful to him. If you ladies should happen to see him, then do by all means tell him so.

JULKA   We won't be seeing your husband any more.

NINA   Oh! Why ever not! So harsh, how terribly unfortunate! He's not that bad! He's no idea what he wants! Voila! There's a man for you! Do not you ladies judge him too harshly – and bear him no grudges. If anyone should, it's me! Well, what's the matter now?

JULKA   Nothing at all! In view of your promising circumstances and your...fortuitous engagement...!

NINA   Perhaps you ladies were thinking I might like Karol back? Whatever next! Whatever for? Ah – I hadn't the faintest idea how to conduct myself with a husband. You see, it all takes practice.

            (To Elka)

            And you, madam, why not talk to him, only from the heart – and he will surely return. No question about it. He just needs sweetening up, that's all. I was so ignorant!

            (Pause)

            Is that all you ladies wanted? I am expecting guests for tea today.

            (To Elka)

            You are frightfully pale. You simply must add herbal essences and fortified wine to everything. I must away! Should I happen to meet the said gentleman, I'll send him along post haste. Thank you – do not by any means go out, madam, because it's frightfully chilly. Adieu!

SCENE 7

(Elka, Julka)

(Elka dumbfounded stares for a while at the door through which Nina has exited – then seizes Julka by the hands)

ELKA   Julka! Can you believe it?

JULKA   I am not surprised, Elka.

ELKA   What do you mean? She forgot about him so quickly – she fell in love with someone else?

JULKA   You don't understand. She's not like you. It'll be etched on your heart, she's different. She'll be off somewhere, searching about...

ELKA   I can see there must be many things about love, and you, that I don't yet understand, because I'm so surprised. But this is quite appalling – to stop thinking about someone so quickly who not that long ago meant everything. That's well nigh impossible.

JULKA   For highly strung creatures, everything is possible.

ELKA   How strange! I thought, that by denying myself Karol, I'd give her every reason to be joyful – that they'd be reconciled...

              (Sits on the couch lost in thought – Julka brings books to the table and begins making notes)

ELKA   *(After a long pause)* Julka!

JULKA   What is it, Elka?

ELKA   Did you notice, Karol looks very unwell?

JULKA   I wasn't paying much attention.

ELKA   He's very pale. There are dark circles under his eyes. He must be feeling guilty, don't you think?

              (Julka is silent)

If he had a clear conscience, he wouldn't have come here, would he ... and then why does he look so ill? Too much eating out, perhaps? Or too much anxiety taking its toll? That does seem more likely. What do you think, Julka?

JULKA   Elka, it's already late, perhaps you should retire?

ELKA   Not yet, let me stay. I wouldn't be able to sleep. So many thoughts! What about that wife of his! Ladies and gentlemen! Engaged!

(Pause)

Am I disturbing you?

JULKA   No, Elka ...

ELKA   I'll be very quiet now – you read.

(Pause, quietly)

Julka – I have a question.

JULKA   Well?

ELKA   (Tentatively) But you won't take it the wrong way?

JULKA   I don't know yet.

ELKA   What ... did the two of you ... talk about? About our marriage – is that right?

JULKA   Yes – about marriage.

ELKA   And how did you react? Did you tell him ... to ... leave us ... and to never, ever come back?

JULKA   (Turning to look at Elka) Elka! What's the meaning of this?

ELKA   (Confused, quickly) Oh nothing, nothing, I only wanted to know, and now I have a thought, that if she doesn't want him either ... he'll ... be all alone ... how sad ...

JULKA   (Rises, goes to Elka, takes her by the hands and says gravely) Elka, do you still love him?

ELKA   (Bursts into tears) I don't know! I don't know!

JULKA	*(Leaning over her)* Think carefully, examine your heart.
ELKA	*(Weeping)* I don't know but I feel sorry for him, he's so pale. Perhaps he regrets it, misses me. When I saw him, everything came flooding back. What do you want from me? I'm not like her. I can't just forget!
JULKA	But of course you must!
ELKA	*(Tentatively)* If he's completely free, if he improves, if he feels regret, then, of course I should, I must forgive him. That's what the priest told me, when he administered the Sacrament of the Sick[76] – he told me it's my duty to forgive...
JULKA	You can and should forgive but you must also forget him.
ELKA	That is impossible to enforce, older sister – can't you see? Impossible to enforce! If you loved, as I do, then you'd understand why I cannot forget!
JULKA	One can love but not as you do! You poor thing.
ELKA	*(Gripping her hands)* A poor thing. You pity me, do you not?
JULKA	I pity you with all my strength!
ELKA	I'm a pitiful creature, I have suffered, been very ill. Give your consent, maybe the pain will stop – you'll see, when he marries me, he'll improve. And I too will be different. I'll do my hair, get dressed in the mornings, I won't contradict him... it was all my fault... my own fault. You heard what she said, he's not so bad! Let me marry him!
JULKA	You? Want to marry him? After all that's happened? Elka... you force me to utter words that will wound you very deeply... it died because of him!
ELKA	*(Quietly)* No, Julka – perhaps I misunderstood him. He only said he wasn't sure if he'd marry me. Perhaps he was thinking that the divorce hadn't gone through yet... and I became so anxious! If he didn't want to marry me then he most certainly wouldn't have come here. He's been waiting outside in the street, you said so yourself!
JULKA	*(Controlling herself)* Elka! Elka! Sometimes the truth is better left buried!
ELKA	I know the whole truth. Julka. You should have spoken to him before. You could have told him that I might change my mind, spared him so much anxiety – you could have explained that I'm not so stubborn after all...

JULKA   I'll say one thing more, Elka. Think carefully. You want to be Karol's wife. Consider...what sort of man he is. Today he prefers you, tomorrow Nina...the day after, someone else...

ELKA   Oh no! From now on, it'll be different. He'll understand how much I love him. In spite of everything, I'll forgive him. From now on, he will love me constantly and faithfully.

JULKA   You want the truth – then listen to me, Elka. Only remember that I'm *forced* to make it clear – you leave me *no choice*. Perhaps only I can cure you completely. But it's going to hurt you very much.

ELKA   *(Distressed, holding her hands at her breast)* It's something horrible...

JULKA   *(Kissing her fervently)* Yes Elka! It's the truth! Karol doesn't love you any more – now I am the object of his affections.

ELKA   *(Distressed)* What? You?

JULKA   He wants to marry you only because I don't want him. He's afraid of cutting a single thread that binds me to him. To that end he has resolved to use you...Have you understood me?

ELKA   *(Stunned)* Yes.

             (Suddenly)

             It's not true! It can't be!

JULKA   *(Gravely)* Elka! You've forgotten that I never lie.

ELKA   I apologize. I'm sorry. Is this really the truth – or an attempt to keep me from him? For my own good?

JULKA   I wouldn't have the strength to invent anything of the sort. Look at this. Here is the frame that held both our likenesses.

             (Picks up double frame - Julka's photograph is missing)

             Just now, when he was alone, Karol stole one of these images. You see – your likeness remains.

ELKA   *(Overwhelmed)* Yes. It's true. Mine remains. And in any case – you never lie.

(Pause)

Did he tell you this himself?

JULKA   Yes, Elka – he at least found the courage to tell me.

ELKA   *(Pale, pressing her face into the cushions)*

I will rest now … I'm so cold …

(Julka kneels beside her)

I can see it all. It's true. He loved to speak with you, for a whole hour or more, he treated me like a child, fussed over me like a lapdog. And when I answered back, he'd say 'hush, quiet now' – you're quite right, he's fallen in love with you … you're understanding, lovely, educated … you are different …

JULKA   Yes, Elka – it's just because I'm different and not because I know a little more than you do! Anyone would have done as a replacement – he can't really tell the difference. He'll break off each of his affairs, drive himself to distraction and then leave in search of another woman.

ELKA   Julka, he'll find no home.

JULKA   He takes pleasure in suffering. He knows how to control it. It will be a hundred times worse for the women he meets on his way. Nina wept, but they're very alike, she's following the same pattern. Yours is a different nature. You've endured the death of *your* child; *your* grief, *your* life – that's the tragedy here!

ELKA   Julka! You speak so kindly. You're very good to me.

JULKA   I stand here before you, Elka, the guilty party. I have a lot to answer for.

ELKA   You?

JULKA   I haven't been a sister to you – I felt … contempt … for your passion, your desire.

ELKA   You were perfectly right, Julka! You should indeed have held me in contempt.

JULKA   No, Elka! I saw with what suffering you paid for that elusive shadow of happiness. Then I came to understand that I was fleeing blindly from my own fulfilment, cowering behind perfect restraint. Next to you, Elka, I perceived my own nothingness. So radiant, you seemed, as you waited for the baby to come … then later, so beautiful in your bitter grief. Please, try to forget my coldness and forgive me. Allow me to still be – your sister.

ELKA   Night stretches before me. I fear the darkness. Sometimes it seems I stand gazing into my freshly dug grave.

JULKA   Will you take my hand? Allow me to be your guide. Now my conscience is clear. You have paid a woman's debt. You did give birth at the edge of a grave. Now you must turn away.[77] Your wounded desires, your injured heart, allow them to kindle your thoughts! Emerge like a phoenix from the flames, into a new morality! I'll lead you towards the things I hold most dear, my ideals, to my world!

            (As she speaks she takes Elka's hand, rises, and slowly moves towards the window leading Elka behind her, who follows her slowly. Julka should speak simply and straightforwardly, but with conviction)

            It is a very different place! No cultivation of personal impressions or intimate little gardens of suffering! There one must work not for oneself, but for new generations. One must unearth and uproot, when required, and subject one's own life to the very same process!

            (She opens the window, a gust of wind blows in, in the distance she can see the city, its houses brightly lit)

            There it is Elka – the new world! All that illumination and yet the contours of tragedy and suffering must still be made visible! I will teach you to hear the voice, which emanates from the depths of that city. I will teach you to understand the force of its reproach and then you will see outlined before you a series of great responsibilities. How your own suffering will seem next to the suffering of the masses! A grain of sand!

ELKA   Is it possible for me, Julka? Is it possible?

JULKA   It is. Your pain will render you robust, like steel, yet faced with the poverty and suffering of others, you'll learn when and how to soften, like wax. I can't experience or understand suffering as you can, Elka. And so, we will go together– into that world filled with reproach.[78] Together we will step into the sea of poverty and injustice. To light our way, let us bear aloft all that we have to offer – your tormented senses, your injured heart…

ELKA   …and to send the shadows flying, your keen, clear mind.[79]

            (They remain like this by the window, gazing intently at the city)

            (Curtain falls)

Notes

1. This is a diminutive of the name 'Julia'.
2. This is a diminutive of the name 'Elżbieta' or 'Elizabeth'.
3. This is the Polish version of the name 'Charles'.
4. It is difficult to say whether Zapolska had a particular urban setting in mind, or a specific partition. There are no street names mentioned in the play, as there are in *Malka*. However, questions concerning how to resist occupation, how to politicize the personal and how to sustain a sense of political activism in troubled times are extremely prominent throughout. We learn that a meeting is disbanded, that it is easier to 'sit on the fence' politically if one is to find work as a journalist, that unemployment is high and that Julka attends lectures at a university, which may be an 'underground' university, though she may also be presented by Zapolska as one of the first women to have gained access to a university place in partitioned Poland (this happened earliest in Galicia). The currency specified is 'Polish' (złotys and grosze) – rather than Russian (roubles and kopeks) or Austrian (kronen and cents), for example – or a combination of two fiscal systems. The 'city' or 'town' (the Polish word 'miasto' could mean either – I have chosen to use 'city' in order to convey a sense of urbanization in an English context) is a strong theme throughout and the sound of a factory siren is specified in the stage directions, which implies increased industrialization. A suggestion may be that Zapolska is aiming for a kind of 'universality' in this text, in terms of the former Polish territories. However, the focus on questions relating to political activism in the form of 'organic work' (gradual social change) and 'triple loyalism' (an acceptance of the state of occupation in an attempt to maintain peace) might also suggest the rooting of the text in Galicia, given that the development of this positivistic intellectual trend is associated most strongly with this area. The literary references in the play – specifically to Adam Mickiewicz's work – imply a strong sense of political association with the Russian partition, but this does not necessarily clearly identify setting. However, Julka also teaches at a school – presumably in Polish – which again suggests Galicia.
5. It is worth paying attention to how characters gain access to the space and how this changes throughout the play. There are times when the doorbell rings, other times when a key is heard scraping in the lock; sometimes characters simply enter because the door has been left open. How access is gained relates very strongly to questions of boundaries in relationships and gendered space and is likely to be highly significant in performance.
6. Karol works as a journalist for a daily newspaper that, it seems, is politically conservative, particularly in relation to the occupying regime. That is at least how Julka perceives it.
7. Questions concerning the relationship between work, politics and the personal are raised at the very start of the play. These must have linked with debates about so-called 'organic work' which were prevalent at the time. 'Organic work' was a mode of resistance suggested by various political activists following the failure of armed struggle for the cause of Polish independence, most particularly the disastrous January Uprising of 1863. Its ideals were somewhat akin to the Fabian notion of consistent and persistent social transformation and thus implied a very particular type of resistance, achieved through 'everyday' social activism, which could also take place 'in secret' – that is, out of the public gaze – rather than revolution or armed resistance and the inevitable resultant loss of life. This led to discourses that strongly politicized the 'personal' sphere when civil liberties were restricted. The concept acquired strong moral undertones and also keyed into debates about national, ethnic, religious and gender identities.

8. The way in which Zapolska portrays Karol's attitude keys into debates about feminism, the role of women in resisting occupation and the 'new woman', as she might be described in Britain, as a figure of fun; man-hating, asexual and somehow unattractive – perhaps even masculine – because she was likely to be intellectually driven. Indeed, Julka is shown as in some ways epitomizing the masculine woman, or, even more extremely, as having absorbed patriarchal modes of thinking and 'being' that are ultimately counter-productive, both personally and politically, and possibly render her ineffectual as a 'sister' on a number of different levels. It may be that ultimately Zapolska portrays Julka as possessing a strong masochistic 'streak', though she also explores the social, political, economic and cultural conventions that may have led to her constructing herself in this way.

9. We learn later that Julka is a teacher. This means that if she married, there would be professional consequences, most likely resulting in her having to give up her job.

10. We never learn exactly why Karol and his wife have separated – though we do get both sides of 'a story'. Additionally, both are constructed as characters whose versions of events are likely to be unreliable or at the very least questionable. The readers/audience are kept guessing. The question of the basis for the divorce is very important in the play because it keys into ideas about what might constitute an acceptable version of events (in terms of both social and religious convention and practice) which in turn will result in the least so-called scandal or damage to the reputations of all those concerned. It appears that Karol might have moved out of his wife's house as a result of his deeply ingrained inability to 'root' himself in the domestic or commit to one person, as well as in reaction to his wife's apparent neuroses. His wife does later confirm that Karol met Elka after he had moved out of her house. What is at stake at this early stage in the play, however, is whether Karol's wife will tell 'the truth', will name Elka and will say that the affair began earlier than it did – that is, while they were still living together. It seems that at this stage she may be maintaining that Elka is responsible for her husband's departure and that she wants to put her marriage back together.

11. He means they are not involved in a full sexual relationship.

12. He is indicating what he perceives to be Julka's left-wing leanings, red being associated with this side of the political spectrum.

13. She seems to be suggesting that he lacks political conviction. In her eyes, at its most extreme, this might render him a kind of collaborator with the occupying regime.

14. We do not learn anything about Julka's romantic past or much about her sexuality but this is a very interesting area for speculation, given her strongly held, often rather dogmatic, beliefs about men. Karol suggests that she might be a virgin, probably in an attempt to find something out; there are various ways of interpreting and constructing this interaction (on p. 173).

15. The characters frequently engage in speculation about the relationship between mind, body and spirit. Indeed, a questioning of whether it is 'healthy' to split and 'label' aspects of an identity according to this model forms an important basis for the play's thematic structure.

16. This is a very interesting comment. It may be that Julka's lecture is being held in secret, in which case, if Karol were to publish it, he would 'out' her as political and possibly jeopardize her day job, at the school. On the other hand, it may be that she would resent having her lecture written about by a journalist lacking, as she sees it, in political conviction. Alternatively, it could be that Karol is suggesting that he would disclose details of Julka's personal life without her permission, given the access he has to information about her life via contact with her sister. Thus, he would write an 'interview' without really having 'interviewed' her. There are other combinations of possibilities.

17. Screens appear frequently in Zapolska's plays. Note the presence of the screen in the final acts of *Małka Szwarcenkopf* and in *Miss Maliczewska*.

18. This section was cut by the censor prior to the play's first performances and does not appear in most published editions.

19. Bourgeois characters close to Nina's 'type' appear frequently in Zapolska's plays. One might consider in this context Juliasiewiczowa in *The Morality of Mrs. Dulska* and the main character in *Little Frog (or Żabusia)*. Neither character is portrayed as neurotic in the same way as Nina, though they all share a love of theatricality and fashion and are essentially fairly robust, wily and hard-nosed (as, ultimately, is Nina). They perform conventional femininity aggressively in order to achieve their ends, often as extremely as Julka performs her opposition to it.

20. Sanctuary lamps are present near the altar in Catholic churches. Their flames are never extinguished. They are intended to symbolize the eternal presence of God.

21. I would describe this sentence as an addition rather than a translation, made in order to theatricalise Karol and Nina's relationship in its new linguistic context.

22. In terms of conventions of beauty in this cultural context, a rosy round face was associated with country girls – therefore peasants – and consequently a lack of sophistication. In *The Morality of Mrs. Dulska*, the bourgeois daughters of Mrs Dulska mock the servant girl Hanka by saying she has rosy cheeks like berry stains.

23. This is a play on words that has emerged in translation, rather than a literal translation.

24. It is important to consider how financial arrangements and ownership of space might shift throughout the play. Both Elka and Julka are employed at this point – we do not know whether they rent the apartment or not but they are clearly financially independent. Perhaps they have inherited it from their parents – their mother is certainly dead (Elka mentions this) and Julka is presented as somehow acting in loco parentis for Elka, even though she seems to have 'come of age', implying a particular kind of power relationship between them. If they do own the apartment – or one of them does – then it is also important to consider what would happen in relation to property rights and inheritance etc. if Karol did marry one of the sisters. It is also interesting to speculate whether his interest in them relates in any way to their financial circumstances and whether, when he does move in to the apartment, he makes any financial contribution towards housekeeping etc. This might also relate to the financial consequences of his divorce from Nina, which we learn nothing about. These issues are alluded to rather than made overt since the play, given its naturalistic form, is grounded in a set of specific social and economic practices that would have been apparent to a contemporary audience. It might also be worth considering in this context Elka's concerns towards the end of the play about whether Karol has contributed money towards the child's funeral and, prior to that, her rather aggressive questioning as to whether they should buy a new samovar when it breaks. Indeed, Elka seems more pro-active in relation to these issues than Julka who is, for a while, the sole bread-winner in the house. A consideration of economic implications is indeed crucial to any reading of the play text.

25. Botticelli's most famous painting is perhaps 'The Birth of Venus', which shows the goddess naked, with very long, wavy blonde hair covering her modesty, emerging from the sea in a shell.

26. The sisters' surname is 'Korecki'. This is a masculine ending that in Polish would change to 'Korecka' for a woman. In this instance I have retained the surname in its masculine form, allowing the word 'Misses' to inflect it. To my ear this sounds better in English than 'Misses Korecka', which mixes an English plural with a Polish singular form, and 'Misses Koreckie', which would be the correct plural

form of the surname but appears illogical. 'Korecki' is perhaps more recognizable as a Polish surname to an English-speaking audience.

27. This is intended as an insult to Elka, who is presumably considerably younger than Julka.

28. This is an interesting comment. She could mean Karol's hands, or else the hands of the lawyers involved in the divorce or the press. There are a number of possibilities.

29. In this scene Julka is constructed as a particularly ambiguous figure, especially in relation to her 'politics'. Her attitude towards Nina and her 'nervous' or 'hysterical' behaviour is interesting and her motivation is complex. What happens to her feminist principles in a situation such as this? Where do her loyalties lie at this point? What motivates her to say what she does to Nina?

30. Nina implies that Elka is offering Karol sexual favours.

31. The use of doors is one of the most important features of the majority of Zapolska's plays in performance but most particularly, of course, those that focus on the domestic. One might consider this in relation to the slamming door in Ibsen's *A Doll's House*, far-reaching in its subsequent literary, theatrical and social impact. However, in Zapolska's work, the door as a device is frequently deployed with self-conscious theatricality in a manner reminiscent of bedroom farce. This becomes particularly evident in plays that centre on one space with several doors leading off it, such as *Four of Them*, which is also about marriage, infidelity and divorce and *The Morality of Mrs. Dulska*, which explores many of the same themes. The apparently private space represented on stage becomes, as a result, a public place of performance on a number of levels. Questions relating to the connection between the personal and the political, and why it is tested during periods of imperialist occupation, are also theatricalised by this means, since what is considered private and what public is expressed spatially and is ideological.

32. It seems most likely that Elka is involved in clerical work.

33. The question of Julka's responsibility towards her sister is paramount throughout the play and relates to the gradual politicization and 'de-naturalization' of their state of 'sisterhood'.

34. Is this statement correct? When is the door locked? When we hear the key scraping in the lock, does this mean that a character has forgotten/does not know that the door has been left open? Why should Karol say this at this point?

35. How much irony does Julka deploy here and what is its target? It might be worth remembering that she is also alluding to the fact that Nina arrived wearing a feather boa – her 'bird-like persona'. Feathers were a frequent addition to women's outfits during this period. Note the reference to feathers and boas in the other two plays included in this edition (the Chanteuses and Stefka's present). In my research productions of Zapolska's plays, there has always been a plethora of fur and feathers – on boas, mufflers, hats, bonnets, collars and gloves. Often at least one of the acts takes place in winter, so these materials conform to both naturalistic conventions of dress relating to season *and* the fact that Zapolska often implies in her stage directions and dialogue that costume might be deployed and read on a more metaphorical or reflexive level.

36. Again, it is worth considering this comment in the light of Julka's tendency to be ironic and in the light of her self-proclaimed feminism.

37. In a literal translation, Karol would refer to the lamps hanging above tables and illuminating family gatherings in the evenings.

38. Karol describes himself as an 'Ahaswer sercowy', or an 'Ahasuerus of the Heart'. This recalls the first title Zapolska gave the play, in which she references the figure of the Wandering Jew of legend, who has no home yet yearns for a Promised Land. I have tried to make this theme explicit in my

translation. My sense is that a contemporary audience would be largely unaware of the implications of such a comment and it would sound too obscure in performance.

39. Young-ish emotionally 'rootless' men, who either verge on or are 'fully' rakish, feature frequently in Zapolska's plays and Karol fits into this mould. Fedycki in *Four of Them*, Zbyszko in *The Morality of Mrs. Dulska*, Wiedeński in *Małka Szwarcenkopf* and Bogucki in *Miss Maliczewska* make for interesting comparisons in this respect. Filo in *Miss Maliczewska* is interesting for his failing performance of this type of masculinity.

40. This is a very childish diminutive of the name 'Karol'.

41. This is an interesting comment. It might be read as an attempt to blackmail Elka emotionally. However, it is also worth remembering aspects of historical context here. If we are in the Russian partition, say in Warsaw, for example, it is the period following insurrection, deportation, exile and the severest political repression. This means that many people of Karol's generation would have experienced some serious disruption or tragedy in their lives relating to the political circumstances in which they were living. His story about his disrupted childhood is plausible in this context, though that does not mean he is not being (perhaps unconsciously) manipulative. Karol's inability to root himself or his lack of desire to do so does not simply lock him into being an example of a particular character 'type' – the playwright may be assuming that the audience understand certain important conditioning factors. If Karol's family, for example, were involved in armed resistance in the 1860s, then this would shed a very different light on his attitude towards politics, and specifically Julka's politics.

42. Zapolska frequently portrays desire, arousal, seduction and love-making in her plays. It is often 'illicit' in some way. Regularly, the situations depicted provide opportunities for visual comedy in performance – I do not think this is the case here. Indeed, this interaction might be described as Strindbergian in tone. The ambiguous power relationship is there (Karol perhaps suggests that there is an equality or balance 'framing' their interaction that does not in fact exist), as is a sense of 'time out of joint'. I am thinking particularly of *Miss Julie* but perhaps even more so of *There Are Crimes and Crimes*, notably Maurice's interactions with Henriette (though the gender roles here are reversed) which are similar in their tone and perhaps the level of risk and sense of transformation expressed by the characters.

43. Elka is pregnant. How heavily pregnant she is becomes significant for a number of reasons, notably in relation to the subsequent seriousness of her illness following her loss of the baby but also the fact that the child is buried and there is a priest present at the funeral. These factors do suggest the more advanced stages of pregnancy.

44. Polish currency.

45. Bom-bet-ski, Dom-bret-ski, Trom-bet-ski.

46. Spooy-na

47. The first part of this name should be pronounced 'bin' as in 'dustbin' rather than as in 'bind together'.

48. These early-morning 'town sounds' appear frequently in Zapolska's plays, including *The Morality of Mrs. Dulska*.

49. The following section, up until the end of this scene, was censored prior to the play's first performances.

50. A sense of political urgency, impending spiritual catastrophe, the suppression of national identity and contained socio-political trauma festering beneath a veneer of performed everyday 'normality' is most strongly expressed here by Julka. Interestingly, Julka appears to be developing an argument that Karol could become a feminist (as he suggests jokingly on one occasion) and that this would

have broader consequences. However, she implies that by focusing on gender differences rather than common humanity, the national cause could be compromised by people who hold Karol's political views and follow his rules of conduct. Julka could be suggesting that dysfunction at the heart of heterosexual relationships is both caused by and perpetuates the broader political situation. She appears to conclude that equality in private and public spheres is inextricably linked. Questions of spirituality rather than religion appear to be significant here and religious imagery is engaged by her in order to develop a socialist discourse.

51. These would probably be glasses that fitted into special metal holders. Tea would also be drunk with lemon rather than with milk.

52. It may be that Julka is referring to the fact that Elka has slept with Karol ('sexual liberation?') as well as the way in which she herself is compromising her feminist principles by writing Karol's articles and pussyfooting around him in order to keep him with her sister in the hope that he will marry her. She may be suggesting that Karol is aware of his new power within this set of relationships and is exploiting it in a number of ways, including via the sharpened mocking tone in which he now refers to her politics. This is perhaps why he then attempts to 'pacify' her.

53. I am using the word 'dinner' here to refer to the afternoon rather than the evening meal. This may be because I am from the Midlands. I also think that 'lunch' sounds rather too contemporary and would say that they might call the evening meal 'supper'.

54. Polish currency – its smallest denominator.

55. This would probably be a musical setting of Psalm 51.

56. In a system that included both, Julka makes a distinction between a day school and a boarding school.

57. The connection Karol seeks to make here between women's intellectual activity and increasing ill health is interesting.

58. This may be more evidence of Karol's desire to construct himself as 'apolitical'. It does not seem that he is required to comment on the 'live' proceedings – as usual he is doing as little as he can get away with and prioritizing the pursuit of women, in this instance, Julka.

59. Karol actually refers to the Polish classic narrative poem *Pan Tadeusz*, written by Adam Mickiewicz (1798–1855).

60. This is an even more extreme diminutive of the name 'Karol' than 'Lolek'!

61. Washerwomen and seamstresses feature regularly as characters in Zapolska's plays; Tadrachowa in *The Morality of Mrs. Dulska* is a washerwoman; Act 1 of *Miss Maliczewska* is set in a laundry; Miss Mania in *Four of Them* is a seamstress.

62. This is ironic given the fact that Karol never seems to do any writing.

63. Early censors of the play cut the following section, up to Karol's cry of 'Delusions!'

64. The section in square brackets could be cut in performance, since it may seem obscure to an English-speaking audience. I have included it because it is extremely important in terms of Julka's developing political discourse. The reference is to a Romantic drama written in several parts (1823, 1832) by Adam Mickiewicz, and entitled *Dziady* (*Forefather's Eve*). This poetic drama has been described as 'the national sacred drama of Poland ... a complex amalgam of patriotic, folkloric and philosophical material written in different times and places, but unified by its pervading national spirit. That nationalism is expressed metaphorically through the *dziady*, a twice-annual folk ritual synthesizing pagan mysticism and Catholicism's All Soul's Day, when peasants would gather in the graveyard and offer a banquet for the spirits of their departed forefathers ... For theatrical purposes, some see

Part III – the dramatic heart of the work – as a self-contained play' (Londres, p. 254). Julka and Karol are here referring to *Part III*, in which the young man disappointed in love – a potentially heroic leader-figure – changes his name from Gustave to Konrad. This signifies his move beyond what Julka would probably call 'selfish erotic affairs' to greater social and political consciousness and responsibility, encouraged by a priest. In this work, Mickiewicz, an exiled writer, develops ideas of 'Polish Messianism' perpetuated by the Romantics during a period when uprising or insurrection was still perceived as a viable strategy for resisting the oppressors and gaining national independence. Following the January Uprising of 1863, this vision of Christ-like, suffering Poland on the brink of resurrection became less viable, as greater political repression ensued. In fact, émigré Romantics like Mickiewicz were accused by some of kindling false hopes of independence in their work. Additionally, Julka and Karol swiftly extend the argument by moving from reference to Mickiewicz's *Dziady* to quoting from his poem, *Konrad Wallenrod* (written in 1828, when the writer was living in exile in Russia). The medieval hero of the poem is based on an actual historical figure, Konrad von Wallenrode, a Teutonic Knight. In Mickiewicz's rendition he is a Lithuanian who was kidnapped as a child and raised by the Teutonic Knights. He is presented as a character who is, culturally and emotionally, in a 'liminal state', pandering to his enemies – whom he secretly wishes to destroy – and revealing his 'heart' only to those closest to him, in private. Julka and Karol use these literary references in order to develop a discussion about Polish masculinity and national identity.

65. I have added emphasis and a suggestion of tone by using inverted commas here.
66. It is interesting to consider Julka's attitude towards religion and sexual morality in relation to her feminism.
67. This interaction is significant because it clarifies the fact that Nina and Karol have not been seeing each other. It may have crossed the reader's mind that they are plotting something together 'behind the scenes'. Zapolska shows us at this point in the action that this is not the case.
68. This implies that a religious body was involved in the divorce proceedings.
69. Pronounced 'Lo-lush' – this is yet another diminutive of the name 'Karol'.
70. The issue here is whether the fact that the child was born prematurely/was stillborn and conceived out of wedlock would mean that a Christian burial was denied. The implication appears to be that some priests would ask questions and that the circumstances would make a difference, also in relation to where in the cemetery the child was buried. Julka seems to be suggesting that the priest was kind because he 'turned a blind eye' to the circumstances – she reports that he made the sign of the cross in order to imply that a ceremony was properly conducted, which is important here in terms of convention because the child was not presumably baptised, though this may also have been accomplished by the same priest. In the most extreme terms, if what Julka says is true, then the child has been acknowledged as a being with a soul and has been blessed, irrespective of its mother's so-called transgressions. It is possible for an actor to deliver Julka's version of events in a number of ways, each implying a particular relationship with her sister at this point.
71. Elka refers to this as a 'kaballah'.
72. Elka implies that in this context the ace of clubs signifies death.
73. This was considered fortifying during periods of indisposition.
74. In this section, Julka once again refers to Karol as the 'Ahasuerus of Lovers', with reference to the Wandering Jew of legend, who was described as cursing Christ on the Cross and consequently being condemned to wander the earth until his second coming.
75. Julka also uses the name 'Ahasuerus' here. See footnote 74.

76. In the Catholic rite, the Sacrament of the Sick is administered when there appears to be a strong possibility that the individual in question could die at any moment. This signifies the seriousness of Elka's condition.

77. The following section, with its political allusions and references to a 'new' world and the city, was severely censored during early performances of the play and is not present in its full form, as it is here, in the majority of published editions.

78. Throughout the text I sometimes use the word 'accusation' to express what Julka says about the voice emanating from the city, and sometimes 'reproach'. I think the sense of what she is trying to convey takes in both these words. I have chosen to use 'accusation' when she is speaking to Karol, and 'reproach' when she is talking to Elka, since this seems appropriate given my interpretation of her character.

79. It is important to remember that Julka is teaching Elka in a way she thinks she will understand. This is an extremely significant aspect of the tone of the ending and should affect the delivery and manner of Julka's speeches. She is, after all, a teacher by profession.

'SISTER OR SERVANT'

Miss Maliczewska (1910)

During the nine years that passed between the creation of *The Man* (1901/2) and *Miss Maliczewska* (1910), Zapolska's health continued to deteriorate and she was bedridden for prolonged periods. She spent months at various sanatoria and wrote only with difficulty. At the same time, there were repeated, sometimes successful, attempts between herself and Janowski to settle their differences.

In 1906 an exhibition of paintings and prints she had collected during her stay in Paris in the 1890s was organized, with her permission, in Lwów. Included in the exhibition were works by Gauguin, van Gogh, Seurat, Pissarro and Sérusier, with whom she had had a love affair. She also wrote a number of plays that had an enormous impact on the development of Polish theatre, most notably *The Morality of Mrs. Dulska* (1906), which secured her reputation internationally and *Ich Czworo* (*Four of Them*) (1907),[1] which, though written for a cast of seven, links very strongly with *The Man* in terms of its dramatic construction around a core quartet of characters. In a surprising and formally inventive departure for Zapolska, *Four of Them* includes a cloaked, green-skinned creature called Mandragora who speaks a prologue and epilogue whilst sitting on the prompter's box.

During the year in which she wrote *Miss Maliczewska*, 1910, Zapolska was feeling more robust and as a result returned, in a more limited capacity, to journalism, working for the popular illustrated daily, *Wiek Nowy* (*New Age*). She wrote a column along the lines of 'Through my window', which had appeared in *Polish Word* in 1900/01. Additionally, during her search for alternative therapies to help her manage her rheumatic, digestive and nervous ailments, she made the acquaintance of a young doctor, Kazimierz Radwan-Pragłowski, who practiced auto-suggestion and hypnosis. This acquaintance led to seemingly intractable problems in her

Figure 25: Note the free standing door-frame in the background. Research performance of Zapolska's *The Morality of Mrs. Dulska*. University of Reading and POSK Theatre, London, 2003/4. Cassie Earl as Juliasiewiczowa, Emma Ankin as Dulska. Photo by Lib Taylor.

relationship with Janowski – in fact, it seems to have been the straw that broke the camel's back. This time it was Zapolska who instigated what was to be their final separation.

She subsequently began work on a play entitled *Metresa* (*The Mistress*). This was the first and preferred title she gave to *Panna Maliczewska* (*Miss Maliczewska*). She was compelled to change this in response to public pressure, following a storm in the press. This was fuelled by articles and letters dwelling on the subject of how offensive it was for the Lvovian public to see 'that word' printed on posters. Zapolska had initially considered calling the play *Panna Malinowska*, then *Panna Maliszewska*, before settling on her final title.

In response to pressure to change the play's title, she wrote:

> Apparently in Lwów there's a big fuss about *The Mistress* – about a play that hasn't been performed yet, which I dared to write and had the misfortune of talking about here and there. I called it *The Mistress* ... and to me this title seemed quite straightforward and natural and not for a moment did it cross my mind that somewhere or other a sinful thought would come into being or that someone's senses would be roused by the word itself. But – I should have remembered, that there are sick people, for whom the sight of a woman's shoe is enough to send them into amorous ecstasies and make them feel 'roused'. What is actually very amusing about all this is the fact that at the moment they are bolstering themselves with 'thousands of schoolchildren' who are supposedly going to be asking their parents what the word 'mistress' means ... I don't pretend to be a laureate of children's literature ...

Figure 26: Note the box set and solid doors. Research performance of Zapolska's *Four of Them*. University of Reading, POSK Theatre London and Łódź Theatre Festival, 2006/7. Robin Owen as the Husband, Harriet Mackie as the Daughter, Sophie Green as the Wife. Photo by Lib Taylor.

And also:

> The Mistress, they say, how pornographic! These things aren't discussed in good company! But they forget how many tears and how much human suffering there is in that pornography...Who cares? To seduce, that's one thing, that's allowed, it's even attractive in a man, but when Maliszewska wants to express something about her life, then the sharp answer is 'silence'![2]

Shortly after the premiere, Zapolska embarked on a trip abroad, which took her to Vienna (where Radwan-Pragłowski was then to be found), Munich, Salzburg and Monte Carlo. Her travels depleted her financial resources and on her return to Poland she sold the three most valuable paintings from her French collection.

The number of performances in Galician cities and towns was limited, whereas in Warsaw the play had an extensive run of around 70 performances. It seems that the play's reputation as 'immoral' put off audiences in Kraków and Lwów, in spite of positive articles in the press that stressed its social agenda. However, Czachowska[3] makes an important qualification; of the 81 plays staged in Kraków that year, only three had longer runs than *Miss Maliczewska*. The conservative press did not spare criticism, however, using graphic descriptions of the play in order to discredit Zapolska's work for *its* apparently graphic – or, as Antoni Balicki[4] put it, 'vulgar' – use of language and taboo themes. Balicki spared no punches. For him, the play was weak, pathetic, banal, filthy, lacking in tact, cheap, rotten and junk.

Figure 27: This is the set for the Łódź performances, which was far more makeshift than the previous box set shown in Figure 26. Research performance of Zapolska's *Four of Them*. University of Reading, POSK Theatre London and Łódź Theatre Festival, 2006/7. Photo by Mike Stevenson.

The conservative press in Warsaw responded along similar lines. Without denying the quality of Zapolska's dramatic construction, the play's banality and the playwright's reliance on caricature was stressed. In the liberal press, on the other hand, complexity of characterization was highlighted. In addition, in conservative papers and journals, it was suggested that the play was rather one-sided in its damning of the male sex, whereas the liberal publications, and those supporting the emancipation of women, hailed it as a realist play with a strong sense of social purpose at its heart.

Rurawski records[5] that between 1911 and 1914, Zapolska further developed her interest in the character of Stefka Maliczewska, sketching ideas for another play entitled *Odwet Panny Maliczewskiej* (*Miss Maliczewska's Revenge*), of which only fragments (Act 2, Scenes 10-14) remain. Stefka, now an experienced prostitute, welcomes Daum and Daumowa into her salon and 'in a calculated way takes her revenge on them for the humiliations she has endured'.[6] Zapolska also wrote a novella about a call-girl in 1910, entitled *Staśka*, in which the protagonist, who gives the play its title, meets her godfather, who wishes to become her lover. Rurawski suggests that in this short story, Zapolska concentrates on the experiences of the male character and that, for this reason, the figure of the prostitute is 'colourless and insignificant'.[7]

During the time I have spent translating this play, several things have struck me, some of which I have already mentioned in my general introduction to this book. The first is the directness and economy of Zapolska's language - perhaps its harshness - as well as its more contemporary, or 'modern', quality. The second is the fact that Stefka does not appear until towards the end of

Figure 28: The setting for the Reading performances. Research performance of Zapolska's *Miss Maliczewska*. University of Reading, POSK Theatre, London, 2007/8.

Act 1 – yet she is repeatedly described during the first scenes and her entrance is eagerly awaited and anticipated. The third are those stage directions relating to aspects of performativity in the play. These suggest that Stefka might make direct contact with 'an audience' or 'an auditorium' while she is represented as present in a naturalistic space, a room. This connects with a very important aspect of this play, namely its potential reflexivity and its emphasis on theatricality. Stefka is an actress *and* a mistress – she 'performs' in a number of different contexts. This is expressed with the greatest wit by Zapolska in the scene where she practices an extract from Shakespeare's *Romeo and Juliet* with Daum, the man whose mistress she has become. He is a lawyer and many years her senior. Perhaps the greatest irony of Stefka's life is that the theatres she aspires to 'perform in' appear to be governed by patriarchal systems very similar to those she finds governing her private life, enacted in a space that increasingly acquires the quality of a stage set for a bedroom farce. In fact, they appear to feature many of the same characters, namely the men who keep her, and whose reported influence on 'the director' is deliberately obfuscated.

When I directed *Miss Maliczewska*, this idea of exploring the interplay between ideas pertaining to 'the theatrical' and 'the real' – in a naturalistic play about performance – became very important and this manifested itself most strongly in the setting I chose to use.

In every other production of a play by Zapolska that I have directed, a box set has either been constructed from conventional theatrical materials or has been alluded to via the same means. *The Morality of Mrs. Dulska* had the parameters of its set defined by a series of large, overtly theatrical door frames that traced an imaginary back wall to the family living room (see Fig. 25). *The Man* was performed in a partial box set constructed from canvas flats, which did not have doors fixed to them but rather, curtained doorways. The box set was located within a much larger black box theatre space, giving the impression that the room had been 'dropped into' the bigger space, was framed by it and by a correspondent darkness beyond the doors (see Fig. 13). *Four of Them* was also played in a fully constructed box set, in a smaller studio space (see Fig. 26). It was more overtly theatrical than the set for *The Man* in the way it was painted, yet it was also more fully realized, given the fact that it had two solid doors leading to outside spaces and two curtained doorways leading to bedrooms. For *Miss Maliczewska*, however, it seemed paramount to have a completely solid space that could resound with the aggression that is palpable in the language and characterization, to hear the slamming of doors, the grinding of keys in locks, the shattering of glass, the sound of footsteps in the hall – to evoke, in short, solidity, harshness and an unyielding quality in the environment (see Fig. 28). For this reason, I used the corner of a studio theatre. In its solid walls, two doors were located, and frequently slammed quite violently by the actors. They formed the walls of a partial 'box set' which shaped the locations of the play, a laundry and Stefka's apartment. At one level, this allowed for a greater level of realism, in terms of the quality of the space and its properties. However, this realism was predicated on the fact that the walls were very literally those of a theatre. The raked audience seating was constructed 'on a corner', and as such spectators formed two walls of a 'box', whereas the other two walls – the solid ones of the 'set' – completed the structure. Consequently, the moments when Stefka appears to directly acknowledge 'the auditorium', or 'the public', as though she is performing to an audience (whether imaginary or real) in a private space, were particularly intriguing and suggestive. For me, these were rather like 'perforations' within an only partially 'constructed' fourth wall. It didn't matter whether the 'auditorium' that Stefka referenced was, to her, imaginary or real, but her consciousness of an observing presence had implications for the performance register within my production. This slippage, or duality, in terms of how the audience might both be read, and read their own function, was also reflected in, or echoed by, the performance space, whose fictional properties were, as a result, problematized. In these moments, there was a conflation of 'real and imaginary states', which I think correlates very strongly with some of the comments about the play's first performances, relating to its 'social value'.[8] The effect of this device must have been especially potent when the characters represented were 'contemporaries' of their audience. In these moments, within this liminal space, the character of Stefka is potentially more 'real', 'material', 'embodied' than the actress. Indeed, the character is also 'playing' an actress. Indeed, the actress playing Stefka could be – could have been – someone's mistress! On this complex relational plane, she 'touches' the spectator. In *Miss Maliczewska*, Zapolska is again testing the limits of naturalism and proposing new possibilities for a realist theatre.

Notes

1. Translated T. Murjas and staged in Reading, London and Łódź in 2006/07.
2. See Czachowska, p. 428.
3. See Czachowska, p. 431.
4. Balicki, A., 'Teatr Krakowski', *Przegląd Polski*, 1910/11, t. 178 z. 533, str. 261–3.
5. See Rurawski, p. 292.
6. See Rurawski, p. 293.
7. Ibid.
8. K.B., *Panna Maliczewska*, Ster, 1911, nr. 1, str. 33–40.

Miss Maliczewska (1910)

A Contemporary Drama

Dramatis Personae
Daum (*pron. Dah-wm*) – a lawyer
Filo (*pron. Fee-loh*) – a student, his son
Edek – a student
Bogucki (*Boh-guts-kee*) – a lawyer
Friends 1, 2, 3 and 4 – Filo's colleagues
Stefka Maliczewska (*pron. Ma-lee-tchev-ska*) – an actor
Daumowa (*pron. Dah-wm-oh-var*) – Daum's wife
Hiszowska (*pron. Hee-shov-skah*) – friend of Daumowa
Żelazna (*pron. Dje-laz-nah*) – a washerwoman
Michasiowa (*Mee-hash-oh-vah*) – Stefka's sister[1]
Bailiff

Figure 29: Edek focuses on his reading. Research performance of Zapolska's *Miss Maliczewska*. University of Reading, POSK Theatre, London, 2007/8. Ben Mitchell as Edek. Photo by Matt Ager.

ACT 1

(The setting is a basement room, very small and very narrow. On the left are two small windows, double-paned, in frames. At the back a stove for cooking and Żelazna's bed, to the audience's right the entrance door, three steps, worn and covered with a cloth, and Stefka's bed, near it a small basket instead of a cupboard, on it a mirror, books, a comb, a very beautiful confectionary box, various flacons, an apple and lots of other clutter. A small, tattered screen stands by the wall, on it hangs a dress and a colourful petticoat, to the left under the windows an oilcloth couch, on it Edek Kulesz's bedclothes, a parcel that has been turned over, a candle, a half-eaten loaf, a torn collar. Under the windows a door, on it pots, books, exercise books. At the back, near the fireplace a wall lamp, above Żelazna's bed – pictures, crepe flowers, photographs and a religious picture,[2] in front of which burns a small lamp. An overall impression of dampness and cramped conditions. The walls should be dark. The floor has been freshly scrubbed, sprinkled with sand, on it cloths and newspapers have been laid out. As the curtain rises Żelazna is

standing by the wash-tub in the depths of the fireplace doing the laundry. Edek Kulesza is sitting by the window at a table, his hands over his ears, and studying out loud. Steam fills the whole room. For a moment Edek's monotonous voice and the drip of the water in the wash-tub is heard: after a while Edek rises, goes to the bread, cuts a slice, eats and returns to his place, all the time muttering and reciting. At last Żelazna approaches the table, begins to rummage and turn everything over, angrily, searching for something)

SCENE 1

(Edek, Żelazna)

EDEK   Good grief!

ŻELAZNA   *(searching the table by which Edek is seated)* Good grief yourself!

EDEK   Stop it, would you ...

ŻELAZNA   Out of the way, Kulesz!

EDEK   Stop it!

ŻELAZNA   There was some laundry dye here – where's it gone?

EDEK   How would I know?

ŻELAZNA   The dye was here. Where is it?

EDEK   Leave me alone, Żelazna – I've got to study.

ŻELAZNA   And I've got to do the laundry. My laundry's worth more than your learning, Kulesz – you'll get nothing for your learning. Where's the dye?

EDEK   *(Beating the table passionately)* Be so kind as to move away!

ŻELAZNA   Tut tut! What's this? Who's mistress here? Me, or Kulesz? Who's got a position – me, or Kulesz? Who's three months in arrears with his rent? Me, or Kulesz? Well? Well?

                (Kulesz is silent)

                Well ... well ... no time to open your big mouth now, is it, when you've got nothing, only thank God I still keep you, because anyone else would have had you out long ago ...

EDEK	(*Quietly*) It'll be paid.
ŻELAZNA	I expect so. I won't be taken advantage of, I work hard.
	(*She goes to the wash-tub, again, splashing is heard and Edek's monotonous voice*)
EDEK	(*Turns towards Żelazna*) Dark already!
ŻELAZNA	(*Drily*) It's only three.
EDEK	It's dark in here, anyway!
ŻELAZNA	(*Drily*) Should move to a palace then and treat yourself to some electricity.
EDEK	(*Studies, takes the bread, eats it, sits at the table by the window, Żelazna takes a bucket of soap suds and exits; knocking is heard at the window, Edek kneels and opens the window*)

SCENE 2

(*Edek, Filo*)

FILO	Hello.
EDEK	(*Mutters*)
FILO	Demosthenes again, is it?[3]
EDEK	(*Carries on muttering*)
FILO	Enough. Coming?
EDEK	(*Holds open his arms*)
FILO	Pity.
EDEK	(*Beating his brow*) It's all too much – I'm getting nowhere, dammit – my brain's bursting.
FILO	Everyone else has gone.
EDEK	(*Bats his hand*)

FILO   *(Looking in)* Hmm ... not here, then?

EDEK   *(Continues to study)* No.

FILO   I brought her something.

EDEK   *(Extends his hand mechanically)* I'll take it.

FILO   No, no – I'll manage.

                (Looks in)

                Old cow not here either?

                (Enters through the window, rushes to Stefka's bed, gets a small bunch of flowers from beneath his cloak, puts them on the basket and returns to Edek, pleased)

Figure 30: Filo arrives with flowers. Research performance of Zapolska's *Miss Maliczewska*. University of Reading, POSK Theatre, London, 2007/8. Michael Day as Filo. Photo by Matt Ager.

That's the ticket! Best way to approach a woman – Nietzsche's rod – wind her in – or else … flowers … I'm a man of experience. Remember that, Kula![4]

EDEK   Last thing on my mind, to be honest …

FILO   Well … sooner or later, it'll catch you up.

EDEK   Won't have any time …

FILO   Can be very time-consuming …

EDEK   Exactly.

FILO   (Sits on the table) What's the problem! You're young, easy peasy. One, two, three, down plops a woman, straight into your arms.

EDEK   What joy!

FILO   Well, it's hardly obligatory – but it's certainly recommended.

            (Sitting on the table, lights a cigarette)

            Want one?

EDEK   Alright.

            (He takes one, they smoke silently for a moment)

FILO   (Looks at Stefka and Edek's corner) Know something, I just cannot believe you could be so close to her and … you know … nothing.

EDEK   (Bursts out) Nothing but filth in your head.

FILO   It's hardly filth – you must admit, that Stefka, she's a top-notch kind of girl.

EDEK   Don't quite see it that way.

FILO   Alright … I know … I know, you don't have to impress me – women are human beings too, we all know that, right! Call that smoking – inhale, man … hear me, inhale?

EDEK   Lay off.

            (He throws the cigarette down and goes to the bread, slices it, starts eating and writes at the table)

FILO   (*Sits on the sofa*) Word of advice – if you don't know how to smoke, then don't.

            (*Pause*)

            She smoke?

EDEK   (*By the table*) Who?

FILO   Maliczewska.

EDEK   Huh!

FILO   I saw her once – leaving a rehearsal – someone – man from the chorus, I think – was smoking, snatched it right from his lips, she did – had a long drag herself.

EDEK   Just one of her pranks. To hell with her, anyway – here's your homework...[5]

            (*Passes him a few sheets of paper*)

            Right then... copy it out – only don't make any mistakes.

FILO   (*Searches his pockets*) Here's twenty.

EDEK   (*Harshly*) You're not serious? And the rest? You still owe me forty from last time.

FILO   (*Ingratiating himself*) Kula, calm yourself, man! I bought her some flowers!

EDEK   Should have given her ready cash!

FILO   Are you mad? Her? An artiste?

EDEK   She's an artiste like I'm a doctor of philosophy. Oh, to hell with it all...

FILO   (*Mechanically slices a piece of bread and eats it*) Got a way with women, I have. No harm in a bit of poetic license. Actually, I did compose some verses. Over there... on a little card, bang in the centre of her bouquet.

            'I only marvel that flowers do not

            Bloom beneath your feet'

EDEK   *(With irony, by the table)*

              'Ah you! My winged bird.

              My paradise...my month of May...my springtime!'

FILO   Ooh! Err!

EDEK   That's it, that's the one, right – Sienkiewicz! Sienkiewicz![6]

FILO   She might not have read it?

EDEK   Not read it? She's digested everything, the complete works – she reads all the time. No discrimination. I did want to guide her – to hell with that idea!

Figure 31: The friends discuss Stefka. Research performance of Zapolska's *Miss Maliczewska*. University of Reading, POSK Theatre, London, 2007/8. Ben Mitchell as Edek, Michael Day as Filo. Photo by Lib Taylor.

FILO   *(Pleased)* So intelligent?

EDEK   Not intelligent, just well read. Would you stop about her, anyway? I've had enough.

FILO   She'll be back when?

EDEK   No idea.

FILO   You're not very polite.

EDEK   *(Sadly)* If you'd holes in your boots, holes in your pants, holes in your brain – if you were miserable and depressed, you wouldn't be so polite either.

FILO   *(Sincerely)* I'd invite you over to my place Kula, God knows I would, and give you everything, only my old folks, regular pair of prigs[7] – you'd never believe it.

EDEK   I know, deep down you're a good man – society you move in – a swamp.

FILO   Right – but I'm a romantic.

EDEK   Like hell you are! You pose as a romantic. Not a shred of sincerity. Well … time you made a move?

FILO   I'll leave her some cigarettes.

EDEK   Capital notion. Go, now.

FILO   Ooh! Look at you! So virtuous!

                (Enter Żelazna and looks angrily at Filo)

EDEK   When do you want them back?

FILO   Take the lot. Don't be shy. I'd only give them away.

SCENE 3

                (Same and Żelazna)

ŻELAZNA   I don't like callers.

FILO   Bye then Edek!

ŻELAZNA	On the paper, if you please – floor's just been washed.
FILO	You'd never guess.
	(*Exits*)
ŻELAZNA	No callers thank you and none through the window. Like some thieves' den not a Christian household!
EDEK	He's not a caller, he's a friend.
ŻELAZNA	Not mine. Want to invite friends, get yourself a palace.

(Edek gets up onto the table, lies propped against the window frame and studies. Only his long legs are visible, dangling, in tattered trousers. Żelazna launders and hums under her breath, some hymn. It grows gradually darker, from the corners emerges the damp, sickly dusk)

Figure 32: Michasiowa has words with Stefka. Research performance of Zapolska's *Miss Maliczewska*. University of Reading, POSK Theatre, London, 2007/8. Sam Tye as Michasiowa. Photo by Lib Taylor.

SCENE 4

(The same, Michasiowa)

(Michasiowa, pale and still quite young – in a kaftanik; carries in a laundry basket covered with a piece of old curtain. In the basket are ballet skirts, a mirror, a box of lipsticks, a corset, some rags. Silently she stands the basket on Stefka's bed, then hangs out the ballet skirts and tights along the screen, at last she goes to the fireplace and warms herself. Michasiowa is silent)

ŻELAZNA	Is it over?
MICHASIOWA	Course it is.
ŻELAZNA	Well – where is she, then?
MICHASIOWA	Chattering with her friends. Wants her milk hot, she says.
ŻELANA	Exactly, conjure money from thin air.
MICHASIOWA	Well it's already lit.
ŻELAZNA	So what?
	(Michasiowa is silent)
ŻELAZNA	Raining?
MICHASIOWA	Not yet.
ŻELAZNA	I pray for rain: good clean water for coloured dyes.
MICHASIOWA	Might even snow.
ŻELAZNA	All I need.
MICHASIOWA	Winter's on its way.
ŻELAZNA	Let's hope it chokes.
MICHASIOWA	Huh – likely story – I might though.
ŻELAZNA	You – don't think so – me, another story ...
MICHASIOWA	Come over all strange.

(Drinks water)

Someone gave her confectionaries again – I over-indulged.

ŻELAZNA   *(With contempt)* Confectionaries!

MICHASIOWA   Yes – well – that's the latest trend!

                 (Glances at the bread)

                 Whose bread is that?

ŻELAZNA   She won't get far with confectionaries.

MICHASIOWA   Whose is that bread?

Figure 33: The ladies arrive to inspect the laundry. Research performance of Zapolska's *Miss Maliczewska*. University of Reading, POSK Theatre, London, 2007/8. Saskia Solomons as Daumowa and Lauren McKinstry as Hiszowska. Photo by Matt Ager.

ŻELAZNA	Oh well... you know...
MICHASIOWA	*(Breaks a piece off and eats it)*
ŻELAZNA	Just help yourself... bless me...
MICHASIOWA	We're only from the same village.
ŻELAZNA	Oh! Is that right?
MICHASIOWA	Mm hmm – tiny place – called Back of Beyond.

MICHASIOWA *(Laughs bitterly)*

That's where all us beggars are born. I'm off! There's more to fetch. Dammit, couldn't put everything in one pile, could she, case her bloody bloomers got rumpled. Huh! Devil take her...!

(Tempers herself)

You won't say anything, Mrs. Żelazna, will you?

ŻELAZNA	Meaning?
MICHASIOWA	That I... was a bit...
ŻELAZNA	I am a Christian woman – I do not gossip.

(Michasiowa takes the empty basket and exits. Żelazna launders for a while, eventually singing a hymn she tentatively approaches the table, looking around, still tentative, at last she picks up the knife, cuts a slice of bread quickly, takes it and pushes it under her pillow, after which, singing all the time, she goes towards the wash-tub)

SCENE 5

(Żelazna, Daumowa, Edek, Hiszowska)

(Knocking)

ŻELAZNA	Who the blazes is that?
DAUMOWA	*(Slides her head round the door)* God be with you!

ŻELAZNA   Amen!

(Both women enter slowly, maneuvering their enormous hats through the narrow door. They are very dressy, their skirts rustle, they are wearing black, they laugh a little, secretively and glance at each other. Żelazna, who at the sight of the ladies has become slightly aghast, begins to quickly move the papers and cloths from the floor)

DAUMOWA   A washerwoman lives here, isn't that right?

ŻELAZNA   That'd be me, Madam, at your service.

DAUMOWA   Splendid, splendid...Why so dark in here?

HISZOWSKA   And close.

ŻELAZNA   Usual thing...in a laundry...as they say...Just a tick, I'll light a lamp.

DAUMOWA   Marvellous. Because we've a pressing enquiry about lace...You do know how to launder lace, I take it?

ŻELAZNA   Plain as day...second nature...

HISZOWSKA   And guipure?

ŻELAZNA   Plain as day...second nature...

                 (She lights a lamp, the ladies look about them, notice the ballet skirts and say to one another)

                 C'est ici, oui, oui...

DAUMOWA   *(Notices Edek's legs dangling from the windowsill)*

                 Ooh! Ah! Whose are they?

ŻELAZNA   Aha...just a tick.

                 (She pulls Edek down)

                 Outside, if you please – I've got business.

                 (Edek climbs down from the windowsill and, still studying and scrutinizing his book, wraps his cloak around him and exits the room carrying Demosthenes)

HISZOWSKA   That your young son, is it?

ŻELAZNA   Hardly ... he's an orphan ... I've taken him in ... like one of my own ...

DAUMOWA   That's lovely, really lovely ...

ŻELAZNA   My Christian duty, madam dear. Like his own birth mother, me. Nothing
             else for it! Care to sit down, ladies ...

             (Passes them stools)

DAUMOWA   Why thank you! A little on the snug side!

HISZOWSKA   *(Quietly, to Daumowa)* Why beat about the ...

DAUMOWA   *(To Hiszowska)* Hist! Don't give it away ... someone else sleeps here, I
             see ...

ŻELAZNA   Oh! She's a lodger ... Miss Maliczewska.

DAUMOWA   I have some recollection – the one from the theatre?

ŻELAZNA   Yes – green around the gills, though – could come to nothing.

DAUMOWA   And she's what? An orphan?

ŻELAZNA   Well I ... I think so ... really couldn't say ...

HISZOWKA   Pays you well, does she?

ŻELAZNA   *(Suspiciously)* Hmm ... I ... it varies.

DAUMOWA   But ... surely ...

ŻELAZNA   Twenty gulden ... food and board ... but why ...[8]

DAUMOWA   Aha ... food and board, is it?

             (To Hiszowska)

             Well ... it's perfectly adequate here ...

HISZOWSKA   I'll add that to the report ...

DAUMOWA   *(Dictating)* Stefania Maliczewska – understudy: accommodation acceptable, sustenance provided...

                  (To Żelazna) My good woman, here we are – best possible reasons... A delegation – from the Society for the Improvement of Women.[9]

ŻELAZNA   *(Slightly unnerved)* You good ladies have permission from the police?

DAUMOWA   *(With a smile)* No, conscience alone is our guide! We discover and document how such and such a girl makes her living... hey ho... Dash it all, let's cut some corners... Does Miss Maliczewska conduct herself well?

ŻELAZNA   *(After a while)* I do look after her.

DAUMOWA   Splendid, splendid, mm, that really is marvellous... but there's always a chance...

HISZOWSKA   Yes or no!

Figure 34: The washerwoman struggles to deal with her visitors. Research performance of Zapolska's *Miss Maliczewska*. University of Reading, POSK Theatre, London, 2007/8. Karina Thresh as Żelazna. Photo by Matt Ager.

ŻELAZNA	No![10]
	(After a while)
	Me, dear ladies, I'm a widow, a Christian widow and I would never suffer anything of the sort under my roof.
DAUMOWA	That's frightfully noble...
HISZOWSKA	So you can vouch for Miss Maliczewska?
ŻELAZNA	To what end? I won't vouch one way or another. All I'm saying is that right now...
DAUMOWA	Very well, that'll do...
	(To Hiszowska)
	Why don't you write 'Miss Maliczewska remains in the care of a fine woman'...err
	(To Żelazna)
	Your surname...it's gone...
ŻELAZNA	Anna Żelazna.
DAUMOWA	*(They look at each other and laugh)*[11] Anna Żelazna! Yes! We might also add that Miss Maliczewska exhibits no indecent tendencies...
ŻELAZNA	Pardon me, what, Madam?
DAUMOWA	Indecent tendencies...well...we do have to formalize it. Society's house style – required for the documentation.
HISZOWSKA	What's that smell?
DAUMOWA	Where?
HISZOWSKA	Ah! That bread! Black bread...it's simply ages since I had some.
ŻELAZNA	Care to, ladies?
HISZOWSKA	Really I...

DAUMOWA	*(Encouraging)* Not the done thing to refuse.
	(Żelazna cuts thin slices and offers them on a dish)
HISZOWSKA	Scrumptious!
DAUMOWA	You're such a child!
	(They laugh)
	In summary, Miss Maliczewska is an honest, decent young girl and her well-being is assured!
HISZOWSKA	Hey ho, our business here is done.
DAUMOWA	Right you are. Since – so far – there's been no…
	(They laugh)

Figure 35: Hiszowska needles the washerwoman. Research performance of Zapolska's *Miss Maliczewska*. University of Reading, POSK Theatre, London, 2007/8. Karina Thresh as Żelazna and Lauren McKinstry as Hiszowska. Photo by Lib Taylor.

HISZOWSKA   Yes, since – so far – there's been no ...

(Looks at her notebook)

We're supposed to be where now? One minute ... aha, her with the tenement building, on the corner of Piaseczna Street.[12]

DAUMOWA   Harder nut to crack. Won't yield ... just won't yield ... I explain to her, slowly, carefully, well, well! Suits her right down to the ground, she says ... what with the tenement building etcetera ... and ... .well, what with the tenement building, suits her right down to the ground.

HISZOWSKA   Shocking! Simply shocking! Dearie me!

(Looks at her watch)

It's late, come now! Our husbands grow impatient!

DAUMOWA   And mine may suspect, last thing we need.

HISZOWSKA   Still against it?

DAUMOWA   Absolutely.

HISZOWSKA   *(Putting on her gloves)* He needs it pointing out – our duty, that's that!

DAUMOWA   His principles. Simply cannot comprehend, terrified I'll get too close, says it rubs off ...

HIZOWSKA   Ha! So melodramatic! Right ... that's covered is it, with Miss Maliczewska ...

DAUMOWA   I'd say it is ...

HISZOWSKA   Dear me! Heaven forbid! Why would she, anyway – she's everything she needs right here ... moral insanity, that's all I can think of.

DAUMOWA   *(Sighs)* There's that ... there is always ... that ...

HISZOWSKA   *(Approaches Stefka's bed)* One last thing ... all this – a single space. Mrs Żelazna, dear woman – just one room here – that is correct?

ŻELAZNA   Just the one ... and, phew, the price ... bless my soul ...

HISZOWSKA	That young man, he stays here too?
ŻELAZNA	What young man?
HISZOWSKA	Well...the young orphan boy...
ŻELAZNA	Oh, Kulesz! Well, yes, he does.
HISZOWSKA	It's all rather...
DAUMOWA	*(Takes the screen and unfolds it)* I'll wave my wand. Here's the screen. A bit tatty... Some sackcloth – metre or two should do it – we'll have it sent over – on the house...
HISZOWSKA	Yes, sackcloth! Not quite so see-through...
DAUMOWA	And Mrs Żelazna will be good enough to ensure that the screen is re-covered and that...that there's always...how can I put it...
	(She spreads her arms above the bed like a guardian angel)
ŻELAZNA	Yes, yes, alright.

Figure 36: Daumowa in furs. Research performance of Zapolska's *Miss Maliczewska*. University of Reading, POSK Theatre, London, 2007/8. Saskia Solomons as Daumowa. Photo by Matt Ager.

DAUMOWA   Well, God be with you, Mrs Żelazna – thanks for the lovely bread.

HISZOWSKA   And we commend Miss Maliczewska to your protection.

ŻELAZNA   Like a mother…like a mother…

               (She bows)

               Most sincere respects…the Lord Jesus go with you.

               (Bowing she sees both ladies out and when they have exited, she mutters
               to herself through her teeth)

               And may you both fall and break your necks.

               (She goes to the window, opens it and calls out)

               You can come back in now!

SCENE 6

(Żelazna, Edek then Michasiowa)

(Edek enters still studying and muttering, he's a little covered in snow, he crosses the stage,
pulls the table up to the lamp, sits, puts his fingers in his ears and studies. Żelazna finishes the
laundry, and begins tidying near the stove, she takes the wash-tub outside)

ŻELAZNA   What's the time?

               (Shouts)

               What time is it?

EDEK   Don't know.

MICHASIOWA   (Enters, carrying a basket, puts it down and shakes out her headscarf)

ŻELAZNA   Not here! Not here! Don't you make this room into a sewer!

MICHASIOWA   What, Easter or something, is it, you and your cleaning up?

ŻELAZNA   Like it or not…that's not permitted…Outside.

MICHASIOWA   My sister pays, so I have permission.

Figure 37: Stefka arrives 'home'. Research performance of Zapolska's *Miss Maliczewska*. University of Reading, POSK Theatre, London, 2007/8. Phoebe Garrett as Stefka. Photo by Matt Ager.

ŻELAZNA	You pay for food and board, not for a floor to dirty.
	(Michasiowa takes out the light dresses and hangs them up, then she puts a beautiful chocolate box on the basket)
ŻELAZNA	*(Looking at the chocolate box)* Must have been quite pricey!
MICHASIOWA	That's right it must! Kindly put it down...
ŻELAZNA	Rubbish! Think I don't know how to handle a box of confectionaries!

SCENE 7

(The same, Stefka)

(Stefka enters quietly, slowly, she moves across the stage in silence; silence, Stefka exhausted sits on the bed, throws off her hat, silence)

MICHASIOWA	Some confectionaries here.
STEFKA	*(Quietly)* Yes, alright! Just leave them! Dammit! Damn it all!
MICHASIOWA	You might give us a tip, Stefka.
STEFKA	*(Quietly)* Oh really. What can you mean? Bite your tongue.
MICHASIOWA	You might give us a tip, Stefka!
STEFKA	Go to hell…I said I haven't got it, so I haven't got it…
	(She lies on the bed)
	I'm completely exhausted.
MICHASIOWA	I'll be going then.
STEFKA	*(Lies like a corpse)* And don't be any later than seven to get the things!
MICHASIOWA	You're on again today?
STEFKA	Yes – it's the opera this evening, right.
MICHASIOWA	But they must have paid you this afternoon.
STEFKA	Mrs Rozental was waiting and she took my wages.[13] Anyway – what the hell – I don't have it.
	(Michasiowa slowly puts on her headscarf and exits. Stefka lies on the bed like a corpse, her jacket unbuttoned and looks at the ceiling. Pause. Żelazna approaches Stefka with a cup of milk in her hand)
ŻELAZNA	Afternoon tea!
STEFKA	*(Quietly)* One minute, I need to get my breath back.

ŻELAZNA	I added some coffee.
STEFKA	My, my! What's the occasion!
ŻELAZNA	Well, it's just... You're going to the theatre what time, Miss Stefka?
STEFKA	Seven.
ŻELAZNA	And it now is?
STEFKA	Five thirty.
ŻELAZNA	Well...
STEFKA	What?
ŻELAZNA	Nothing... nothing...

Figure 38: Michasiowa holds the chocolates. Research performance of Zapolska's *Miss Maliczewska*. University of Reading, POSK Theatre. Sam Tye as Michasiowa and Phoebe Garrett as Stefka. Photo by Lib Taylor.

STEFKA	*(Leaps up)* I've got my breath back.
	(She runs to Edek and covers his eyes)
	Hello there!
EDEK	Lay off!
STEFKA	My, my! I won't bite you, Mr Untouchable!
	(She looks at the bread)
	How come your bread has shrunk?
	(She cuts a piece and eats it)
	Perhaps you'd like some confectionaries?
	(Edek without breaking off stretches his hand out behind him. Stefka puts a couple of sweets in his hand)
STEFKA	*(Laughing)* There you are! Sample those! The fruits of my disgrace!
	(She laughs)
	Know what, my feet are agony today.
ŻELAZNA	Because you're over-working.
STEFKA	Why so sweet Mrs Żelazna, today!
ŻELAZNA	As always.
STEFKA	You don't say!
	(To Kulesz)
	It's not the same bread as usual.
EDEK	Because it's black bread; I buy from the soldiers now – lasts longer.[14]
STEFKA	And fills you up more. What've you been scribbling today. Anything?
EDEK	Three.

STEFKA	*(Sits on the table where Edek is writing)* Shifted any?
EDEK	One, but he hasn't paid. I've still got two in the 'very good' category and one 'excellent'.
STEFKA	What's today's topic?
EDEK	Utter drivel. 'Imagine you are a father and your son has the plague. In 2,000 words describe your experiences.'[15]
STEFKA	You're not serious!
EDEK	As God is my witness. They're the essay topics that idiot professor gives.
STEFKA	And you've had to experience a father's pain three whole times?
EDEK	Four! Three times for upkeep and an extra helping for myself.
STEFKA	You don't charge enough.
EDEK	They'd never pay…Well…move aside…I've got work to do… Demosthenes, remember?[16]
STEFKA	*(Pushes herself further onto the table)*
	Hey – who's Spinoza?[17]
EDEK	A philosopher.
STEFKA	A Jew – first name, Baruch.
EDEK	A Jew.
STEFKA	What's he done?
EDEK	A phi-lo-so-pher! Where did you hear it?
STEFKA	It's Miss Osterlo, the chorus girl, got this part today. We talked about it quite a lot. None of the girls knew. Write it down on a scrap of paper – I'll tell them. Alright? I'll give you some confectionaries. That Osterlo's a lucky one. She said they gave it to her because the costume involves a lot of hosiery, and her legs are straight up and down. That's rubbish – plain as day to me…She only has a lover, who's 'like that' with the director, and

Figure 39: Stefka taunts the conscientious student. Research performance of Zapolska's *Miss Maliczewska*. University of Reading, POSK Theatre, London, 2007/8. e, London, 2007/8. Ben Mitchell as Edek, Phoebe Garrett as Stefka. Photo by Lib Taylor.

of course she's a protégé. Damn it all, if I could only find someone who's 'like that' with the director!

(Rolls around on the table)

If only I could!

EDEK   Watch what you're doing!

STEFKA   *(Lying on the table)* If they'd only give me one part, they'd be convinced I've got talent... one part would do it...

(She lifts her leg, looks attentively at her shoe)

Oh! I'd be rich! I'd drink coffee every day, I'd ride in a trap with rubber tyres and I've give you great big coins – I'm telling you, it would be – well!

(Scrutinizing her shoe)

Oh dearie me!…mm hmm…

(Suddenly)

Got any card?[18]

(She rises and stands centre stage)

EDEK   Take one of the book covers. I always sole my shoes with book covers – thick ones…

STEFKA   Today I'm playing a lady, so I have to wear my own shoes – and we kneel down with our backs to the audience.

(She takes off her shoe, stuffs in the cardboard)

Give me some ink!

(She rubs it in)

EDEK   Wait!

(He also rubs ink over a hole in his shoe)

STEFKA   What are you doing – straight onto your sock like that?

EDEK   *(Mournfully)* Fool! Straight onto my bare flesh! – Flowers for you over there!

STEFKA   Huh! To hell with flowers. I'm done for today.

EDEK   One must have courage.

STEFKA   *(Sadly)* You, Edek, big words – always at the ready…

EDEK   *(Bitterly)* That counts for something…

(In the meantime Żelazna has folded laundry into the basket)

ŻELAZNA   Going up to the attic.

(Exits)

Figure 40: Stefka performs for Edek. Research performance of Zapolska's *Miss Maliczewska*. University of Reading, POSK Theatre, London, 2007/8. Phoebe Garrett as Stefka. Photo by Lib Taylor.

STEFKA   Go then and may you break your neck.

EDEK   Right...get up, I need to gather my papers.

                (Stefka slowly rises from the table)

STEFKA   Ugh...like I've been punched in the stomach!

                (Knocking)

SCENE 8

(Stefka, Edek, Bailiff, then Żelazna)

BAILIFF   Miss Maliczewska live here?

STEFKA   Your business, sir?

BAILIFF	From the court…have to write everything down.
STEFKA	*(Cajoling)* You're a man of letters?
BAILIFF	I have to make an inventory.
STEFKA	*(Winks at the audience)*[19] I see! From the court!
BAILIFF	Complaint brought by Icek Eisenstein. Sum of twenty-seven kronen, fifty-eight halers…let's keep everything by the book…
	(Goes to the table)
	I need to make an inventory…
STEFKA	*(Uncaring goes to the bed and lies down on it)*
	So make one sir!
	(Żelazna bursts in)
ŻELAZNA	*(Shielding the furniture)* What's that? From the court? I won't allow it. It's all mine. Miss Maliczewska owns absolutely nothing. She's sub-letting…
BAILIFF	News to me…let's keep everything by the book!
ŻELAZNA	I'll swear an oath. The furniture's mine, it's all mine!
STEFKA	*(Amused)* Well I never…well I never…
ŻELAZNA	And that's mine! And that is!
	(Edek takes his papers and exits)
ŻELAZNA	*(To Edek)* I need you out 'til after seven, I've got business.
BAILIFF	Pine kredenzer.[20]
ŻELAZNA	*(Rushes to the kredenzer)* It's mine! I swear it!
BAILIFF	You can appeal. By the book.
	(Approaches the bed and takes the ballet skirt)

Figure 41: Holes in their shoes. Research performance of Zapolska's *Miss Maliczewska*. University of Reading, POSK Theatre, London, 2007/8. Phoebe Garret as Stefka, Peter Dodds as the Bailiff, who has come to find out what she owns. Photo by Matt Ager.

STEFKA	*(Jumps up)* Put that down, if you please – tools of the trade.
	(Takes tights)
	Hands off...tools of the trade...
	(Humming)
	You...mm, you....are the man...of my dreams...la, la, la...
BAILIFF	*(Writing)* Pine table, settee, oil cloth cover, hay stuffing...right-o! That should do it...

(Formalizes document, adds stamp)

Yes.

STEFKA	*(Dances around the stage)* You married, sir?
BAILIFF	By the book!
STEFKA	Blessed with children?
BAILIFF	By the book! Care and responsibility for items listed belongs to the said Stefania Maliczewska, as specified in paragraph ...
STEFKA	You've done this before.

(She puts on her ballet shoes, the Bailiff exits)

Kind respects to your wife, kiss your children from me, and mind as you go, good sir, there's a muddy patch just out there ...

(Dances in front of Żelazna)

Oh valiant granny, I am the custodian of your junk!

ŻELAZNA	It's not funny. You could have paid that Jew up front, Miss Stefka.
STEFKA	*(Saddens immediately)* It's obvious I couldn't.
ŻELAZNA	That's no good, you should be prepared.
STEFKA	Can't you see I've got nothing?
ŻELAZNA	I don't know, but this will not do.
STEFKA	*(Suddenly becoming serious)* Don't I know myself that it just won't do!

(Throws herself onto her bed)

I want to sleep! Żelazna! Have you any spirits for the curling tongs – I've nothing for my hair.

ŻELAZNA	No I do not.
STEFKA	What's to be done! I keep on borrowing from other people.

ŻELAZNA   It's beyond me.

                 (Looks out into the entrance hall)

STEFKA   (Drags herself up from the bed) I'll go ask the barmaid – she might slip
                 me enough.

                 (Drags herself out of the room, wrapped in something or other)

SCENE 9

(Żelazna, Daum)

(After Stefka's exit Żelazna lights the lamp in front of the picture, tidies the room a little; she listens, knocking at the door, she rushes quickly, enter Daum in a fur and a hat)

DAUM   Well?

ŻELAZNA   How do you do, sir.

Figure 42: Research performance of Zapolska's *Miss Maliczewska*. University of Reading, POSK Theatre, London, 2007/8. Ben Mitchell as Edek, Phoebe Garrett as Stefka. Photo by Matt Ager.

DAUM *(Pushes her aside with his stick)* Yes, yes... well... where is she?

ŻELAZNA Gone out. She'll be right back.

DAUM Will she now.

ŻELAZNA Oh sir... but... she will... she will... How impatient you are. Perhaps you'd care to sit down.

DAUM *(Sits in his fur and hat)* Yes, yes, quite so.

(Pause)

DAUM And... she has been warned?

ŻELAZNA But of course... of course.

DAUM She has agreed?

ŻELAZNA Naturally.

DAUM Well then, can't be very virtuous can she, so quick...

ŻELAZNA What do you mean quick? You've no idea sir, what went on... She practically fainted... cried out... but in time... you catch my meaning, sir... honest young lady, that girl... so she's obliged to umm and ahh...

DAUM *(Pushes her away lightly)* Yes, yes... quite so.

ŻELAZNA Only to begin with she'll pretend she knows nothing. You know, sir – a bit like a comedy.[21] So she never knows you have my consent, sir. Until she grows to like you, after about, quarter of an hour...

DAUM *(Frowns)* What for?

ŻELAZNA And you do the same, sir, as if you don't know a thing.

DAUM Yes, yes... quite so.

ŻELAZNA *(With a smile, quietly)* And... with regard to the er...

DAUM *(Takes fifty kronen out of his wallet and gives it to her)*

ŻELAZNA But that's only fifty.

DAUM	(*Quietly*) Another fifty ... tomorrow ...
ŻELAZNA	Sincere respects ... sincere respects!
	(*Pause*)
DAUM	Not here is she.
ŻELAZNA	She'll be back ... wink of an eye ... just popped over to the public house on the corner ...
DAUM	(*Wincing*) A drinker?
ŻELAZNA	Saints preserve us, such a lovely girl! Some spirits to crimp her hair,[22] that's all ... Most natural thing in the world ... she's young ... flirtatious ...
DAUM	What age?
ŻELAZNA	Nineteen.
DAUM	Are you sure?
ŻELAZNA	Couldn't be surer. Got my hands on her birth certificate.
	(*Pause*)
DAUM	(*Rises*) Someone's coming I think.
ŻELAZNA	(*Looks towards the entrance door*) Only the neighbour. Any problems, say you've come to look at the tenement building, as a potential buyer.
DAUM	Best if no-one comes in.
ŻELAZNA	I'll make sure of it, that I will, sir. When she gets back, I'll lock the door, myself, I'll sit in the hallway.[23]
	(*Pause*)
ŻELAZNA	Here she comes!
	(*Daum sits near the stove still dressed, enter Stefka*)
ŻELAZNA	I'm off to the tobacco shop.
	(*She sidles out of the room. At first Stefka doesn't see Daum, who is sitting still near the fireplace in his fur and hat, suddenly Stefka notices him*)

Figure 43: The washerwoman defends her territory. Research performance of Zapolska's *Miss Maliczewska*. University of Reading, POSK Theatre, London, 2007/8. Karina Thresh as Żelazna, Pheobe Garret as Stefka, Peter Dodds as the Bailiff. Photo by Lib Taylor.

SCENE 10

(Stefka, Daum)

STEFKA   What can I do for you, sir?

DAUM   Nothing.

STEFKA   That's not much.

                (She bustles about her theatre things, arranges her ball dress, fan, flowers in the basket, stands, looks at Daum a while then suddenly bursts out laughing)

DAUM   *(Remains seated)* What's so funny, miss?

STEFKA   You've a fine head on your shoulders sir.

              (Pause, Stefka sits and begins to tack ribbons onto her ballet skirt, she has her back turned to Daum, at last she turns to look at him)

STEFKA   No really – what do you want?

DAUM   Buying a tenement building. Looking round.

STEFKA   A whole tenement building? You must be rich.

DAUM   So, so.

STEFKA   No such thing as 'so so'. Either you're rich or not. Best to say it straight, sir.

              (Pause)

              Are you married?

DAUM   Yes.

STEFKA   Children?

DAUM   Yes.

STEFKA   What's your wife's name?

DAUM   Ewa.

STEFKA   *(To the audience, her voice thickens)*[24] As in Genesis?

DAUM   I beg your pardon?

STEFKA   Ah! You haven't read it. You don't look the bookish type.

DAUM   *(Entertained)* And what do I look?

STEFKA   Well…someone who hit the jackpot, anyway. What's the time?

DAUM   Six thirty.

STEFKA	Damn and blast, last thing I need.
DAUM	What?
STEFKA	Oh this...
DAUM	Why do it yourself? No seamstress round here?
STEFKA	Could I afford it!! Really![25]

(Rises, goes to the fireplace, takes the milk, drinks)

DAUM	What are you drinking?
STEFKA	My afternoon tea and liquid supper.

(Runs to Edek's bread, cuts a piece and throws the rest to Daum in passing)

Care for some too – black bread...

DAUM	Pardon me?
STEFKA	*(Childishly, laughing)* Why what did you do?

(Pause)

(Daum lights a cigarette, Stefka gestures that she would like one)

DAUM	*(Taunts her with the cigarette, like a small animal)* Say if you please!

(Stefka takes a cigarette, but is afraid of him and goes back to sewing her skirt)

DAUM	You're performing today?[26]
STEFKA	Precisely! Some performance! I'm an understudy...three years already, but what's the use? No patron...nothing...and of course I could perform.

(Rises suddenly and goes to Daum)

You know the director, sir?

DAUM	I know him.

STEFKA	Only – the two of you are like *this*.[27]
DAUM	Yes we are.
STEFKA	*(Goes to the fire, kneels and heats her curling irons)* Not pulling my leg, are you.
DAUM	No!
	(Looks at the irons)
	Oh! Ah!
	(He puts out the cigarette, a key is heard in the lock)
STEFKA	*(Indifferent, still by the fire)* What's going on? Someone's locked the door...
DAUM	Right then ... enough of this comedy ...
	(He turns down the lamp, darkness fills the den, dim rays of light barely shining through the little window, Daum throws himself at Stefka from behind)
DAUM	Right then ...
STEFKA	*(Helpless and shocked, with arms by her sides, at present failing to understand)* What do you ... what?
DAUM	Quiet! Keep it down!
STEFKA	*(Shouting – she has understood)* Let me alone! Get away! Get away!
	(She tears herself away, he catches her up, grabs her by the hair, pulls her backwards)
STEFKA	Jesus! It hurts!
DAUM	Quietly!
	(Stefka throws herself towards the window, jumps onto the table, beats the window pane, breaks the window, bloodies her hands)
DAUM	You've gone mad!

STEFKA	Save me! Anyone! Save me!
DAUM	Shut your mouth, you little bitch!
	(He wants to pull her off the table, she with bloodied hands beats his face and arms and pushes him over, the door opens, Żelazna bursts in)
ŻELAZNA	*(In a whisper)* God in heaven! You can hear everything outside!
STEFKA	*(Weeping genuinely, moves away, throws herself onto her bed weeping)* You monster! You criminal! Criminal!
ŻELAZNA	*(In a whisper, turns up the lamp)* Quiet, nothing has happened.
DAUM	*(To Żelazna)* This is a pretty tale! What a mess...
ŻELAZNA	*(In a lowered voice)* My dear sir, I had no idea...
DAUM	*(Livid)* You, madam, told me she'd been warned... Some warning!
ŻELAZNA	My good sir, upon my honour!
DAUM	I need something to wipe myself...
	(Żelazna gives him water, he washes his hands with the gesture of Pontius Pilate)
	Well – it's hardly my fault.
	(He takes out his wallet and takes out English sticking plaster, sticks it on his wound and loses ten kronen, when he's dressed to go out he says)[28]
	Now give it back.[29]
ŻELAZNA	*(Bowing)* My good sir! Expenses!
DAUM	*(Pushes her away)* Yes, yes... quite so.
ŻELAZNA	*(Stops him at the exit)* And for the window pane, sir?
DAUM	Go to hell!
	(Exits slamming the door)

Figure 44: Stefka escapes Daum's clutches. Research performance of Zapolska's *Miss Maliczewska*. University of Reading, POSK Theatre, London, 2007/8. Phoebe Garrett as Stefka. Photo by Matt Ager.

SCENE 11

(Stefka, Żelazna then Edek)

ŻELAZNA   *(Goes to the bed, takes a pillow, climbs onto the table and blocks up the window)* Miss Stefka you broke the window, please pay for it tomorrow ...

STEFKA   *(Quietly)* I'll pay.

ŻELAZNA   A double pane ... Two kronen ...[30]

STEFKA   I will pay!

                 (Żelazna bustles about for a while, she leaves muttering. Stefka lies down for a while, at last she rises, sits and finishes her dress, Edek enters, cold, goes to the table)

EDEK   What's all this? Was there a fire! My books, oh! Notes and even borrowed ones! Was it you?

STEFKA	*(Quietly)* It was me!
EDEK	*(Crying)* Lord! You know what … this is … it's disgusting!
STEFKA	*(Suddenly rising)* Leave me alone! If you only knew what's happened here.
EDEK	Ha! This is disgusting! Things are hard enough for me.
STEFKA	You fool … I'll pay you back … If you only knew … I can't tell you … I'm so ashamed …
	(Cries)
EDEK	*(Interested, approaches her)* Well?
STEFKA	*(Throws herself into his embrace and says through her tears)* This old man was here … an old pig[31] … so high … in a fur coat … he grabbed me by the hair … pulled me along the ground …
EDEK	*(Idiotically)* What did he want?
STEFKA	Oh you idiot!
EDEK	Oh!
	(Pause)
	What did you do?
STEFKA	*(With pride)* And, well, I escaped his clutches.
EDEK	*(Gives her his hand)* That was brave! At last I can see you as a person …
STEFKA	Let me alone, I've cut my hand.
EDEK	Never mind! It's a baptism … you'll come out of this more courageous.
STEFKA	Fine words!
	(Goes towards the fire, in order to turn up the lamp and notices the ten kronen banknote on the ground)
STEFKA	He lost this … must have been … oh! Got blood on it …

Figure 45: Stefka pursued by Daum. Research performance of Zapolska's *Miss Maliczewska*. University of Reading, POSK Theatre, London, 2007/8. Phoebe Garrett as Stefka. Photo by Lib Taylor.

EDEK   Get rid of it!

STEFKA   So much money!

EDEK   Get rid of it! Burn it!

STEFKA   Are you out of your mind!

EDEK   That is dirty money.

STEFKA   No. A little muddied, a little bloodied ... but ... it's ...

              (She wipes it)

              There! Can't even see it! Good!

              (Runs to the basket, folds her ballet skirts, covers them with a curtain, hurriedly puts on her shoes, jacket and hat)

EDEK   This is about moral filth.

STEFKA   Huh! Why don't you get stuffed? When Michasiowa comes, let her take
                the basket and carry it to the dressing room...

                (Runs towards the exit)

EDEK   Wait! Where are you going?

STEFKA   *(Triumphantly, already on the steps)* I'm going to pay off my debts.

                (Springs out)

EDEK   *(Alone, looks at her with contempt, spits and bats his hand)*

                That's all we need to know...a woman.

                (Goes to the table, looks for his bread, then under the sofa, at last in tears)

                What the hell happened to my bread?

                (Curtain falls)

Figure 46: The aftermath. Research performance of Zapolska's *Miss Maliczewska*. University of Reading, POSK Theatre, London, 2007/8. Phoebe Garrett as Stefka. Photo by Lib Taylor.

ACT 2[32]

(A room in Stefka's apartment. Ordinary Jewish-style furniture, universal, the sort usually available as part of rental. Two wardrobes – a chaise longue, tables – a commode, a rocking chair, two baskets covered in small rugs. A cheap rug on the floor. To the audience's right a curtained window. In front of it a light jardinière[33] with a few dried flowers. Lots of tasteless cheap objects. A pink bedroom lampshade hanging from the ceiling. At the back, a curtained alcove. When the curtains are undrawn, a metal bedstead is visible, quite neatly made up, with a pink cover, a stove – at the back an entrance door, to the left a door to the kitchen. In the main playing space a small table, as the curtain rises Michasiowa is kneeling by the stove and lighting it. Dusk – the only light comes from the stove)

SCENE 1

(Michasiowa, Daum)

(Michasiowa, dressed a little better, has a silk blouse, blue, old, with lace – a torn skirt and she is barefoot. When she has lit the stove she sits for a while on the ground and looks into the flames. A key is heard grinding in the main hallway door, the door opens and Daum enters with a heap of parcels and two bottles. Michasiowa, who has dozed off – wakes up)

MICHASIOWA	(Humbly, but in a bad temper) My good sir…how do you do…how do you do…
DAUM	(Moves her aside with his stick) Alright, alright…she's not in?
MICHASIOWA	She's at a rehearsal.
DAUM	For what?
MICHASIOWA	Something sad I think. To do with a man from Spain…
DAUM	The table needs moving out…
MICHASIOWA	(In a bad temper) Right…well…the leg's coming off.
DAUM	(Livid) Again? I won't pay for your damages.
MICHASIOWA	But my dear sir! This is worthless junk – it's rotten and worm-eaten.
DAUM	Not true.
MICHASIOWA	They won't give anything even half decent to lodgers.[34]

DAUM   Silence! Lay the table!

                (To Michasiowa, who is lighting the lamp)

                I'll do it myself.

                (He takes off his overcoat and climbs up onto the chair)

                Why light it anyway? Waste of naphthalene!

MICHASIOWA   *(Exiting to the kitchen)* She pays for naphthalene herself!

                (Exits – after lighting the lamp Daum climbs down from the chair and walks round the furniture, checking that it's stable, and mutters. Michasiowa returns with a table cloth, lays the table. Daum opens the packages)

DAUM   Be so kind as to lay three places.

MICHASIOWA   What's going on?

DAUM   Well…here we have three forks…three knives…

Figure 47: Setting the table. Research performance of Zapolska's *Miss Maliczewska*. University of Reading, POSK Theatre, London, 2007/8. Sam Tye as Michasiowa. Photo by Matt Ager.

MICHASIOWA	Don't overdo it.
DAUM	Right – that'll be adequate for three people …
MICHASIOWA	Someone coming to supper, then?
DAUM	Be so kind as to bite your tongue and just lay the table … Sardines … here … like so … leave that there … this is caviar …
MICHASIOWA	Right … yes …
DAUM	Wine bottles, on the window ledge … keep them chilled …
MICHASIOWA	Wine bottles? One's enough to start a fight!
DAUM	Yes, yes, quite so …
	(Goes to the stove)
	Why's it so cold in here?
MICHASIOWA	Well, because we light it once a day and it's frosty out there.
DAUM	It really ought to be warmer.
MICHASIOWA	I'd say so. And in the mornings I have to chop ice away from the kitchen porch just so I can open the door. But we have to economize on everything, there's no way round it.
DAUM	*(Smokes cigarettes, after a while)* Anyone come here?
MICHASIOWA	Dear God! You keep on asking the same question. Who on earth would come here? She's bored as a lapdog, she is …
DAUM	She should do some reading.
MICHASIOWA	Dearie me! And what will she do in her old age?
DAUM	I can see you're giving her notions.
MICHASIOWA	*(Upset)* Hardly! What do I care! She does what she wants with her life.

(Pause)

Well... what's for supper?

DAUM   There must be something left over from dinner.

MICHASIOWA   Right you are. Such huge portions.

DAUM   Besides, it's not supper – just an informal spread...

MICHASIOWA   Because I might be able to get hold of some nice chops...

DAUM   No need for that... no need... just a light sort of buffet.

MICHASIOWA   Whatever you say.

DAUM   *(Rises and sees a court summons on the side table)* What's this?

MICHASIOWA   From the court again.

DAUM   *(Livid)* What? Again? I won't pay! By God, I will not pay!

MICHASIOWA   So don't pay then... dearie me!

DAUM   How much is it for?

MICHASIOWA   Eighty...

DAUM   What? Gulden?

MICHASIOWA   No, no! Kronen! Dearie me!

DAUM   What's it for?!

MICHASIOWA   She has to wear something on the stage. Two dresses tomorrow – for that, apparently.

(Pause – Daum sits by the stove)

Shall I make some tea?

DAUM   Yes, only brew the one I brought, in the packet – not yours...

SCENE 2

(Michasiowa, Daum, Stefka)

(Stefka bursts in, dressed a little better, has a giant hat with feathers)

STEFKA   *(Singing)* Platz da! Jetzt kommt die Grette![35]

DAUM   At last!

STEFKA   What do you mean 'at last'? Long rehearsal … burned the candle at both ends, thought we might have to stay the whole night long.[36]

                 (To Michasiowa, throwing her hat)

                 Right, get rid of that rag.

Figure 48: A bad atmosphere. Research performance of Zapolska's *Miss Maliczewska*. University of Reading, POSK Theatre, London, 2007/8. Dan Harding as Daum, Phoebe Garrett as Stefka. Photo by Lib Taylor.

(Pointedly)

And I've had it up to here with a certain someone.

DAUM	Who, me?

STEFKA   *(Powdering her nose and combing her hair)* Yes … well … possibly … why hasn't this person seen the director? Leading me on, all the time.

DAUM   What do you want Stefka? You've got a part haven't you?

STEFKA   That's not a part, it's a scandal. Anyway it had nothing to do with this certain person – it was an act of God, who arranged that Milowicz should sprain her ankle and I be asked to stand in for her.

DAUM   *(Lying on the sofa)* But they did let you.

STEFKA   But I did ask – for you to go to the director and request for my name to be put on the poster and what did they do – leave Milowicz on!

DAUM   I'm in no hurry.

STEFKA   But I am. Only someone or other is afraid of compromising himself.

DAUM   *(Frowning)* What do you mean? Have I got something to boast about? Besides, no skin off my nose, I didn't promise a thing.

STEFKA   *(Sadly)* But I made myself a promise.

(To Michasiowa)

What're you laughing at?

MICHASIOWA   You're just imagining it, miss.

STEFKA   I've got perfectly good eyesight. Go to the kitchen …

(Affecting threat)

… and sharpen a knife …

MICHASIOWA   Christ Jesus! What for!

STEFKA	(*Laughing*) I'll cut both your throats! Well, hurry up! Off you go! And let this certain person thank God that a certain other person has an angelic disposition, because any other woman might well raise hell...so you'd never believe it...
DAUM	Wouldn't be seeing a lot of me then.
STEFKA	Dearie me! How exceedingly tragic!
	(*Michasiowa exits, Daum pulls Stefka towards him. Stefka delicately withdraws to say something, flees to the table*)
	What's with the tip-top spread?
DAUM	(*On the sofa*) If Stefka promises to be well-behaved then maybe, just maybe, one of my friends will show up for a bite to eat.
STEFKA	If he's anything like a certain person...
DAUM	That's not the point. However – since she is always pointing the finger, complaining that she's bored, then if, I repeat, she can behave herself half-decently, not stick her tongue out...
	(*Stefka sticks her tongue out*)
	...not turn her nose up...
	(*Stefka turns her nose up*)
	...not play the fool...in a word...have some kind of dignity...
STEFKA	To hell with dignity! If your friend is coming here then he knows what I am and all about my pre-dic-a-ment!
DAUM	Dignified and decent behaviour is possible in every situation. Look at me – do I get up to the sort of pranks you do? No – and why not? Because I know what dignity is!
STEFKA	You can really talk for that long?
DAUM	What I intend is that this friend of mine should leave here with the appropriate impression.

STEFKA	If he drones on like a fat old bore as well then let him stay where he is. I've no desire to go grey with boredom
	(Sweetly)
	And now – please leave ...
DAUM	Where to?
STEFKA	Onto the street or something – because my guests will arrive shortly.
DAUM	What guests?
STEFKA	Mine. My applause. For tomorrow. Why? If a certain person doesn't take the trouble to secure my position, then I must. Tomorrow after the couplets I will have much murmuring and approving applause. I have to organize it – and I've managed to do that after some considerable effort and difficulty. Any minute now my applause will get here and I have to offer them something ...
	(She looks around sadly, there's nothing – suddenly clocks the table – to the kitchen)
	Michasiowa! Bring out a tray, would you! Yes! This will make tip-top sandwiches ...
DAUM	Pardon me – this is a snack intended for my friend.
STEFKA	To hell with that!
	(Michasiowa carries in a tray. Stefka puts what's on the table onto it)
	That's the ticket! Sardines, ham ... butter ... tip ... top ... yum ... yum ...
DAUM	Please do not touch that – its caviar!
STEFKA	Sheer decadence! Give the caviar to me! There simply must be an avalanche of sandwiches ...
DAUM	Wait! I'll do it!
	(They all rush into the kitchen – pause – doorbell – Michasiowa rushes back in, thrown out by Stefka, who, standing in the kitchen doorway, with a knife in her hand, says, 'Ask them in, let them wait')

Figure 49: Here comes Miss Stefka! Research performance of Zapolska's *Miss Maliczewska*. University of Reading, POSK Theatre, London, 2007/8. Andrew Baker and Matt van Niftrik as Friends, Michael Day as Filo. Photo by Lib Taylor.

SCENE 3

(Filo, Friends 1, 2 and 3, others with mandolins, then Stefka)

(Daum's hand is seen gesticulating urgently to Michasiowa from the kitchen)

DAUM   My overcoat! My overcoat!

              (The youths enter, look around)

FILO   We're here to see Miss Maliczewska. Is she in?

MICHASIOWA   She is. She's asked for you to wait!

              (Exits to the kitchen)

FRIEND 1   *(To Filo)* Well…not exactly chic, is it, really.

FILO   Well…what do you want, it's respectable.

FRIEND 2   Maybe this is just the entrance hall?

FILO   No. There's only a kitchen, through there.

FRIEND 3   I thought she'd have better living quarters.

FILO   Her behaviour is beyond reproach.

FRIEND 1   But…

FILO   That's how it is. I know! She never steps out with anyone. Not even actors. Now then, so we don't forget each other's names. You…

                (To Friend 1)

                … are Drwęski.[37]

FRIEND 1   Rwęski,[38] I said – not Drwęski.

FILO   Alright then, Rwęski it is. You…

                (To Friend 2)

FRIEND 2   Norymberski.[39]

FILO   That's not a surname. We mustn't make her suspect we've changed our names…How about Januszewski?[40]

FRIEND   Agreed.

FILO   You! Jastrzębski.[41]

FRIEND   How about a count's name or something?

FILO   Not a hope. She'll sniff you out straight away.

FRIEND 1   So cunning?

FILO   O, ho! You – Gwaranz, you – Młodziejewicz…you…[42]

FRIEND 1   Something with a coat of arms.

FILO	You ... Pomian ... you ...[43]
FRIEND 1	Something animal-like.
FILO	You – Miałkowski. Purr-fect![44]
FRIEND 1	How about you? Filo – what'll you change yours to?
FILO	Me? Jaroszewski.[45] Remember! Don't give the game away. And – you know what... she's a decent girl! And don't get in my way – help me along – because I love her! Quiet! Stop arguing! Here she comes!
STEFKA	(Enters with dignity, as the artiste, she doesn't know what to do with her hands, like a debutante) Gentlemen!
FILO	Allow us to introduce ourselves. These are my friends – the ones I told you about. They're all at your disposal. Here is – my friend – ah – Drwęski...
FRIEND 1	Rwęski.
FILO	Norymberski... ah no – Pomian, Gwaranz...
	(To his friends)
	... come on then – brain like a sieve!
	(Each one mutters something and bows)
STEFKA	A pleasure! Really! You gentlemen are so gracious, took the trouble to come all this way.
FILO	The privilege is all ours.
	(Long pause – no-one knows what to say, Stefka is troubled – suddenly she says with a smile)
STEFKA	Be so kind, gentlemen, as to take a seat!
	(The youths sit, chairs break beneath two of them – consternation – suddenly Stefka bursts out laughing and nearly chokes)
FRIEND 2	I'm so terribly sorry, Madam...
FILO	Really... such behaviour... be so kind as to break a seat![46]

STEFKA	*(Laughing)* It's nothing, really, this is furniture from Noah's ark. Not for sitting on. Jewish manufacture. No-one Jewish here, is there? Haven't offended anyone? Let's just sit on the floor! That way nothing will collapse. Well? Not so bad, is it.
FILO	It's heavenly!
	(They sit in a circle on the floor, Stefka among them – she throws them some cushions as they sit)
STEFKA	Like in the East! And if everything collapses, then down we go, bang, straight into the cellar. Ha, ha, ha!
	(They all laugh heartily, childish laughter)
FILO	I would rescue you.
FRIENDS	And I would! Me too!
STEFKA	How would you manage that?
FILO	I'd catch you mid-air.
STEFKA	Like the princess from the Glass Hill.
FILO	And the Prince of the Moon.
STEFKA	*(To the friends)* And these are our courtiers ... and this the shortest fellow ... is a pageboy. Well! All that's missing is a golden coach.[47]
FRIEND 1	We'll build a flying machine.
STEFKA	From a spider's web – and you'll hammer it together with diamond nails and the engine will be made of gold – and instead of fuel ...
FILO	Dew from the flowers.
STEFKA	We wouldn't get very far.
FILO	The sun would drink the dew.
FRIEND 1	And you would use the diamond nails as earrings, miss.
STEFKA	*(Sadly)* Huh! No!

(Revives)

Wait a minute ... we'll have something to eat!

(She jumps up, runs to the kitchen door)

Service!

(She carries out a tray of sandwiches, behind her Michasiowa with a couple of plates)

Please! Help yourselves!

(She offers them around, the boys take them – to Filo)

Here's the best one ... for you sir ... here come the napkins!

(She rushes to the kitchen)

FILO	*(To friends)* Well? Was I right or what?
FRIEND 1	She seemed bigger to me on stage.[48]
FRIEND 3	And younger.
FRIEND 2	Actually I'd say she looked older.
FILO	Fools, the lot of you. She's delicious.[49]
FRIEND 1	Mmm ... well ... Milowicz is better looking.[50]
FILO	Hardly!

(Stefka returns – casts the napkins about)

STEFKA	There we are! Ah! One other thing! ... Michasiowa! The corkscrew ... glasses ...
MICHASIOWA	*(Quietly)* There's only two.
STEFKA	Well then, two there shall be!

(To the boys)

Right – let's drink something nice!

(*Michasiowa returns with two glasses, Stefka takes a bottle from the window ledge and wants to open it*)

FILO   Allow me!

MICHASIOWA   (*To Stefka, quietly*) Your patron wants his overcoat.

STEFKA   (*As above*) No idea where it's gone, do I?

                (*Putting glasses on the table*)

                Right – here – two more glasses – and here's an egg cup – here's a sort of deeper ashtray and here's a small vase … Yes! Gypsy style!

                (*They sit and huddle close together*)

FILO   Gentlemen! Let us drink the health of the lady of this household and her impending success!

STEFKA   That rests entirely in your hands!

                (*She clinks glasses with them*)

                Michasiowa! Sandwiches!

                (*Michasiowa passes the tray around again*)

                It's true, you gentlemen really can make sure I land on my feet.

                (*Stefka says this with bewitching charm*)

FRIEND 1   We'll see to that. We'll give you a first class round of applause.

STEFKA   Only it shouldn't be too much.[51]

FILO   (*Knowingly*) We've had practice.

STEFKA   Yes – it's one of your hobbies.

FILO   That's right. Only we don't organize an ovation for just anyone.

FRIEND 1   Absolutely not.

(Stefka runs to the door – calls out 'sandwiches' – Daum's hand appears through the door in its shirt sleeve, holding a tray of sandwiches)

STEFKA   Dearest sirs do help yourselves! And a little wine! Now it's my turn to toast you! Long live my clappers!

(One of them strums his guitar)

Wine! Music! Dancing! Laughter! Lord! How good I feel – how strangely well I feel!

(The friends begin to play The Mistress waltz)[52]

FILO   *(To Stefka)* At your service, ma'am!

(They dance)

FRIEND 1   *(Jumps in)* Now it's my turn!

(Grabs Steka, Filo plays on the mandolin for a while, at last he takes Stefka away from his friend and dancing says in her ear)

FILO   You're delicious!

STEFKA   *(Laughing)* So are you!

FILO   You've such delicious eyes!

STEFKA   You've such delicious lips!

(The short friend dances on his own, they bump, dancing, into the friends, laughter, suddenly Stefka grabs the youngest and shouts)

With the pageboy! Small fry!

(She begins to twirl, shouting, laughing, other friends get up, some play, others dance, childish and jolly pranking, enter Michasiowa)

MICHASIOWA   Pardon me Miss!

STEFKA   What!

(She stops, they all stop)

Figure 50: A toast. Research performance of Zapolska's *Miss Maliczewska*. University of Reading, POSK Theatre, London, 2007/8. Michael Day as Filo, Sam Tye as Michasiowa, Phoebe Garrett as Stefka. Photo by Matt Ager.

MICHASIOWA	Your auntie's asking for you a minute, Miss.
FILO	You have an auntie?
STEFKA	*(As though waking from a dream)*
	But … er … what does she want?
MICHASIOWA	Auntie's asking for a bit of quiet.
STEFKA	*(As though in a fever)* Huh! Stuff her! Carry on! Small fry! Take Michasiowa!
	(One of the friends grabs Michasiowa, twirls her around, Stefka grabs Friend 1, Michasiowa pulls away and exits to the kitchen, shouting begins, play and noise, after a while Michasiowa returns with a funereal expression and says)
MICHASIOWA	Pardon me Miss.
STEFKA	*(Angry)* What this time!

MICHASIOWA	Auntie is very ill – she has a migraine – and she is very angry.
STEFKA	(Breaks off and sobers up) You say – she's angry.
MICHASIOWA	(Meaningfully) Extremely![53]
STEFKA	(Confused) Ah well! In that case, pardon me, gentlemen … only …
FILO	(And friends, also confused) But we understand perfectly … we're very sorry Miss … on behalf of my friends … thank you so much for entertaining us … so well …
STEFKA	I'm terribly sorry, I …
FRIEND 1	But honestly Miss, we were going to leave in any case …
FILO	Yes! That's right!
FRIEND 1	And now! As a farewell! The waltz.
	(They being to play a waltz, Stefka leads them towards the door)
STEFKA	I commend myself to you – for tomorrow – after the third couplet … my darlings …
FRIEND 1	Allow me to put your mind at rest – you'll be hearing from us!
	(They laugh and exit, playing)

SCENE 4

(Filo, Stefka)

(The stage is empty. Stefka leans against the stove and remains there, depressed. Filo sidles in and speaks quietly, against the backdrop of the waltz)

FILO	Are you sad?
STEFKA	(By the stove) I feel as though …
FILO	A moment ago you were so happy.
STEFKA	(Sighing) Well? One moment does not resemble another.

Figure 51: Daum is getting angry in the kitchen. Research performance of Zapolska's *Miss Maliczewska*. University of Reading, POSK Theatre, London, 2007/8. Phoebe Garrett as Stefka, Sam Tye as Michasiowa. Photo by Matt Ager.

FILO	Thank goodness. Variety! Like a wild-flower meadow. Full of contrasts!
STEFKA	Yes... for you...
FILO	And you?
STEFKA	Oh! Me, I...!
FILO	What are you missing? You're young, beautiful, an artiste, what more do you want! Not been through anything yet, have you – me, well, that's different...
STEFKA	Really.
FILO	I may be young in years. But what have I been through. I'm practically an old man.
STEFKA	Hm. It's the fashion to say such things.

FILO	I'm beyond that…don't be sad.
STEFKA	At your command?
FILO	Yes – at my request.
STEFKA	What's it to you?
FILO	Because as soon as the lights went out behind your eyes I became forlorn…your eyes were so delicious when you were dancing the waltz.
STEFKA	Ha! If we could only dance the waltz for an entire lifetime!
FILO	You can…so to speak! Such intoxication, such joy, it can last a whole lifetime.
STEFKA	And then such sadness!
FILO	Why think about what comes later? Today belongs to us! Long live today! How very lovely you are!
STEFKA	You keep on repeating that.
FILO	I don't know any other way. Me, God only knows how long I've felt like this about you…when you were still living in that basement…
STEFKA	Ah! It was you who gave me flowers, care of Kulesz?
FILO	It was!
STEFKA	I didn't know, because he never said, who brought them, just 'a friend' – you didn't sign your name under the poems either. I don't even know what your name is?
FILO	(Smiling) My name is…springtime! (Pause – Stefka repeats quietly, 'springtime' and then, expressively)
STEFKA	But – honestly now?
FILO	(Pause) Januszkiewicz.[54]
STEFKA	And your first name? What do they call you at home? Your mother?

FILO	Mama? Filo…
STEFKA	Like in the play, 'Balladyna'…[55]
	(Enter Michasiowa)
MICHASIOWA	Pardon me Miss?
STEFKA	(As if in a dream) Ah! What is it!
MICHASIOWA	You're auntie's asking for you to come at once.
FILO	I'll be going then… goodbye, miss…
STEFKA	(With regret) What a shame! It's so good to talk to you! And what's Kulesz doing - is he well?
FILO	Oh - he's scribbling away…
STEFKA	And doing your homework for you?
	(Laughs)
FILO	(Laughing) Sshh! It's a secret.
STEFKA	Huh! Even the sparrows are twittering about it!
FILO	Is that right!
STEFKA	Here's to your conscience! Goodbye now!
FILO	Goodbye!
	(Grabs her by the hands and kisses her arms and elbows)
STEFKA	(Laughing) What's all this!
	(Throws him out)
	Alright! Alright! Enough, enough!
	(Filo is moved and she also, they laugh nervously, Filo exits, Stefka looks after him, returns to the stage, tidies the furniture, through the kitchen door Daum enters carefully, looks for his overcoat)

SCENE 5

(Daum, Stefka, Michasiowa)

DAUM   *(Frowning)* Where's my overcoat?

STEFKA   *(Finds it, puts it on, it is enormous, and jumps up and down in front of Daum)*

                Your rightful property is restored to you, sir! My patron's overcoat! Here it is!

DAUM   *(As above)* Kindly give it back. I have to go and buy another lot now, there's hardly a thing left.

                (Stefka takes off the overcoat, gives it to Daum with exaggeration)

STEFKA   But the sandwiches really were tip…top…

DAUM   I'll be right back. Leave the chain off.

STEFKA   God go with you! I'll miss you…

                (Daum exits, Stefka runs to the alcove and quickly begins to change out of her dress into a kimono-style dressing gown, hums The Mistress[56] waltz, enter Michasiowa, tidies)

                Who's there?

MICHASIOWA   Me!

STEFKA   What do you think? Good looking, that boy who left last.

MICHASIOWA   Doesn't count.

STEFKA   *(Laughing in the alcove)* And why not?

MICHASIOWA   Because Stefka, you either grub about and find some old toadstool – or else something with milk still under its nose.

STEFKA   So – it evens out.

MICHASIOWA   Right.

STEFKA	Oi! Stop being so poisonous! Been sulking again? You're unbearable. I'll have to throw you out.
MICHASIOWA	Right-o.
STEFKA	Why shouldn't I? Just because you're my sister I'm supposed to keep you at my side?
MICHASIOWA	God has ordained it. All you have to do is pay up monthly and I'll get out from under your feet.
STEFKA	Right.

(Quietly)

(Knocking at the kitchen door)

MICHASIOWA	What's got into the kitchen?

(Michasiowa enters after a while, quietly)

Stefka – there's some lady in there and she wants to talk to you.

STEFKA	A lady? For me? From the theatre?
MICHASIOWA	Hardly. She's dressed like someone really sort of … and she wants you to be alone.
STEFKA	(Intrigued) In that case, ask her in!

(Hurriedly buttons the dressing gown at her breast)

SCENE 6

(Daumowa, Stefka, Michasiowa)

DAUMOWA	Is Miss Maliczewska in?
STEFKA	That's me.
DAUMOWA	Would it be possible to speak with you safely for a while – with no interruptions, that is.
STEFKA	Aha. Alright then.

Figure 52: A discussion about morality. Research performance of Zapolska's *Miss Maliczewska*. University of Reading, POSK Theatre, London, 2007/8. Saskia Solomons as Daumowa and Phoebe Garrett as Stefka. Photo by Lib Taylor.

(Goes to put chain on entrance door, to Michasiowa, quietly)

Go and stand by the gate and if the old fellow should come tell him to take a stroll somewhere and not come up yet. Madam – now we are alone.

(To Michasiowa)

I'll shut the kitchen door behind you.

(Stefka and Michasiowa exit to the kitchen – then Stefka returns)

Here I am!

DAUMOWA	*(Thrown a little off course)* You're still very young.
STEFKA	*(Laughing)* No – it's an optical illusion.
DAUMOWA	And very jolly?
STEFKA	Why should I be sad?
DAUMOWA	Well – everyone has some reason to be sad. Let's sit down, alright?
STEFKA	Here then, on the chaise … that's safest.
DAUMOWA	*(Sitting on the chaise)* You're probably curious as to why I'm here. And so – let me tell you – you interest me a great deal.
STEFKA	Why so?
	(She takes one of the chairs from next to the table and pulls it in front of Daumowa)
DAUMOWA	You see – there are a few of us women – ladies really – we've set up a sort of society.
STEFKA	*(Sitting carefully on the chair)* Aha! You're having a collection. Thin pickings here though.
DAUMOWA	Not at all. We don't collect anything. We look after single women who for reasons we care little about have, so to speak, gone off the rails … and … well …
STEFKA	I see … and what's it to you ladies?
DAUMOWA	We're following the dictates of our conscience.
STEFKA	I'd much rather do something else.
DAUMOWA	Oh, dear Madam – it's a great joy when you manage to awaken self-respect in someone – a sense of decency …
STEFKA	Tact … morality …
DAUMOWA	*(Thrown off course)* Tact … exactly … exactly …
STEFKA	I hear that every day.

DAUMOWA	Who from? First time I've been here.
STEFKA	*(Her voice thickening)* But I have a sort of resident barrel organ.
	(Thinly)
	Pardon me, madam.
DAUMOWA	So much the better, that there's someone here to take up the cause of human dignity. Because the kind of life you're leading really cannot make a person happy. The decadence that surrounds you, that can't be enough. You must feel a deep sense of inner disquiet…
STEFKA	Of course I do – because – I have debts.
DAUMOWA	That's nothing compared to the crimes you inflict upon yourself.
STEFKA	*(Slides off the chair)* Me?
	(Sits on the ground)
DAUMOWA	You stand at this moment beyond society.
STEFKA	*(Laughing)* To hell with that.
DAUMOWA	Society is necessary.
STEFKA	For what? Horseradish sauce! Will society pay my debts?
DAUMOWA	But it will shroud you in respectability.
STEFKA	Ha! What luxury! When you have everything you need, then you can afford a portion of respectability.
DAUMOWA	That's right. But by then it may be too late.
STEFKA	*(Sadly)* Ah well, no unfilled vacancy in heaven, then.
DAUMOWA	But surely – if you wanted to – abandon this way of life and return…
STEFKA	*(Rather violently and gloomily)* And return? To where? To a basement? Oho! Not a chance. It's bad for me here, really…but there…o, ho!
DAUMOWA	I went there – you had everything – a roof over your head, a life…

STEFKA	*(Very bitterly)* Well – if you had to live like that, in a place like that – I'm curious, how long you'd stick it out.
DAUMOWA	You had protection – you know the lady I mean.
STEFKA	*(Covers her eyes to hide her tears – when she pulls her hands away, her gaze falls on Daumowa's fur)* Precisely – you've hit the nail on the head – I hope you don't mind my asking – is that made of mink or seal?
DAUMOWA	*(Nonchalantly)* Seal.
STEFKA	*(Reaches out her hand hesitantly and strokes it)* Goodness me! That must have cost a huge amount of money.
DAUMOWA	Not so expensive. One thousand five hundred. *(Smiling)* A gift from my husband – for bearing him a son…
STEFKA	*(Smoothing the fur)* You have a husband?
DAUMOWA	I do.
STEFKA	*(In a childlike tone)* A good one?
DAUMOWA	Very – a most worthy man.
STEFKA	And a son?
DAUMOWA	And a little boy.
STEFKA	What age is he?
DAUMOWA	Oh, he's a grown man.
STEFKA	Good looking?
DAUMOWA	Very.
STEFKA	And what do you call him, at home?
DAUMOWA	Filo.

STEFKA	I know a Filo too – Filo Januszkiewicz.
DAUMOWA	(Laughing) That's not my son. Well – you see, if you knew how to conduct yourself, you would have, as I do, a good husband, children…
STEFKA	Huh! My husband would never give me a coat like that.
DAUMOWA	(Spreads out in her coat) Well, who knows? In any case – does this coat equal happiness?
STEFKA	But you did want a coat like that…
DAUMOWA	Very much so… but…
STEFKA	But what? I'm a woman, same as you – don't you think? Fashioned from different clay, perhaps?
DAUMOWA	I didn't pay with my dignity.
STEFKA	Madam – it was a man who gave you that fur coat.
DAUMOWA	(Taken aback, after a while) My husband.
STEFKA	Well – because you had a dowry, so you had something to buy a husband with – and me, a poor girl, I didn't have a dowry, and so I was bought.
DAUMOWA	(Lost for words) Difficult to get to the point with you.
STEFKA	(Gets up off the floor) Ah well!…
DAUMOWA	(Rises, politely) I'm leaving! But I will be seeing you again. I hope you'll ponder my words…
STEFKA	(A little seriously) Let me tell you something. You should have come to see me earlier. It's too late now.
DAUMOWA	It's never too late.
STEFKA	I'm afraid…
DAUMOWA	(Pointedly) In any case, the way we organize our society means that we take action only after a given individual has irrevocably stepped off the right road.

STEFKA	*(Sniffing)* Condiments after dinner.
DAUMOWA	We don't interfere with anyone's secrets. We don't get involved in gossip about the whole affair. We're not remotely bothered who it is…it's enough that…the matter is illegal, shocking…
STEFKA	*(Naively)* Madam – if only the society were able to settle debts.
DAUMOWA	One simply shouldn't get into debt. It's an affront to human dignity.
	(Daumowa moves towards the door, Stefka follows her)
STEFKA	He who is satisfied does not believe the hungry. You don't use scent, do you, Madam?
DAUMOWA	*(In spite of herself, affected by her wit)* No. My husband doesn't like it. He has forbidden it.
STEFKA	Someone forbids me from using scent as well. I'm told only coquettes perfume themselves. Let me teach you a thing or two. Spray the edge of your dress with scent until it's moist then at every step you take there'll be a waft of perfume.
DAUMOWA	*(Laughing)* That would be subterfuge!
STEFKA	*(Laughing)* So be it!
DAUMOWA	Really! I feel so sorry for you! I've liked you terribly.
STEFKA	*(Pointing at her)* I've liked you too.
DAUMOWA	*(Offended, straightens up)* Madam – Miss Maliczewska – she is a persona non grata.[57]
STEFKA	*(Offended)* Ah – dear madam – sticks and stones.
DAUMOWA	May I leave safely – and unseen?
STEFKA	I should hope so! Best if you go through the kitchen.
	(Doorbell)
DAUMOWA	And why? So I don't get caught red-handed!

STEFKA	This way! Fare you well, madam!
	(With irony)
	You'll forgive me for not being able to return your call – but – I don't even know your name.
DAUMOWA	*(With superiority)* That's irrelevant.
	(Politely)
	I'll be seeing you again – fare well – please do think about what I've said...[58]
	(Doorbell – exits to the kitchen, Stefka sees her off, Stefka's voice is heard, 'Straight through, if you please – and downstairs through the courtyard on the left – sincere respects', Stefka returns, sticks her tongue out after Daumowa and runs to the entrance door, opens it but does not lift the chain. Bogucki's voice is heard, 'Does Miss Maliczewska live here?', Stefka takes off the chain, enter Bogucki, stylish, man of 35, carrying flowers)[59]

SCENE 7

(Bogucki, Stefka)

BOGUCKI	Miss Maliczewska?
STEFKA	*(With charm)* That's me.
BOGUCKI	*(Looking around)* He was supposed to be here...
STEFKA	Our mutual friend. But he went off to get some air in his lungs. Why not take off your coat and wait?
BOGUCKI	I see you've been forewarned of my visit.
STEFKA	He's been trumpeting your arrival like you're an archangel or something.
BOGUCKI	*(Removing his coat)* You'll pardon me...
STEFKA	You'll pardon me – for not having an entrance hall.
BOGUCKI	*(Introduces himself in perfect form)* I am Bogucki.

Figure 53: First meeting with Daum's friend. Research performance of Zapolska's *Miss Maliczewska*. University of Reading, POSK Theatre, London, 2007/8. Michael Muncer as Bogucki, Phoebe Garrett as Stefka. Photo by Matt Ager.

STEFKA   Take a seat, do! Oh! Not there! Not there!

BOGUCKI   Why not?

STEFKA   Because everything is broken. Well – this seems to be holding together...

                (Bogucki sits on the chaise – Stefka stands by the table)

                I know you from somewhere.

BOGUCKI   Maybe you've seen me from the stage. I'm often at the theatre.

STEFKA   In the front row?

BOGUCKI   Naturally.

STEFKA	Oh! Oh! Wait a minute … now I know! It was you with Milowicz …
BOGUCKI	*(Laughing)* It might have been!
STEFKA	*(Rushes towards him and leaps onto the chaise)* Oh yes! Yes! You'd come to meet her and wait near the women's dressing rooms.
BOGUCKI	Long time ago now!
STEFKA	Three years ago … I was still a slip of a thing in the ballet then …
BOGUCKI	I don't recall …
STEFKA	Because there's nothing to recall …
BOGUCKI	*(Rises – going to coatstand – handing her the flowers)* You'll accept these flowers, Madam …
STEFKA	*(Overwhelmed and delighted)* Thank you so much … I'll put them right here in a very prominent spot …
	(Runs to the alcove, takes a jug of water, puts on the table)
BOGUCKI	*(Following her)* Why so?
STEFKA	Because he never, ever buys me a single flower.
BOGUCKI	You don't mean it!
STEFKA	Oh! Mm, hm! You don't know him! Only thank God you're the friend …
BOGUCKI	Why's that?
STEFKA	Because you seem so down-to-earth, a people's man. I was afraid it might be yet another stuffed-up mortician – like him.
BOGUCKI	Is he that dull?
STEFKA	Sir! Dull is the very least of it! Just as well I've got an angelic disposition and can put up with him.
BOGUCKI	Well, if that's how it is – just leave him.
STEFKA	Right. Hah! Let's talk about something more cheerful.

(Takes his arm)

That Milowicz used to trick you good and proper.

BOGUCKI   *(Laughing – they go towards the chaise)*

What are you saying?

(They sit)

STEFKA   *(Laughter rising)*

For the love of God, I remember one time, it was raining...after an operetta...you sir, were supposed to wait outside our dressing rooms and she left from the men's side. And you waited and waited and the rain poured. We were looking out of the window, laughing 'til our sides split! What a joke!

BOGUCKI   That was rather nasty of Milowicz.

STEFKA   Why – when she'd had you up to here?

BOGUCKI   And I was being so faithful to her as well.

STEFKA   I see...you look the type...

BOGUCKI   *(Edging closer to her)*

Why don't you find out...

(Grinding of key in the lock)

SCENE 8

(Daum, Stefka, Bogucki then Michasiowa)

(Daum enters with parcels – stands in the doorway unimpressed by the pair seated in close proximity – he says with affected joviality)

DAUM   Aha! Here already I see? Apologies – I had to go out.

BOGUCKI   *(Greets him)* No harm done. We've become acquainted.

STEFKA   And fallen in love...

(Sticks out her tongue. Daum makes despairing faces)

BOGUCKI   *(Laughing)* Oh – if only ...

DAUM   Please take charge of supper – actually it's not really supper ...

               (Michasiowa enters)

STEFKA   *(Next to the table with Michasiowa)* Only ... an informal sort of snack ...

DAUM   *(To Bogucki)* I sent you a financial breakdown yesterday ...

BOGUCKI   Thanks – difficult to pull it off though ...

DAUM   Why's that?

BOGUCKI   I propose arranging a sort of fictional sale – would make things much easier.

               (Stefka butts in)

Figure 54: Let's do business. Research performance of Zapolska's *Miss Maliczewska*. University of Reading, POSK Theatre, London, 2007/8. Michael Muncer as Bogucki, Dan Harding as Daum. Photo by Matt Ager.

STEFKA	(Childishly) No – don't talk business – talk about something cheerful.
DAUM	I said – remember – I told you distinctly… be so good as to recollect…
STEFKA	My good sir – it has slipped my mind.
DAUM	(Irritated) Shame. I did ask…
BOGUCKI	(Rising) What's going on?
STEFKA	This good gentleman made a request that I should behave myself in a dignified fashion. But that's boring. Well? It'll bore you sir and you're such a merry fellow…
BOGUCKI	But of course it will!
	(They sit in their old place together – Daum oversees Michasiowa's laying of the table)
	Do tell me, Madam, why Milowicz'd had me up to here? Did she say anything?
STEFKA	Well – because you were jealous and used to make scenes.
BOGUCKI	That's not true! She was just boasting. I don't have such ugly inclinations.
STEFKA	That's good.
	(Looks at Daum)
	Jealousy is a beastly inclination.
DAUM	(Butting in) Dress your caviar with lemon juice, shall I?
BOGUCKI	Alright then!
	(To Stefka)
	In any case, I know the whole story.
STEFKA	(Interested) And about Bucholtz too?
BOGUCKI	And Winnicki…[60]

STEFKA	You're not serious! But there's one you knew nothing about, I'll wager...
BOGUCKI	Alright, let's bet on it.
DAUM	*(Butting in)* Prepare some sheep's cheese for you with cornichons, shall I?[61]
STEFKA	Oh do stop interrupting. Right... bet's on, then.
BOGUCKI	The stakes?
STEFKA	Discretion.
BOGUCKI	And if you happen to be indiscreet?
STEFKA	It'll be hard luck...
	(They laugh)
DAUM	*(Angry, by the table)* Miss Maliczewska - would you be so gracious as to tell me where you put that glass?
STEFKA	Well I was drinking out of it... and it broke!
DAUM	Marvellous! But there were two...
STEFKA	*(Jumps onto the chaise - jumps off and runs to the kitchen)* Wait a minute!
BOGUCKI	*(Sitting back in his place, watching her go)* She's got a lovely shape to her... and very smooth.
DAUM	So so. Cigarette?
	(Passes his cigarette case)
BOGUCKI	*(Takes the cigarette, laughing)* What's with the long face? Nice cigarette case.
DAUM	A present.
	(Bogucki examines it - Stefka returns)
STEFKA	Here's one more.

(Sits beside Bogucki)

So now I'll tell you, sir, about Miss Milowicz's lover – only about the real one ... That's nice.

(Takes Daum's cigarette case)

BOGUCKI	It's Daum's.
STEFKA	Never seen it before.

(Puts it down on the chaise)

A theatre man.

BOGUCKI	Huh!
STEFKA	Hardly that! Because it's our own we really love.
BOGUCKI	In that case, perhaps I should be in the operetta?
STEFKA	No – straight plays – you can take lessons with me. I'm training for the drama. I already know Desdemona and Klara – only Juliet left to go ...[62]
BOGUCKI	You don't mean it?
STEFKA	I swear. Just Juliet left and then I'll be ready ...
DAUM	*(By the table)* Ladies and gentlemen, refreshments are served.
STEFKA	You think I'm too young?

(She stands on tiptoe)

BOGUCKI	On the contrary. You're frightfully lithe and you've got first-class eyes.
DAUM	Your refreshments await you.
STEFKA	Precisely – in a drama, it's all about the eyes. In the ballet, it's legs, in opera, the throat – in drama – your sparklers.
BOGUCKI	You've got the right expression and frame – can't tell what colour though ...

Figure 55: Daum in a pickle. Research performance of Zapolska's *Miss Maliczewska*. University of Reading, POSK Theatre, London, 2007/8. Dan Harding as Daum. Photo by Matt Ager.

STEFKA	Black ... here ... take a look.
	(She covers her eyes with her hand, Bogucki moves it away, she slaps his hand, Daum is livid, moves to the table, takes a newspaper, sits away from them and begins to read)
DAUM	Whenever you feel like it – help yourselves ...
STEFKA	And what colour eyes do you have?
BOGUCKI	Sapphire blue.

STEFKA	You can't be serious?
BOGUCKI	Take a look!
	(Daum clears his throat meaningfully – they look at him)
STEFKA	(Quietly to Bogucki) He's angry.
BOGUCKI	So it seems.
STEFKA	Let's go and eat. Shouldn't be provoked.
BOGUCKI	Let's go.
STEFKA	(Laughing) Doctor's orders … he shouldn't …
	(Takes Bogucki's arm and the proceed in Daum's direction – they bow to him deeply)
	Let us attend this informal gathering.
DAUM	Well – at last.
	(Rises and goes with them to the table – they sit, Stefka in the centre)
	A little cognac!
BOGUCKI	Of course! But I couldn't eat a thing – had something earlier …
STEFKA	And its rations for me, is it?
DAUM	Help yourself. But just the one.
BOGUCKI	Why's that?
STEFKA	(To Bogucki) You married sir?
BOGUCKI	Over my dead body.
STEFKA	Children?
DAUM	(Horrified) Miss Maliczewska!

STEFKA   Well – what? So if you're neither the first nor have the second – then we're both bachelors!

                (They clink glasses – Daum tries to join in)

BOGUCKI   Not your business – you're not a bachelor.

STEFKA   Yes! That's right! Just the two of us!

DAUM   *(Resisting)* But ... whatever.

BOGUCKI   Bit of ham.

STEFKA   Some mustard – I'll fetch it.

                (Rushes to the kitchen dancing and singing)

BOGUCKI   *(Looks after her admiringly, then at Daum)* You're getting sourer by the minute. What's the matter? Jealous?

DAUM   *(Superior)* Me? Jealous about some mistress? What do you take me for?

BOGUCKI   That's better. No need for me to hold back then ...

Figure 56: Research performance of Zapolska's *Miss Maliczewska*. University of Reading, POSK Theatre, London, 2007/8. Dan Harding as Daum, Phoebe Garrett as Stefka, rehearsing the balcony scene. Photo by Matt Ager.

DAUM	Well...maybe after...
BOGUCKI	You see! You see!
STEFKA	(Bursts in, stepping out the mazurka)[63]
	What's so funny? She doesn't know – she wants to join in...
BOGUCKI	Do sit down. When you're not here, the room darkens.
STEFKA	(Enraptured) Dearie me! You will come more often? Won't you?
BOGUCKI	Of course I will. If you'll permit me!
	(Daum clears his throat)
	...if the gentleman and the lady will allow it...perhaps one day we could all step out together...
STEFKA	(Joyfully) Oh my God! Anything for some distraction...
DAUM	Out of the question I'm afraid. My position precludes foolish pranks of that nature.
BOGUCKI	Well – I do understand that. But when it's dark – in the evening – out of town – in a closed carriage...
STEFKA	(Angrily) Huh! Like a funeral procession.
DAUM	Even that would be risky.
STEFKA	See what a merry life I lead, sir.
DAUM	It is unfortunate. There's no other way.
STEFKA	(To Bogucki) Pour me some cognac, would you?
DAUM	No – anything but that.
BOGUCKI	Why not?
	(Pours)
	Here's to indiscretion!

STEFKA	(Sprawled out at the table) Alright.
	(They drink)
	I really liked you a lot sir.
BOGUCKI	I liked you a lot too, madam.
STEFKA	(To Daum) Well? You see? Not a shred of dignity and he liked me anyway. Pardon me, sir – but do you happen to know the director of the theatre?
BOGUCKI	I do.
STEFKA	(Kneels on the chair and leans against the table, Daum contemplates her, she sticks out her tongue at him) Are you on first name terms?
BOGUCKI	No.
STEFKA	Hm.
BOGUCKI	But if that's of any importance to you I can always drink a 'brüderschaft' with him some time.[64]
STEFKA	My hero! Do that – then I'll explain what I'm after …
BOGUCKI	Very well – I'll look for him today.
STEFKA	My hero!
	(Bogucki rises)
DAUM	What's this? You're leaving?
BOGUCKI	I have a very important rendez-vous …
STEFKA	With a woman?
DAUM	Madam Maliczewska!
	(Stefka turns her nose up)
	Madam Maliczewska!
BOGUCKI	(Dressing) But I'll certainly be back … with your permission Madam.

STEFKA	*(Near the door, hands him his hat)* Dear sir! Do come back! And quickly! Quickly!
BOGUCKI	With your permission?
DAUM	*(Sourly)* Feel free!
BOGUCKI	*(Laughing)* So little enthusiasm. No matter.
	(To Daum)
	Staying?
DAUM	For a bit.
BOGUCKI	See you again.
STEFKA	Yes. See you soon.

SCENE 9

(Stefka, Daum)

(Michasiowa clears the table – Stefka runs close to Daum and turns her nose up)

STEFKA	Can you credit it! I made a conquest!
DAUM	Right. When you left the room – he said he was shocked and disgusted.
STEFKA	Lying dog. Because, he said, I've got a good shape, I was eavesdropping! Now then, at the double, I have to learn Juliet, get me a balcony! Tomorrow's homework, right then, a table...
	(She shifts the table into the centre of the room – throws the script to Daum and shouts)
	You read Romeo and prompt me...come on...
DAUM	*(Sourpuss)* Haven't got my glasses.
	(Stretches out on the chaise)
STEKA	*(Politely and affectionately)* Whatever. Well...for me...

DAUM	*(Threatening)* You don't deserve it.
	(Reading)
	'But soft! What light through yonder window breaks?
	It is the east and Juliet is the sun!' etcetera...[65]
STEFKA	*(On the table)* Alright, now it's me.
	'Tis but thy name that is my enemy;
	Thou art thyself though, not a Montague.
	What's Montague? It is nor hand nor some foot,
	Nor arm, nor face, nor any other part
	Belonging to a man. O! be some other name:
	What's in a name? That which we call...'
DAUM	Nor foot...
STEFKA	Yes I already said that.
DAUM	But you said 'nor some foot'!
STEFKA	Give it a rest... now it's you.
	(Indicates him with her foot)
DAUM	Wait.
	(Reads)
	'Her vestal livery is but sick and green,
	And none but fools do wear it; cast it off.
	It is my lady; O! it is my love...'
STEFKA	Where are you up to? Where? You've gone backwards...

	(Doorbell)
	Who's that?
DAUM	The chain? The chain!
	(Michasiowa rushes onto the scene – Stefka still standing on the table)
	Don't take off the chain!
MICHASIOWA	I know, I know!

SCENE 10

(Same, Bailiff)

BAILIFF	Miss Maliczewska live here?
MICHASIOWA	She does – why?
BAILIFF	In the name of the law – business.
	(Michasiowa gloomily lifts the chain)
MICHASIOWA	Bailiff's here…
	(Stefka turns to Daum – Daum grabs his fur coat and hat and flees through the kitchen)
STEFKA	(Helpless for a moment – jumps off the table – rushes to the door) Over my dead body!
BAILIFF[66]	(Entering) Miss Maliczewska? Stefania? Here on behalf of Ryfke Rosenbusch – Modern Fashion Emporium – sum of fifty-three kronen…
STEFKA	(Recognizing him) Hello there Brzezina![67] Come inside, come on! Old friend of mine, aren't you! How's it going! Nothing here of mine though…
BAILIFF	Again?
STEFKA	(Laughing) Always.
BAILIFF	(Walks around, notices Daum's silver cigarette case on the chaise and throws himself upon it like a predator) Ahh… and this…

STEFKA	(Motions, as though to rescue it, then remembers herself) Oh that! Help yourself! Take it! Do take it sir!

(To Michasiowa, bubbling over with laughter)

The old goat's cigarette case! God's punishing him!

(Spins Michasiowa around, who is also laughing – and begins to dance the cancan, tearing her dress about with childish enthusiasm, singing full throttle 'God's punishing him' until the curtain has fallen completely)

ACT 3

(The same décor – daytime, Stefka is sitting near the side table doing her hair)

SCENE 1

(Stefka, Michasiowa)

MICHASIOWA	(Bustling about the room) You might give us a tip, Stefka.
STEFKA	(In a thin blue cotton blouse and a short grey woollen skirt) Nothing to give.
MICHASIOWA	Still?
STEFKA	That's right. And if it's so bad – just leave.
MICHASIOWA	Of course it's bad – if I was in service with strangers I'd earn my keep…

(Doorbell – Michasiowa goes to the door)

Might be him.

STEFKA	Hardly! He only crawls by quietly in the evenings…
MICHASIOWA	Mostly – but he's already been here twice in the daytime.
STEFKA	Well – who is it?

(Michasiowa holds the door ajar – the messenger passes her a bouquet and a letter)

Probably from that one who hasn't been weaned yet. Don't want them! Give them back!

MICHASIOWA	But the messenger's already gone.
STEFKA	I told you not to accept anything from that whelp…
MICHASIOWA	Why not? You can accept it.
STEFKA	I don't want to! I bet the kitchen door's open again.
MICHASIOWA	It's shut! You should see what he's written.
STEFKA	Oh really. I wouldn't dream of it.
MICHASIOWA	So I'll read it!

(Sits by the table and reads Filo's letter)

I will bind your slender wrists with pearls

And spread your golden hair over them…

(She sighs)

He writes nicely, it's a bit difficult to read.

STEFKA	Wonder where he stole this one from?
MICHASIOWA	Why would he steal something? Nothing with the letter except flowers.
STEFKA	What use are those weeds to me!
MICHASIOWA	So why don't you tell him Stefka that instead of flowers he should send perishable goods… that would be a better investment.
STEFKA	You're so stupid.
MICASHIOWA	What – speak for yourself… that's one form of currency.

(Begins to read)

I will bind your slender wrists…

STEFKA	What a drag…
MICHASIOWA	Or for him to pay for my lodgings…

STEFKA	Don't you dare mention it to him – not him or the old fellow ...
MICHASIOWA	Course not. If I passed as a sister, it wouldn't do to ask – but like this – as a servant – what does it matter if I speak up for myself!
STEFKA	I'll pay you.
MICHASIOWA	On the Day of Judgment – when the sky falls down. You might be better off telling the gentleman I'm a sister, then perhaps he'd get ashamed and pay up.
STEFKA	God save us! He let me know clearly didn't he that I should never mention my relations. I laid it down for you as a condition straight away. If you want to be here with me, fine. But – as a servant – you agreed. And so – keep your mouth shut ...
MICHASIOWA	(Gloomily) Because I thought you'd be rolling in it here.
STEFKA	Oh, that's right! Led by the nose. (Doorbell) Who's there? (Michasiowa goes to the door)

SCENE 2

(The same, Filo in a suit)[68]

FILO	Anybody home?
STEFKA	(In one move leaps off the sofa) What? What is it?
FILO	(Much altered) Two words. Something about a premiere. When? We want to arrange an ovation ...
STEFKA	Stop pulling my leg! You know I'm not in this premiere and that I'm sick and tired of your ovations. I forbade you from coming here! It's not what I want! I don't like it when people trail around after me ...
FILO	I don't trail around, because I am your shadow.

STEFKA	(Returns to the chaise) Lucky aren't I. And please don't send flowers, because you don't have the money...
FILO	That's not your concern. I'd steal the stars, so I could cast them under your feet.
STEFKA	(Laughing) And in the meantime you sell your textbooks...
FILO	Not true. I have my sources of income. My father gives me an allowance.
STEFKA	Five kronen...
FILO	A bit more than that.
STEFKA	It's all the same. It's not for you to buy flowers with. In any case... it's not what I want... not what I want...
	(Stamps her feet and runs to the window)
FILO	Hard luck. Neither of us can do anything about it. I'll love you 'til I die and since love elicits love you'll also come to love me...
	(Sits on a chair in the centre and looks askance at Stefka)
STEFKA	I hate you more and more.
FILO	(Hands in his trouser pockets) I love you more and more for it.
STEFKA	Why don't you go to school?
FILO	(Gloomily) I am in fact attending – the school of love.
STEFKA	(Returns to the chaise) I'll write to your parents, sir.
FILO	So much the better – the situation will be clarified at once.
STEFKA	What situation?
FILO	Mine and yours. I'll go through horrific battles, through hell – but I'll overcome it all and forge out a path for the two of us...
STEFKA	Where to?
FILO	Mutual co-existence.

STEFKA   (Goes to the mirror) You're sick in the head.

FILO   (Gloomily) But I won't manage to overcome all the obstacles – we'll perish together.

STEFKA   (Winks) Right-o.

FILO   You really believe I'd leave you here in this world alone? Never! Everything preys on your charm, innocence, your youth. Everything! Even now they're making horrific accusations – they're saying terrible things about you ...

STEFKA   (Interested) What are they saying?

FILO   (Rises but stays in the centre) I'd never repeat such slander for fear of upsetting you. But let me put your mind at rest. I don't believe a thing! I'm the only person in the world who knows you and what you are. And I will always rise up in your defense, even were I to lose my life. I would call up death itself and overcome it. Please believe me.

STEFKA   (Sits with her feet on the sofa) Must you keep talking about death!

FILO   Because it doesn't frighten me.

STEFKA   And if it actually came here, you'd hide behind the stove ... What's death anyway! If some professor turned up here, you'd take to your heels.

FILO   Never! You don't know me.

                (Doorbell)

STEFKA   Well ... well ... might be a professor.

FILO   (Doesn't move, his hands in his trouser pockets) I call upon the entire world to rise in your defense, Madam ...

                (He sits down on the chair)

                And anyway I'm not afraid of anyone, just because I'm wearing a suit.

STEFKA   In the meantime why don't you scarper through the kitchen ...

FILO   (Sits still) Wouldn't dream of it.

                (Doorbell)

STEFKA	Please – it might be one of my girlfriends...
FILO	(As above) Invite her in.
STEFKA	I don't want to start any gossip.
FILO	(As above) Just let her try – I'm perfectly capable of defending you.
STEFKA	Dear God!
	(Pause)
	Aha! And maybe I'm jealous and I'm scared she'll take you away from me...
FILO	(Jumps up) If that's it... I'll go... but I'll be back!...
STEFKA	Not today – I ask you!
FILO	No holding me back. I... will return!
	(Doorbell – Michasiowa goes to answer the door)
MICHASIOWA	I wouldn't advise you to stay here.
FILO	I'm going! Reluctantly...
	(Exits)
STEFKA	(Quickly) Don't you dare let him in here again! Open it!
MICHASIOWA	What's the big hurry? Probably someone with a bill.
	(Holds door ajar on the chain, Bogucki is visible)
BOGUCKI	Is the young miss at home?
MICHASIOWA	One minute!
	(In a whisper to Stefka)
	Are you in or not?
STEFKA	To whom?

MICHASIOWA   That gentlemen – old fellow's friend...

STEFKA   Of course I am – ask him through!

MICHASIOWA   (Opening the door) The young miss is in.

              (Bogucki enters holding a parcel)

SCENE 3

(Bogucki, Stefka, Michasiowa)

STEFKA   Why so early?

BOGUCKI   (Politely) Wanted to bring it as soon as I could – you know what I
              mean...

STEFKA   Oh! Oh! Oh!

BOGUCKI   There you are!

Figure 57: Cockerel feathers. Research performance of Zapolska's *Miss Maliczewska*. University of Reading, POSK Theatre, London, 2007/8. Michael Muncer as Bogucki, Phoebe Garrett as Stefka. Photo by Lib Taylor.

	(Hands her the parcel)
STEFKA	*(Unwraps it – a feather boa – she throws the paper onto the ground near the chaise)* Luxury!
	(She throws her arms round his neck and kisses him – takes a closer look)
	These are cockerel feathers!
BOGUCKI	*(Confused)* That's what you wanted ...
STEFKA	*(Her better half winning)* I said ostrich feathers ... never mind.[69] It's lovely.
BOGUCKI	And may I say that on a certain little person it looks particularly lovely ...
STEFKA	Not too big is it? Well? I think I look like mutton dressed as lamb ...
	(She jumps onto the sofa, regards herself in the mirror, without removing the boa)
	... you sit here too ...
	(Bogucki sits next to her)
	When the old fellow asks me, where I got it, I'll say you gave it to me. Let him be ashamed that he's so stingy and other gentlemen give me presents.
BOGUCKI	I fail to understand how it's possible to deprive you of anything. It's the greatest joy surely to surround a woman with fine goods and luxury ...
STEFKA	Well – my dear sir ... look around you ...
MICHASIOWA	*(From the alcove)* I can't even be bothered to dust this junk any more.
STEFKA	*(Sternly)* Go and look in the kitchen would you Michasiowa – check to see if I'm not in there ...
	(Michasiowa exits)
BOGUCKI	You deserve to be put in a display cabinet, like a porcelain figurine ...
STEFKA	*(Saddening all the while)* Not that. But do you see, sir, I would at least in my situation like enough money to be able to shut people up. Like this,

they maltreat me twice as much and it seems that everyone resents me for having so little money ... Whoever wants to can take it out on me and exploit me ... And the caretaker, and the lodgers, and the landlord, and of course I pay more than others.

(Pause)

I give you my word – all this is worth less than nothing.

BOGUCKI   I keep on saying that you need to be surrounded by wealth.

STEFKA   Let me tell you that even that isn't really necessary. I know how to talk my way round a lot of things. If I don't have it – well, I don't have it. But, you see sir, I have ambition ...

BOGUCKI   What?

STEFKA   Am-bi-tion. If I could only scrape something together in the theatre, then at once I'd be able to make my own way in life ...

(Pause)

And you ... saw the director, did you, sir?

BOGUCKI   I'm supposed to be seeing him tomorrow morning.

STEFKA   And you'll tell him about me?

BOGUCKI   Of course.

STEFKA   *(Rises and goes to the table, sits near to him)* Because if I have a position – then I'll be free to do anything I want – right? That's how the world works. I see that ...

(Bogucki follows her, takes her hand and kisses each finger)

Only Daum doesn't want to see that. Lord! He's so ashamed of me, you've no idea sir. In any case, everyone is ashamed of me. You too sir ...

BOGUCKI   *(Stands beside her)* What do you mean? If you loved me – I'd boast about it – sheer joy.

STEFKA   But ...

BOGUCKI   I give you my word.

STEFKA	Would you walk with me arm in arm?
BOGUCKI	Both my arms through both your arms!
STEFKA	In broad daylight?
BOGUCKI	The broadest.
STEFKA	*(Jumps up)* Let's go then!
BOGUCKI	Pardon me! There's a difference. You don't love me Stefka …
STEFKA	Huh! What use is my love to you?
	(She goes to the chaise and sits in her place)
BOGUCKI	Of course it's some use – more than some – much more …
	(He strokes her hair)
	My own little Stefka! So young, so lovely …
STEFKA	*(Lies down like a child and shuts her eyes, her back to the audience, slowly she turns over and her closed eyes are visible)*
	Carry on talking …
BOGUCKI	*(Sits next to her on the inside)* If she were mine – I'd carry her in my arms, help her, watch over her – nurse her …
STEFKA	*(Her eyes closed)* Carry on talking …
BOGUCKI	I'd take care of her, love …
STEFKA	*(As above)* She would have a position.
BOGUCKI	… a first-rate position …
STEFKA	*(As above – quietly, sweetly)* And no debts.
BOGUCKI	And no debts … He would give her all these things, if only she were his.
STEFKA	*(Opening her eyes, in a childlike voice)* So let him take her …
BOGUCKI	*(Leans towards her, aroused)* Stefka …

STEFKA	*(Sobers up – pushes him away and after a while, hugging herself)* No…oh no…Let him take her away from here…let him take her forever…forever after…
BOGUCKI	*(Cooling)* That would take some thought.
STEFKA	*(Sighing)* Yes!
BOGUCKI	First of all I need proof that you love me, Stefka.
STEFKA	*(Looks at him bluntly, then jumps up)* Aha! No idiots here thank you.
	(Winks – runs to the table)
BOGUCKI	*(Rises)* You shouldn't talk like that, it spoils everything.
STEFKA	*(By the table)* Lots of things spoil everything for me too.
	(Bursting out)
	Huh! I can see now, that I'll perish here…
BOGUCKI	Oh! Oh! Such grand phrases already…
	(Grinding of the key in the lock – the door is ajar – Daum is visible trying to get in, the chain is on)

SCENE 4

(Daum – the same)

DAUM	*(Behind the door, livid)* Miss Maliczewska! Miss Maliczewska! Please take off the chain.
STEFKA	*(Agitated)* Wait! So much yelling!
	(Lifts the chain)
	If you please! What's brought you here, good sir?
DAUM	What? Straight after…
	(Notices Bogucki)
	Ah! It's you? What are you doing here?

BOGUCKI	Paying a visit.
DAUM	(Angry) Really? Bit early, isn't it?
BOGUCKI	Since you're also here …
DAUM	I'm here because I've a bit of free time in court and …
	(To Stefka)
	You're not dressed?
STEFKA	I'm in my negligee. Huh! Don't go on at me. You show up, and straight away …
DAUM	(About the boa) What kind of an eiderdown is that?[70]
STEFKA	(Pulling it away from him) It's my boa.
DAUM	Hideous, only tarts wear those.
STEFKA	(Irritated) Most appropriate then.
DAUM	(Gravely) I had you down as something better. Might do to remember that.
STEFKA	(Increasingly goaded) The first shall be last.
DAUM	(To Bogucki) You'll forgive us, dear sir, for the turn this conversation has taken.
STEFKA	(Very excited) Thou shalt not corrupt the little ones.
DAUM	(Looks at her angrily – and says sharply) Where's my inhalation?
STEFKA	(Hangs her head, depressed, and says quietly after a while) Just a minute!
	(Exits to the kitchen)

SCENE 5

(Bogucki, Daum)

BOGUCKI	What inhalation?
DAUM	Sore throat – during my break I come here for an inhalation – closer than going home.

BOGUCKI	You don't make much effort. That could well offend a young girl.
DAUM	I'm not afraid. She knows they're practically beating down my door. Anyway...
BOGUCKI	Come on – you're not serious! I'm thinking of her.
DAUM	Oh! Incidental.
BOGUCKI	You pretend not to care.
DAUM	*(Needling)* How are your wedding plans coming along?
BOGUCKI	Not sure yet.
DAUM	Now, now. Not a bad match. Take my advice...
BOGUCKI	So eager to marry me off? Don't worry – I'm not in your way.
DAUM	I repeat – I'm not afraid of anyone.
BOGUCKI	That's how you keep her?
DAUM	Maybe!
	(Goes to the kitchen)
	Well?
STEFKA	*(Offstage)* It's ready.
DAUM	*(Exiting, to Bogucki)* You'll forgive me – it's important...
BOGUCKI	Feel free. I'm going anyway...
	(Stefka comes out)
	I want to say goodbye.
STEFKA	*(From a distance)* Bye bye!
BOGUCKI	*(Grabs her, bends her back and kisses her on the lips)* Yes! Like this! Yes!
STEFKA	Let go of me sir! He's performing his ablutions in here.
	(Enter Daum, grumpy, sets up his apparatus for inhalation and sits by the small table)

STEFKA	*(Angry, to Bogucki)* It's ugly, what you're doing.
BOGUCKI	*(Pretends to be interested in the apparatus)* Oh! That's what you do.
DAUM	*(Looks at Stefka)* Why is your left cheek so red?
STEFKA	*(Who has approached and is passing him a cloth)* Because my right cheek isn't.
BOGUCKI	So the steam comes from this bit?
DAUM	You'll forgive me ... I'm not going to talk ...
BOGUCKI	No ... no ... I'm leaving.
	(Daum waves his hand – Stefka leads Bogucki to the door)
BOGUCKI	*(Quietly to her)* When he leaves, I'll come back.
STEFKA	Come tomorrow – straight from the director's.
BOGUCKI	No – I must see you before then.
	(Exits)

SCENE 6

(Daum, Stefka)

DAUM	It's ruined ... ruined ... someone must have fiddled with it.
	(Stefka kneels silently and fixes the apparatus)
DAUM	*(Livid)* This costs money ... one really shouldn't ...
STEFKA	It's fixed now.
	(Takes the boa and looks at it)
DAUM	And I won't be paying for that boa! Need it, did you? Not enough useless frippery?
STEFKA	I get cold at rehearsals.

DAUM	So wrap a scarf round your neck.
	(Stefka sits on the chaise and stays like this, very still, looking in front of her)
DAUM	(After a pause) And now you're sulking, putting on airs and graces. And that's what you call an angelic disposition! I did tell you – I won't suffer any funereal expressions and I need to be entertained, that you should be merry in my presence…I did tell you. Yes or no?
STEFKA	(Quietly) Yes.
DAUM	Well then – adapt to my demands.
STEFKA	Just a minute!
	(Stretching)
	I'm the one supposed to say something jolly?
DAUM	Could do…
STEFKA	But I don't sort of feel like it today…
DAUM	I heard you behind the door enjoying yourself.
STEFKA	Well…because…
DAUM	Because Mr Bogucki was enjoying himself too? That what you wanted to say?
STEFKA	(Agitated) Maybe.
DAUM	(In a sudden outburst) I forbid you to have visitors. I forbid you. I said at the start – no visitors. Yes or no? Did I say so?
STEFKA	Yes but you did! Yes!
DAUM	(Putting on his fur) So please adapt to my demands. I've no desire to encounter similar scenes.
STEFKA	(From the chaise) What scenes? We were only talking.
DAUM	Quite so. That's a real possibility, is it – to only talk with you.

STEFKA	*(Upset)* And why not?
DAUM	Because she's not made for talking.
STEFKA	*(Very upset)* You're wrong, Mr Bogucki talks to me and enjoys himself with me a lot.
DAUM	That he enjoys himself I've not doubt – but not by talking.
STEFKA	*(Increasingly roused)* Perhaps he's in love with me?
	(Daum bursts out laughing)
STEFKA	*(Livid, wounded to the bottom of her heart)* Why? What are you laughing at? Why shouldn't people love me?
DAUM	Because you love your own family – you love your profession, you love your honour, you love your dignity.
STEFKA	*(Increasingly livid)* But someone like me you don't love…
DAUM	This is terribly comical…
	(Looks at his watch)
	I'm going.
STEFKA	*(Advancing on him)* Aha! Aha! Let him know this – that people love me and not only Bogucki… but others too… young people… with hair on their heads and with their own teeth…
	(Practically sobbing)
DAUM	*(Moves her away with his stick)* Move aside! Now she's ugly! … I'll be back in an hour for my inhalation.[71] She should be at the ready. And I'd ask for the room to be warmed – because it's cold in here.
STEFKA	*(Gloomily)* I don't have any money.
DAUM	Here's thirty – let Michasiowa bring a half-pile of wood and light the stove.
	(Puts on his coat and top hat and calls)
	Michasiowa!

SCENE 7

(The same, Michasiowa)

MICHASIOWA   *(With irony)* Sincere respects to the good gentleman.

DAUM   Go and see would you Michasiowa that there's no-one on the stairway.

MICHASIOWA   Just a minute.

(Exits onto the stairway)

STEFKA   *(By the window)* Best not to come here in the daytime.

DAUM   I do as I please! And I'll thank you not to use that tone because I don't like it.

(Michasiowa returns)

MICASHIOWA   No-one there!

DAUM   Splendid!

(Exits)

(Stefka looks after him for a while, at last runs away from the window throws herself onto the chaise and begins to weep quietly)

MICHASIOWA   *(Nonchalantly)* What's the matter? Well? You'll get a fat swollen nose.

STEFKA   *(On the sofa, crying)* I am offended … deeply offended … my pride has been hurt …

MICHASIOWA   What do you mean?

STEFKA   *(With profound heartache)* He told me no-one can ever love me.

MICHASIOWA   *(Standing)* Love you how?

STEFKA   Well … honestly … well – love me.

MICHASIOWA   *(With irony)* Oh … that's different. You wouldn't want that kind of love, Stefka, because you're not made for it, only for the other.

STEFKA   *(Quickly)* Why not? Why not?

MICHASIOWA	*(Needling)* Because – you're … already beyond … company … Stefka …
STEFKA	*(Quickly)* What do you mean?
MICHASIOWA	*(Proudly)* Ah well … you know … beyond good company. What's to be done? I'm still among people and so really I can still be loved honestly, as you might put it …
STEFKA	*(With irony)* You can?
MICHASIOWA	*(In an outburst)* Well yes! Well yes! Even though I'm scarred from the smallpox and my nose goes red – but I'm still among people …
	(She bends towards her sister with hatred, they both look into each others eyes intently, Stefka lowers her eyes first)
STEFKA	Don't talk nonsense …
MICHASIOWA	*(With malicious, nervous laughter, leaning over Stefka, turned to face her)*
	I'm the sort of person people can visit in the daytime if they want to, but to Stefka they come quietly, when no-one's using the stairway, and in the night … there …
STEFKA	Why are you latching onto me? What have you got against me?
	(Michasiowa holds her gaze for some time, at last she wraps her shawl around her head, goes to the alcove, takes her long stockings, stained with ink, from the basket)
MICHASIOWA	Nothing at all!
	(Long pause)
MICHASIOWA	*(In her former tone)* You shouldn't always rub ink over the holes in your shoes Stefka because it's impossible to wash it out.
STEFKA	*(Depressed, lies down on the chaise)* Be quiet – give me something to eat …
MICHASIOWA	There is nothing. The good gentleman ate the rest of the rolmops yesterday.[72]
	(Doorbell)

STEFKA   *(Lying on the sofa)* Who's that?

MICHASIOWA   *(Looks out over the chain)* The one with the poems.

                  (Into the hallway)

                  The young miss is not in.

STEFKA   *(Lying down)* You idiot! Let him in!

MICHASIOWA   What for?

STEFKA   Let him in!

SCENE 8

(The same – Filo)

FILO   I'll only be a minute.

STEFKA   Come here, sir – closer – sit down … Yes … and now tell me one thing. Is it really possible to be in love with me?

FILO   *(Sits on a chair near the chaise on the audience's side)* But I …

STEFKA   *(Kneeling on her heels on the chaise)* Only not like anyone, with anyone. But honestly … well, like you love your women?

FILO   How can you ask that? I worship you. For me you're the epitome of love, beyond you I …

STEFKA   That's tittle-tattle. What I'm asking, is whether it's possible to love me honestly?

FILO   Any other love would be an insult to you, Miss!

STEFKA   And so I'm not beyond good company?

FILO   You stand beyond ordinary people – amongst the angels.

STEFKA   *(Stamps her feet)* No … no … I want to be in good company, with ordinary women – those you can love, get engaged to, marry …

FILO   *(Looks closely at her)* Yes … you said a great word there. A great word …

Figure 58: A declaration of undying love. Research performance of Zapolska's *Miss Maliczewska*. University of Reading, POSK Theatre, London, 2007/8. Phoebe Garrett as Stefka, Michael Day as Filo, Sam Tye as Michasiowa. Photo by Lib Taylor.

STEFKA	*(Looks at her sister)* Because everyone belittles me, they tell me, that I'm the sort no-one loves ...
FILO	And who could be worthy of love, if not you? Where is there a creature more pure, more perfect, than you? *(Slides down in front of the chaise onto his knees)* Stefka, our love ...
STEFKA	Why do you keep on saying 'our love'?! I don't love you.
FILO	The bonds of our love must never be broken. I'm sitting my exams this year – then I'll do the right thing and train as a lawyer ...
STEFKA	And I'll do the wrong thing ...
FILO	I'll finish that – and then – Stefka – then we'll be together always! Happy – inseparable – I'll lift you right up to the clouds, dress you in blue skies – illuminate you with stars ...

Figure 59: Another declaration of undying love. Research performance of Zapolska's *Miss Maliczewska*. University of Reading, POSK Theatre, London, 2007/8. Phoebe Garrett as Stefka, Michael Day as Filo, Sam Tye as Michasiowa. Photo by Lib Taylor.

STEFKA   *(Gets up and runs to the table)* That will be quite … quite …

FILO   *(Follows her)* I've thought it through. I won't leave you in the theatre. It's a filthy, rotten ditch. Not the place for you, not you … you just lose your dignity there …

STEFKA   *(Stands by the window)* It's … all dignity has abandoned this place …

FILO   *(By the table)* Even if you didn't want to …

STEFKA   Well then … enough … I'm bored of this. You can leave. I only wanted certain people to overhear …

                (Looks at Michasiowa, who is darning stockings backstage)

                … that it's possible to really love me, honestly.

FILO   Who doubts this? Let him step forward … Stefka! … take this ring … take it … wear it as a symbol of our engagement …

STEFKA	Leave me be, sir...
FILO	As for my father, my mother – don't be afraid. I have a way, I'll tell them something that'll force them to turn to you themselves and never seek to sever our attachment. It may be a terrible, painful way – but it's foolproof. One of my friends tried it – in the same situation – he got engaged – his parents threatened him – he used this method – and everything changed...
MICHASIOWA	(From the window, interested) He got married?
FILO	No – because she ran away with someone else. But I do know how to disarm my parents...
STEFKA	(Bored) I forbid you sir!
	(To Michasiowa)
	Please leave us.
	(Michasiowa exits – Stefka goes to the chaise)
FILO	Whether you like it or not I'm going to do it! I'm only apologizing in advance! I kiss the hem of your dress... the clouds will cover the sun momentarily, a fleeting blot on the landscape... but I know that when I've won our happiness in this way – you'll forgive me... Ah! One more thing! Listen! Stefka... I tricked you, I lied to you... in the madness of youth... the folly... I didn't use my own name – when we were introduced.
STEFKA	(By the mirror) Oh my God! I so do not care.
FILO	It's not Januszkiewicz – my surname is Daum.
STEFKA	(Quickly) It's what?
FILO	Daum – Gustaw[73] Daum...
STEFKA	The son of old Daum?
FILO	The lawyer...
STEFKA	(Abruptly) What? What!
	(She runs to the door and puts the chain on)
FILO	You know my parents?

STEFKA	*(Shouting)* No...no...no...but I don't want to know you either! ...I don't...I don't...
	(Escapes to the window)
FILO	*(Runs after her)* What is this?! Why not? What's happened?
	(Wants to take her hand)
STEFKA	I don't want you...get out of here...get out...
FILO	I know my father doesn't have a particularly good reputation, but that's in politics – he changed sides...but that, Stefka, happens in even the most decent families; why should I be punished? He's basically a very decent man, of peerless morality, Stefka, he would...
STEFKA	*(Covers her ears, runs to the kitchen)* Shut up! Shut up! Get out of here!
	(Calling Michasiowa)
	Do something...get rid of him...
MICHASIOWA	*(Bursts in – to Filo)* Best if you go sir – when she falls into a temper, God help us...best for you to go now...
FILO	*(Energetically)* I'll go...I'll look for my father...I'll bring him right here – and all together we'll go to my mother's. You'll see how pleased he'll be! I'm off...but I'll be back...
	(Wants to leave via the main staircase)
MICHASIOWA	No that way – through the kitchen...
FILO	*(With pathos)* Alright – but I'll come back through the main entrance, openly and in a decent manner befitting us both.

(Exits quickly, decidedly)

SCENE 9

(Stefka, Michasiowa)

STEFKA	*(Agitated)* Don't you ever let him in here again!
MICHASIOWA	Best not to start anything with a child like that in the first place.

STEFKA	Be quiet!
	(After a while, snorts with laughter)
	Don't you answer back! You took the poems yourself.
MICHASIOWA	I just collected the post...
	(Doorbell – Michasiowa goes to the door – lifts the chain)
	Just a minute...
	(To Stefka)
	...the friend...
STEFKA	*(Pleased)* Ah! Ask him in!
MICHASIOWA	*(In a whisper)* And you be careful – a bird in the hand is worth two in the bush...
	(Stefka runs to the door – opens it)

SCENE 10

(The same – Bogucki)

BOGUCKI	Here I am!
STEFKA	Thank God!
BOGUCKI	*(Flirtatiously)* Really?
STEFKA	*(Sincerely)* Truly – when I see you sir – my heart at once feels lighter. Life with you must be terribly pleasant.
BOGUCKI	*(Sweetly)* I do my best.
STEFKA	And that's why women like you sir.
BOGUCKI	*(Laughing)* They don't like me – they go mad for me.
STEFKA	*(Exaggeratedly)* Ah...yes...
BOGUCKI	*(Going towards the chaise)* And you as well Stefka...you go mad for me...

STEFKA   *(They sit - Stefka on a chair)* I wouldn't dream of it. In any case, I'm not free to ...

BOGUCKI   *(On the arm of the chaise, turned towards Stefka)* Ah! Such fidelity. A lot will come of that, Stefka.

STEFKA   Well ... there's always ...

BOGUCKI   Wouldn't say it if you were Daum's wife, but this ...

STEFKA   Well - and if it was you instead of Daum, and if I was being unfaithful to you, then ...

BOGUCKI   Ha! That's different ...

STEFKA   Because it's you ...

BOGUCKI   No - but, you see Stefka, there's a difference between me and Daum. If you betrayed me, Stefka, you'd have no excuse, but betraying Daum, anyone would forgive you ...

STEFKA   *(Sadly)* There's some truth in that ...

BOGUCKI   There is ... yes ... profoundly so ... Just you try betraying Daum, Stefka ...

                (He pulls her off the chair towards him)

STEFKA   With you sir ...

BOGUCKI   *(Tenderly)* I should think so! You'll see Stefka how straight away your life will brighten ...

STEFKA   You know that, sir.

                (Sincerely)

                I've no talent for betraying people ...

BOGUCKI   What a shame ...

STEFKA   I'd prefer things straight down the line, honest - without betrayal ...

BOGUCKI   Naturally, naturally ... who knows how things might turn out.

                (Pause)

Perhaps your life would take a completely different course, Stefka...I for example know very well what Stefka needs...I've done a lot...a very great deal...even things that Stefka hasn't been expecting...

STEFKA   *(Taken in, against her will drawn to him)* Tell me then sir...what have you done?

BOGUCKI   *(Slyly)* I'd prefer not to say, but as always I'm well aware of my responsibilities towards a woman who loves me and is generous towards me. I am a gentleman and as such I know who and what I ought to be...

STEFKA   *(Pause)* Know what sir...I might think again...

BOGUCKI   Yes – that would be best. Wouldn't force a woman to do anything against her will. On her own, all on her own, that's my system...

                    (Embraces Stefka and kisses her)

                    Dear, darling Stefka...as she likes and when she likes...though I at once am all yours...and I'll have a chat with the director...and all the rest...Stefka...my sweetness...so pretty, so lithe...maybe she'll visit me today?...I'll be here at the court...send a card with the doorman...Michasiowa can arrange it...warn me...how lithe you are...I'm telling you Stefka, everything...everything...

                    (Grinding of the key is heard in the lock, the door is rattled on the chain, Daum is visible behind it)

SCENE 11

(Daum, Stefka, Bogucki)

STEFKA   There! Here he is!

DAUM   *(Behind the door)* Please remove the chain.

STEFKA   *(Elevated)* What is it? What do you want? Is there a fire?

                    (Goes to open the door)

DAUM   *(Enters, spots Bogucki)* I was sure of it.

BOGUCKI   *(With irony)* Glad not to disappoint you – I'm leaving – Miss Stefka...see you again soon...

DAUM	*(Angry)* Scaring you off, am I?
BOGUCKI	*(Getting dressed)* Not at all – I'm going to the courthouse.
DAUM	*(With intent)* I just ran in to your future fiancée.
BOGUCKI	*(Laughing)* That's right – she was just about to go to an exhibition – with your wife ...
	(To Stefka)
	Miss Stefka! I await your decision.
STEFKA	*(Laughing)* Who knows – you might have to wait a long time sir.
DAUM	What is the meaning of this?
STEFKA	*(Drily)* That's our business!
	(Sees Bogucki to the door, he exits – smiling at her meaningfully)

SCENE 12

(Daum, Stefka)

STEFKA	*(With irony and drily)* If you really thought I'd believe that Bogucki has a fiancée you were wrong.
DAUM	Keep your mouth shut – and get me my inhalation.
STEFKA	*(Points to the apparatus with her foot)* Get it yourself.
	(Begins to dress very quickly in the alcove)
DAUM	What?
STEFKA	*(With fury and brutally)* That!
DAUM	*(Takes the apparatus himself and prepares the inhalation)* If you think you'll get far with this you're mistaken. We didn't make any vows ...
STEFKA	What a relief!
MICHASIOWA	*(Goes into the kitchen)* You should go to the theatre to pick up your wages – it's the fifteenth and we have to pay for the suppers.

(Notices Daum)

Sincere respects to the good gentleman!

DAUM   How much for the suppers? I'll pay.

STEFKA   (Rapidly) No need... I'll do it myself... I don't want...

(Dresses in her jacket and hat)

DAUM   Shouldn't you stay at home, since I'm here?

STEFKA   (Rapidly) I should or should not do anything, anything!

DAUM   I'm simply drawing attention to the main tenets of common decency...

STEFKA   (Rapidly but not trivially) Why don't you partner up with a dog and dance the polka down our main street...[74]

DAUM   What? What did you say?

STEFKA   (Opens the door and adds) Perhaps not – I'd feel sorry for the dog!

(Rushes out like the wind through the kitchen – Michasiowa looks after her)

DAUM   What's the matter with her?

MICHASIOWA   Mm hm!

DAUM   Sharpening her little claws again...[75]

MICHASIOWA   Tell you the truth, she's always been that way.

DAUM   I'll wear those down again in no time...

MICHASIOWA   Vicious little thing – always has been, always will be. Shall I light the stove?

DAUM   I did give you something for the wood. It's like a morgue[76] in here, I have to put my coat on.

(Puts on coat)

MICASHIOWA   But we don't have any matches.

DAUM	Here.
	(He takes them from his coat pocket and throws them onto the floor – Michasiowa picks them up)
	As for Stefka, best if I leave her an ultimatum in writing. This is the way things have to be ... and if not ... that's up to her ...
MICHASIOWA	*(Sizing up Daum with concealed rage, lights the stove)* You'd throw her over, would you, good sir?
DAUM	*(Writing)* That's my affair.
MICHASIOWA	*(By the stove)* Seems to me you'd not be able to live without her any more, sir.
DAUM	What's that? Why so articulate today?
	(Through the kitchen door Filo sidles in)

SCENE 13

(Filo, Daum, Michasiowa)

MICHASIOWA	*(Collects herself abruptly)* What are you doing here?
FILO	The door was open.
	(Notices his father)
	Father!!
DAUM	You? Here? I'm ... buying a tenement building ... looking round ... but what are ... what are you doing here? ...
MICHASIOWA	Dear God in heaven! I'll go and get her!
	(Rushes out)
FILO	I don't know father ... all I can think of is ... you've been following me ... that's bad ... personal freedom ... never mind. It's a matter of form – I can forgive you. This is the main thing. What am I doing here! And so – I prefer to tell you straight away – I've come to see Miss Maliczewska ...
DAUM	*(Affecting nonchalance)* Who's that?

FILO

(*Decisively, building up courage*) That is the woman, I love, who loves me and who after finishing my training I will marry.

DAUM

(*Backing away but not giving full voice immediately*) Who? Her?

FILO

(*Increasingly bold – though his voice wavers*) Yes. And it's pointless. Whatever you want to say. Social position? Doesn't exist for me! Her surname? Better than ours – ends in 'ski' – and as for her own person ...[77]

DAUM

(*Breaks off – shortly, sharply*) Silence! And get yourself out of here!

FILO

I can see that the eternal misunderstanding begins again ... fathers ... children ... never mind ... you force me to ... say something I wouldn't normally say. But – I'll speak in my father's own language.

(*Pause*)

You – father – have an elevated sense of honour, dignity. So have I. Would you instruct me to pay a debt I had run up at cards?

DAUM

What are you getting at?

FILO

A debt that's been run up with a woman is of infinitely greater significance. Miss Maliczewska and I ... that is I ... have certain responsibilities towards her ...

DAUM

(*Pales, backs away and says hoarsely*) You? You do?

FILO

Forgive me, father ... youth ...

DAUM

(*In a whisper*) And her ... she ...

FILO

She is not guilty. Only me ...

DAUM

Shut up. Shut up!

(*Sits practically unconscious, covers his face*)

FILO

I suppose that now ...

DAUM

Shut up – let me gather my thoughts.

(*Pause – Filo stands motionless by the wall – Daum has covered his eyes and remains seated*)

FILO	(Quietly) Father!
DAUM	(As though sobering up) Above all you must leave this place…
FILO	But…
DAUM	(Feverishly) And me – I will leave too. In a minute.
FILO	Do you want to talk to my fiancée?
DAUM	(Feverishly) Yes…yes…that's right…
FILO	(Childishly) Be kind to her. She's so shy, though on the face of it she's bold; but since you think its necessary – I'll go. I trust you and I see that you acknowledge my human rights. I respect you for that. Tell her that…
DAUM	(In a whisper) I know what I need to say – you go!
FILO	(Steers himself towards the front door) It's locked…
DAUM	Wait!
	(Mechanically he takes the front door key from his pocket, remembers himself and hides it)
	Perhaps there's another way out…
FILO	Yes – through the kitchen.
	(Goes to the kitchen)
	It's open.
	(Sincerely, to his father)
	I'll be waiting downstairs…
DAUM	No…no…go home.
	(After a while he looks at him, takes his head in his hand and kisses his son's forehead)
	You didn't know…you're not to blame…
FILO	No father…it's me, me…she's not guilty…

DAUM	No...no...go...go...

(Filo exits. Daum remains alone for a while, looks around muddled, wants to sit, rises, takes his hat and stick, sits again on the chaise, footsteps on the stairs, Michasiowa bursts in through the front door, unlocking them with the key she has with her)

SCENE 14

(Daum, Michasiowa then Stefka)

MICHASIOWA	She's on her way...she didn't want to but I persuaded her, she's just now stopped downstairs...she's talking to...the young gentleman.
DAUM	(From the chaise) Stop her! Stop her!...let her not talk to him...
MICHASIOWA	But she loves him, if you please, sir.
DAUM	(From the chaise) This is not about her, this is not about her...

(The front door opens and Stefka bursts in, Daum flings himself towards her, as though he wants to beat her, she cries out)

STEFKA	Ah...

(Wants to say something, suddenly backs away to the window and stays there immobile, with her fists clenched near her lips, Michasiowa beside her, as though to defend her)

DAUM	(After a pause, hoarsely – quietly) I've found out...such things...such things, the very thought of them makes me shudder...

(Moment of silence)

DAUM	(As above) I didn't have a very high opinion of a certain person's morality...but this exceeds all boundaries – this is filth...it's...
MICHASIOWA	(Quietly to Stefka) Tell him the truth Stefka, nothing happened did it...
STEFKA	(Quietly, through clenched teeth) I will not! Let him think it...then he'll leave...I'll write to him tomorrow...but let him finish with me...
DAUM	(As above) I'm leaving...for good...in a state of great contempt...with disgust...just one thing...reparation on behalf of my son! I won't give it...I will not!

(He steers himself towards the door, stops suddenly and turns towards Michasiowa)

My inhalation device - pack it - I'll take it with me.

(Michasiowa packs the apparatus using the paper discarded from the boa ... silence throughout - at last Daum takes the apparatus and leaves, hunched, aged, in passing he says bitterly, looking at Stefka)

In return for so many kindnesses!!

STEFKA   *(To Michasiowa quickly)* The key! Get him to give back the door key!

(Michasiowa runs out and returns after a while with the key)

STEFKA   *(Animates like a mad woman and begins dancing around the room)*

He's gone! He's gone! What joy! What happiness! He's not here! He's not here! He won't come any more ... oh no, no ...

(She cries and laughs nervously, to some degree Michasiowa's words put a damper on this laughter)

MICHASIOWA   *(Grumpy)* Fat lot to be pleased about.

STEFKA   *(Laughing spasmodically)* Of course there is! Oh! I loathed him ... how I loathed him ...

MICHASIOWA   *(Quietly)* Tomorrow the Jew will be here for his quarterly payment, for the furniture - and well ... a whole month's worth of suppers - the washerwoman's cost us over ten gulden - you've run up debts in all the shops - on the sixteenth they'll alight here like crows. Wonder what'll happen ...

STEFKA   *(Extinguished, quiet - sits on the chaise)* God only knows ...

MICHASIOWA   The apartment's ours for another two weeks ... it's worst of all with the seamstress - today a little girl came three times with the bill ... she's started playing up on the stairs now ...

STEFKA   *(Quietly, uncertainly)* So send for the watchman, let him throw her out.

MICHASIOWA   The watchman's angry too - he says that Stefka owes him too ... and as for me, I'm not saying a thing, only that boarding house, well ...

STEFKA   *(Falls on her face onto the chaise)* Well - what shall I do! What! ...

MICHASIOWA   You should have patched it up...not broken it off...

                    (Doorbell)

                    He hasn't come back has he?

STEFKA   (Gets up) I won't have it! I'll suffer the worst...but not this...

                    (Stops up her eyes)

SCENE 15

(The same, Bogucki)

BOGUCKI   She here?

MICHASIOWA   The friend!

STEFKA   (Leaps up) Manna from heaven!

                    (Throws herself towards him)

                    I meant to send a card...

BOGUCKI   (Quickly) I came out of the courthouse – I see Daum in a carriage
                    frightfully pale – he turned away from me – what is it?

STEFKA   (With enthusiasm) What it is – is that I'm free...free...no-one has any right
                    to me...I can do as I please...

BOGUCKI   (Surprised) It's been broken off?

STEFKA   (Energetically) Once and for all! Daum has been overcome! Just a pile of
                    tatters – that's Daum!

BOGUCKI   But why?

MICHASIOWA   (Quickly) It's because of your sir – because that gentleman was jealous
                    of you, sir...

BOGUCKI   (Suspiciously) Oho! Ha! I really...

STEFKA   (Quickly) Doesn't matter whether it's this or that – enough, that I'm
                    free...And I'll tell you right now, that I am very happy, that I don't need
                    to betray him with you.

(With the charm of a child)

Because I would have betrayed him, and that's ugly isn't it ... always ... and so it's better if it's out in the open, right, and honest ...

BOGUCKI   (Without enthusiasm) Well ... yes ...

(To Michasiowa)
Leave us, Michasiowa, I want to talk to the young miss.

(Michasiowa exits saying to herself)

MICHASIOWA   (To herself) God save us, maybe we'll scrape through somehow ...

STEFKA   (Childishly and sincerely) You're pleased, sir, that now I'll be entirely yours?

BOGUCKI   (Slyly) Very ... But sit down now Stefka, opposite me and let's talk sensibly. If it's going to happen that I'll be taking Daum's place - then it'll have to be within my means. I'm saying this openly - I can't do much, maybe even less than Daum. But I like clarity. Exactly like him. Right! Now you've separated - and since he promised you nothing ...

STEFKA   Oho! Ha! The things he promised! ...

BOGUCKI   (As though cutting through it with a knife) But on the whole! Nothing for certain. You've separated with no bad feelings ... The same with me. No bad feelings.

(Rises, looks into the kitchen, into the alcove)

The apartment can stay the same, because that's most practical - in case I have to take a trip ... any debts?

STEFKA   (Sits quietly on the chaise and looks at him) Yes.

BOGUCKI   (Sits on the arms of the chaise) Many?

STEFKA   (As above) One hundred and eighty zlotys.

(Quickly)

But not everything needs to be paid straight away.

BOGUCKI	It'll be settled – but I'm saying right now – I won't pay any more – nothing above that amount – remember that Stefka. Also…no relatives, is that clear…! I don't like it. And one final request – I come here and that fact remains completely secret…completely…
STEFKA	*(Sadly)* So you'll be visiting in the dark again?
BOGUCKI	*(With a complacent smile)* Well…naturally, I'm building up a position…I need to cultivate good opinion.
STEFKA	*(Tentatively)* And you won't take me anywhere with you?
BOGUCKI	*(Like a great lord)* Sometimes, maybe…out of town…in the evening…
STEFKA	*(With irony)* With the hood up…Ah! You strolled out with Milowicz even in the daytime.
BOGUCKI	*(Evasively)* I was a few years younger, these days I have foresight and must think about the future.
STEFKA	*(Increasingly sad)* And will you meet with the director?
BOGUCKI	Naturally…if the occasion should arise…
STEFKA	*(Tentatively)* And you'll tell him about me?
BOGUCKI	*(Evasively)* Through a friend. Personally isn't appropriate right now…What's this? Bad mood?
	(Rises)
	Ah! Not on the menu, I'm afraid. You should smile, always, and greet me merrily because I myself occasionally experience moments of terrible agitation and require some distraction – That is my ultimatum. Well – is it a deal?
STEFKA	*(Sadly)* It's a deal!
BOGUCKI	Oh! I'm not keen on that…merrily…well…and with a smile…
STEFKA	*(Smiling wanly)* It's a deal!
	(Bogucki kisses her, she surrenders passively – Bogucki looks at his watch)

BOGUCKI	Oho! Three o'clock. I'm off to the chambers, I'll be back this evening, I'll bring my own supper, just a little something ...
STEFKA	(With irony) Informal snack ...
BOGUCKI	(Getting dressed) Yes ... that's right ... well ... bye then! How lithe you are ... how lithe ... (kisses her) 'til this evening! Call Michasiowa!
STEFKA	What for?
BOGUCKI	Is there by any chance someone on the stairway?
STEFKA	(Shakes her head) Ah well! (She goes out herself and looks) ... there is! The landlady's dog.
BOGUCKI	Ah, How witty you are Stefka! Bye bye my precious kitty! Bye bye my sweet! Bye bye! Wait for me and long for me! (Moves her towards him) Love me?
STEFKA	(With her whole disappointed soul) I wanted to ... not any more ...
BOGUCKI	(As if to a child, off hand) She will do ... she will ... goodbye. (Exits)

SCENE 16

(Stefka, Michasiowa)

MICHASIOWA	(In a whisper) Well – what's going on?
STEFKA	Ah, well ... what could I do? (Sits on the chaise with her feet up)
MICHASIOWA	(Pulls up a chair) Right you are. Knife to the throat. What should I be? Sister? Servant?
STEFKA	A servant. He'll lay no claim to family.

MICHASIOWA	(Livid) Would you look at that! Just the same ...[78]
STEFKA	Let me alone would you Michasiowa. My head hurts.
MICHASIOWA	It's from hunger – mine does too. I won't go for dinner without any money, because they're calling me names and I'm ashamed. Did you bring something from the theatre?
STEFKA	(Quietly) Nothing. Rosenbusch took it. She was waiting for me in front of the theatre. Let's hang on 'til the evening – he'll bring some supper ...
MICHASIOWA	(Simply) As long as it's not always sardines, like the last one. Well ... let's hang on 'til then ...
STEFKA	(Sleepily) Get some sleep!
MICHASIOWA	(Sits on the ground by the stove) Good idea. I wonder, who best to approach for favours now?
	(Exits)
STEFKA	(Alone, in tears, wraps her shawl around her and settles down to sleep) For an entire lifetime, just like this ... damn it all ... an entire lifetime ...[79]
	(Curtain slowly falls)

Notes

1. The name 'Michasiowa' is not a first name; it functions rather more like a surname, though it is not strictly a surname either. Crucially, it implies that Stefka's sister has been married, to someone called Michał (a man's first name – Michael) which has been feminized via the ending to 'label' the woman in a particular way. We never learn anything about Michasiowa's husband throughout the play – he may have died, he may have left her, he may have emigrated; these are just some of the possibilities. Michasiowa appears completely reliant in her own way on Stefka and this is one of the most important issues at stake in the text.

2. Arguably one of the most common religious images to be found in Polish households is that of the Black Madonna of Częstochowa.

3. Demosthenes was a prominent Greek statesman and orator of ancient Athens. For a time he made his living as a professional speech writer and a lawyer. It seems that Edek may be trying to learn some of his speeches, which were written down.

4. This is most probably a reference to the golden fishing rod mentioned in Nietzsche's Thus Spoke Zarathustra (1883-5).

5. Edek actually refers to Filo's 'Polish'.

6. Henryk Sienkiewicz (1846-1916), Polish journalist and Nobel prize-winning novelist. This poem is included in one of his two, paired short stories entitled Bez Dogmatu, which were published in book form in 1891.

7. He actually says 'A pair of Dulskis', with reference to Zapolska's 1906 play *The Morality of Mrs. Dulska*!

8. This reference to currency clues us into the fact that the play is set in Galicia.

9. Literally, the 'lifting up' of women, implying that they are falling and need 'raising'.

10. Meaning 'no, she is not a prostitute'.

11. Literally translated, the washerwoman's full name is 'Iron Anna' (Mrs Iron). This is what the women laugh at. If correctly pronounced, the names partially rhyme and so in English, in performance, this can become the focus for their laughter, since names have not been translated.

12. 'Pyah-setch-na'. Piaseczno is actually a town in central Poland, about 20 km from Warsaw. However, this play is not linked to this town, since it was part of Prussia during the third partition of Poland, and there are references to Austrian currency in the text. However, 'Piaseczna' is quite a common street name in Poland.

13. This would be one of the local tradespeople or money lenders.

14. Edek means that he buys the soldiers' rations.

15. I have added the final sentence in order to make it perfectly clear that Edek is writing essays for other students.

16. See footnote 3.

17. Baruch Spinoza (1632–77) was a Dutch rationalist philosopher of Portuguese-Jewish descent.

18. Note that Elka in *The Man* also discovers a hole in her shoe. In Zapolska's short story 'The Anti-Semite', the journalist Szatkiewicz marvels at the fact that the actress he is involved with, Irma, has shoes that are not falling apart.

19. This is an interesting stage direction – Zapolska includes several that are similar throughout the play. Whether Stefka is winking at 'the audience' (or 'publiczność' – 'public') sitting watching a performance of the play, or whether she is pretending to be on stage or performing within the room to an imaginary audience, or whether she is treating the other people in the room as her 'audience', or a combination of these, is not made clear. The distinctions may seem quite subtle but are highly significant given the fact that the play is about performance and performativity.

20. A type of sideboard.

21. Note the theatrical metaphor being used in this context, particularly in relation to footnote 19.

22. Alcohol was used to set the hair.

23. By locking the door, the washerwoman is implying that Daum can do as he pleases. Since she has set the scenario up as some kind of 'performance' (see footnote 21) and is of course fully aware that Stefka knows nothing, she is most likely aware that the possibility of Daum raping Stefka exists.

24. See footnote 19 – this could also translate as 'an audience' or 'the public'. If Stefka really does wink at the audience present at a performance, then there might be an attempt to align their perspective with hers. It is worth considering these stage directions in relation to Małka Szwarcenkopf's 'asides' or 'partial soliloquies' in the play of this title.

25. Actresses were expected to provide their own costumes, unless they were of star status. This is partly why Stefka is so frequently in debt. Michasiowa acts as the equivalent of her 'dresser' and the women fix as much as possible themselves. Zapolska herself documents how difficult this situation made the life of an actress starting out in the theatre. In her short story 'The Anti-Semite', for example, Szatkiewicz is described falling asleep in the actress Irma's lodging whilst she is sewing sequins onto a costume for a performance the next day.

26. The strength of this sexual allusion is more evident in translation than in the original, however, it serves the purpose of the scene well.

27. Stefka is a poor girl with no connections – she is attempting to make some here, since the advancement of her career appears to depend on it.

28. The Austro-Hungarian Gulden was replaced by the Krone in 1892 at a rate of 2 Kronen = 1 Gulden.

29. He means the 50 kronen he gave her when he first arrived.

30. This means one pane 'behind' another, what we might now call double glazing, rather than two panes next two each other – 'lagrowana'.

31. Stefka calls Daum a 'horse' (probably a cart horse – ungainly, brutish) but I believe 'pig' sounds more to the point in English.

32. We learn nothing about what happens between Acts 1 and 2 – we see Stefka exiting with a bloodied hand, having been pulled along the ground, to pay off her debts with dirty money, and the next time we encounter her she is set up as Daum's mistress. However, directorial decisions concerning events that have taken place in the interim must and will affect the way in which relationships are represented in the following acts.

33. A large stand or cabinet for plants and flowers.

34. It is implied in the play that the sisters are renting the apartment from Jewish property owners.

35. Stefka is probably singing a line from her rehearsal. I have been unable to determine which text or libretto this is from. It translates roughly (from the German) as, 'Stop everything! Here comes Grette!'

36. 'Przez alembic'. An alembic was a lamp. My translation expresses the equivalent sense; the rehearsal may have lasted so long that the lamp burnt out.

37. pron. Dr-ven-ski

38. pron. R-ven-ski

39. pron. No-rim-bear-ski

40. pron. Ya-noo-shev-ski

41. pron. Yas-tchem-bski

42. pron. Gva-rantz and Mwod-jay-ev-itch

43. pron. Pom-yan

44. The surname Wołowski is used. The root of this surname is 'wół' which means 'ox'. I finally searched for an equivalent joke in English and devised the surname 'Miałkowski', which is pronounced 'miaow-kov-ski'. This makes the surname animal-like in a different way – and then the word 'purr-fect' follows on nicely.

45. pron. Ya-ro-shev-ski

46. I have added this joke – I think it helps with the dynamic of the scene.

47. *The Princess on the Glass Hill* is a Norwegian fairy tale collected by Peter Christen Asbjørnsen and Jørgen Moe in *Norske Folkeeventyr* It recounts how the youngest son of three obtains a magical horse and uses it to win the princess.

48. This is clearly a joke. In my research production, this became a reference to Stefka's chest size.

49. The word Filo uses is 'cudowna'. The root of the word, 'cud', means 'miracle'. I have opted for delicious because I think it is useful in evoking the right kind of tone in English, given the nature of the scene, Filo's character and his relationship with the friends.

50. This is Bogucki's ex, as we have previously learnt.

51. Stefka is anxious that the applause doesn't *seem* 'contrived', even though it is. If it seems natural and spontaneous, presumably the management of the theatre are more likely to take notice.

52. 'Metresa'. *The Mistress* was Zapolska's first title for the play, which she removed as it was considered too risqué.

53. Daum is clearly a potentially aggressive man but there is also the danger that he will withdraw his so-called patronage if he is pushed too far.

54. pron. Ya-noosh-kyev-itch. This is not the surname Filo invented for himself with the friends.

55. Juliusz Słowacki's 1834 play *Balladyna*, written after the failure of the November Uprising. It features a character named Filon.

56. It has been difficult to determine which waltz this is a reference to. It may have been one of Johann Strauss the Elder's waltzes, since he left his wife and family to live with his mistress and it was she, reportedly, who created the dance. It would presumably have been recognized by a contemporary audience of *Miss Maliczewska* as a piece of music bearing this title.

57. 'Sans gene' – in other words, not fitting any category.

58. This is in fact the last time Daumowa makes an appearance in the play. The interaction is a difficult one to gauge. It seems possible, though unlikely, that Stefka might have an inkling as to Daumowa's relationship to her patron, though it is clear from later interactions that she has no idea of Filo's relationship to either Daum or Daumowa until he does actually say what his real surname is. Crucially, Daumowa does not mention her surname, and Zapolska makes this completely explicit in the dialogue, leaving an air of mystery about her. It seems more likely to me that Daumowa suspects something about Stefka but does not know for sure. If neither woman is entirely sure – indeed, if Stefka is oblivious – then the interaction might arguably become far more interesting – a sort of game of chess without either player really knowing whether they're in the same game! Daumowa certainly might be 'feeling her way' and 'performing' through the interaction. The scene represents one of the greatest challenges in performance in terms of establishing motivation and yet is in some ways is its lynch-pin, since it occurs roughly halfway through.

59. Bogucki is probably considerably younger than Daum. Why does Daum invite him to the apartment? Is it to show off his mistress? Is it to broker a not strictly kosher deal? Is it to test Stefka? It seems possible to me that it is a combination of these factors – they end up not discussing business because Stefka interferes, as does Bogucki's interest in Stefka and Daum's jealousy.

60. pron. Vin-nits-kee

61. Cornichons are small pickled cucumbers.

62. She is referring to Desdemona from Shakespeare's tragedy *Othello* and Klara from Aleksander Fredro's *Śluby Panieńskie* (*Maiden's Vows*) (1833).

63. A mazurka is a stylized Polish folk dance in triple meter with a lively tempo that has a heavy accent on the third or second beat.

64. This means 'brotherhood' in German. Bogucki is suggesting a pledging of brotherhood over a drink, with the director of the theatre.

65. What is significant here is the 'play within a play'. They are quoting from a play that is famous for its portrayal of romantic love, in the form of star-crossed lovers Romeo and Juliet. This contrasts sharply with their rather cynical financial and sexual 'arrangement'.

66. It is interesting to note that the Bailiff often appears not long after Daumowa has departed.

67. This is the only time the Bailiff's name is used.

68. Literally, 'in civilian clothes'. This means he is not wearing his uniform.

69. These would have been more expensive.
70. An early version of the duvet, filled with feathers of the eider duck.
71. As the scene progresses this statement clearly acquires sexual overtones. The machine breaks etc. etc. – one does not get the impression that Stefka is achieving any personal erotic satisfaction from this so-called relationship. The situation with Bogucki is slightly different, since she does appear to find him physically attractive. However, her growing cynicism prevents her from taking this 'as it stands'. She becomes increasingly aware of the way in which she is valued in the 'economies' of the world she inhabits.
72. Herring wrapped around a pickle and marinated with onion, pepper, lemon and seasonings
73. Pronounced 'Gustav'.
74. 'Pies niech polkę z nim tańczy przez Wały Hetmańskie.' Literally, 'may he dance the polka with a dog down the Hetman Embankment' (in Lwów, which was then part of Poland).
75. 'Różki odrosły'. Literally, 'her little horns have grown back'.
76. 'Psiarnia', literally 'a dogs' home'.
77. Consider this comment in relation to Maurycy Silbercweig's desire to change his surname in Act 1 of *Małka Szwarcenkopf*.
78. 'Taki drugi Protazy' – literally, 'yet another Protazy'. Protazy is character from *Pan Tadeusz*, an epic poem by Adam Mickiewicz, published in 1834 in Paris. He carries a big bunch of keys. Michasiowa is saying that Daum was like Protazy, in that he kept the keys to the household, and that Bogucki has turned out to be more or less a replica of Daum.
79. It is interesting to consider the ending, with the two sisters left on stage, in relation to the final act of *The Man*, written ten years earlier.

BIBLIOGRAPHY

Selected Books

Bartoszewski, W. & Polonsky, A. (eds), *The Jews in Warsaw*, Oxford: Blackwell, 1991.

Bashevis-Singer, I., *A Day of Pleasure*, New York: Farrar, Strauss & Giroux, 1986.

Basnett, S., *Translation Studies*, London: Routledge, 2003.

Berkowitz, J., *Yiddish Theatre*, Oxford: Littman, 2003.

Bieniasz, J., *Gabriela Zapolska*, Wrocław: Zakład Nar. im. Ossolińskich, 1960.

Bienka, M., *Warszawskie Teatry Rzadowe: Dramat i Komedia*, Warszawa: Instytut Sztuki PAN, 2003.

Boase-Beier, J., *Stylistic Approaches to Translation*, Manchester: St. Jerome, 2006.

Borzymińska, Z., *Szkolnictwo Żydowskie w Warszawie 1831–1870*, Warszawa: Żydowski Instytut Historyczny, 1994.

Braun, K., *A Concise History of Polish Theater*, Lewiston: Edwin Mellen, 2003.

Brodzki, B., *Can These Bones Live?* California: Stanford University Press, 2007.

Carsin, S., *Warsaw before the First World War*, New York: Boulder, 1989.

Chwalba, A., *Historia Polski 1795-1918*, Kraków: Wydawnictwo Literackie, 2000.

Czachowska, J., *Gabriela Zapolska*, Kraków: Wydawnictwo Literackie, 1966.

Davis, K., *Deconstruction and Translation*, Manchester: St. Jerome, 2001.

Davies, N., *The Heart of Europe*, Oxford: OUP, 1986.

Dylewski, A., *Śladami Żydów Polskich*, Bielsko-Biała: Pascal, 2002.

Getzler, E., *Contemporary Translation Theories*, London: Routledge, 1993.

Gitelman, Z., *The Emergence of Modern Jewish Politics*, Pittsburgh: University of Pittsburgh Press, 2003.

Hatim, B. & Mason, I., *Translator as Communicator*, London: Routledge, 1997.

Hermans, T. (ed.), *Translating Others*, Manchester: St. Jerome, 2006.

Hermans, T., *Translation in Systems*, Manchester: St. Jerome, 1999.

Heylen, R., *Translation, Poetics and the Stage*, London: Routledge, 1993.

Hoffman, E., *Shtetl*, London: Vintage, 1999.

Hutnikiewicz, A., *Mloda Polska*, Warszawa: Wydawnictwo Naukowe PWN, 2008.

Johnston, D. (ed.), *Stages of Translation*, Bath: Absolute Classics, 1996.

Kallas, A., *Zapolska*, Warszawa: Renaissance, 1931.

Lefevre, A., *Translation, Re-writing and the Manipulation of Literary Fame*, London: Routledge, 1992.

Kłosińska, K., *Ciało, pożądanie, ubranie*, Kraków: eFKa, 1999.

Krajewski, S., *Żydzi, Judaizm, Polska*, Warszawa: Vocatio, 1997.

Londré, F & Berthold, M., *The history of world theater: from the English restoration to the present*, Continuum International Publishing Group, 1999.

Malinowska, E., *Feminizm Europejski*, Łódź: Łódź University Press, 2000.

Michalski, J. (ed.), *Lud Żydowski w narodzie Polskim*, Warszawa: PAN, 1984.

Murjas, T (ed. & trans.), *The Morality of Mrs. Dulska by Gabriela Zapolska*, Bristol/Chicago: Intellect, 2007.

Nathans, B. & Afran, G., *Culture Front*, Pennsylvania: University of Pennsylvania Press, 2008.

Nussbaum, H., *Szkice historyczne z życia Żydów w Warszawie*, Warszawa: Wydawnictwo Artystyczne i Filmowe, 1989.

Pajaczkowski, F., *Teatr Lwowski pod dyrekcja Tadeusza Pawlikowskiego*, Kraków: Wydawnictwo Literackie, 1961.

Polonsky, A., *The Jewish Community in Warsaw*, Oxford: Blackwell, 1988.

Rurawski, J., *Gabriela Zapolska*, Warszawa: Wiedza Powszechna, 1981.

Sikorski, R., *The Polish House*, London: Phoenix, 1997.

Sivert, T. (ed.), *Teatr Polski w latach 1890-1918*, Warszawa: Wydawnictwo Literackie, 1988.

Szydlowska, M., *Cenzura teatralna w dobie autonomicznej 1860-1918*, Kraków: Universitas, 1995.

Zamoyski, A., *The Polish Way*, London: John Murray, 1993.

Zapolska, G., *Panna Maliczewska*, Kraków: Universitas, 2003.

Zapolska, G., *Szkice Powieściowe*, Kraków: Wydawnictwo Literackie, 1958.

Zapolska, G., *Utwory Dramatyczne*, Warszawa: Lektor, 1923.

Zapolska, G., *Utwory Dramatyczne*, Warszawa: Książka i Wiedza, 1950.

Żarnowska, A., *Workers, Women and Social Change in Poland, 1870-1939*, Burlington VT: Ashgate, 2004.

Selected Newspaper Reviews
Małka Szwarcenkopf

Arsztein, M., *Izraelita*, 1901, nr. 22, str. 259.

Błeszyński, J., *Kurier niedzielny*, 1897, nr. 30, str. 354-6.

Bogusławski, W., *Gazeta Warszawska*, 1897, nr. 183, str. 3.

Chołoniewski, A., *Dziennik Polski*, 1897, nr. 279, str. 2-3.

'D.S'., *Gazeta Polska*, 1897, nr. 156, str. 2-3.

Dobrowolski, A., *Kurier poranny*, 1897, nr. 190, str. 4-5.

Grabowski, I., *Kurier Warszawski*, 1897, nr. 11, str. 10-11.

Koneczny, F., *Przegląd Polski*, 1897/98, t. 126, str. 536-44.

Korycki, W., *Niwa*, 1897, nr. 31, str. 612.

Kościelecki, Ł., *Kurier Codzienny*, 1897, nr. 190, str. 3.

Krechowiecki, A., *Gazeta Lwowska*, 1897, nr. 229, str. 4-5.

Lange, A., *Głos*, nr. 32, str. 779.

Lew, H, *Izraelita*, 1897, nr. 29, str. 285.

'Minos', *Glos Narodu*, 1897, nr. 237, str. 5.

Rajchman, A., *Echo*, 1897, nr. 29, str. 344.

Szczepański, L., *Życie*, 1897, nr. 5, str. 8-9.

See also Czachowska, J., pp. 171-84.

The Man

Beaupré, A., *Głos Narodu*, 1902, nr. 15, str. 6.

Bissinger, J., *Dziennik*, 1902, nr. 43, str. 3.

Bogusławski, W., *Gazeta Warszawska*, 1902, nr. 258, str. 3.

Ehrenberg, K., *Nasz Głos*, 1902, nr. 104, str. 5.

Feldman, W., *Słowo Polskie*, 1902, nr. 36, str. 1-2.

Gawalewicz, M., *Słowo*, 1902, nr. 223, str. 1.

Łoziński, J., *Kurier poranny*, 1902, nr. 269, str. 3.

Prokesch, W., *Kurier Teatralny*, 1902, nr. 4, str. 50-51.

Rabski, W., *Kurier Warszawski*, 1902, nr. 269, str. 1-3.

S.K., *Niwa Polska*, 1902, nr. 1, s. 5.

S.R, *Dziennik Polski*, 1901, nr. 148, str. 2.

Womela, S., *Kurier Lwowski*, 1902, nr. 30, str. 6-7.

See also Czachowska, J., pp. 251-62.

Miss Maliczewska

'K.B', *Ster*, 1911, nr. 1, str. 33-40.

Balicki, A., *Przegląd Polski*, 1910/11, t. 178, z. 533, str. 261-3.

Barwinski, E., *Gazeta Narodowa*, 1899, nr. 141, str. 1.

Daszyńska-Golińska, Z., *Prawda*, 1910, nr. 49, str. 9-10.

Dobrowolski, A., *Dziennik Polski (Literatura i Sztuka)*, 1910, nr. 44, str. 700-03.

Ehrenberg, K., *Scena i Sztuka*, 1911, nr. 4, str. 5.

Feldman, W., *Krytyka*, 1910, t. 4, z. 12, str. 350.

Jankowski, C., *Tygodnik Ilustrowany*, 1911, nr. 5, str. 94.

Makuszyński, K., *Świat*, 1911, nr. 2, str. 11-12.

Rabski, W., *Kurier Warsawski*, 1911, nr. 18, str. 2-4.

Rakowski, K., *Czas*, 1910, nr. 496, str. 1.

See also Czachowska, J., pp. 427-42.

Newspaper Articles

Crace, J., 'Move over, Ian Rankin', g2 (*The Guardian*), 23.01.09, p.14.

... Dig out some elevated historical moment and write. Ah! If I were a poet I'd write such wonderful tragedies in verse... Not contemporary ones, though, because it's useless, when today's people chatter away in verse. You really need costumes for that...

Gabriela Zapolska to Ludwik Szczepański, 1899
(trans. T. Murjas)

Figure 60: The cast members receive balloons during a standing ovation in Łódź. Research performance of Zapolska's *Four of Them*. University of Reading, POSK Theatre London and Łódź Theatre Festival, 2006/7. Ben Mitchell as Mandragora, Liz Gaubert as the Widow, Andrew Parsons as Fedycki, Sophie Green as the Wife. Photo by Mike Stevenson.